REGULATING THE CHANGING MEDIA

Regulating the Changing Media

A Comparative Study

Edited by

DAVID GOLDBERG
TONY PROSSER

and

STEFAAN VERHULST

CLARENDON PRESS · OXFORD
1998

Oxford University Press, Great Clarendon Street, Oxford OX2 6DP

Oxford New York

Athens Auckland Bangkok Bogota Bombay Buenos Aires
Calcutta Cape Town Dar es Salaam Delhi Florence Hong Kong Istanbul
Karachi Kuala Lumpur Madras Madrid Melbourne Mexico City
Nairobi Paris Singapore Taipei Tokyo Toronto Warsaw
and associated companies in
Berlin Ibadan

Oxford is a registered trade mark of Oxford University Press

Published in the United States
by Oxford University Press Inc., New York

British Library Cataloguing in Publication Data
Data available

Library of Congress Cataloging in Publication Data
Regulating the changing media : a comparative study / edited by David
Goldberg, Tony Prosser, and Stefaan Verhulst.
p. cm.
Includes bibliographical references and index.
1. Mass media—Law and legislation. I. Goldberg, David.
II. Prosser, Tony. III. Verhulst, Stefaan (Stefaan G.)
K4240.R44 1998
343.09'9—dc21 98-24189
ISBN 0-19-826781-9

1 3 5 7 9 10 8 6 4 2

Typeset by Best-set Typesetter Ltd., Hong Kong
Printed in Great Britain
on acid-free paper by
Biddles Ltd., Guildford and King's Lynn

Preface

This book is the outcome of a research project funded by the UK Economic and Social Research Council (grant no L126251021) as part of its Media Economics and Media Culture Research Programme. We hope that it will contribute to the growing body of literature on the 'new' media in several ways. Firstly, it provides a 'snapshot' of media developments in a number of widely different countries at a time of great media change. The coverage is (unless otherwise indicated) as at the end of October 1997, although in places it has proved possible to incorporate some particularly important later events. Secondly, we have suggested possible ways in which the regulation of the media may develop to take into account these new developments; we regard the view that the changing media will make regulation redundant as profoundly mistaken, although this does not mean that future regulation will simply replicate that of the past. Thirdly, two of us are academic lawyers and we are particularly interested in the future role of law in such regulation; again we do not accept that we shall witness 'the end of law' but it is likely that legal intervention will also be different in the new media world.

We would like to make a number of important acknowledgements. Firstly, we thank the Economic and Social Research Council for funding this work, and in particular the Director of the Media Economics and Media Culture Programme, Professor Simon Frith, for his support. We would also like to thank the Faculty of Law and Financial Studies at the University of Glasgow for some financial support in order to permit brief continuation of work after the Research Council funding had ended.

The project administrator and secretary was Gill Kane, and we are most grateful for her contribution without which the project would certainly have descended into chaos. We are also grateful to our national reporters who have contributed chapters to this book for all their work and for the timely completion of the reports. The European Audiovisual Observatory in Strasbourg, and in particular Ad van Loon, offered help to us in many valuable ways, including hosting a meeting of the contributors and this proved most valuable in completing the project. Support has also been given in a number of ways by Christophe Poirel in the Council of Europe, and we are particularly grateful to the staff of the European Commission whom we interviewed in the course of our work. We would also like to thank the contributors at our conference held in Glasgow in June 1997. Finally we would like to thank Tom Riley for general support and for his agreement to contribute a Foreword to this book.

The work which is included in this book is part of continuing research by the IMPS group in the School of Law at Glasgow University. Further details can be found from our website at <http://www.imps.gla.ac.uk/>

David Goldberg, Tony Prosser, Stefaan Verhulst
Glasgow and Oxford
December 1997

Foreword

New digital technologies have become almost invisible in our society and commonplace in its usage. In societies where the information and communication technologies are predominant we are witnessing a major shift in human history. The question as to whether this change is a positive one is far from being determined and will be debated for decades to come. The information and communications technology revolution of the past decade has brought new challenges to governments around the world. The social changes that these technologies are bringing are only beginning to surface.

This book is timely in illustrating the multitude of legal responses to this changing media. Further value is added to this comprehensive international report in that the authors, each in their own way, illustrate how cultural differences between nations drive not only the legal approaches but also the content of this changing media. The following chapters will draw out how different governments, driven by their own unique legal, cultural, economic, and political ethic, are attempting, with varying degrees of success, to control content. The research behind this book is invaluable as it points out the diversity of our world nations. While there have been many arguments positing that the dominance of American culture is creating an unwanted uniformity around the world, there is much evidence to suggest that the contrary is happening. Although the new technologies, especially the Internet, are global in nature, regional voices are continuing to become stronger; witness the ethnic conflicts around the world as a manifestation of the desire for maintaining racial or ethnic identity.

The rise of the Internet has led to the idea that this medium will eventually replace television and succeed, where the latter has failed, in creating a proactive citizenry engaged in the cut and thrust of governance on a daily basis. In the past few years a Utopian rainbow has been created across the Internet. A few dreamers and hopeful visionaries are suggesting that this free and almost anarchistic medium will lead us to new forms of improved democracy. Many foresee a knowledge-intensive society composed of an enlightened citizenry. Proponents subscribing to this believe that borders will disappear in this new and evolving world, the role of governments will diminish, and society will evolve into new forms which we can only begin to conceive. Data coming from recent studies and early proponents of these theories are now beginning to manifest doubts about this supposed Utopia.

For example, recent surveys on the population of the Internet suggest that there are now approximately 86.1 million people connected to, and using, the Internet (NUA Surveys, November 12, 1997). People are using the Internet as a tool to enhance the interests that drive them in their daily and professional lives. Many also use it for political activism, to get government information, or to have services delivered electronically. Evidence is surfacing that suggests the Internet will not replace television. Rather, it will evolve as a medium unique unto itself, but not necessarily create a world alien to the one we currently occupy.

One worry is that, while the Internet is a ubiquitous medium, spanning the globe and connecting millions of computers, it is also an isolating technology. People connect with other people in cyberspace but, as often as not, it is a solitary medium engaged in by an individual sitting alone in front of a terminal, removed from the experience of group interaction. The dynamics of one-on-one interaction in a physical environment are far different from interaction with faceless identities. There are benefits to the latter, such as being exposed to a diversity of cultures around the world and not tagging the invisible person at the other end by gender, sex, race, or age. But the problem goes deeper and could result in serious repercussions for society if we produce millions of people whose contact with society is mostly through the computer. Television has contributed significantly to the decline of community activities and volunteer groups, according to studies conducted in North America. The Internet, and the possible convergence of the TV and the Internet, could compound this even further.

This phenomenon has raised anxieties beyond the early concerns about the divisions in our society leading to the 'information rich' and the 'information poor'. While we already know that we are evolving a society that will be divided by the degree to which one is computer literate, there are even deeper concerns surfacing about the negative social impacts for societies. Fragmentation in the world of television has meant we no longer share the experience of common events, whether it is in news, sports, or entertainment. The same principle applies to the Internet, an even more distancing technology. As our access to the world of information and multimedia grows further and further apart amongst our citizens, what impact will this have on nation states in the future? Ironically, the very media that are creating the fragmentation also have within them the capacity to impose strict, authoritarian controls never dreamed possible by tyrants of the past. Privacy advocates constantly present niggling worries about the potentials for a surveillance society in which the individual is controlled and manipulated through the use of the millions of bits of our personal information stored in thousands of networks around the world. Perhaps the concern should not be so much about the censoring of content in the new media, but rather about what checks and balances we should be putting in place, legal and technological, to protect our freedoms?

There has been more information generated in the 1990s than all the information produced prior to 1990. We are awash with information. Yet, this rise in the production of information has not brought with it a concomitant rise in literacy. In fact, studies in the United States and Canada have shown not only increasing illiteracy in the general population but an appalling lack of knowledge at the University level about general historic events, our political leaders, or system of government. This has educators and thinkers questioning the wisdom of rushing to put computers into schools, when the answer lies in how the content is presented and organized. Many object to the theory that a combination of the television and access to the Internet in schools will offer all the information a student can possibly need, and ask whether this will bring knowledge. Information presented in pieces and organized to illustrate its meaning can be used to formulate a knowledge base; this has been the role of a good curriculum presented by a good teacher. The rise of illiteracy itself needs to be addressed by getting to the root causes of the illiteracy, not, say many educators, by putting more computers into the classroom. This is not to say that all these new technologies should not be used to enhance our activities in the workplace, the schools, and the home. Rather, it means that we need to take stock of the meaning of technology and infuse it with the spirit of life that humans bring to technology.

There is a notion abroad in the world that these new technologies, by their mere existence and emergence into society, offer answers and bring with them wisdom. It is only individuals, with foresight, intelligence, imagination, and creativity that bring wisdom.

The Internet is a revolutionary medium that has afforded the opportunity for millions of people to open themselves to a rich panoply of information and services. The benefits of the Internet are legion, as anyone who has used it will realize. But it is equally important to understand the issues which it is raising for society. For example, there is a new political philosophy emerging on the Internet based on the uniqueness of the medium (commonly referred to as the 'Net'). Many occupants of the Net believe that this is a new Commons, an electronic public space, in which the rules of the physical world do not necessarily apply. These active citizens of the Internet (referred to as 'Netizens'), will consistently fight against any attempts by government to restrict what they see as their new form of democracy. People who subscribe to this emerging political philosophy, which we can refer to as 'cyberism', passionately believe that the Net will find its own way of dealing with the problems emerging in their particular society. Yet, even now the common ills of the physical world have found their way onto the Internet, and these same Netizens are agreeing that old solutions still apply. However, there is no doubt that, from this new medium, the politics of cyberspace will take wider and wider hold. There is already extensive activism on the Internet, in which groups and individuals take online actions to lobby all levels of government, from the local to state/provincial, national, and international. The politics of cyberspace are beginning to impinge on the real political world. The question becomes to what degree will the young Netizens of today change the political world of the future?

What is needed is intelligent debate and discussion about the directions that we as a society are taking. By offering widely different approaches to these new media and the issues surfacing in different countries, this book presents a substantive background of fact and analysis, in which readers can decide for themselves the future impact that emerging technologies will have on the world. It represents a significant and important contribution to that debate.

Thomas B. Riley
Visiting Professor, School of Law, University of Glasgow
President: Riley Information Services Inc, Ottawa, Canada
Author: *Living in the Electronic Village: The Impact of Information Technologies On Society: Volumes 1 to 4 (1993–1997)*

Contents

Foreword   vii
  THOMAS B. RILEY
List of Tables   xiii
Notes on Contributors   xv

1 Regulating the Changing Media   1
  DAVID GOLDBERG, TONY PROSSER, STEFAAN VERHULST

2 Germany   29
  WOLFGANG KLEINWÄCHTER

3 Italy   61
  GIUSEPPE DALLERA, MARIA VAGLIASINDI,
  PIETRO VAGLIASINDI

4 The United Kingdom   101
  STEFAAN VERHULST

5 The European Institutions   145
  STEFAAN VERHULST AND DAVID GOLDBERG

6 Hungary   177
  ILDIKO KOVATS

7 The United States   201
  PETER JOHNSON

8 Australia   247
  MARK ARMSTRONG, TREVOR JORDAN,
  MICHAEL HUDSON

9 Conclusions   295
  DAVID GOLDBERG, TONY PROSSER,
  STEFAAN VERHULST

Index   315

List of Tables

Chapter 2: Germany

2.1: Advertising in private television (in million DEM for 1996)   30
2.2: Participation of print media in the broadcasting sector
    (examples)   31
2.3: German network operators (as expected by 1 January 1998)   32
2.4: Viewing rates for the main television stations (per cent)
    in 1997   33
2.5: Advertising revenue of public broadcasters (in million DEM)   34
2.6: Cost of TV rights for the premier football league/*Bundesliga*
    (in million DEM)   35
2.7: On-line use (in million users) in 1996   39

Chapter 3: Italy

3.1: Expected changes in the fixed network infrastructure market   69
3.2: The national television sector in Italy   70
3.3: Mobile telephone tariffs   73

Notes on Contributors

Mark Armstrong is Professor of Communications Law and Director of the Media and Telecommunications Policy Group at RMIT University. His publications include *Communications Law and Policy in Australia* (1987–97) and *Media Law in Australia* (1995). He was chairman of the Australian Broadcasting Corporation (1991–96).

Giuseppe Dallera is Professor of Public Finance and Financial Law at the Faculty of Law of the University of Perugia, and Head of the Institute of Economics and Finance. He studied at the University of York and has published widely on themes related to Public Finance.

David Goldberg is a Senior Lecturer, School of Law, University of Glasgow. He is a Co-Director of IMPS and the Founding Editor of *Tolley's Communications Law*.

Michael Hudson is a Research Associate with the Media and Telecommunications Policy Group at RMIT University. He was formerly associate to the Honourable Justice Northrop at the Federal Court of Australia and was a solicitor at Blake Dawson Waldron in Melbourne.

Peter Johnson is an associate with the law firm of Debevoise & Plimpton in New York City. His published articles include 'Pornography Drives Technology: Why Not to Censor the Internet' (1996); 'The Irrelevant V-Chip: An Alternate Theory of TV and Violence' (1997); and 'The Scotch Whisky Trail' (1987).

Trevor Jordan is a Research Fellow at the Media and Telecommunications Policy Group at RMIT. He has extensive experience in the engineering and regulatory aspects of the telecommunications industry in Australia. He was previously the Regulatory Manager of the Interconnect Unit at Telstra.

Wolfgang Kleinwächter is Director of the NETCOM Institute in Leipzig/Germany and President of the Law Section of the International Association of Media and Communication Research (IAMCR) since 1990. His recent publications include 'Broadcasting Legislation in Central and Eastern Europe' (1996) and 'Regional Development and Information Society' (1997).

Ildiko Kovats is a researcher in the Research Group for Mass Communication Studies at the Budapest ELTE University, and author of numerous articles on Hungarian communication policy, new communication technology development, international communications, and professional journalism.

Tony Prosser is John Millar Professor of Law at the University of Glasgow. His publications include *Law and the Regulators* (1997) and *Privatizing Public Enterprises* (1991, with Cosmo Graham).

Maria Vagliasindi is Lecturer in Economics at the University of Edinburgh. She studied Industrial Organisation and in particular regulation at the Universities of Oxford and Warwick. She has been involved in several research projects on the interactions between regulation and competition and the economics of new media.

Pietro A. Vagliasindi is adjoint Professor of Public Finance and Law at the University of Pisa, and studied economics at University College, London and at the London School of Economics. In Italy he has been involved in many research projects, publishing on topics related to the public sector and public intervention and acting as economic adviser for the Treasury, the Parliament, and the Ministry of Finance.

Stefaan G. Verhulst is Programme Director of the Programme in Comparative Media Law and Policy (CSLS, Wolfson College, University of Oxford) and was until recently senior research associate at the School of Law, University of Glasgow. His latest publication is *Broadcasting Law in India: Reforms and Debates* (1997, with Monroe E. Price).

1

Regulating the Changing Media

DAVID GOLDBERG, TONY PROSSER, STEFAAN VERHULST

1 INTRODUCTION

One of the areas of contemporary life which is changing most rapidly is that of the media.[1] It includes rapidly changing technology; even more importantly, it bears with it economic and social change which is widely claimed to be revolutionary.[2] The aim of this book is to assess the effects of these changes on the capacities of law to regulate the media and, in particular, to examine the extent to which it remains possible for governments and other public authorities to shape the changing media in such a way as to ensure that important social values are not neglected. Such shaping is one role of law, both in its formal sense of constitutions, legislation, and courts, but also through the operation of regulatory authorities established by law. In this book the capacity of radically different legal and administrative systems to cope with fast moving and radical change will be compared with the aim of understanding more about law, regulation, and the media themselves.

The changes, initiated by digitalisation and compression, affect all levels of the media value chain—content, distribution, and interface—and thus lead to media convergence. The computer storage, manipulation, and display of text, pictures, and sound in a common digital form makes possible new forms of media—'multimedia'—and thus new products or services and new markets. Firstly, different services that had previously been carried by different physical media may be carried by a single medium (for example CD-ROM); and secondly, a service that had

---

[1] The issue of definitions was discussed in Wallis R, *Lack of clarity in multimedia definitions can hinder development of useful applications* <http://www.city.ac.uk/multimedia/ftnewslt.htm>

[2] The daily press coverage of changes in communications technologies plays neatly on the words 'revolution', 'evolution', and so on. However, the present 'revolution', if such it be, is one of investment and of transformation of scale rather than technological innovation. Indeed, the history of the technologies of information reveals, rather, a gradual change. It has also been suggested that forecasts and expectations are inspired by the desired (r)evolution and not the real ones. Anyone who tries to make an analysis of the changes in the communications landscape must be well aware of these possible pitfalls. See Goldberg, D, Prosser, T and Verhulst, S, *The Impact Of New Communications Technologies On Media Concentrations And Pluralism* (1997, Strasbourg: Council of Europe), 2.

previously been carried by a single medium may be distributed through several different physical media (for example the electronic newspaper).[3] The movement from a single purpose network or transmission mode towards multipurpose networks is another consequence of this process.[4] No longer do the separate media involve physical carriers with widely differing characteristics: all new communications services can be delivered in an off-line mode, and through packaged media (for example by CD-ROM), or in an on-line mode, or through delivered and network media (for example over the Internet).[5] Later in this chapter we shall describe these technological developments in more detail; but even here we must stress that they are not merely technical in effect. Already they have had profound effects on the economic structure of the (broadly-defined) media industries. In some respects they may have appeared to make it more pluralistic through the lowering of entry barriers and through the growth of small companies such as Internet service providers and software houses. However, in other respects they have encouraged consolidation through alliances between different companies, each trying to dominate emerging markets and to achieve a synergy of different but interdependent parts of the market such as telecommunications, broadcasting, and information technology. This raises far-reaching questions about how competition is to be maintained and policed. Even more profound are the social implications; current uncertainty is shown by the range of predictions as to what they may be. On the one hand, these include visions of an 'information society' with a new diversity of information sources permitting vastly enhanced consumer choice and so enriching democratic debate and cultural diversity. On the other, they envision a society profoundly divided between 'information haves' and 'information have-nots', and so increased political and cultural alienation. Moral and social fears about pornography, particularly child pornography, on the Internet have also pointed to a dark side of the new diversity, suggesting that the freedoms involved can never transcend more established social concerns.

One theoretical reflection should however be expressed at the outset of this book. There is an assumption implicit in much work about this topic which posits a causal relationship between technological developments and social impact. We do not accept such a causal relationship; as a recent writer has put it, '[i]t is indisputable that digitalisation has advanced

---

[3] 'Crossroads on the information highway; convergence and diversity in communications technologies', *Annual Review of the Institute for Information Studies*, 1995, p. xiii.

[4] Ducey, RV, *A New Digital Marketplace in Information and Entertainment Services: Organizing Around Connectivity and Interoperability* (Washington DC: NAB, 1995), 3.

[5] Van Bolhuis, HE and Colom, I, *Cyberspace Reflections* (European Commission, DG XII, Social Research Unit, 1995), p. X.

rapidly in the media industries, but it is an unwarranted leap of logic to see convergence as the determining factor in the ongoing concentrations of capital, and the tempestuous merger activity in the communication industries'.[6]

If the media are the subject of unprecedentedly rapid technological, economic, and social change, law as a regulatory technique is coming under increasing scrutiny and more and more limits on its capacity to police change are suggested as new challenges arise. In one sense this work will attempt to answer the question posed by European Commissioner Bangemann opening the Global Information Networks Conference:

Traditional borders between telecommunication, audio-visual and publishing are blurring. What must the new regulatory framework look like that stimulates rather than hinders the cross fertilisation between these sectors, leading to radically new concepts of multimedia content and services, a potential source for many new jobs?[7]

Uncertainty about the regulatory framework applies to traditional legal forms such as criminal law; much difficulty has already been encountered in attempts to control pornography on the Internet. Other forms of law also face difficulties. For example, attempts to ensure diversity of media ownership on democratic grounds are increasingly questioned as being unnecessary in a world of new diversity of output, as being unenforceable, and as hindering the competitive opportunities of enterprises on a world scale. Even more strikingly, attempts to guarantee universal provision of public services including broadcasting and telecommunications have been criticised as reflecting an outdated and complacent unitary conception of national culture and as neglecting consumer sovereignty through treating the citizen as a passive recipient of public services defined paternalistically. In a radically different area, intellectual property law is a cornerstone of the law relating to on-line services and especially the Internet, and one of the major debates surrounding recent developments in the media is the extent to which in its existing form it can serve a useful purpose in the common digital environment.[8] Finally, as some of these examples vividly show, the historic concentration on the use of law by national authorities to resolve national problems has become outdated with the development of industries to which national boundaries are irrelevant; the very liberation that this represents, it is claimed, makes

---

[6] Schiller, H, 'United States', in *Media Ownership and Control in the Age of Convergence* (London: IIC, 1996), 249.

[7] Dr Bangemann, M, Opening Speech <http://www2.echo.lu/bonn/openspeech.html>

[8] See Charlesworth, A, 'Theft by Many Other Names', in *Times Higher Education Supplement*, 12 Jan 1996.

regulation a historical throwback rather than a practical task for the future.

At the same time as the potential of law to regulate the changing media is increasingly doubted, there have been suggestions at a highly theoretical level that law is profoundly unsuited to the regulation of other social systems. Of particular importance has been work drawing on the theory of autopoiesis.[9] As one commentator on this theory has put it:

[t]here have proved to be a number of problems . . . with the Utopian vision of law as an effective regulator of social behaviour. Not least of these was the growing evidence of law's failure to fulfill the high hopes that had been expected of it. Attempts to regulate social systems through law often seemed to work effectively for a short time and then would produce consequences which were unanticipated by legislators and would-be reformers.[10]

This is largely attributable to the fragmentation of modern societies into differentiated functional systems and subsystems, including law, politics, and the economy, between which direct communication is impossible. The answer is not, however, to end legal regulation in any form but instead to develop a new form of reflexive law which, rather than seeking to intervene directly in other social sub-systems, seeks to establish more indirect means of involvement such as the creation of procedural opportunities for influencing their development. The same theme has been mirrored in other work, suggesting that traditional techniques of 'command and control' regulation are less effective than mechanisms for self-regulation, including 'enforced self-regulation' or 'coregulation' by which the state requires an industry to set its own standards if it is to avoid harsher and less appropriate standards set by the state itself.[11] We shall see examples of these techniques in the national chapters which follow; the validity of the general critique of the regulatory capacity of law will be assessed in our conclusion. For the moment, the point of importance is that the rapid change in the technology, the economics, and the social role of the media has been accompanied by growing caution about the regulatory capacities of law.

---

[9] For a very clear introduction to autopoiesis see King, M, 'The Truth about Autopoiesis' (1993) 20 *Journal of Law and Society* 218; for an earlier example with some direct relevance to regulation see Teubner, M, 'Substantive and Reflexive Elements in Modern Law' (1983) 17 *Law and Society Review* 239; and for later development see Teubner, G, 'Juridification: Concepts, Aspects, Limits, Solutions' in Teubner, G (ed), *Juridification of the Social Spheres* (Berlin: de Gruyter, 1987) and his *Law as an Autopoietic System* (Oxford: Blackwell, 1993). For a direct application to regulatory concerns see Black, J, 'Constitutionalising Self-Regulation' (1996) 59 *Modern Law Review* 24–55. The literature is enormous.

[10] King (n 9 above), 222 (footnote omitted).

[11] See Ayres, I and Braithwaite, J, *Responsive Regulation: Transcending the Deregulation Debate* (Oxford: Oxford University Press, 1992), esp ch 4.

2 OUR METHODOLOGY

It was partly in response to these developments that the British Economic and Social Research Council commenced in 1995 a research programme on *Media Economics and Media Culture*. As part of the programme we commissioned the national studies which form the heart of this book. By choosing to obtain a snapshot of developments in radically different legal systems at one particular point during rapid change, we hoped to move beyond the abstraction of much of the debate about the role of law and of regulation. It seemed at least an arguable hypothesis that the reactions of, for example, the legal systems of the United Kingdom, the United States, and Hungary would reveal very different capacities and techniques for coping with the change. Such study would also provide us with an opportunity to contest the technological determinism underlying some debates on the changing media, a determinism which would suggest that much the same changes would occur everywhere irrespective of culture. By contrast, we expected that the studies would reveal important differences in the way in which the changes were taking place as well as in national patterns of regulation.[12]

The methodology used is thus based upon comparative research in general and comparative law in particular.[13] There is an increasing demand today for comparative research, partly due to growing internationalisation and the concomitant export and import of social, cultural, and economic manifestations across national borders. When analysing media developments and the legal responses thereto, comparison is even more necessary since media are at one and the same time major forces behind, and the products of, globalisation. This is our justification for adopting the comparative research method in this book. Comparisons can lead to fresh, exciting insights and a deeper understanding of issues that are of central concern in different countries. They can lead to the identification of gaps in knowledge and may point to possible directions that could be followed, and of which the researcher may not previously have been aware. They may also help to sharpen the focus of analysis of the subject under study by suggesting new perspectives.[14]

However, comparative research poses certain well-known problems,

---

[12] For the importance of national culture in shaping regulation see eg Hall, P, *Governing the Economy* (Cambridge: Cambridge University Press, 1986); Levy, B and Spiller, PT (eds), *Regulations, Institutions and Commitment* (Cambridge: Cambridge University Press, 1996).

[13] Earlier notable contributions which compare media laws are Barendt, E, *Broadcasting Law* (Oxford: Clarendon Press, 1993) and Hoffman-Rheim, W, *Regulating Media* (New York: Guilford Press, 1996).

[14] See Hantrais, L, 'Comparative Research Methods' (1996) *Social Research Update*, Issue 13.

for example accessing comparable data and comparing concepts and research parameters.[15] In many cross-national projects, national experts are required to provide descriptive accounts of selected trends and developments derived from national data sources. The co-ordinators then synthesise information on key themes and issues. Since much of the international work is not strictly comparative at the design and data collection stages, the findings cannot then be compared systematically. Data collection is strongly influenced by national conventions. Their source, the purpose for which they were gathered, the criteria used, and the method of collection may vary considerably from one country to another, and the criteria adopted for coding data may change over time.[16] Moreover, attempts at cross-national comparisons are still too often rendered ineffectual by the lack of a common understanding of central concepts and the societal contexts within which phenomena are located.

In an effort to overcome some of these problems in relation to the national reports which follow, a template was distributed seeking information in a standard form. This covered the general trends in media development, largely in order to establish the extent to which convergence was actually taking place rather than being merely prophesied. There was also coverage of the ways in which market structures were being shaped by the strategies of actors within the changing media and the effects of this on concentration and pluralism. Detailed analysis was also required of the regulatory institutions and tools used. It must be stressed that this is a snapshot taken in 1997; the media have continued to change rapidly since this snapshot in all the jurisdictions studied, and indeed regulatory institutions and techniques are themselves continuing to develop. Of course, the snapshot does not cover all the myriad developments in equivalent detail; for example, personal mobile communications and electronic commerce are not fully discussed but we hope to look at them in more detail in later work. Nevertheless, we hope that this snapshot will permit some conclusions to be reached about underlying trends in media development, in regulation, and, perhaps most importantly, in the capacities of law in a rapidly changing world.

Six countries were selected, with the following justifications. The UK, apart from the obvious advantage of accessibility of information to the main researchers, has pioneered the development of competition in some key areas, especially telecommunications services and networks. Combined with this liberalisation is a particular form of constitutional structure which permits considerable scope to a government with a majority in the House of Commons to engage in policy experiment without the incon-

---

[15] Based upon Hantrais, L and Mangen, S, *Cross-National Research Methods in the Social Sciences* (1996).

[16] ibid.

venience of constitutional constraint and with minimal use of legal challenge (through there are signs that in some areas this is changing). Thus this means that we can study policy making on a particularly 'heroic' scale in this jurisdiction.[17] Of the other European jurisdictions studied, both have a much greater role for constitutional norms and institutions in shaping policy, whilst both have been implementing similar policy changes to those observed in the UK. Germany has swiftly deregulated its telecommunications system both because of privatisation and because of the impact of European Community policies. In the past, the Federal Constitutional Court has had an important role to play in defending public service broadcasting,[18] and constitutional factors also seriously complicate the regulatory structure with a division between Federal and *Länder* responsibilities. Germany has also seen important and controversial alliances and mergers in the media sector. Italy has had a long history of constitutional and political arguments about broadcasting concentration and public service; whilst some of the new technologies are not yet so advanced there, it also has had to come to terms with increasing competition and the creation of new regulatory authorities. Because of the peculiar nature of Italian politics, this process has been the opposite of 'heroic' with serious delays and difficulties experienced in the formation and implementation of policy, including difficulties on constitutional grounds. As is already clear, underlying many of the developments described in this book has been the role of the European institutions, both as policy initiator in, for example, telecommunications deregulation, and as a policeman of national policies, for example in competition matters. It was thus essential to include an overview of the role of these institutions in this book, both for the European Community and for the Council of Europe.

Hungary is included because it raises further interesting concerns. Although change has been rapid in other nations, the countries of the former Eastern Bloc have had to move from state-controlled media to a more pluralistic structure with enormous speed and have had to create regulatory institutions virtually from scratch. These countries have also faced the problem of gaining the enormous amount of investment needed for the new services, and this has meant in practice depending largely on foreign investment, raising serious problems of potential limits to pluralism. The existence of an outdated infrastructure also raises the question of the extent to which new technology provides an alternative form of delivery in nations making a rapid economic leap forward.

---

[17] For further discussion of the peculiar constitutional freedom of UK policy-makers see Graham, C and Prosser, T, *Privatizing Public Enterprises* (Oxford: Clarendon Press, 1991), esp chs 1, 2, 8.

[18] See Barendt (n 13 above); the key cases are discussed in the chapter on Germany below.

Outside Europe, Australia was chosen as it is a common-law based system—in this respect similar to the UK—and one in which considerable liberalisation has already taken place. However, it has a rather different role for the courts and one which has meant that they have been more active in this field than in the UK; it has also chosen to approach some regulatory issues differently. Moreover, Australia's Pacific Rim geo-political context has some bearing on its policy and regulation. Finally, the choice of the USA was an obvious one. It is the home of much of the new technology underlying the changes to be described in this book and has had a long history of high-profile regulatory authorities, which have been characterised by important differences in regulatory style from those in Europe.[19] However, the traditional regulatory approach has come under attack recently with a greater emphasis being placed on competition and this has led to experimentation with new, and possibly less intrusive, forms of regulation. It also has an exceptionally strong role for the consti-tution and for the courts, being in this respect the polar opposite to the UK, and at the time of the study key decisions were being made by the Supreme Court on issues central to our work.

The information we received from each of the countries analysed will be set out and analysed in the chapters below and supplemented with fur-ther information obtained as a result of interviewing, for example, those responsible for media regulation in the European Community institu-tions. Before doing so, however, we need to explain the technological change which has happened in the media in greater detail as well as the effects of this and other influences on industry structure. It will also be useful to describe in general terms some different purposes of regulation of the media and the different institutional structures through which this may take place.

3 MACROTRENDS IN THE CHANGING MEDIA

A number of trends are apparent across the media and communications markets.[20] The most well-known example is that of digitalisation and related technical advances such as compression, optical fibre, and ex-tended switching. This is taking place at all levels of the media value chain; for example, in the form of convergence of the content of media or

---

[19] See eg Vogel, D, *National Styles of Regulation* (London: Cornell University Press, 1986).
[20] See *The Future of the UK Media Industry* (London: FT Telecoms & Media Publishing, Oct 1996).

of media forms (the creation of multimedia), the convergence of delivery channels (the shift of single- to multi-purpose networks) and the convergence of customer interfaces (for example the teleputer encompassing a super telephone, PC, and television). The process leads to the convergence of industries (telecommunications, IT, and media) and markets and the creation of a new media consumption environment,[21] in turn producing a multiplication of distribution channels (or the creation of the so-called Information Superhighways) and the prospect of fierce inter-modal competition (for example wired versus wireless, satellite versus cable) as well as intra-modal competition and the involvement of non media groups (rail companies, electricity suppliers, etc). Further implications are firstly the re-use and re-packaging of content for multimedia purposes and vertical integration, and secondly increased customer contact through two-way communications or interactivity leading to customisation or personalisation of the information and to 'narrowcasting'. It is these developments above all which have led to predictions of the coming 'information society'.[22]

There are, of course, dangers in over-stressing the convergence factor, and it would be foolish to suggest at this stage that a coherent industry will arise incorporating electronics, information technology, carrier, entertainment, and information businesses. Nor, in the first instance, will the amalgamated turnovers, competitive strengths, and employment capacities of each sector be combined to form a super-industry with a huge influence upon the rest of economy and society.[23] More realistically, three elements have to be taking into account when analysing those trends. Firstly, market development is expected to be evolutionary. Television services will merge with on-line services as and when telecoms networks are sufficiently advanced, although this may not occur in the near future,[24] and whether these trends will take place at all, in the UK for example, is still uncertain. A recent report published by the UK Department of Trade and Industry[25] stated that the main characteristic of the current situation is a general uncertainty about the shape of the so-called Information Society.

[21] See Garnham, N, 'What is Multimedia?', in *Legal Aspects of Multimedia and GIS*. Lisbon 27/28 Oct 1994, Legal Advisory Board Conference (DG XIII), 10; <http://www.2.echo.be/lab/>
[22] See Carruthers, S and Smith, S, *The Information Society: Meeting the Social and Economic Challenge* (UK Information Society Project, Tagish, 1995), 3.
[23] See *The main events and developments in the Information Market 1993–1994* (Luxembourg: IMO, Oct 1995).
[24] Jameson, J, *Convergence and the New Media: a Roadmap* (London: IPPR, 1995), 4.
[25] Not only is there uncertainty about the end target but there is also debate about the routes ahead. See *The Development of the Information Society: an International Analysis* (London: HMSO, 1996).

The uncertainty is only too obvious if the track records of other technologies are considered. Implementation of ISDN, EC-promoted unified telecoms, high definition television, UK cable television, a UK fibre-optic network, etc, has dragged on for years.[26] Kenneth Baker, former Minister for Information and Technology predicted as long ago as 1982 that, 'by the end of the decade multi-channel cable television will be commonplace countrywide . . . TV will be used for armchair shopping, banking, calling emergency services and many other services.' In reality by the end of the 1980s, cable TV had reached 1 per cent penetration in the UK and the vision of armchair shopping has yet to be realised.[27]

Secondly, we can still observe two distinct and competing service categories within the new communications services which dominate the present debate in the UK: *TV-type services* (such as near video on demand, and digital terrestrial television) versus *on-line type services* (the Internet). In the long run they could converge or at least be linked via gateways; at present, however, the on-line and TV-communities still have different cultures and their actors still operate differently. Moreover, a recent report included a third critical area and competing service to the two: the *off-line multimedia* (CD-ROM, CD I, etc), and stated '[e]ach of the three areas has reached different stages of development, has different technical, marketing and financial constraints, and is approaching the future from different angles. Each, though, has the same digital destination.'[28] Indeed, at present the most popular delivery medium for multimedia (both to the home and the office) is undoubtedly the CD-ROM, due to its large storage capacity and the low cost associated with producing disks.[29] In the long term however, both consumer and business markets are likely to turn to broadband networks (telephone, cable, fibre, wireless) for the delivery of new communications services.[30]

Finally, as hinted above, the 'convergence' model is misleading since it suggests 'narrowing'. What really happens in the market is diversification and the creation of new industries and sectors. Computers, for example, diversified into hardware and software, and into mainframes and PCs.[31] In addition to broadcast TV, there now exists satellite TV, global TV, digital TV, interactive TV, and narrowcast TV. Telephone companies have become telcos, resellers, Internet services providers, network providers,

[26] See Cawkell, AE, 'The information superhighway: political realities and the time factor', *Journal of Information Science*, 21(1) 1995, 61–2.

[27] See Harrison, F, 'The Future of New Media', *Admap*, Nov 1996.

[28] See *The Future of Multimedia* (London: FT Telecoms & Media Publishing, Oct 1996).

[29] See *The Emergence of a Mass Multimedia Market* (Luxembourg: IMO Working Paper 95/6, Dec 1995), 3.

[30] See Goldberg, D, Prosser, T and Verhulst, S (n 2 above), 4.

[31] See Mitchell, H, *What is 'convergence'*, ISPO-discussion group, 5 May 1996; <http://www.ispo.cec.be/>

etc. This may have considerable implications for the ways in which competition and pluralism are regulated.

The new services

Convergence will lead to new and more numerous services. Because digital data and transmission occupy much less space than analogue, media capacity will be much increased. One result will be a major reformulation of entertainment and information delivery as described above. Another will be a whole raft of new services. These will be both *multimedia* (ie using text, sound, and video in combination) and *multiple media* (involving several media such as broadcast and telecommunication). Moreover many non-media services such as home shopping will be bolted on the new capacity in interactive formats. However, what demand there will be for the new services and what the so-called 'killer' application will be is still unknown. Most studies suggest that there is no 'killer' application and that a combination of applications (as described below) is needed to support the successful diffusion of services. There is however an emerging new theory that the 'killer' application for the Internet might come not from games and information, but from 'intranets' (private, corporate Internets) and electronic commerce.[32]

Types of application, while often sharing similar enabling technologies, are differentiated by a mix of technical requirements and characteristics suited to different users' needs.[33] Important categories are firstly *entertainment services*, the area growing from interactive TV applications, where the main confrontation between telecom and cable and TV companies will take place to conquer new revenues from the residential market. Secondly, *communication services* include the advanced services where content is provided by the users interacting between themselves, while, thirdly, *information services* are characterised by access to remote databases and interaction by users with service suppliers. In this area off-line CD-ROMs are likely to be a competitive or complementary technology to on-line services. Fourthly, *transactional services* are characterised by the presence of financial transactions with specific security requirements, and fifthly, *professional services* include applications such as teleworking and co-operative working. Finally, *public and social services* include services provided by public administration organisations and services with social relevance in certain vertical markets (such as telemedicine or distance learning for universities) which may be supplied by public or private organisations.

[32] See *The Future of Multimedia* (n 28 above).
[33] See *Review of Developments in Advanced Communications Markets in Europe* (London: Databank Consulting, 1996), 20.

The new communications industry

In order for advanced information and entertainment services to be developed and deployed, a suitable multimedia delivery market structure needs to be in place. The current view is that there will be at least five markets and layers of participants.[34] The five layers are firstly, *content providers* (creators and owners) who develop multimedia information or own elements of it (for example in digital picture archives), including publishers, TV producers, software companies, music companies, news services, and even advertising agencies who as a result of copyright legislation can claim to be rights holders. This group also encompasses, of course, individual creators. Secondly, *content and service producers* and packagers, who gather information and entertainment content and add value by merging or packaging them into bundled interactive offerings for delivery via the access application providers (for example database compilers, publishers, on-line service providers, broadcasters, record companies, etc). Thirdly, *network builders* who develop and deploy the integrated broadband communications infrastructure in the form of electronic information distribution networks, including network switching equipment, satellite communications systems, wireless network systems, fibre-optic cable, and other external plant facilities (for example telecommunications, satellites, cable operators) as well as other forms of distribution, such as CD-ROM.[35] Such a distribution network can be regarded as the 'pipe' that conveys the message.

Fourthly, *network operators or service providers* who manage the networks and provide new communications services by transporting information and entertainment content and/or communications (telephony and datacoms), together with call monitoring and customer billing. This layer is divided into two elements: national distributors (for example BT, Mercury, resellers, and satellite distribution services) and local distributors (networks operated by local exchange carriers, competitive access providers, cable television systems, wireless systems, and local radio and television broadcasters). Service providers may run their own 'servers' connected directly to distribution networks, or use others' servers. Some may control their own gateways and control systems; others may depend

[34] Quelin, B, 'Mouvements strategiques et frontières des activités: La formation d'une nouvelle industrie', *Communication et Strategies*, no 19, 3ème trimestre 1995, 25–43; KPMG. Ashurst Morris Crisp and Prof G Yarrow, *Public policy issues arising from telecommunications and audiovisual convergence. Convergence between telecommunications and audiovisual: consequences for the rules governing the information market* (Brussels: LAB, 30 Apr 1996); Wallis, R and Cross, T, *The Common Digital Environment and Industrial Convergence*; <http://www.city.ac.uk/multimedia/cvrgnc3.htm>

[35] *Beyond the telephone, the television and the PC* (London: OFTEL, 1995).

on those of third parties. Some may collect bills, recruit advertisers, and run navigation systems. Equally, these functions may be carried out by network builders and owners.

The fifth and final layer is that of *access application or site equipment providers*. These are the third parties who provide information and entertainment service access. Access applications incorporate such elements as consumer electronic devices (such as PCs, PC-TVs, set-top boxes, personal mobile communicators, etc), application software (information/entertainment navigation, selection, retrieval, viewing, browsing, billing, etc), massively parallel databases, interactive multimedia servers, and data encryption. Some elements of this market are already well developed, for example the PC market. Others are less well so, such as the intelligence linking customer apparatus to the distribution network through set-top converters, modems, and conditional access systems. As customers may be understandably reluctant to purchase such equipment before services are well developed, service providers and network builders may have to play a part in supplying apparatus; an example to be considered below of such arrangements are those proposed by BSkyB involving subsidy for the initial development of decoders by other companies in return for their involvement in interactive services such as home banking and home shopping.

It would of course be quite misleading to suggest that the technological development described above has had a direct causal relationship with economic and social developments; one of the unspoken assumptions in much of the literature which we wish to contest is that of such technological determinism.[36] However, there is no doubt that strategies within the media industries have been profoundly affected by the developments described above. In one respect, of course, the new technologies might seem to offer greater pluralism through diversification and permitting the delivery of a greater range of services more closely targeted to individual needs whilst lowering entry barriers and so permitting greater competition. Indeed, examples of such new entry are not hard to find, especially in the area of the newer services, such as the boom industry of Internet service providers. However, there is also a contradictory tendency towards increased concentration. Underlying this are a number of incentives. These include the need to redefine corporate missions or to reposition as a result of the blurring of boundaries between previously distinct industries, the need for partners as a precondition of developing new broadband networks because of the high costs of investment and the removal of intermediaries from the industry value chain. This has found

---

[36] And see eg Schiller, H (n 6 above).

expression in the development of alliances or external ventures and these may take place both horizontally and vertically. For example, relations between content creators and producers and between service providers and network builders are characterised by strong vertical agreements, in addition to the more traditional horizontal integrations in the form of media conglomerates. This is certainly the case in for instance the US, where the industry is dominated by four giant corporations. Time Warner is one of them. The company owns for example Turner Broadcasting (a giant in itself), it publishes books, music, and magazines, produces motion pictures, has ownership interests in cable channels, and owns extensive cable franchises. Such a pattern of concentration should be enough in itself to alert us to problems of competition law and policy. It also, however, has the further consequence of blurring the distinctions between different markets so that it becomes more difficult to measure and control market dominance. Thus tests of ownership and of share in a single market are likely to prove impossible to apply, or to be misleading as indicators of entry barriers or pluralism of the media. The traditional limits on cross-media ownership are also increasingly inappropriate as they are based on the assumption of a relatively small number of distinct media markets, notably television or radio and the print media. As new markets develop and convergence proceeds it becomes more and more difficult to maintain these assumptions. A possible response is to develop a 'media exchange rate' attempting to measure influence across markets, as was proposed by the UK government in 1995.[37] However the difficulties of establishing a non-arbitrary means of assessing the comparative influence of different media are formidable and, after facing extensive criticism, this proposal was quietly shelved.[38] Another approach, and one which does seem to be in the process of becoming more popular, is that of concentrating on key elements of the markets which can give the greatest competitive advantage, for example through the 'gatekeeping' function of controllers of access to bottlenecks, such as conditional access systems, subscription management systems, navigation systems, and new and intelligent broadband networks.[39] These will be analysed in detail in the chapters below, but the point should be made here that an effect of the combination of changing technology and changing market structures has been to suggest that some traditional regulatory tools are inappropriate whilst other regulatory techniques may become more useful.

---

[37] Department of National Heritage, *Media Ownership: The Government's Proposals*, Cm 2872 (1995).

[38] For a general discussion of this issue see Graham, A, 'Exchange Rates and Gatekeepers' in Congden, T *et al* (eds), *The Cross Media Revolution* (London: John Libby, 1995), 38–49.

[39] ibid.

4 PURPOSES OF REGULATION

We have now gone some way to explain the developments in the media which lie behind our study. It remains for us to discuss the other key element; the concept of regulation used. One preliminary point needs to be made. This is in part a study of the law relating to the media, but it is only concerned with part of that law. Thus private law is generally outside the scope of this work, as is the operation of the ordinary law on such matters as contracts. Rather, law is of interest as a regulatory tool through which public authorities implement policies relating to the media. So what can we characterise as regulation? In our template for information on each nation studied we deliberately used a wide concept of regulation, characterising it as technological regulation concerned with infrastructure and standardisation, economic regulation concerned with market structure and remuneration and finance, social regulation of content including defamation and security, and user protection covering privacy and equity and access to the media. These categories cover a vast area, of course; is it possible to be more precise about a concept of regulation and its purposes?

It would certainly not be possible to claim that the concept of regulation has been neglected either in academic discussion or in political and industry debate.[40] However, we would suggest that the experience to be described in this book suggests that much discussion of regulation has been oversimplified. In particular, regulation has usually been defined by its opposite, free markets, and has been seen as necessary only when markets cannot work successfully either for reason of monopoly or oligopoly power or because of the need for public interest interventions by the state.[41] Media regulation has also been shaped by the social and political value accorded to a free media in particular and to freedom of speech in general. The principle is recognised in all Western industrialised countries, but most societies value freedom of speech not as an end in itself but rather as a means to reach normative objectives such as self-fulfilment, discovery of truth, etc, and above all the promotion of democracy.[42] The protection of the principle has been a topic of a revived debate as a result of the rapidly changing media, and it is interesting to note in the following chapters the difference in interpretation of the principle in, for instance, the US and the UK.

There is a considerable literature on possible justifications for

---

[40] For a comprehensive account see Ogus, A, *Regulation* (Oxford: Clarendon Press, 1994).

[41] For an example of such a view see the speech of Rupert Murdoch reported in the *Financial Times*, 28–9 June 1997.

[42] See Hoffmann-Riem, *Regulating Media* (n 13 above).

regulating the electronic media, but much of it is of limited relevance to this study because it is based on justifications which no longer exist. The first was the existence of spectrum scarcity; the second the particular pervasiveness or intrusiveness of broadcasting.[43] A further justification was the concept of public service broadcasting. This latter did itself tend to be a rather vague justification for regulation which was not often subject to detailed analysis, especially when public service broadcasting was the business of government and so did not involve the development of separate regulatory institutions. Nevertheless, in the past it was seen as the only guarantee of broadcasting which catered for a variety of different interests, including those of minorities, and as permitting participation in a common culture. However, to a very large degree spectrum scarcity no longer exists and it is arguable that the growth of new services means that there is no longer any special pervasiveness or intrusiveness for broadcasting. Moreover, it is argued that a future proliferation of channels to be brought about by digital technology will produce diversity beyond that ever dreamed of by public service broadcasting. If we wish to analyse regulation properly it is thus necessary for us to reassess reasons for regulating the media. We would suggest that at least four distinct regulatory rationales can be found.

The most familiar type of regulation in discussion of broadcasting (though not of the print media) is social regulation of content. Of course, this includes restrictions on sexual and violent material; however, it may also include issues of defamation and breach of confidentiality. It is striking that these concerns remain at the heart of debate around the changing media. One immediately striking example is that of Internet content, for example in the attempts of authorities in Germany to close down access to some servers, and even the attempts to make executives of Compuserve subject to criminal liability. In the United States this has also been a high-profile issue, most importantly with the successful challenge to the provisions of the Communications Decency Act discussed in detail in Chapter 7 below. In assessing the future of regulation of this kind, however, there are important distinctions to be made between different types of medium. The proliferation of digital channels may make less necessary some controls on content, for example those concerning issues of balance in coverage. However, concerns about violent or sexually explicit content show no signs of decreasing, as is evidenced, for example, by successful attempts to prevent the reception in the UK of pornographic services from overseas.[44] This shows clearly how important international controls will be to make future content regulation effective. The same is true of the Internet. Apart

[43] For discussion see Barendt (n 13 above), 3–10.

[44] For a recent UK example see Department of National Heritage Press Release DNH 067/97 of 5 Mar 1997, relating to 'Satisfaction Club'.

from attempted controls on pornography discussed earlier, there are examples of the Internet successfully breaching limits applied to other material; one example is the publication there during a ban by the courts of a book by President Mitterand's doctor describing his fight with cancer.[45] In view of the nature of network architecture, it seems that, even in a national context, content regulation of the Internet will prove very difficult. Moreover, the international nature of the Internet and of other forms of new media will mean that future controls will have to be international in nature or involve self-regulation by parts of the industry itself. New attempts at content regulation are thus likely to look very different from techniques adopted in the past. One of the purposes of the national reports in this book will be to examine the extent to which content regulation is still attempted and what techniques may be most appropriate to implement it.

The second type of media regulation is radically different. This is regulation for competition, and has also been highly controversial lately in relation to concentration of ownership, mergers, and joint ventures, and more specific trade practices such as the selling of tied programming rights and 'bundling' of channels or control of conditional access systems. In a deeper sense, some form of regulation of this type could be seen as a presupposition for the operation of any forms of market at all; for example, the establishment of processes for the allocation of the frequency spectrum, administratively or by auction, is necessary for the existence of dispersed property rights in it. Similarly, it is difficult to envisage any efficiently functioning market for information without a system of intellectual property rights enforced by the public authorities.

In one sense regulation for competition is not as controversial as content regulation, as it is not specific to the media but instead an application of broader competition policies applying across different product markets; though, as we shall see, there are fuller and more detailed controls over the media for the separate purpose of protecting media pluralism. Even in the field of regulation for competition, however, there are problems in coping with the new media landscape. Firstly, it has already become evident that much of recent media activity has been international, both in terms of the markets served and the companies involved. However, transnational attempts to preserve competitive markets are in their infancy. Partial exceptions to this are the attempts by the European Community both to liberalise and to re-regulate telecommunications, and by the European Commission to police mergers and anti-competitive practices in the media field. These have had some notable successes, but only affect a very small proportion of overall media activity. The alternative to

---

[45] See http://www.nb-pacifica.com/reg/bannedmitterandbookon_494.shtml

international regulation, that of concentrating on national markets, not only misconceives the nature of much of the media industry but has been alleged to prevent the growth of large enterprises able to compete in world markets, a concern not limited to the media but also applying to other industries such as civil aviation.

Secondly, even in Western Europe some nations do not have an effective system of domestic competition law. This is partially compensated by use of Community law, but elsewhere this is not possible, so leaving few weapons to combat market concentration and unfair trade practices. The nations surveyed in this book mostly do have workable systems of competition law, but this is not necessarily true in other parts of the world. Thirdly, the instruments used even in the more sophisticated systems of competition policy are often crude and outdated. Thus much competition law, especially in relation to the media, is based on relatively simple tests of ownership or market share, often blurring regulation for competition and the protection of pluralism of information. Such controls may still have an important role now when convergence is still incomplete, but are difficult to apply to the new media markets for two reasons. Firstly, as already suggested, there are serious difficulties of measurement of influence across different types of media and hence the difficulties with the concept of a 'media exchange rate'. Secondly, the control of key access points in the new media can give an influence over other commercial actors far beyond anything suggested by simple ownership statistics. Examples are systems of conditional access for subscription services and search engines for use on the Internet. In relation to the former, the European Community has already taken action to ensure that access is afforded fairly; in the UK this is implemented by the Office of Telecommunications, the specialist telecommunications regulator. There is reason to believe that such tasks are best entrusted to such specialist bodies rather than to generalist competition authorities; however, outside the Anglo-Saxon world and now Germany, France, and Italy, regulatory authorities of this kind are rare and raise the further problem that telecommunications and broadcasting have normally been regulated separately (except in the USA) whereas technology has converged.

These problems do not mean that regulation for competition will be unimportant in the developing media world. It will retain a major role in ensuring transparency of ownership and control, interconnection and interoperability of systems, and in the different form of the distribution of intellectual property rights. Indeed, as examples of developing markets worldwide show, the successful resolution of these questions is a prerequisite for the establishment of competition, not a form of control after it has been established. For this study, other central questions are whether it is possible to develop more accurate tests of influence in media markets than the traditional tests of ownership, what are the most important access points and gateways which will need greater regulatory attention, and which types of institution are best suited to carrying out the remaining regulatory tasks.

Despite these complexities, regulation for competition is in principle no different in the context of the media from regulation of other industries. However, it is easily confused with a different from of regulation which has been extremely important in the past and has justified special controls on media ownership and, to some degree, on content. This is the need to ensure plurality and diversity in the media on democratic grounds, and can itself be broken down into several distinct categories.[46] It has particular importance in the context of news and current affairs, attempting to secure that different political and social viewpoints are fully represented. It has also applied across programming as a whole in order to ensure that such programming covers a range of interests rather than offering only content which is cheap to produce or designed to appeal only to audiences most likely to attract advertisers. This principle of diversity has in some cases been elevated to constitutional status, emphasising its importance, as occurred in Germany and Italy. Thus *internal pluralism* within a service is the first type of pluralism which regulation may seek to protect.

Closely related to it is *external pluralism*, concerned not with the content of a particular service but with the maintenance of a range of different services. This is clearly related to the competition goals of regulation discussed above in that it is used to justify controls on concentration of ownership, but goes further than this. In the words of the (generally pro-competition) Conservative Government in the UK in its 1995 proposals on media ownership:

[g]eneral competition legislation is mainly concerned with securing economic objectives, although it can also encompass other non-economic objectives. However, wider objectives are important so far as the media are concerned. A free and diverse media are an indispensable part of the democratic process. They provide the multiplicity of voices and opinions that informs the public, influences opinion, and engenders political debate. They promote the culture of dissent which any healthy democracy must have. In so doing, they contribute to the cultural fabric of the nation and help define our sense of identity and purpose. . . . Special media ownership rules, which exist in all major media markets, are needed therefore to provide the safeguards necessary to maintain diversity and plurality.[47]

---

[46] For basic distinctions between different types of pluralism see Council of Europe Steering Committee on the Mass Media (CDMM) (96) 20, 12; and Goldberg, D, Prosser, T and Verhulst, S (n 2 above), Part 4.

[47] Department of National Heritage, *Media Ownership: The Government's Proposals* (n 37 above), para 1.4.

Thus there is an accepted case for stronger controls than those suggested by competition policy to protect external pluralism on democratic
grounds.

There is now an influential trend of opinion suggesting that new developments in the media are making this type of regulation redundant. The
development of digitalisation and the potential for an enormous growth
in the number of channels available, it is argued, will provide a diversity
of different viewpoints without the need for regulatory intervention.
Moreover, the development of new forms of delivery will lower entry
barriers so that a healthy diversity of participants in the media market will
continue to exist, and that will in turn ensure a continued diversity of
information representing a wide range of viewpoints. Thus neither internal nor external pluralism will be dependent on regulatory intervention.
One of the points which will emerge in the national chapters later will
indeed be the difficulty of implementing regulatory controls in a rapidly
changing media environment. However, there may also be at least two
reasons for caution before abandoning them. Firstly, the development of
a large number of channels and indeed of a large number of companies
does not in itself guarantee impartiality, especially in the provision of
news and current affairs programming. To give a deliberately exaggerated example, a profusion of channels each controlled by a different
Christian sect would not ensure fair coverage of other religions. Secondly,
the model of consumer choice offered in the new markets is not the only
sort of diversity. Even if it succeeds in providing the consumer with the
opportunity to select from a wide range of channels in which he or she can
find one or several precisely reflecting his or her interests, this is to treat
those choices as preformed and unchangeable. In fact, one of the advantages of the 'old' media and of public service broadcasting was to provide
a different form of diversity through a mixture of programming through
which one could learn and develop tastes through coming across the
unexpected; in other words, to act as a participant in a culture rather than
as a consumer or 'rational economic man'.[48] Thus there may be a case for
encouraging the continuation of something resembling traditional public
service broadcasting alongside the new media plurality, even if such
plurality does indeed come into existence. Thus important questions to be
examined in later chapters will be the extent to which, in practice, pluralism requires further controls than those of competition policy, whether
growth in the number of available channels and of new forms of delivery
can be translated into diversity of viewpoint and of content, and what role
public service broadcasters should have in the new environment.

[48] See Hollis, M and Nell, E, *Rational Economic Man* (Cambridge: Cambridge University
Press, 1975).

The final type of regulation which can be identified here is one which has been less explicitly protected in the past, but which is coming more to the forefront of debate now. This is that of regulation for access. One form of access regulation has already been noted in our discussion of competition policy; that of providing access to competing but interdependent systems through interconnection rights. This is probably the most important issue of all in the rapidly developing field of telecommunications competition, and is a further prerequisite for the establishment of competitive markets, as we shall see in later chapters. Another form of access is, however, radically different and is based on social rather than economic rationales. This attempts to shape the availability of new services so that we do not have a society divided between information 'haves' and information 'have-nots' resulting in social division. The theme has been very important in telecommunications regulation where it is labelled 'universal service' and includes both geographic access (itself aided by technological developments such as satellite delivery) and 'affordable tariffs'.[49] Indeed, important recent debates in the UK, in the European Community institutions, and in the US Government and regulators have concerned the degree to which guarantees of service should be developed beyond basic voice telecommunications to include data services which will provide access to the Internet. Particularly important has been the issue of access to the new forms of media by training and educational institutions; examples of work have included a detailed rule-making procedure by the US Federal Communications Commission on the matter of which telecommunications services are essential to education, public health, or public safety and a controversial promise by the Labour Party in the UK before it entered government that British Telecom would be given greater freedom to provide entertainment services if it provided free Internet access for schools or libraries (something which anyway seems likely to be implemented by the cable networks for commercial reasons).[50]

In the more conventional broadcasting environment, issues of access are linked to competition concerns and the role of 'gatekeepers' controlling key elements of technology which could be used to prevent access to the services of competitors, and also to pluralism with its concern to provide access to programmes for citizens with a wide range of different tastes and interests. A particularly fraught example of an access controversy is that

---

[49] For a taste of a huge literature on this theme see eg Office of Telecommunications, *Universal Telecommunications Services* (London: OFTEL, 1997); *Communication from the Commission of the European Communities on Universal Service for Telecommunications*, COM (96)73 final (1996); Federal Communications Commission, *Report and Order in the Matter of Federal-State Joint Board on Universal Service*, FCC 97–157 (1997).

[50] See FCC (n 49 above); Office of Telecommunications, *Information Highways: Improving Access for Schools, Colleges and Public Access Points* (London: OFTEL, 1997).

concerning sports rights and the movement of sporting events to subscription or pay-per-view services.[51] This has been regulated in a number of countries through the specification of 'listed events' protected against exclusive broadcasting on subscription and pay-per-view services, and the European Community has very recently taken steps to ensure that Member States are permitted to continue this practice.[52] It has also been accepted that universal service is one of the characteristics which should form part of public service broadcasting, both in the sense that geographical coverage is as extensive as possible, and also that the range of programming is such as to cater for as many different interests as practical. Recent regulatory interventions to protect this principle include the 'must carry' rules under which new forms of delivery such as cable or digital broadcasting must provide viewer access to the public service channels as part of the service. These have a long history in the United States but have also been included in the terms on which new broadcasters can operate.[53]

We will thus need to consider the extent to which universal service principles can be developed from telecommunications and from public service broadcasting and applied to the environment of the changing media. One answer might be simply to leave this to competition law as a matter of access to competing systems in the market place; however, the discussion above suggests that universal service goes well beyond this. A related issue showing another side to access is also becoming of considerable importance; that of encryption and rights to privacy—does access imply a right to limit the access of others on privacy grounds, in particular the rights of the state? Again this contains several strands, but one of the most controversial is that of whether encryption will be permitted on the Internet in forms which prevent access by public authorities. The development of electronic commerce will be dependent on the achievement of effective encryption, but governments are extremely reluctant to permit systems which could be used for terrorism, espionage, or indeed money laundering outside the control of the authorities. It also must not be forgotten that data protection and privacy concerns are profoundly affected by the development of the new media forms, and these areas of user protection will also be addressed in the national reports. Important recent examples of action include that taken by the UK Data Protection Registrar, the US Department of Commerce and Federal Trade Commission, and the European Community.

---

[51] For an overview of the issues see Cowie, C and Williams, M, *The Economics of Sports Rights* (Oxford: RPRC, 1997).

[52] *Television Without Frontiers Directive*. In the United Kingdom the relevent provisions are ss 97–105 of the Broadcasting Act 1996; see also the Independent Television Commission, *ITC Code on Sports and Listed Events* (London: ITC, 1997).

[53] For UK examples see the Broadcasting Act 1996, ss 28–32.

Much public discussion about the development of new forms of delivery and of media convergence has suggested that these technological developments increasingly make regulation impossible as new forms of delivery escape effective regulatory control. This may be true about some types of content regulation, especially on the Internet, and, as we have seen, simple tests of ownership as the basis for maintaining pluralism are likely to become inappropriate because of the difficulties of separating overlapping markets and of measuring the influence of different forms of media. However, we hope to have shown something of the complexity of regulatory purposes; even if we disregard spectrum scarcity and pervasiveness, other regulatory goals are likely to retain their importance. Thus regulation for competition, especially of key access points to ensure open access for competitors, will be of greater, not lesser, importance, as will technological regulation, for example to ensure standardisation in liberalised markets. Secondly, there is no certainty, even if we do see a proliferation of new delivery forms and of channels, that this will ensure the provision of a plurality of views necessary for democratic health, and it is possible that this may require the continuance of something resembling existing public service broadcasting. Finally, maximising access to the changing media through universal service principles is emerging as an important regulatory principle; this has another side concerning questions of privacy and the right to refuse access to others. What we see in this overview of regulatory purposes is a mix of different concerns; some based on ensuring that markets can operate effectively, for example regulating gatekeepers and interconnection terms. Others are based on rights such as the right to privacy and the right to free speech.[54]

5 REGULATORY INSTITUTIONS

A point which is probably more striking in media regulation than in any other form of regulatory activity is the diversity of the institutions and of the instruments used. This may produce considerable complexity as divergent attitudes towards the changes in the media structure may have to be understood within the frame of the different logic employed by different actors, and the media involve convergence of a number of different regulatory systems including telecommunications as well as more traditional media regulation.[55]

Often regulation is thought of as the province of governments or

[54] For the relationship between economic principles and rights in regulation see Prosser, T, *Law and the Regulators* (Oxford: Clarendon Press, 1997), esp chs 1 and 10.

[55] McQuail, D and Siune, K (eds) *Changing Media Politics. Comparative Perspectives in Western Europe* (London: Sage, 1986).

bureaucrats, but this conceals radically different types of actor with differing styles and varied institutional capacities. It will be useful at this point to outline briefly some of the actors involved and the national chapters will provide more details.

Starting at the national level, the courts have been more closely involved in media regulation than in most other forms of regulation.[56] This is largely because media regulation raises more directly some key constitutional rights, most notably the right to freedom of expression. As Chapter 7 will show, this has been fundamental in setting out the basic framework within which regulatory controls operate. The rights protected are not limited to the example of freedom of speech or to the highly rights-conscious United States; further rights such as a right to privacy or even a right to public service broadcasting have been defined in other jurisdictions, as for example in Germany by the Fourth Broadcasting Verdict of the Federal Constitutional Court and in Italy by the 1974 ruling of the Constitutional Court. Thus the first role of the courts has been to create and police a framework of basic rights within which both the media and the public authorities must operate. This has not been so developed in all jurisdictions; for example, the peculiar constitutional traditions of the United Kingdom have restricted such an explicitly rights-based judicial role, although, as we shall see, such a role is now developing through the European jurisdictions. Secondly, the courts have clearly played a role in settling ordinary civil disputes including the allocation of property rights. This may concern the basic principles of competition, for example determining interconnection conditions, or reviewing the legality of regulatory interventions. Finally, in a few areas the criminal courts have had a role to play, notably in relation to obscenity where direct regulatory controls are supplemented by criminal provisions and sanctions. This has become of considerable importance in the case of the Internet where criminal prosecutions have been employed after child pornography has appeared on sites, and raises important questions of how far such liability extends to the various participants in the provision of services and networks. It has been argued recently that one of the preconditions for successful regulation is the existence of an independent and reliable system of courts; the role of the courts will be one of the major concerns of this book.[57]

More conventionally, regulation is also the business of governments. However, this can also raise considerable further complexities. The extent to which government is directly involved varies considerably from nation

---

[56] See Barendt (n 13 above) and Craufurd-Smith, R, *Broadcasting Law and Fundamental Rights* (Oxford: Clarendon Press, 1997).

[57] Levy, B and Spiller, P, *Regulation, Institutions and Commitment* (Cambridge: Cambridge University Press, 1996).

to nation, as we shall see, as do governmental concerns and the government departments involved. For example, one department may be concerned with cultural matters, another with competition, and a third with the promotion of industry, including the media and telecommunications matters. This can give rise to serious internal conflicts. Just as importantly, responsibilities may be further complicated by a Federal structure. This is most noteworthy in the case of Germany, where media regulation remains the responsibility of the *Länder* or states, in some cases acting jointly. Telecommunications regulation, in contrast, is a matter for Federal authorities. The scope for further conflict is obvious, and illustrates once more how regulatory responsibilities need not match the development of the changing media. Similar problems have arisen in the United States, where for example the implementation of the universal service provisions of the Telecommunications Act 1996 was in part entrusted to a federal–state joint board.

The United States of course has been the home of the regulatory agency, acting at various degrees of 'arm's length' from the executive government. In the area of the media, the key example is the Federal Communications Commission, which has the advantage of combining responsibility for broadcasting with that for telecommunications. The agency model is being increasingly adopted elsewhere, though not necessarily with the same combination of responsibilities. For example, in Germany a new Telecommunications Regulatory Authority has recently been established at Federal level, but it has no responsibility for media matters which remain in the hands of the *Länder*, themselves in some cases acting through their own joint institutions. Competition regulation remains to a large degree the responsibility of the Federal Cartel Commission. In some cases this division of responsibilities may be extraordinarily complex; for example, in the United Kingdom at least fourteen statutory or self-regulatory bodies have been identified claiming jurisdiction over aspects of new media delivery.[58] Apart from the complex question of the division of functions, the existence of regulatory agencies raises important questions relating to their real independence from government and the extent to which they have autonomous powers to make and implement policy.

A further type of regulatory institutional form is that of self-regulation, and this is growing in importance. It is essential to stress that this can cover a number of radically different approaches to regulation. The most common usage refers to regulation by professional associations or by participants in a particular industry rather than by the state or by formal legal norms. Examples often given are those of the press or financial

---

[58] Murroni, C, Collins, R and Coote, A, *Converging Communications: Policies for the 21st Century* (London: Institute for Public Policy Research, 1996), 49.

services in the UK. However, even these cases should alert us to the fact that self-regulation is a highly complex phenomenon. Firstly, it is not a useful way of characterising a whole regime of regulation, as almost invariably self-regulation is mixed with more direct interventions by the public authorities including use of criminal or civil sanctions; self-regulation is a technique of regulation, not an alternative to it.[59] Secondly, where strong elements of self-regulation do exist, this does not indicate a lack of interest by the state. In many cases, self-regulatory techniques have been adopted in order to avoid the alternative of direct public intervention. Indeed, a convincing case has been made for the conscious development of 'enforced self-regulation' involving negotiation between the state and individual firms to establish appropriate standards and regulation, which can then be publicly enforced.[60] The distinction between public regulation and self-regulation is thus by no means a watertight one, and further examples of the overlap will be given later in this book.

This discussion does not of course exhaust the issues raised by a study of regulation; other matters include the use of different techniques such as fiscal norms, subsidies, and 'command and control' regulation, and some reference to these will be made in our national studies.[61] Nevertheless, enough has been said to indicate the complexity of regulation, both in terms of the purposes followed and the institutions used.

6 CONCLUSION

In the first part of this chapter we described the changes currently shaping new forms of media. Despite their far-reaching nature, we advised a degree of caution in claiming that we are in a process of revolutionary change with the beginning of a new 'information society'. Instead the process seemed much more contingent and evolutionary. This in itself is a strong argument for a comparative study of the type made here, for such contingency suggests that the peculiarities of national culture will have an important determining role in the evolution of the new media and of its market structure.

If the development of the new media seems more complex and contingent than is often suggested, the same is true of regulation. Our preliminary analysis would suggest that regulation is a much more complex

---

[59] See Prosser, *Law and the Regulators* (n 54 above), 271. For a similar point in relation to the regulation of financial services, see Treasury and Civil Service Committee, *The Regulation of Financial Services in the UK*, HC 332, 1994–5, para 25.

[60] Ayres, I and Braithwaite, J (n 11 above), esp ch 4.

[61] For an exhaustive study of different concepts of regulation and the associated techniques, see Daintith, T, *Encyclopedia of Comparative Law: vol XVII, State and Economy*, ch 10 'Regulation' (Tübingen: Mohr, 1997).

phenomenon than is often suggested, especially by the proponents of radical deregulation as a response to rapidly changing market structures. In particular, a variety of purposes are reflected in regulatory policies, both concerned with 'public interest' objectives and with the proper functioning of markets themselves. Similarly, there is a large variety of different types of institution involved in the regulatory process. This suggests two further hypotheses. Firstly, once again national and cultural characteristics will be of considerable importance in shaping regulatory demands and outcomes. Secondly, we are unlikely to find a general withering away of regulatory intervention through law; given the plurality of regulatory purposes, we may find shifts in content and in regulatory styles, but no process of simple deregulation. Now it is time to turn to the national studies through which we shall see if these hypotheses are borne out.

2

Germany

WOLFGANG KLEINWÄCHTER[1]

1 MEDIA DEVELOPMENT

General trends in media development

Germany, one of Europe's biggest media markets, is undergoing a deep transformation of its media system in the last decade of this century. For over forty years, since the end of World War II, the general political and legal framework for the media was stable and remained relatively unchanged with only one main innovation in the 1980s: the introduction of private broadcasting.

Now, in the 1990s, two main events have challenged the established system. In the early 1990s the consequences of the unification of the two German states called for new media policies and regulation. Moreover, since the middle of the 1990s the consequences of the technological convergence of mass media, data and telecommunications services, as well as the 'digital revolution' have led to new approaches, new concepts, and new legislation. However, whilst Germany's unification in the field of broadcasting was mainly managed within the existing legal framework,[2] the 'digital revolution' has rocked the traditional legal media institutions. In particular the electronic media are now in a permanent process of change.

There are four main trends which dominate the present media development in Germany:

- a shift from the public to the private sector combined with commercialisation
- growing economic concentration
- technological convergence and the emergence of digital television and other new broad and narrowband services
- growing globalisation versus growing regionalisation.

---

[1] This chapter covers developments up to 1 October 1997.
[2] See Kresse, H and Kleinwächter, W, *Die Rundfunkordnung in den neuen Bundesländern* (Stuttgart: Schäfer & Pöschel, 1992).

Table 2.1: Advertising in private television (in million DEM for 1996)

Channel	Advertising income
RTL	1.960
SAT 1	1.624
PRO 7	1.334
RTL 2	0.327
Kabel 1	0.151
VOX	0.113

Source: *Media Perspektiven*, 6/1996

Market participants and other interested parties

The main participants in the German media market are the *public and private broadcasting institutions*. The public broadcasters, financed mainly by licence fees, are a major economic interest with more than 10 billion DEM income annually: in the public sector there are nearly twenty TV channels and more than fifty radio channels. In the private sector the two giants 'Bertelsmann' and the 'Kirch group' are the main players with more than two dozen TV channels, and are both very active also in the publishing field (the Kirch group mainly via the Springer Verlag and Bertelsmann via its own global publishing network). Advertising in private television reached nearly 6 billion DEM in 1996. Advertising in the main thirty-six private radio stations reached nearly 742.9 million DEM in 1996.[3]

The *print sector* plays a significant role in the German electronic media sector. Besides Bertelsmann and Springer there are numerous medium sized companies, like Bauer, Burda, Holtzbrinck, WAZ, Gong and others, which have also entered the broadcasting market since the early 1990s.

Consumer electronics companies, which have had little influence on media policy and legislation so far, are still an important factor on the media market, but face strong international competition. Germany's TV maker Grundig has lost substantial market share over the years and is struggling for survival. Telefunken, another traditional German consumer electronics producer, disappeared years ago. Siemens AG stopped the production of consumer electronics in 1996. On the other hand, Siemens is more aggressive in the computer market, having entered also the production of servers, set-top boxes, and equipment for digital broadcasting.

[3] *Daten zur Mediensituation in Deutschland 1996*, Frankfurt, 1997, 19.

Table 2.2: Participation of print media in the broadcasting sector (examples)

Publisher	Radio	Television
Bertelsmann AG	RTL Radio	RTL
	Radio NRW	RTL 2
	Klassik Radio Hamburg	VOX
		Premiere
Springer/Kirch	Antenne Bayern	SAT 1
	Radio PSR	PRO 7
	Radio Nora	Kabel 1
	Antenne Radio Stuttgart	DSF
		HOT TV
Holtzbrinck	Antenne Sachsen	SAT 1
	Radio Brocken	Ntv
	Antenne Thüringen	
	Radio Gong München	
	RadioRPR/Rheinland-Pfalz	
Bauer	Radio Hamburg	TM 3
	Radio Nora	RTL 2
Burda	Antenne Bayern	Focus TV
	Klassik Radio München	Kabel Plus
	Ostseewelle Schwerin	

Source: Daten zur Mediensituation in Deutschland 1996, Frankfurt, 1997

Network operators will also become important players in the German media market. Germany's information infrastructure is one of the best in the world. Fibre-optic cable systems and a high level of digitalisation have created a network which allows all kinds of basic and value added broad- and narrowband interactive services. Additionally the cellular network and the satellite system offer alternative opportunities. A central player in the future media market will be the German Telekom AG (TAG). TAG is not only the owner of Germany's main telecommunications network, it also owns a fully developed mobile phone system (D1), an On-Line Service (T-Online) and Germany's biggest cable television network. It is entering new fields both in services, multimedia software development, and, via its consumer electronics subsidiary BOSCH, equipment production. How far the telecommunication newcomers like 'o.tel.o' (VEBACOM/RWE/Telliance), 'ARCOR' (DEBEKOM/Mannesmann), and INTERCOM (VIAG/British Telecom), all three already active in mobile telephony (D2, Eplus, E2) will also enter the media market remains

Table 2.3: German network operators (as expected by 1 January 1998)

Network operator	Partner	Main basic networks	Mobile telephony
Telekom AG	Telekom	Telephony	D 1
o.tel.o	RWE/VEBA	Electricity	E Plus
ARCOR	Mannesmann/ DEBAKOM	Railway	D 2
INTERCOM	VIAG/BT	Electricity	E 2

to be seen when liberalisation of telecommunication commences on 1 January 1998.

New entrants are the *service and Internet access providers*. German Telekom AG started with its 'T-Online' in 1996. 'CompuServe', one of the first entrants in the German On-Line market, was overtaken recently by America On-Line. Its German subsidary, a joint venture between AOL and Bertelsmann AG under the name 'Alles On Line' (AOL) has meanwhile got a substantial market share with more than 1.5 million customers. Microsoft Network, Eunet, X-Link, and others are also competing for a fast growing market which is still in an early stage of development. The German problem is that the infrastructure sector is much better developed than the applications and services sector. While the level of digitisation of the networks is relatively high, Internet penetration is lower than in other European countries, and far behind the US and Scandinavia.

Another group of players in the German media market is that of the numerous small and medium sized enterprises in the *software development and multimedia content production*. SAP is one of the biggest companies in the field, also playing an international role.

Growing privatisation and commercialisation

The main trend in the German broadcasting landscape is determined by more private broadcasting and growing commercialisation, in particular in television. The public broadcasting sector, which until the middle of the 1980s was in a monopolistic position, has come more and more under pressure. Public television is still strong and distributes in total eighteen full programmes. Besides ARD and ZDF, the two national channels, there are eleven so called 'third programmes': Mitteldeutscher Rundfunk (MDR), Westdeutscher Rundfunk (WDR), Süddeutscher Rundfunk (SDR), Ostdeutscher Rundfunk Brandenburg (ORB), Sender Freies Berlin (SFB), Norddeutscher Rundfunk (N3), Bayern 3, Hessen 3, Südwest 3, Radio Bremen, and Saarländischer Rundfunk (SR). Additionally, the public broadcasters have two specialised channels for children (Kinderkanal)

Table 2.4: Viewing rates for the main television stations (per cent) in 1997

RTL	ARD	SAT 1	ZDF	ARD III	PRO 7	RTL 2	Kabel 1	VOX	Super RTL
17.8	15.0	14.1	12.4	10.5	9.0	4.0	3.9	2.9	2.2

Source: *Funk-Korrespondenz Cologne*, 19/97, 9 May 1997

and for information (Phoenix), and three international cultural and news programmes (EURONEWS with the European Broadcasting Union, ARTE with France and 3SAT with Austria and Switzerland). However, ARD and ZDF have lost their dominant position in the national television market. The private RTL, partly owned by Bertelsmann AG and CLT, gained market leadership from 1994.

Additionally the public sector is confronted with a deep financial crisis as a result of substantial losses in revenues from advertising and soaring prices for film and sports rights. More and more money from advertising has moved to the numerous new private television stations. Besides the 'big three' private television channels RTL, SAT 1, and PRO 7, there are nearly a dozen new national stations and numerous regional channels which have entered the market since 1990, among them RTL 2, Super RTL, Kabel 1, ntv, VIVA, VIVA 2, VOX, Eurosport, DSF, HOT TV, B 1, IA, TM3, TV Blau-Weiß, and others. All the private channels are free-to-air TV while there is currently only one pay-TV channel on the German television market, Premiere, jointly owned by Kirch and Bertelsmann.

Competition between the public and the private sectors is becoming tougher from year to year. The public broadcasting system is under constitutional protection and it is seen as a fundamental element of the democratic system, guaranteeing the right to freedom of expression and offering basic services in culture, education, and information. The Constitutional Court in its nine broadcasting decisions since 1961 and the existing legislation of the *Länder* has always confirmed that the public broadcasting service has 'the right to exist and to develop' (*Bestands- und Entwicklungsgarantie*).[4] Nevertheless the pressure is growing and lawyers of the private sector are arguing that 'the right to exist and develop' does not imply any privileges in market competition.

A symbol of the changing environment is the coverage of main national and international sports events. Some years ago ARD and ZDF lost the rights to the premier football league, the *Bundesliga*, the most important

---

[4] See Decision of the Constitutional Court of the Federal Republic of Germany, 5 Feb 1991, BverfGE 57, 295f.

Table 2.5: Advertising revenue of public broadcasters (in million DEM)

	1990	1991	1992	1993	1994	1995
ARD	732.1	761.2	576.8	444.9	335.8	345.1
ZDF	1.444.1	1.480.0	1.297.8	815.3	591.6	646.8

Source: *Daten zur Mediensituation Deutschland 1996*, Frankfurt, 1997

sports event in Germany, and to other major sports events like tennis from Wimbledon, boxing, and the Formula I World Championship, but they still kept their rights to other international highlights in sports like the Olympic Games or World and European Championships for Football and Athletics. Now this is also ending. The right to the European Champions League, Europe's most prestigous annual football event, are already with RTL. In competing for the rights to cover football's World Cup Championships in 2002 and 2006, the public sector lost after aggressive bidding against the Kirch group.

1996 saw another step in the commercialisation of Germany's sports television. For the first time a key football game in the European Cup, the semi-final between FC Bavaria Munich and FC Barcelona, was not shown on free TV but only on the pay-TV programme Premiere. Regardless of numerous protests by the general public, the event indicated that commercialisation of public sports events will continue and will lead to more costs for the viewers. Even if there is still a general consensus that the main sports events of 'general interest' should be accessible for the public in an open channel, as declarations of the Kirch group with regard to the World Football Championships have indicated, there are no guarantees that this will continue beyond the year 2000. A broad debate has started around the so-called 'list of important sports events' which should be accessible on free TV, in particular with a view to the Football World Championships in 2006, where Germany is a candidate to host the event. But Germany abstained in the voting over the *Television without Frontiers* Directive of the European Union because there was no consensus among the German *Länder* about this list.

Moreover, rights to new films are becoming extremely expensive. The big private companies, in particular the Kirch group, have bought exclusive rights to new films and have formed joint consortia with the major studios in Hollywood which give them special access to huge archives and new film stocks. The public sector has growing difficulties in obtain-

Table 2.6: Cost of TV rights for the premier football league/*Bundesliga* (in million DEM)

Year	Cost	Channel
1985/86	12	ARD/ZDF
1990/91	50	UFA (RTL/ARD/ZDF)
1994/95	140	ISPR (SAT 1)
1997/98	280	ISPR (SAT 1)

Source: Amsieck, M, 'Der Sportrechtemarkt in Deutschland', in *Media Perspektiven*, 2/1997, Frankfurt/Main, 64

ing similar rights and in offering an attractive programme with top international films.

Growing concentration and 'low quality' programmes

The German televison market looks very diversified and pluralistic with more than thirty full free public and private German language channels. But regardless of this quantity of channels there is a growing concentration of ownership which leads to less diversity and lower quality of programme content.

Two market leaders own the overwhelming majority of the private channels. The Kirch Group and Bertelsmann AG, partly in combination with other minor shareholders, control all the main private channels. Kirch controls SAT 1, PRO 7, DSF, and ntv. Bertelsmann controls RTL, RTL 2, Super RTL, and VOX. Content of the programmes becomes more and more unified. The multiplication of channels has led to much 'more of the same'. Endless series of soap operas, talk shows, game shows, and old films dominate the different channels. One can find sensational programming and eccentricity as well as extensive coverage of trivial events but few cultural and educational programmes. Although the three market leaders have tried to develop their own 'information competence', the general profile of the channels is more that of a 'tabloid paper' than of a 'quality paper'. For the viewer it becomes more and more difficult to see differences between the thirty channels.

This mainstream has also influenced the content of public television programmes which, in competition for higher viewing rates, have followed the general trend towards the 'middle of the road' aimed at 'majorities'. Experts like Lutz Hachmeister, former Director of the Adolf Grimmer Institute in Marl, see in this trend a danger that programme quality standards are undermined and that the interests of minority groups are either totally ignored or that relevant programmes for special interest groups, including political features and current affairs programmes, are shown not in prime time but only in slots after midnight. Broadcasting could lose its constitutional role as a fundamental element in the democratic process.[5]

Development of new services

While Germany lagged behind for many years in the development of new services, since the middle of the 1990s growing competition and many innovations have changed this situation. Although some pilot projects of 'video on demand' (VOD) have so far failed and tests with 'digital audio broadcasting' (DAB) and 'digital television' (DTV) did not produce the expected results with a mass audience, numerous new on-line and off-line services have been developed which have enriched the German media market and changed its structure. Against the background of the highly developed and modern digital information infrastructure in Germany the convergence of networks is leading to a growing diversity of services which goes beyond traditional radio and television and opens new opportunities for old and new players in the field.

Since 1994 a number of plans have been developed for the introduction of digital television. Original ideas for a joint project among Telekom, Bertelsmann, and Kirch were blocked by the Bundeskartellamt and the European Commission for anti-trust reasons. Later two competing groups were formed. On the one hand a combination of Bertelsmann AG, the German public broadcasters ARD and ZDF, the French Canal Plus, and German Telekom created 'MBGG', a company with its own programme package and its own model for a set-top box. On the other hand the Kirch group pushed its alternative project forward. In early 1996 MBGG collapsed after some internal conflicts and divergent interests, while Kirch continued to implement its plan and started in July 1996 its own 'DF 1' project during the Formula I motor race at Hockenheim. DF 1 was designed as a 'bouquet' of about twenty channels for individual choice. Consumers could buy a standard package and had to pay for additional services on a 'pay per view' basis.

Two weeks before Kirch started, Bertelsmann decided to leave the 'digital race' and to give up earlier plans for a similar digital 'RTL Club'. Bertelsmann argued that the introduction of digital television was premature and that Germany, where more than thirty channels are freely accessible, was not yet prepared for pay-TV.

---

[5] See Hachmeister, Lutz, 'Mein Feind, das Medium: Mentalität und Management im deutschen Fernsehsystem', in *Funk Korrespondenz Köln*, 38/97, 19 Sept 1997, 3ff.

Kirch's early start raised a lot of speculation over an uncertain market. Optimists and pessimists expressed totally opposite views about the future of digital broadcasting in Germany. While there was a basic agreement that in the long run there is no alternative to digital television, the disagreement was on the 'when' and the 'how', and for what price.

One year after Kirch's start DF 1 collapsed. Kirch's hope of attracting more than 200,000 viewers within one year failed totally. He lost about one billion DEM. Kirch, who is a joint shareholder with Bertelsmann in Premiere, entered into negotiations with its 'archenemy' on the future of digital television in Germany. After months of secret negotiations behind closed doors both sides came out with a surprising agreement. In late August 1997 Kirch and Bertelsmann (CLT/UFA) announced that they would join their forces to develop the German digital pay-TV market. The withdrawal of Canal Plus from Premiere, the only pay-TV channel in Germany so far, produced the opportunity to rearrange the shares among the other shareholders, Kirch and Bertelsmann. Both parties agreed to take 50 per cent of Premiere. Part of the deal was also that the services, developed under DF 1 will be included in a special Premiere package. The argument of the former enemies was that the digital pay-TV market in Germany is too small and needs a pooling of resources. Either there will be no digital pay-television in Germany or only one. Premiere has so far 1.6 million customers.[6]

But competition cannot be avoided. The public broadcasters ARD and ZDF started their own 'digital bouquet' during the International Broadcasting Fair 'IFA' in Berlin, in late August 1997. The difference is that the public broadcasters offer their additional services 'free of charge'. It remains to be seen how attractive the new services are and how the consumer reacts.

The problem is, that there is so far no agreement between the public and the private broadcasters on a joint set-top box. Kirch, Bertelsmann, and German Telekom as the main cable network provider have agreed to use the 'd-box', developed by Beta Research, a subsidary of Kirch and Bertelsmann, and produced by the Finnish Nokia company. ARD and ZDF had developed their own system which is not compatible with the d-box. The public broadcasters are arguing that the d-box would create a 'monopolistic situation' which violates anti-trust legislation. Although Bertelsmann and Kirch have promised to develop software which would make the different systems compatible as soon as possible, ARD and ZDF are criticising the time-lag as a competitive advantage for the private broadcasters and are calling for discrimination-free access to the set-top

---

[6] See 'Digitales Fernsehen in Deutschland—der aktuelle Stand', in *Medienforum Berlin-Brandenburg*, 2–4 Sept 1997, Berlin, Dokumentation; see also 'DF 1 ist gescheitert: Premiere übernimmt Kirch', in *Funk Korrespondenz Köln*, 36/97, 5 Sept 1997, 13.

boxes. Whether anti-trust legislation is violated or not is under investigation both at the national and the European level.

Additionally, many new legal questions raised by digital television are not yet settled in the German broadcasting legislation; for example, packaging, conditional access, navigation, and others.

Digital radio is another uncertain test field. Pilot projects for digital audio broadcasting (DAB) started in the early 1990s and continue on a broader basis in nearly all *Länder*. However, the equipment both for producers and consumers is rather expensive, attractive value added services are not yet developed, and the market is very thin. A general breakthrough for digital radio is still far away. Nevertheless the IFA 97 saw the market introduction of DAB.[7]

Converging technologies have also stimulated the development of new non-broadcasting services, and in particular access to the Internet. As in other countries, academic institutions were the 'door opener' for the Internet and the World Wide Web. The German Telekom AG started in 1996 its 'T-Online' service, which is at the moment the most successful on-line service in Germany. After the merger of AOL and Compuserve in 1997, the joint venture with Bertelsmann AG and America On-Line will become a strong competitor with about 1.5 million users in Germany. Bertelsmann's plan is to develop 'AOL' (Alles On-Line) into the 'RTL of the on-line market'. 'Europe On-Line', a newly established on-line service with Burda and other European investors, failed and stopped most of its activities in 1996.

All major public and private broadcasting companies, from the ARD-Tagesschau via MDR-Sachsenspiegel to SAT 1 Harald Schmidt Show, have their own homepages on the World Wide Web and offer information additional to their programmes via the Internet. A dispute arose in the summer of 1997 when ZDF started its new Web Page in co-operation with Microsoft and NBC. Private broadcasting companies argued that the ZDF Web Page goes beyond 'programme support' and offers value added services which would be a misuse of licence fees, going beyond 'the right to develop'. The case is still pending. Radio over the Internet is becoming more and more popular, in particular with the younger generation. On-line services are also offered by all the major German newspapers. According to *Media Perspektiven* there were more than seventy dailies on-line at the end of 1996.[8]

Besides the broadcasting corporations, the computer and telecom com-

---

[7] See Müller-Römer, Frank, 'Das "digital radio" ist da: Die Markteinführung des multimedialen Systems DAB beginnt', in *Medienforum Berlin-Brandenburg*, Berlin, 2–4 Sept 1997, 191ff.

[8] See Riefler, K, 'Zeitungen online—Chance oder Risiko?' in *Media Perspektiven*, 10/96, Frankfurt/Main, 537ff.

Table 2.7: On-line use (in million users) in 1996

Internet	T-Online	CompuServe	MSN	AOL
2.87	2.73	1.13	0.38	0.18

Source: MC Online-Monitor I/96

panies are now searching for additional markets in new fields which did not belong to their traditional core business in the past. German Telekom, owner of Germany's largest television cable system, is investigating opportunities to go beyond its role as a network operator and to enter the broadcasting field as a service provider as well. Siemens AG is also developing new service departments which investigate further business opportunities in the new markets.

In the satellite field, ASTRA and EUTELSAT have the dominant market positions, while the Kopernikus project, once seen as the major project, is of less importance today. Thirty-three million households in Germany have access to satellite programmes via 10 million satellite dishes. This is one third of all households.[9] Both satellite operators offer nearly 100 television and 80 radio programmes in a dozen languages. They have also started to offer capacities for digital radio and television, which opens new opportunities and will stimulate the introduction of new services in the long run. Astra has now entered a joint venture with the US chip producer Intel called 'European Satellite Multimedia Service' (ESM). ESM will develop ASTRA NET, which is aimed to bring satellite services directly to PCs and to allow interactive communication via satellites.[10]

Growing globalisation versus growing regionalisation

The German television market is mainly a national and regional market, although there are visible trends towards growing internationalisation. One barrier keeping the German market as national as possible is the legal system which is based on the principle of federalism. Broadcasting federalism, which means that each of the sixteen *Länder* has its own regional media legislation and its own broadcasting and licensing authority, makes it rather difficult and expensive for foreign stations to compete for and to get a national broadcasting licence.

Although the European Television Directive *Television Without Frontiers* opens in principle the opportunity to distribute European

[9] See *Daten zur Mediensituation in Deutschland 1996* (n 3 above) 9.
[10] See 'Astra-Net: Technologie & Dienste', in *infosat*, No 109, Apr 1997, 12ll.

programmes in the whole European Union, no foreign competitor has a substantial share in the German television market. No significant changes with regard to foreign programmes have been seen since the 1970s, regardless of the fact that numerous American, English, French, and other programmes like CNN, NBC, Sky News, TV 5, Nickleodeon TV, etc are easily accessible today via cable or satellite.

On the other hand, both Kirch and Bertelsmann have broadened and deepened their international co-operation and are operating in the global market. Bertelsmann, the world's second largest media corporation, has entered several joint ventures with US companies. The large merger between UFA, a subsidary of Bertelsmann, and CLT in early January 1997, created one of the world's largest electronic media companies. UFA and CLT now combine nineteen television stations and twenty-three radio stations in ten European countries with a total turnover of 5 billion DEM per year. Bertelsmann also co-operates (despite controversies in 1996 on digital television and other issues) with the French Canal Plus. Bertelsmann and its print subsidiaries (Gruner & Jahr) and broadcasting subsidiaries (UFA) also have stakes in the United Kingdom, Spain, Poland, the Czech Republic, Slovakia, Hungary, and other countries.

Kirch has moved into co-operation agreements with Time Warner, Disney, and other US companies. Co-operation with Berlusconi's Finninvest includes stakes in Mediasat and TELEPIÙ in Italy. It also has stakes in the Swiss Teleclub, in Spain's Tele Cinco, in the French Hexatel SW.A. and Tricon S.A., and in others.[11] How far the global playing of the two German giants will go, and what consequences this will have for the German television market, for programme content, and for television viewers in Germany, remains to be seen.

It is also unclear what consequences for the television market will arise from further European integration. So far the language barrier and also the more traditional approach of the German audience has kept the German television market rather national in character. European channels such as Euronews or Eurosport, which also offer a German language version of their programmes, remain marginal in market share. Even in the music sector, once dominated by English-American MTV, the German language VIVA and VIVA 2 became the most successful competitors.

Central and Eastern Europe, an area which was already covered for some years by the Astra satellite with many German television channels, was seen by many experts as a natural German broadcasting backyard because of the high percentage of German-speaking people in those countries, the wide range of German businesses there, and the many German

---

[11] See 'Medienkonzerne: Beteiligungen und Unternehmensdaten', in *Daten zur Mediensituation in Deutschland 1996* (n 3 above) 28ff.

tourists spending holidays in the Tatra mountains, at the Balaton, or at the Black Sea. However, despite this background, the German private broadcasters have shown little engagement in the new emerging private broadcasting markets in these countries so far.[12]

In the broadcasting sector Bertelsmann competed for a licence (as part of a joint venture with a Polish corporation) for the first private television station in Poland, but the Polish Broadcasting Authority preferred that a purely national company become Poland's first private television station. Bertelsmann was more successful in a bid in Hungary when, after the adoption of the broadcasting law, the new broadcasting authority licensed two private television channels. UFA as part of a Hungarian consortium won the competition and in October 1997 started its private television programme on the so-called 'third channel' in Hungary.

Kirch has not entered a major competition in the East so far. There are only minor German broadcasting activities in the Czech Republic, and no real engagement has been seen in the new emerging private broadcasting sector in the Slovak Republic, in Romania, Bulgaria, and Slovenia. In none of the former Soviet republics have major German investments been undertaken, although all of them have introduced private broadcasting during recent years. Negotiations in the Russian Federation, to enter one of the biggest television markets in the world with about 70 million TV households, have so far failed.

In the print sector the situation is rather different. German publishers have major stakes in the newspaper and publishing field in Poland and in the Czech Republic as well as in Hungary. In particular, in Hungary the national press market is subdivided between Bertelsmann and Springer. While Bertelsmann owns '*Nepszabadsag*', the main national daily newspaper, Springer is the main owner of regional newspapers in the country.

International co-operation in the public sector takes place mainly within the framework of the European Broadcasting Union, although this has not reached a very high level in recent years. Besides some co-productions by ARD and ZDF with partner organisations, the two channels '3 SAT' (a joint programme of ARD and ZDF with ORF from Austria and SRG from Switzerland) and 'ARTE' (a joint programme from ARD and ZDF with the French public channel) symbolise the 'international openness' of German

---

[12] See Kleinwächter, W, 'Broadcasting in Transition: Media Freedom Between Political Freedom and Economic Pressure in Central and Eastern Europe', in Bailie, M and Winseck, D, *Democratizing Communication? Comparative Perspectives on Information and Power* (Cresskill New Jersey: Hampton Press, 1997), 243ff; see also Kleinwächter, Wolfgang, 'Rundfunkrecht in Osteuropa—Der mühselige Weg vom Einheitsrundfunk zum dualen System', in Dörr, D and Hümmerich, K, *Osteuropa zwischen Deregulierung und neuer Ordnung*, Schriftenreihe des Instituts für Europäisches Medienrecht Saarbrücken, Vol 7, Saarbrücken 1993, 19ff.

public television, but only with limited viewing figures. In Euronews the German public broadcasters ARD and ZDF decided not to participate as official partners. Co-production between German public broadcasters and public channels in Central and East European countries, where low production costs and high professional standards offer special financial and artistic incentives, remain more the exception than the rule.

Globalisation on the one hand is mirrored by a growing regionalisation in broadcasting on the other hand. This can be seen in particular in the public sector. The regional so-called 'third programmes' of the public broadcasting sector, which once had only a marginal importance, have grown in the 1990s substantially and now offer full 24-hour programmes with substantial success. In some regions, in particular in the new German *Länder*, the regional public television station (MDR or ORB) is seen by many people as their 'first channel'. The majority of the 'third programmes' are meanwhile also distributed via satellite and cable so that they cover the whole Federal Republic. Some *Länder* have started a debate about the future of the ARD and its first programme, which is a joint venture of the broadcasting stations of the *Länder*. Although it is not to be expected that the first programme 'ARD I' will disappear, the debate indicates a general shift in favour of the regional broadcasting stations in the public sector.

In the private sector, high costs and low viewing figures prevented the development of regional television in the past. While the licensing authorities obliged private broadcasters to include 'regional windows' in their programmes and to co-finance local and regional broadcasters, no real progress was seen until the middle of the 1990s. This could change in the future. In some regions with a population of more than two million, regional stations such as TV Blau-Weiß in Munich, TV Puls in Berlin, and IA in Hamburg have started with innovative programmes but low viewing rates have prevented a commercial success so far.

Local television has also grown since the middle of the 1990s. With falling production costs dozens of small local stations, using low power transmitters or free channels in some cable systems, distribute their programmes within small communities. In the Free State of Saxony alone about 100 local TV companies have been licensed by the '*Sächsische Landesanstalt für privaten Rundfunk und neue Medien*' (SLM), but all have to struggle for their daily survival.

2 REGULATION AND OTHER MEDIA POLICIES

Challenged by technological innovations and global developments, the German media law system, which was stable for nearly half a century since World War II, has started slowly to move towards de-regulation, liberalisation, and privatisation. Traditional legal theories and practical approaches are changing while legal barriers (which had been erected to make a revival of a centralised media system, as under the 'third Reich', impossible) to protect the public interest, and to avoid concentration and monopolisation, have been removed step by step. Legislators are more or less following what technology and the market determines.

The years 1996 and 1997 marked a watershed for legislation in the field of media and telecommunication in Germany. After years of controversial discussion, the German *Bundestag* adopted the new Telecommunications Act on 25 July 1996.[13] The Telecommunications Act deregulates and liberalises the German telecommunication market, both with regard to networks and services. Parallel to this, a new Broadcasting State Treaty,[14] which is the main agreement among the sixteen *Länder* on basic principles and frameworks for broadcasting in Germany, was elaborated in 1996, ratified by the parliaments of the *Länder*, and entered into force on 1 January 1997. The new Broadcasting State Treaty reaffirms the dual broadcasting system, but gives private broadcasters more opportunities to compete in global markets by lifting some restrictions concerning cross-ownership and concentration.

In 1997 a new Federal Law on Information and Communication Services[15] and a State Treaty on new Multimedia Services[16] were adopted by the Bund and the *Länder* creating a new body of multimedia legislation, which removed unnecessary restrictions on the introduction of new information and communication services of all kinds. The Federal Law, adopted 22 July 1997 liberalises 'Tele Services'. According to Article 1, § 3, no licence is needed to start such a service. The State Treaty, which entered into force on 1 August 1997, deals with 'Media Services' where a licence is needed if the 'media service' is for a mass audience and comparable to 'broadcasting'. The two legal instruments do not make it clear where a 'tele service' ends and a 'media service' starts, but the intention of both documents is to make the legal environment for new services as flexible as possible, taking into account that the responsibility of the *Länder* for 'media questions' in general is a highly respected

[13] *Telekommunikationsgesetz* (TKG, Telecommunications Act), 25 July 1996, BGBl. 1996, Part I, No 39, 31 July 1996, 1120ff.

[14] *Rundfunkstaatsvertrag* (RStV), 31 Aug 1991 in the third version of the *Rundfunkstaatsvertrag*, 26 Aug 1996–11 Sept 1996, quoted in *Funk Korrespondenz Köln*, 52/1996, 27 Dec 1996, 1ff.

[15] *Gesetz zur Regelung für Informations- und Kommunikationsdienste (Informations- und Kommunikationsdienste-Gesetz—IuKDG)*, 22 July 1997, *Bundesgesetzblatt* 1997, Part I, No 52, 28 July 1997, 1870ff. Draft (April 1997).

[16] *Staatsvertrag über Mediendienste (Medienstaatsvertrag/MDStV)*, quoted in *Funk Korrespondenz Köln*, 35/1997, 29 Aug 1997.

constitutional and cultural value. Practice will show where the line is drawn.

The Federal Law also includes regulation of electronic signatures, which is seen as a legal innovation. According to Article 3, § 3, a special 'certification institution', linked to the new Telecommunication Authority, will allocate certificates with a signature code. Detailed rules will guarantee the security of transactions.[17] The law also includes new articles for data protection, the criminal law, youth protection, and copyright. Legal efforts have been undertaken also in other fields like encryption, distribution, packaging, and navigation. Several draft laws are under consideration in parliamentary committees.

The Telecommunications Act, the Broadcasting State Treaty, and the two multimedia instruments are the cornerstones of the new emerging legal framework for media and information services in Germany. This framework, which is widely deregulated, liberal, and flexible, is aimed at preparing Germany for the information age and its new emerging markets. Legislation has followed technological development and market pressure, while basic public interests, endangered by commercial forces, have received only a minimum of legal protection.

Types of regulation and other policies

The German media law system is based on federalism. Federalism means that the sixteen *Länder* of the Federal Republic have their own media sovereignty. They regulate their regional broadcasting system, adopt broadcasting laws for both the public and the private sectors, and have their own regional broadcasting institutions and licensing authorities. The federal government or the federal parliament have no competences in the field of broadcasting. The *Länder* agree in so-called state treaties upon general principles and frameworks so that in all the sixteen *Länder*, on the basis of regional diversity, the same principles are adopted and a common broadcasting standard is guaranteed.

This system was introduced mainly by the three western allies after World War II. The centralised 'propaganda machinery' of the 'Third Reich' was seen as partly responsible for the crimes of German fascism. One consequence of this evaluation was that the allies pushed forward the introduction of a decentralised media system in post-war Germany. The German Constitution, the *Grundgesetz* of 1949, reflects this approach.[18]

Regulation is different in the field of telecommunications, which is a federal responsibility. The distinction between broadcasting and telecom-

[17] See IuKDG (n 15 above), 1872ff.
[18] See *inter alia* Herrmann, G, *Fernsehen und Hörfunk in der Verfassung der Bundesrepublik Deutschland* (Tübingen, 1975).

munications was clear in the past: all content-related issues, which could be linked to culture, were the responsibility of the *Länder*. All network-related issues, which could be linked to technology, were the responsibility of the federal institutions. According to some decisions of the Federal Constitutional Court, it was a public duty of the state owned telecommunication system to serve the broadcasters.

This is changing now. New regulation has privatised and liberalised both networks and services in the field of telecommunications. Traditional legal boundaries as well as established judical competences are becoming undermined.

The emergence of new services which could be defined both as broadcasting services and/or telecommunications services became the subject of a controversial public debate between the institutions of the *Länder* and the *Bund* in 1996. While the federal government announced a plan for drafting a Federal Multimedia Law, the *Länder* questioned the constitutional competence of the *Bund* and drafted their own State Treaty on Multimedia Services. While the *Länder* argued that multimedia services are an extension of broadcasting services and so belong to the competence of their parliaments and governments, the federal government argued that multimedia services are an extension of telecommunication services and so belong to the competence of the federal institutions.

As mentioned above, the outcome was the adoption of two legal instruments, a Federal Law and a State Treaty, which regulated tele-services and media services, taking into account the different responsibilities. But this 'administrative compromise' was questioned in general by the media industry which asked whether there is any need to adopt new 'multimedia legislation'. According to it, no new laws are needed, neither on the federal nor on the regional level.

Structure and institutions

According to the federal system each of the sixteen *Länder* has its own media legislation and institution. The parliaments in each of the sixteen *Länder* have adopted one law on public broadcasting and another law on private broadcasting.

The laws on *public broadcasting* establish a public broadcasting company and allocate frequencies to this company to guarantee 'basic services', in particular for information, culture, and education. The public broadcasting companies are financed by licensing fees, collected in the *Länder*. The amount of the licence fee is agreed upon in a Broadcasting Financing State Treaty among the sixteen *Länder*, on the basis of recommendations by the independent Broadcasting Finance Commission (KEF). The Broadcasting Finance State Treaty is part of the general Broadcasting State Treaty and has to be ratified by the regional parliaments.

A Broadcasting Council representing the public is the highest supervising authority of each of the regional broadcasting companies (*Landesrundfunkanstalten*). The councils elect the director-general (*Intendant*) and oversee the general activity of the public broadcasting company, in particular the programming. The public broadcasting law defines the number of representatives in the council, which are different from *Land* to *Land*. The members of the council come, as a general rule, mainly from the following four sectors:

(a) the political sector (government and political parties, represented in the parliament, city councils, etc)
(b) the social sector (the churches, social groups, trade unions, and industrial associations, etc)
(c) the cultural sector (union of journalists, associations for culture and science, universities, etc)
(d) the civic groups (interest groups, NGOs, individuals, etc).

The system with broadcasting councils, representing 'the public' at large, was introduced to guarantee also distance from the state (*Staatsferne*). That is why the representation of the political sector should not normally be higher than a maximum one third of the membership of the council. But very often party representatives 'ride tickets' from organisations representing the social, cultural, and civic sectors.

Some *Länder* have agreed to establish joint public broadcasting stations (*Mehrländeranstalten*) especially in regions where different *Länder* have similar cultural roots. Another reason for the establishment of *Mehrländeranstalten* is an economic one. Bigger entities collect more licence fees which gives them sounder financial and economic backing. In the North of Germany the four *Länder* of Schleswig Holstein, Lower Saxony, Hamburg, and Mecklenburg-Vorpommern have established the 'Norddeutscher Rundfunk' (NDR). In the south of former East Germany the *Länder* of Saxony, Thuringia, and Saxony-Anhalt have established the 'Mitteldeutscher Rundfunk' (MDR). The 'Südwestfunk Baden Baden' is another joint station between Rheinland Pfalz and Baden-Württemberg, although Baden-Württemberg has with the 'Süddeutscher Rundfunk' (SDR) its own broadcasting station. While each broadcasting company has its own budget, based on the licence fee of its region, rich stations help poor stations by the transfer of financial resources, so that all public broadcasting companies can meet similar standards.

ARD, Germany's first television channel, is based on a special state treaty among the sixteen *Länder*. Programming is produced by the eleven regional public broadcasting stations of the *Länder*, which agree about the division of labour, the share of programme content within the 'first programme', and the financial transfers. The director-general of ARD (ARD *Intendant*) is elected, on the basis of rotation, for two years, from the director-generals of the eleven regional broadcasting stations. (1989/ 90: Kelm/Hessischer Rundfunk; 1991/92: Nowottny/Westdeutscher Rundfunk; 1993/94: Plog/Norddeutscher Rundfunk; 1995/96: Scharf/ Bayrischer Rundfunk; 1997/98: Reiter/Mitteldeutscher Rundfunk.)

The second German television channel, ZDF, was also established by a special state treaty among the sixteen *Länder*. Based in the city of Mainz, ZDF has television studios in each of the *Länder*. In the 'ZDF Broadcasting Council', which has similar competences to those of the broadcasting councils of the public broadcasting stations of the *Länder*, all sixteen *Länder* are represented on an equal footing. The Council is the highest authority of the ZDF. It elects the director-general (ZDF *Intendant*) and oversees the programming.

The *Länder* laws on *private broadcasting*, which are based on the common principles laid down in the Broadcasting State Treaty, are different from *Land* to *Land*. A key element of all private broadcasting laws is the establishment of a *Länder* Broadcasting Authority (*Landesmedienanstalt*) which is both the licensing as well as the controlling authority. The highest body of the *Landesmedienanstalt* is the Council (*Landesmedienrat*) which is composed of representatives of the public, similar to the broadcasting council for public broadcasting. The Council for Private Broadcasting is responsible for issuing calls for the allocation of new frequencies, and for licensing and overseeing the programming of the private broadcasters. The council also has the right to punish private broadcasters if they violate the law (financial fines can reach, according to the new Broadcasting State Treaty, an amount of up to 500.000 DEM). The Council also elects the Director of the *Landesmedienanstalt*, who operates and manages its day-to-day business.

There is no restriction on forming 'joint broadcasting authorities' for private broadcasting among the *Länder*, but so far only Berlin and Brandenburg have agreed on a common *Landesmedienanstalt*, the 'Medienanstalt Berlin-Brandenburg' (MABB). All the other fourteen *Länder* have their own *Landesmedienanstalten*. The system is more and more heavily criticised by the private sector. Private companies have to go around and to negotiate with fifteen authorities to get a nationwide coverage. They are calling for a harmonised approach and a unified procedure.

According to the general rules and principles of the Broadcasting State Treaty, which includes a special section on private broadcasting (Section III, §§ 20–40), the sixteen *Länder* co-operate with their *Landesmedienanstalten* to guarantee the adoption of the same policies and criteria with regard to the further development of private broadcasting in Germany, by taking into account and respecting regional differences and interests.

The new Broadcasting State Treaty establishes[19] two joint institutions for private broadcasting by the sixteen *Länder*: the Conference of the Directors of the *Landesmedienanstalten* (KDLM) and the Media Concentration Commission (KEK).[20] While the KDLM is the political co-ordinating body, the KEK has to oversee the development of media concentration in the private sector. The KEK has six members, who have to be independent experts, nominated by the prime ministers of the *Länder*. According to § 26 of the Broadcasting State Treaty, the KDLM has to publish every three years a report by the KEK on media concentration in Germany.

There is no federal institution which has a responsibility for the media in Germany. Media commissions, established by the German *Bundestag* or the federal government, have no legislative or executive competence. Their conclusions or recommendations are not binding and are very often received with mistrust from the *Länder*, which keep a close watch for secret or silent interference in their media sovereignty.

The only federal institution with competence over the media is the Federal Constitutional Court in Karlsruhe. The *Grundgesetz*, the German constitution, protects in Article 5 both freedom of the media and the individual right to freedom of expression. Both rights are seen as sensitive in view of German history, where individual freedoms and media independence were ignored by several political regimes earlier this century. If media-related actions by institutions of the *Bund* or the *Länder* (including the broadcasting laws adopted by the parliaments of the *Länder*) and other events and developments give the impression that they could lead to a violation of Article 5, the Federal Constitutional Court is the highest authority to make a final judgment. Decisions of the Federal Constitutional Court have the same legal value as a federal law and are binding on all institutions.

Since 1961, when the Federal Constitutional Court rejected the ambitions of the Federal Government under Chancellor Konrad Adenauer to launch a state-owned television (the decision of the Court later paved the way to the establishment of ZDF as the second German television channel), the Court has adopted about ten special decisions concerning broadcasting.[21]

Besides the constitution itself, the broadcasting laws of the *Länder*, and

---

[19] § 35.
[20] See *Rundfunkstaatsvertrag* (n 14 above), 10.
[21] A key decision was the so-called '6th broadcasting decision', adopted 5 Feb 1991. The decision summarises the main principles and guidelines for the constitutional organisation of broadcasting in Germany; see BVerGE 57, 295ff.

the Broadcasting State Treaty, the broadcasting decisions of the Federal Constitutional Court are the most important legal sources which constitute the legal framework of the media in Germany.

One of the key principles laid down in the Court's decisions from 1961 is the principle that broadcasting has to be organised free from governmental control. Although political parties as well as regional and federal governments, like everywhere in the world, have tried from time to time to influence television programming and to obtain control over broadcasting institutions, German public television is still relatively free and independent. Nevertheless, political parties have managed, not without success, to obtain some influence via the public broadcasting councils. Thus political majorities in the *Länder* are very often reflected in the programme policy of the public broadcasting station. In Bavaria, where the conservative CSU has an absolute majority in the parliament, the Bayrischer Rundfunk (BR) has a more conservative image ('*Schwarzfunk*'), while in Nordrhine-Westphalia, where the Social Democrats have for decades had a parliamentary majority, the Westdeutscher Rundfunk (WDR) is more left wing oriented ('*Rotfunk*').

Moreover, private television is far from being politically neutral. Although their main business is entertainment, SAT 1 and RTL in particular have a growing influence on public opinion in Germany. They are also playing a political role more and more. While they have no direct linkage to a political party, it is an open secret that, on the one side Bertelsmann AG, owner of RTL and based in Nordrhine-Westphalia, has closer relationships to the Social Democrats, whilst on the other side the Kirch group, owner of SAT 1 and based in Bavaria, has better relations with the conservative parties of the CDU and the CSU.

The private media industry, and here in particular Bertelsmann AG and the Kirch Group, has won more and more influence in media legislation in the last decade. The argument of the big players is that to keep German broadcasters competitive on the global market calls for deregulation and the removal of legal barriers against cross-ownership and concentration; this was widely reflected in the new Broadcasting State Treaty.

Instruments of policy and their objectives

Pushed forward by technological innovation and market developments, media policy in Germany has had to modernise the dual system and to move it into the new environment of the coming information age. On the one hand media policy has to protect the public broadcasting system; this is a constitutional duty to guarantee basic information rights and freedoms. On the other hand, media policy has to take into account the special interests of the private broadcasters and the developments in the new emerging media markets, which represent a sector of growing importance for the whole national economy, and this is influenced by European and global challenges.

As far as the public broadcasting system is concerned the Federal Constitutional Court has decided in several rulings that, even against the background of a changing technological and economic environment, public broadcasting has a constitutional guarantee of its existence and further development. This includes a sound financial basis as well as the right to participate in new technological developments, and to enter new service areas. The new Broadcasting State Treaty reaffirms this constitutional principle. It allocates the necessary frequencies and funds to the public broadcasters and allows them to broaden their activities by launching two new channels for children (Kinderkanal) and information, education, and culture (Phoenix). Public broadcasters also have the right to enter the digital age by experimenting in this new area. Public broadcasters started their digital television project in August 1997, as mentioned above.

The private sector is hostile to this 'right to development' of the public sector. The German Association of Private Broadcasters (VPRT) has protested against the two new specialised channels and considers this decision to be illegal and unfair competition. A legal dispute arose when Nikelodeon and ntv, the German private news channel, brought the case to the European Court. Both television stations see in Kinderkanal and Phoenix an anti-competitive measure which is not covered by the constitutional protection for the *Grundversorgung* (basic service). The case is still pending and a decision is not expected until the end of 1997.

As far as the licence fee is concerned, the amount of the monthly fee for the period 1 January 1997 until 31 December 2000 was fixed at 28.25 DEM. A licence fee has to be paid by everyone who owns a radio or television set, regardless of whether she or he is listening to or watching public radio or television programmes or not. Some smaller groups have advocated the introduction of a system which would allow people not to pay licence fees because their television sets will block the reception of public programmes, but their arguments have not obtained wider support. When the multimedia legislation was adopted in August 1997, a discussion began over whether owning a PC, which is able to receive broadcasting programmes over the Internet, should also entail having to pay licence fees. The debate was watered down immediately both by the federal government and by the private companies, but the issue could return to the agenda with further progress of Web Television and other innovations in the context of growing convergence.

A second source of income for the public broadcasters is advertising. Advertisements in public broadcasting are limited. There are no advertisements on Sundays and public holidays. No advertising is allowed after

8.00 pm. Rules for advertising in public broadcasting are the subject of permanent discussion. On the one hand, public broadcasters want to remove the 8.00 pm barrier. On the other hand, private broadcasters want to eliminate the right to advertising on public broadcasters altogether. They see the right to collect licence fees in combination with the right to advertise as unfair competition which violates market mechanisms and gives public broadcasters an unjustifiable protected status. Against the background of shrinking advertisement income in public television, the public broadcasters themselves have started a debate about the future of advertising. The new ARD Chairman, Udo Reiter, has proposed to give up the right to advertise if there is compensation in the form of a higher licence fee. Negotiations for a new fee will start not earlier than 1999, but higher broadcasting licence fees are seen as socially unacceptable. They would also reduce the willingness of a broad audience to move slowly towards the acceptance of pay television and digital services, which have to be paid for additionally to the licence fee.

Politicians have to find a balance between the public interest and market pressure. With the entering into force of the Broadcasting State Treaty a certain balance, which is supported both by the public and the private sector, has been achieved, but more conflicts will come with further development of new information and communication services. Potential controversial issues will be the allocation of frequencies for digital video services, new rules for advertising, the definition and introduction of new services, and, maybe, the implementation of the now adopted anti-concentration rules (see below). Other issues like packaging or navigating are also controversial among public and private broadcasters.

Broadcasting legislation is more and more influenced by telecommunications legislation. The new Telecommunications Act has changed Germany's telecommunications landscape and will also have profound consequences for the relationship between Telekom AG and the public and private broadcasters. The Act has clear universal service obligations,[22] but it also gives Telekom AG the right to raise funds by offering its cable network to the broadcasters. Here a new area of conflict has arisen in 1997. While costs are still under discussion, capacities and competences are becoming another hot issue. The existing broadband cable network, owned mainly by Telekom, has only limited capacities. With the emergence of more and more channels, newcomers have only limited opportunities to reach the viewer via the existing cable systems. Public and private broadcasters are calling for a demonopolisation of the cable system in Germany and want to prevent Telekom from starting to play a role in selecting programmes on their networks. While Telekom denies that it

---

[22] See *Telekommunikationsgesetz* (n 13 above), § 117–22, 1126ff.

wants to play a role as a content provider, discussions continue to strengthen the legislation to guarantee that the distributor remains a neutral platform open to all and with no discrimination. After the first German 'Cable Summit' in May 1997, Telekom offered to broaden its network for two additional channels, but no final agreement on the other controversial issues could be reached.[23]

There is no agency like the American Federal Communications Commission in Germany with competence over both telecommunications and broadcasting. The new Telecommunications Act establishes a new independent Telecommunications Regulation Authority.[24] This new authority has no competence over broadcasting, but with continuing convergence between broadcasting and telecommunications some aspects of the new media, relevant also to broadcasting, could fall within the competence of the new telecommunications authority. Proposals are already circulating to reorganise the whole system and to combine the fifteen private broadcasting authorities of the *Länder* with the new telecommunication authority of the *Bund* as a German 'FCC'. While at the moment it is rather unrealistic to expect such a reorganisation in the next five years, growing market pressure could challange the existing system again.

Proposals for change

During the negotiations on the new Broadcasting State Treaty all the new issues emerging from the changes in policy, economy, and technology in the last five years have been covered and incorporated into the new Treaty, which entered into force on 1 January 1997. No further changes are needed for the moment. The new Treaty has to be tested through its practical implementation in the coming years before proposals for new changes can be made.

Nevertheless, some future changes have already been proposed indirectly in the text of the new Treaty. A key question for the future will be the structure of the ARD and the public broadcasting corporations of the *Länder*. The general principle of 'one *Land*, one broadcasting station' is under growing pressure, in particular against the background of more and more financial restraints. Rich *Länder* argue that they will no longer be prepared to subsidise poor stations if these stations are not ready for fundamental reforms and restructuring. In particular, Saarländischer Rundfunk (SR) from the Saarland, Radio Bremen (RB) from Bremen, and Sender Freies Berlin (SFB), are all small stations and highly dependent upon subsidies and so under attack. The proposal is to establish more

---

[23] See 'Runder Tisch Kabelnetzpolitik', in *Funk Korrespondenz Köln*, 20/97, 16 May 1997, 36ff.
[24] See *Telekommunikationsgesetz* (n 13 above), § 66–72, 1139ff.

Mehrländeranstalten to save money by reducing bureaucracy and by creating more economically-oriented units.

A first signal came already in early 1997 when the two *Länder* Baden-Württemberg (governed by the Christian Democrats) and Rheinland-Pfalz (governed by the Social Democrats) agreed to merge Süddeutscher Rundfunk (SDR) and the Südwestfunk Baden-Baden into a joint Südwestrundfunk (SWR). A state treaty among the two *Länder* was signed in April 1997.[25] There are discussions between Ostdeutscher Rundfunk Brandenburg (ORB) and Sender Freies Berlin (SFB) to merge and to create a strong broadcasting company in the new capital of Germany, which will become the seat of the federal government in 1999.

Another controversial issue, which was not settled by the multimedia legislation, is the definition of new multimedia services. What is a 'teleservice' and what is a 'media service'? This is not only a question of the competences of the *Länder* and the *Bund*, it is also a challenge for the whole legal system for the media. Does a home shopping television channel need a licence, for example HOT TV, which has asked the *Bayerische Landesanstalt für privaten Rundfunk and neue Medien* (BLM) in Munich for a television licence? When does an information and communication service with video clips, offered by German Telekom AG within T-Online, enter the area of broadcasting? Is digital radio over the Internet a 'tele- or a media service'? How are we to guarantee equal access rights for viewers, if more and more partners such as cable operators, packagers, navigators, etc are entering the chain which links the broadcasters with the viewers? Debate in Germany has started, but no solutions have been reached so far.[26]

The general trend, in Germany as in the European Union, is to define all the new services as trade issues and no longer as media issues. Although mass media are still seen as a cultural good, in practice the new services (and even the traditional broadcasting services) are seen mainly as a commodity which follows different rules. A legal consequence of that approach is that legal norms derived from trade law, industrial law and competition law are more applicable with regard to new information and communication services than is traditional media law. And, as far as conflict resolution is concerned, instead of the Federal Constitutional Court, the Anti-Trust Authority, the *Bundeskartellamt*, would become the final arbiter for settling disputes.

---

[25] See *Staatsvertrag über den Südwestrundfunk*, 15 Apr 1997, in *Funk Korrespondenz Köln*, 17/97, 25 Apr 1997, 3ff.

[26] See Kurp, Matthias, 'Gesetze mit begrenzter Haltbarkeit? Probleme und offene Fragen bei der Regelung von Multimedia', in *Funk Korrespondenz Köln*, 35/97, 29 Aug 1997, 3ff.

Topics and issues

Technological regulation

Innovations can be expected as a result of the new Telecommunications Act, adopted on 25 July 1996. The Act enters into force in two stages up to 1 January 1998. The principal aims of the Act are to stimulate competition, to guarantee universal service in the field of telecommunications, and to use the frequency spectrum efficiently. The entry of new competitors into the field of telecommunications services can also have long-term consequences for the German media market. In particular cable television will have to be reconsidered against the background of new services, including the offer of digital packages.

Another key issue is standardisation. Set-top boxes are seen as the main gateway for the new services within individual households. So far no regulation of this exists in Germany. There are debates around the need to agree upon an open standard to avoid a situation in which one company can determine the number of television programmes channelled via a set-top box into a given household. The exclusion of other programmes via a particular technical standard violates principles of diversity, pluralism, and media freedom in general. Regulation is needed to avoid restrictive practices and closed systems which reduce individual opportunities for access to and participation in communication. The case of the 'd-box', as mentioned above, is an illustration of what is at stake.

Economic regulation

The main new regulatory element in the Broadcasting State Treaty is the regulation of media concentration. The system introduced is rather complex. It is aimed at avoiding a situation where a single media corporation obtains a dominant position in the German media market. Several models and mechanisms have been discussed over the years to find a balance which would avoid the emergence of *de facto* monopolies on the one hand, but stimulate the further development of private broadcasting on the other. Finally the so-called 'viewer share model' was adopted.[27] According to this model, an illegal level of media concentration is reached if one media company (not a single channel) has more than 30 per cent of the annual viewer share for the totality of channels controlled by that company. A new Media Concentration Commission (KEK), which has six independent experts as members, nominated by the prime ministers from the *Länder*, will oversee developments in this area.[28]

Section 27 of the Broadcasting State Treaty regulates how the viewer

---

[27] See *Rundfunkstaatsvertrag* (n 14 above), § 26, p. 8.
[28] ibid, § 35, para 3, p. 11; the Commission started its work in June 1997.

shares will be determined. Section 28 defines which channels have to be included in the shares of a media company. Besides other criteria, 'family relationships' have to be taken into consideration. This special rule in § 28, para 4 refers to the fact that the owner of PRO 7, Thomas Kirch, is the son of Leo Kirch. Theoretically, PRO 7 is an independent broadcasting station, but in practice it is seen as a part of the Kirch empire. As far as Bertelsmann AG is concerned, the viewer shares of RTL, RTL 2, Super RTL, VOX, and Premiere have to be combined to determine the viewer share of the company. At the moment neither of the two German giants come close to the 30 per cent mark. It remains to be seen what will happen if one of the two should go beyond the 30 per cent frontier. And it is also unclear what the joint venture between Kirch and Bertelsmann in the area of digital television will mean against the background of this regulation. Anti-trust authorities at both national and European level have started to investigate the consequences of the case.

The general philosophy behind the 30 per cent rule is to guarantee a minimum of democratic pluralism and media diversity whilst allowing the maximum development of big media players to enable them to compete on the emerging global media markets against other global players, in particular from the USA. The structure of the system does allow three big players up to 30 per cent (in practice Kirch, Bertelsmann, and public broadcasting) with a remainder of a little more than 10 per cent for different minority groups.

If a media company should go beyond the 30 per cent barrier, the *Landesmedienanstalten* have the right to ask the corporation to sell parts of its company or to undertake 'special measures' to reduce the market share.[29] This could be a warning or the withdrawal of the whole licence for the company's channels to bring the viewer share into line with the 30 per cent figure. The KEK has to produce a general report every three years which has to include an analysis of the cross ownership (horizontal, vertical, and diagonal) situation and of international linkages. The KEK report will be the basis for further evaluation and new legislation.

Stronger anti-concentration regulation has been introduced for information-related programmes. Here the limit is a viewer share of 10 per cent (§ 28, para 5). If an information programme goes beyond 10 per cent, it has to give up programme time to third parties and independent producers in order to reduce its share below 10 per cent, otherwise it risks losing the licence.

The anti-concentration rules of the Broadcasting State Treaty are linked to measures guaranteeing pluralism and diversity *within* the programmes of the private market leaders also. According to § 30 of the Treaty, the

---

[29] ibid, § 26, para 4, p. 8.

private broadcasters have to open programme windows for independent producers, so-called 'third parties' (*unabhängige Dritte*).[30] A private channel is obliged to reserve a weekly programme time of 260 minutes. Seventy-five minutes of this amount have to be in prime time between 19.00 and 23.30. The media company has a right to discuss with the *Landesmedienanstalt* which independent third producer will get the right to the production window, but if there is no consensus between the private broadcaster, the independent producer, and the *Landesmedienanstalt*, the *Landesmedienanstalt* will make the final decision (§ 31, para 4).

Another instrument for promoting pluralism and diversity within the programmes of the private media companies is the obligation to establish a 'programme council'.[31] The programme council should represent the general public, but will be selected by the company itself. The Council has the right to obtain exclusive information from the Board of the private company and to give recommendations. In cases of conflicts between the council and the company, recommendations of the 'programme council' can be overruled by the Board with a 75 per cent majority (§ 32, para 4).

The new Broadcasting State Treaty does not explicitly regulate pay-television. Premiere and also the new digital television services act within the general broadcasting legislation. The public broadcasters are also considering opportunities for pay-TV. This option was sharply criticised by the private broadcasters, who argue that it goes far beyond the basic service (*Grundversorgung*) which justifies the collection of licence fees. If these fees are used to regroup existing programmes, to mix them with new elements and to sell the result to the audience, this would violate fair competition and has to be regarded as a misuse of the fees.

Social regulation

The guarantee of universal and basic service is a cornerstone of the German media law system, even if the principle has come under growing pressure through the changing technological and economic environment and market forces. The Broadcasting State Treaty, in its 'Preamble', reaffirms this constitutional obligation and calls for information pluralism and a broad range of cultural programmes.[32] In the new Telecommunications Act also, 'basic service' is identified as a key element of the new, deregulated telecommunication system.[33] While stable licence fees will allow public broadcasting to continue with basic services, special

[30] See *Rundfunkstaatsvertrag* (n 14 above), § 31, paras 1–6, pp. 9f.
[31] ibid, § 32, p. 10.
[32] See *Rundfunkstaatsvertrag*, 'Präambel', para 2, p. 2.
[33] See *Telekommunikationsgesetz* (n 13 above), §§ 17ff, pp. 1126ff.

obligations and the introduction of a 'Universal Service Fee' for new private telecommunication companies which do not offer universal services[34] will guarantee the continuation of that service in the field of telecommunications. How the new legal mechanism will work in a deregulated and market-dominated information and communication environment has still to be seen.

The content-related regulations in the Broadcasting State Treaty follow international standards, laid down in the Human Rights conventions of the United Nations and the Council of Europe. Section 3 of the Treaty defines the content categories which it is forbidden to distribute via broadcasting. Among them are hatred, war and racial propaganda, and pornography. Special regulations to protect children and young people prohibit programmes which undermine morals and decency. Programmes with a sexual content can be distributed only after 11.00 pm.

A new debate started in 1997 when Premiere started the distribution of semi-pornographic films after 11.00 pm in its pay-TV service. The *Landesmedienanstalt* of Hamburg (HAM), where Premiere has its licence, attacked the channel, but Premiere argues that there should be a difference between free TV and pay-TV as far as this kind of film is concerned because access is not free and under conditional control. An adult should have the right of 'free choice', as in a pay-TV programme in a hotel or in a video shop.[35]

While the other content-related regulations in the Broadcasting State Treaty are widely accepted, it is unclear how this regulation will be adopted for new on-line services. The opportunity to gain access to child pornography and neo-Nazi propaganda via the Internet provoked a court decison in Bavaria against the on-line provider CompuServe which was forced to block access to the incriminated services and had to pay a fine in 1995. The *CompuServe* case provoked an international debate on whether such a control is technically possible, and the question whether exclusion of certain content-related services violates the universal right to freedom of expression will need more discussion. Recommended remedies such as 'Clipper Chips' and 'Proxy Servers' are seen as a threat to data protection and information security. The new federal multimedia law clarifies the situation a little by stating that 'service providers are not responsible for the content of services of third parties' (Article 1, § 5.3).[36]

Both issues were also discussed in the Telecommunications Act debates. They are again on the agenda in the discussion of pending legislation

---

[34] Part 2, Section II, § 17–22 of the Telecommunications Act (*Telekommunikationsgesetz*) (n 13 above).

[35] See 'HAM contra Premiere: Streit wegen Pornographie eskaliert', in *Funk Korrespondenz Köln*, 35/97, 29 Aug 1997, 8.

[36] IuKDG (n 15 above), 1871.

concerning encryption and electronic signatures. The minister of the interior, Mr Kanther from the Christian Democrats, has called for a 'second key' which would give governmental institutions access to all files, including personal and economic data, to prevent crime; however, the Free Democrats, partners in the coalition government, see this as a threat to individual rights, economic freedom, and privacy.

In the Telecommunications Act the government has obtained far reaching access rights to all data transferred via telecommunications networks. Network operators and service providers are obliged to keep all data of their clients. Under certain conditions they have to guarantee access to the police, to the courts, and to other governmental institutions responsible for internal and external security, free of charge.[37]

No special legislation exists for non-commercial broadcasting in Germany. Non-commercial radio broadcasters in particular have called for legal guarantees for use of a special part of the frequency spectrum for their services. But although some *Länder* have in their legislation provision for a so-called 'open channel', which would give ordinary citizens the opportunity to produce and distribute their own radio and television programmes, there is no special regulation of non-commercial private broadcasting in the State treaty.

3 CONCLUDING REMARKS

Even in the early 1990s, the German media law expert Wolfgang Hoffmann-Riem prophesied the 'end of the media law' in Germany. Although the adoption of the new Broadcasting State Treaty and the redrafting of numerous regional media laws in the *Länder* since 1990 give a different impression, media practice in Germany shows that regardless of all regulatory efforts the legal system for the electronic media has become more and more weak, and although regional governments try to keep sovereignty (and control) over media policy in their *Länder*, the media market develops its own dynamism which calls for more and more deregulation.

Because the media industry is seen as a major source of new jobs, policy will follow this market pressure and will further liberalise the existing system step by step. The process will gain further momentum from the emergence of new, liberalised legal frameworks for telecommunications and trade in information services. If traditional broadcasting becomes integrated into an 'Integrated Digital Service Network' (ISDN) it is unavoidable that an integrated network of legal norms will be established.

---

[37] See *Telecommunications Act* (n 13 above), § 90, p. 1146.

Such a new system of norms will go beyond traditional broadcasting and press legislation, telecommunication regulation, and computer laws. It will combine traditional constitutional norms like the right to freedom of expression and universal services with new norms, taking into account the changing economic and technological environment. A new branch of law, the 'Law of Information and Communication Services', will emerge. This new legal system will consist of a stable legal framework which defines the general rules and principles, and a number of more specific norms and institutions, which will be partly self-regulatory both to meet the speed of change in the economy and technology and also to keep the new complex information and communication system workable.

Further European integration and general globalisation of networks and services will lead on the one hand to a greater 'internationalisation' of German media legislation. International norms, negotiated within the ITU, the WTO, or the European Union, will make some national regulation obsolete. But on the other hand this will not undermine the role of the *Länder* in the media sector. On the contrary, European integration will lead to a greater role for the regions. The Maastricht Treaty has introduced the principle of subsidiarity as a cornerstone of a further deepening of European integration. Subsidiarity will strengthen the role of the regions, as can be seen also in the new offensive role of the Committee of the Regions of the European Parliament. In fact many regions of the European Union have defined their new role in the context of the coming information age. A number of regional initiatives, partly sponsored by the European Commission such as the Inter-Regional Information Society Initiative (IRISI), Teleregions, Telecities, European Digital Cities, and others, have defined the multimedia content industry (which also includes broadcasting) as a key element of their regional strategy.[38] Regional content is seen as one of the most lucrative resources within the coming information economy.[39] Against this background the German *Länder* will undoubtedly redefine their future role. Until the end of 1996 nearly all German *Länder* had developed so-called regional initiatives for the information society such as 'media nrw', 'Bayern on-line', or the 'Saxonian Information Initiative (SII)', which also includes media issues.[40]

As far as media legislation is concerned, the growing role of the regions will probably not lead to a new, regionally-oriented re-regulation. It is

[38] See 'Regional Development and Information Society', Conference sponsored by DG XIII and DG XVI of the European Commission, Brussels, 30–31 Jan 1997.

[39] See Tapscott, D, *The Digital Economy: Promise and Peril in the Age of Networked Intelligence* (New York: McGraw Hill, 1996).

[40] See Kleinwächter, W, 'Regional Development and the Information Society—The IRIS-Initiative as a Pilot Action of the European Union', in Kahin, B, *National and International Initiatives for the Information Society* (Cambridge: Harvard University Press, 1996), 426ff.

more realistic to expect further deregulation, or self-regulation which takes into account different regional cultures, behaviours, and experiences. Self-regulation could become an appropriate instrument in the area of content for instance, combining the respect for certain common standards with a flexible response to the needs of new technology. In this context the role of civil society and of consumer groups will grow.[41]

[41] See Miller, S, *Civilizing Cyberspace: Policy, Power and the Information Superhighway* (New York: ACM Press, 1996).

3

Italy

GIUSEPPE DALLERA, MARIA VAGLIASINDI,
PIETRO VAGLIASINDI

1 MEDIA DEVELOPMENT

Comparing Italy with other major countries—even only European partners—it is evident that the diffusion of the so-called 'new media' and the development of multimedia has been very slow.[1] In 1996, despite the uncertain economic situation, the information and communication technology (ICT) market in Italy increased by 7.8 per cent; a good achievement when compared with 7.2 per cent for the EU.[2] The most impressive progress relates to telecommunication (TLC) growing at 10.6 per cent, far above the world-wide rate of 3.6 per cent—coming to over £17 billion, while IT has been growing at 4.3 per cent reaching £10 billion, and office products have decreased by 1.2 per cent, maintaining around £1 billion. The free-to-air national television sector—satellite is a brand new development and cable-TV only exists in Italy at an experimental level—completely dominates the scene in the media world and will continue to do so in the near future. This is true from all the major perspectives (economic, socio-political, and legal) which we are going to examine.

A plausible reason for this slower evolution is perhaps to be found in the initial State monopoly which hindered the diffusion of technological progress and cost reductions. In this context, major changes are expected since large-scale cabling is planned by Telecom Italia, the Italian public operator, privatised in October 1997. At present new media developments have not stimulated political debate or governmental action, probably because of our current backwardness.[3] For instance no system for enhancing competition or for regulating existing oligopolies has been devised.

---

[1] According to OECD and other studies, Italian figures (for PC penetration, internet host, pay-TV subscribers, CD sales etc.) on average compare very unfavourably with the Finnish, Norwegian, German, French, and British ones (not to mention USA, Canada, Japan, and New Zealand). IT expenditure in 1996 was 1.4% of GDP in Italy compared with 3.1% in the US and 2.8% in the UK; moreover, in Italy we have 8 PCs for 1,000 inhabitants against the 33 in the US.

[2] Hereafter the figures are expressed in sterling, unless otherwise stated. Estimates are from the European Information Technology Observatory (EITO).

[3] To be fair we should add that in Italy it is very popular always to blame the State and the government either for being too much involved or for not caring at all.

TV-frequencies have been allocated without the use of any economic mechanism such as auctions with competitive bids. Undoubtedly, such a solution would be strongly opposed by public and private concessionaires (RAI, MEDIASET, TMC). The new law—named after 'Maccanico', the TLC Minister—may represent a first step towards more competition in that it establishes a new Authority and designs a general telecommunication regulatory framework.[4]

In what follows our general aim is to gain a greater understanding of media developments, outlining recent socio-economic and legal evolution (section 1.1), describing the development of new services (section 1.2) and finally analysing market players with particular attention to the television sector (section 1.3).

1.1 General trends in media development

Overall, in Italy there is a slowly emerging tendency towards deregulation, expanding competition, and growing concentration of media companies. Pay-television will start contributing to the growth of the TV sector, but will not become comparable in terms of value added contributions to free-to-air-television. Because of linguistic and cultural barriers in Europe, globalisation will not immediately determine major changes either in the broadcasting and information system, or in the new media.

Information networks such as Lan (Local Area Network), Wan (Wide Area Network), and Internet are changing everyday life. However, notwithstanding the progress of digitalisation, industry (media, TLC, and IT) and market *convergence*—together with the creation of new delivery channels and multimedia—seems relatively slow. Hence it remains appropriate to distinguish TV-type services from internet-type (on-line) and multimedia CD-type (off-line) services. This depends on the uncertainty about the evolution of technologies and standards, apart from our backwardness in TLC infrastructure. The installation of fibre-optic cable, needed to create a diffuse broadband network so as to bring interactive multimedia services into all Italian homes, has already started but will probably take more than ten years to be completed. Some convergence is brought by market diversification. For example, Telecom Italia—the first company to enter mobile telephony with Telecom Italia Mobile (TIM)—has become one of the most important Internet service providers and seems very interested in entering the cable-TV market.

The television sector is the most relevant for its economic size and social

---

[4] Among the numerous previous reports see Barile, P and Zaccaria, R (eds), *Rapporto '93 sui problemi giuridici della radiotelevisione in Italia* (Turin: Giappichelli, 1994).

relevance.[5] In the last decade the public broadcaster RAI (holding three channels and previously a monopolist) has faced increasing pressure from public opinion (favourable to its privatisation) and political parties, and also fierce competition from private firms. In the expanding private sector there has been a growing concentration, primarily in the national TV sector which has led to an unbalanced duopoly between MEDIASET (previously Fininvest) holding three channels (Canale 5, Italia 1, Rete 4, formerly independent networks) and TELEMONTECARLO with two small channels (TMC 1 and TMC 2, formerly the separate groups TMC and Video Music). On the pay-TV side TELEPIÙ owns three channels, TELEPIÙ 1, 2, 3, and has become a digital satellite television broadcaster (DStv).

Currently, globalisation seems not to have introduced major changes because the broadcasting system was already importing programmes from other European countries, the US, and Japan. The difficulties are mainly due to linguistic and cultural barriers. Nevertheless, the satellite television international channels (such as CNN International, BBC Word, Discovery Channel, MTV Europe, Cartoon Network) currently broadcast in Italy.

In 1996 the growth of ICT (TLC plus IT) was due mainly to the TLC market, which is around twice the IT one (more than £17 billion and less than £10 billion). Fixed and mobile net services increased by 8.6 per cent (with a revenue of £12.7 billion), public net infrastructures by 14.7 per cent (reaching £2.7 billion) and private systems by 18.8 per cent (around £2 billion). In the IT market, hardware grew faster (4.5 per cent, around £3 billion) than software services and assistance (4.1 per cent, around £7 billion).

Telecom Italia's privatisation represents the final step in eroding the state monopoly in the telecommunications sector. In this context, joint ventures between electric utilities, railways, and television companies with international partners to provide expertise are in embryo. In mobile telephony there is a duopoly, but new joint ventures will soon enter the market.

Taking advantage of its monopoly position in traditional telephony services, Telecom Italia entered the Internet market designing different services for families, professionals, and firms. On the whole, while the institutional side of the Internet is quite well developed, the Internet

---

[5] For more details see Monteleone, F, *Storia della radio e della tv in Italia: società, politica, strategie, programmi 1922–1992* (Venice: Marsili, 1992). For an overview of the evolution in the EU see Rath, CD (ed) *La televisione in Europa* (Turin: F. Angeli, 1990) and Barberio, R and Macchitella, C, *L'europa delle televisioni* (Bologna: Il Mulino, 1989). Recent evolution of satellite is to be found in *Satellite Info Point* (<http://www.cdc.polimi.it/~piu1837/main.html>).

market is small. However, its commercial use is rapidly growing and Internet voice connections are emerging as a threat to international calls. Digital press is developing as well. Alongside big consolidated editorial groups like Rizzoli and Mondadori—which recently entered the digital press market—new pioneering groups (such as Giunti Multimedia), whose quality is good relative to European standards, are active in the market. The recent increase in PC sales is under the influence of multimedia applications and network connection. At the end of 1996 the EU growth rate (40 per cent) was below the US one (around 70 per cent). In Italy, despite Olivetti and IBM's resistance, Compaq became the largest seller in the first half of 1997 (increase of 44 per cent) according to SIRMI (86,500 against 84,500 for IBM and 80,000 for Olivetti which decreased by 11 per cent). Hewlett Packard (around 70,000) is the fastest growing at a rate of 82 per cent. As far as distribution is concerned Vobis (31,000) Computer discount (22,000) and Video Computer (16,000) are the most important companies.

On the regulatory side, political fights over media ownership still dominate the scene. They are mainly due to the political involvement of Mr Silvio Berlusconi, the owner of Fininvest and MEDIASET. A clear and final solution has not yet been reached. Only recently have issues related to multimedia, Internet and network started to be dealt with. Overall few changes have taken place, mainly inside the existing legal framework and the usual categories of communication, broadcasting, copyright, and obscenity. Currently, waiting for the appointment of the new authority, these are responsibilities of an independent authority, the *Garante per la radiodiffusione e l'editoria* (Watchdog for broadcasting and publishing).[6]

Despite some tendencies towards federalism, legal and administrative powers remain the responsibility of the Government and the Parliament. Comprehensive legislation is now in place, but in the past specific issues have been dealt with as they became economically or, more often, politically relevant. The new regulatory framework has finally emerged after several parliamentary discussions and official reports. For instance, the Special Parliamentary Committee proposal of 20 July 1995 came up with a new unified discipline. Many of the ideas proposed by the Special Parliamentary Committee have been incorporated in the recent Government proposals, and have now been finally translated into a new law.[7] In

---

[6] More details on its functions can be found in section 2.1.2 below. For a general overview of the past regime on media and TLC see Pace, A, *Comunicazioni di massa. Diritto* (Enciclopedia delle Scienza Sociali, Vol II: Rome, 1992); Corasaniti, G, *Diritto dell'informazione* (Padua: CEDAM, 1995); Cardarelli, F and Zeno-Zencovich V, *Il diritto delle telecomunicazioni* (Bari: Laterza, 1997).

[7] Such proposals include the institution of a Council Authority (17 July 1996) and more general telecommunication reform (25 July 1996).

the new scheme the Council is composed of i) a Commission for infra-structure and network (determining the allocation of frequencies, criteria for interconnection, access, and 'universal service' obligations) and ii) a Commission for services and products (supervising concessions, owner-ship transfers, advertising, and fairness). The Council determines the general principles on concessions such as accounting separation for access and interconnection, the cost of universal service and infrastructure with bans on cross-subsidies and discriminatory practices, and takes over all functions performed by the *Garante* as well as anti-trust powers. Conces-sions to any single operator cannot exceed 20 per cent of broadcasting capacity and revenues are limited to 30 per cent.

1.2 Development of new services

New 'off- and on-line' services have been offered, but have not reached the largest part of the population, stimulating only minor discussions or legal responses. The most notable exception, due to a strong demand from public opinion, is represented by the interactive telephony service—in particular those similar to *hotlines* and *chatlines* characterised by the prefix 144—whose delivery system was changed (becoming available only on written request). The new multimedia reality is thus emerging, but at a slow pace. In fact, Italy is still behind its major European partners (Ger-many, Great Britain, and France) even though it is starting to gain ground. For instance, Giunti Multimedia, the Italian pioneer digital press firm (which produces many CD-ROM titles), having entered the market after the French Grolier Hachette and the German Bertelsmann, still remains substantially a small firm.

On the other hand, the quality of Italian firms is well appreciated in Europe. For instance, a consortium led by Giunti Multimedia was chosen by the EU for the project 'Ortelius' (a data bank for university teaching). 'Time on line' (the Internet on-line news site of Mondadori Multimedia based on the innovative software Illustra of Informix) was awarded the Emma Award at the Frankfurt Fair as the best multimedia product in Europe. Rizzoli New Media entered the market exploiting the Internet for distributing its services. In fact it has developed the new *Enciclopedia Rizzoli '97* on CD-ROM for PC, whose monthly updates will be distributed via the Internet thanks to a partnership with Telecom online (Tol). Lately, major digital publishers such as (Mondadori, Opera Multimedia, and Rizzoli New Media) are investing steadily in 'high sales' CDs (around 100,000 copies), many coming from abroad.

Another small but relevant phenomenon is the diffusion of on-line newspapers. The *Unione Sarda* was the first to publish an Internet edition on Vol.it; now all the major newspapers (*Il Corriere della Sera, La Stampa,*

L'Unita', *La Repubblica*, *La Gazzetta dello Sport*, etc.), press agencies (ANSA, ASCA, ADNCRONOS, AGI . . .) and national channels (RAI, MEDIASET, etc.) appear on Internet sites. The majority of them run daily editions (with full stories) and many press agencies show news in real-time. Archive research is also provided, usually as a complementary commercial service, and economic, financial, and tax on-line consulting services are currently offered. However, by the end of September 1997 only forty among the 160 most important periodicals and fourteen out of the fifty newspapers have active web pages and only nine use advertising in their pages. *La Gazzetta dello Sport* on-line (www.gazzetta.it) seems to be the most visited Italian Internet site (with 250,000 pages read each day and more than one million contacts). On the whole the Internet market is still quite limited and its commercial use is just starting. According to an ANEE (Associazione Nazionale Editori Elettronici) research, among all registered web sites (9275 in September 1997) around 11 per cent (1138) offer editorial services. Among those (i) 234 belong to national editors, while 400 belong to service providers, the remaining to new editors, (ii) 476 are financed by advertising, 22 by subscription, (iii) 842 use only Italian, 264 also offer an English web page, (iv) 464 are dedicated to IT, 328 to local news, 290 to sport and leisure, 286 to culture and art.

Nevertheless commercial use is becoming more and more important, being characterised by fast growth and declining costs. Currently it is not entirely clear where the real Internet business lies. According to LOTTOR, by July 1997 there were around 112,000 web sites; 98,000 more than in January (in the US 10.8 million; an increase of 3 million from January). Probably in the near future the most relevant issue to be resolved is that of providing access to such services. In fact, half of the revenue coming from the Internet software market that is currently dominating the scene is attributed to the interconnection market.

Despite the low prices of services major Internet access providers (such as Video Online and Agora) have not met a sufficient demand to pay out initial investments. Consequently, the quality of connection is still quite low. The total of paying subscribers in 1996 was below 50,000 while free users totalled 450,000. The Internet provider association estimated the Internet market value to be more than £10 million in 1995 and around £25 million in 1996. By 1997 the £60 million ceiling will be probably reached. According to a Demoskopea investigation for Alchera Strategic Vision, by September 1997 46 per cent of 'technology oriented' firms (with at least ten workers) and around 11 per cent of all firms are connected to the Internet, and users are around 5 per cent (ie around 2,348,000 against 1,377,000, ie 2.1 per cent in March 1997), with 700,000 being computer connected. However, we are still very backward in the EU for the number of hosts in the network (less than five per 1,000 inhabitants, just above Portugal and

Greece), for paying subscribers (around 300,000) and for PC penetration (14.8 per cent).

Matters have improved since the major Italian phone company Telecom Italia entered the market with three different services: (i) Video Online will remain at a low speed for families, (ii) Telecom on line (high speed) has been created for professionals and amateurs, and finally (iii) Interbusiness designed for firms. It is expected that demand, prices, and quality will grow in the near future. Telecom estimates the number of future total paying subscribers will be more than one million in the year 2000, whereas the Internet providers association forecast more than five million users. This will constitute an important market for advertising as well. In the US the CNN Internet site is currently earning around $600,000 through advertising. This represents half of the earnings of the greater browsers and software producers like Netscape. Providing services to firms is also thought to be profitable (as proved by Netscape in the US). The Internet site may represent not only an important tool for communicating to the public, but also a starting point for rebuilding an internal network (Intranet, which uses the same software) for a firm's internal organisation purposes. Agora 2000 (99 per cent of which is held by Veronica Berlusconi) operates under the direction of Silvio Pesenti in connection with the Fininvest group and the Mondadori Editor. Currently it has put on-line the Mondadori *Pagine Utili* (Useful Pages), which constitute the new telephony directory entering the market in competition with the *Pagine Gialle* (Yellow Pages).

Currently the Internet is also fast developing on the institutional side. Bankitalia and the Finance and University Ministries have web pages. On-line services are provided by the Public Administration (tax forms and tax instructions are currently available via the Internet). It is increasingly used by the academic world (applications for national research funds are currently made via the Internet). Most Italian universities are connected and have Internet sites; also Departmental web pages are copious. Banking, public, and social services seem also most promising in playing a major role in the Internet market in the near future. Banks are starting commercial applications and public web sites have been rapidly appearing in the north (and in Tuscany) especially in big cities with universities. The use of Internet and Intranet is seen as a way to improve efficiency in the public administration, but it is still not used by high levels in public administration (PA) and it is hindered by bureaucratic procedures. In this respect the recent directives on informatic documents (implementing the so-called 'Bassanini 1'; L. 15.3.1997 n. 59) seem to mark the beginning of a real PA informatic revolution. Many civic networks now offer on-line services. This experience started in 1995 with 'Iperbole' Bologna. As at March 1997, 18 Regions, 39 Provinces, and 295 cities (60 in Tuscany) have their own web sites. However, 43 per cent still have no policy and 34 per cent are not co-ordinated.

In this respect the Internet may have limited uses due to the restricted and highly selective make-up of users. Italian users have very distinctive characteristics: 51 per cent live in the north, 79.3 per cent are under forty, 92.6 per cent are males, 93.8 per cent have higher education or university qualifications, and 45.9 per cent have a management position. The commercial use of Internet sites poses major security problems. Even the American Central Intelligence Agency was obliged to close temporarily its Internet site to delete an external message ('welcome to the Central Stupidity Agency') inserted by a hacker. The operations of an Italian press agency have also been suspended for a week by a supposed terrorist organisation (*Falange Armata*). This is a serious threat also for commercial use and for the development of banking and shopping via the Internet. Newspapers and periodicals are the most active in the multimedia market; providing videos, CDs, cassettes, and floppies as special supplements, generating substantial competition with the original markets, and legal controversies.

Another line of convergence is (mobile) telephony. New cellular phones and pagers are designed to be able to connect with the Internet and in particular with electronic mail. Currently we have a duopoly of TIM (Telecom Italia Mobile) and Omnitel, but new joint ventures are planning to enter the market soon. For instance, MEDIASET together with BT, TELENOR and BNL seems ready to apply for the third mobile radio licence. In the light of deregulation, new joint ventures (electricity utilities, the railway company, TV and international partners to provide experts) are also planning to enter the market in the longer run. MEDIASET joined Albacom (the BT and BNL telecommunications venture) in fixed telephony.[8]

To complete this brief outline, let us take a look at the network infrastructure market prospects. In Italy, as in the EU, we experienced first a technology-driven change (related to hardware manufacturers) followed by a knowledge-based one focused on satisfying consumers' needs, which appeals mainly to the software industry. The ultimate challenge is to meet the ever-increasing communication demands, from traditional voice telephony to multimedia and the Internet.

As Table 3.1 shows, access networks, intelligent networks, telecom management systems and customers represent a faster growing part of the market compared to traditional switching and transport systems (which are performed in a less expensive way by sub-contractors).

[8] MEDIASET has currently a 30% stake in Albacom, the BT and BNL telecommunications venture (£22 million), that will drop to 19.5% after ENI's subscription to part of the reserved capital increase.

Table 3.1: Expected changes in the fixed network infrastructure market

Decreasing	Increasing
Transmission	Broadband switching
Narrowbank switching	Network intelligence
Other (generic access, etc)	Telecom management

1.3 Market participants and their strategies

Table 3.2 outlines the main broadcasters in the television sector in 1997. The dimensions of the national television market in 1996 can be summarised by the following figures:

- 17 million subscriptions to RAI (a personal licence fee of £68 per annum, in the form of a 'property tax' which gives a revenue of around £1.19 billion).
- £1.8 billion classic advertising investments (of which more than 30 per cent belong to RAI and 60 per cent to MEDIASET). TV has around 60 per cent of the total spending.
- 0.9 million subscriptions to pay-TV (2.7 million expected by 1999). 100,000 subscriptions for digital-TV (300,000 expected by the start of 1998; 60,000 seasonal for football). One million parabolic antennas (one-quarter in condominiums, one-fifth dual-feed, ie receiving Eutelsat and Astra).

In practice the Italian market is an oligopoly with two dominant firms (RAI and MEDIASET). Publitalia—the greatest private advertising agency, collecting mainly for MEDIASET—had a major role in the concentration process of Canale 5, Italia 1, and Rete 4. More competition should improve the situation, at least in theory, because the coverage of the whole national territory is not guaranteed by all national channels.

MEDIASET SpA is the Fininvest group's arm in the television business. Apart from holding concessions for the broadcasting of three networked television stations, MEDIASET owns Videotime (which produces television programmes for its channels), Publitalia '80 (dealing with advertising) and Elettronica Industriale (which runs broadcasting signals, receivers, and transmitter equipment). It also has various interests in the music, insurance, building, and printing industries and owns *Il Giornale*, a national newspaper ranking fifth in the circulation list. In 1996 it had more than 4,000 employees and produced around 48 per cent of the 13,000 hours of programmes. MEDIASET's consolidated net turnover in 1996 totalled £659 million (an increase of 7.4 per cent), and net profit close to

Table 3.2: The national television sector in Italy

RAI	3 channels: RAI 1, RAI 2, RAI 3 (public held through IRI)
MEDIASET (Fininvest)	3 channels: Canale 5, Italia 1, Rete 4
TELEMONTECARLO	2 channels: Tmc 1, Tmc 2 (VideoMusic)
RETE A	1 channel (tele-sales)
TELEPIÙ	3 channels: TELEPIÙ 1, 2, 3 (pay-TV)

+870 local concessionaires = Italian television sector

£216 million (an increase of 17.7 per cent). The Cecchi Gori Group (producer and distributor of films) is the owner of the smaller national broadcaster TMC. The presence of a film producer/distributor as the new market entrant suggests the advantages of combining film and TV activities. Finally, RETE A, the last national concession, is practically irrelevant being mainly a tele-sales specialist.

The TV audience dropped in the eight months from October 1996 to May 1997; for instance from 27 million in November to 24 million in May (during peak hours, ie from 20.30 to 22.30). The share for the average day of the main channels in 1996–7 (1995–6) was 23.8 per cent (23.8 per cent) for RAI 1, 21.9 per cent (21.7 per cent) for Canale 5, 15.4 per cent (15.25 per cent) for RAI 2, 10.3 per cent (12 per cent) Italia 1, 9.5 per cent (9.6 per cent) RAI 3, 9.15 per cent (8.75 per cent) for RETE 4 and 9.9 per cent (8.9 per cent) for all the others (including TMC). This invariance (in the presence of a global decrease) is a strong indication of how the main channels have perfect knowledge of their customers, so that notwithstanding strong competition average quotas stay the same. The only major difference, the decrease in Italia 1's audience, is due to an attempt to create a 'thematic' channel specifically addressed to younger generations. This failed attempt to target the young public shows how the near future still belongs to channels aiming at a relatively broad audience.

A duopoly structure also characterises television advertising. However, Publitalia has a dominant position in the market; £0.8 billion advertising investments in the first eight months of 1997 (increase of 9.6 per cent), compared with Sipra £0.47 billion (increase of 9.1 per cent). In fact, as we will see in what follows, RAI has greater restrictions on advertising time, since it is financed through licence fees. This attracted advertising producers and wholesalers to MEDIASET which has been accused of progressively absorbing the greatest part of the financial resources, once belonging not only to other television broadcasters and radio (itself now quickly increasing by 14 per cent, £0.08 billion advertising investments, in the first eight months of 1997), but more generally to the press (slowly increasing by 3.5 per cent, £0.78 billion).

The public broadcaster RAI faced an increasing strain from fierce competition by private firms (namely MEDIASET at national level) reporting major losses. However, RAI's financial situation has improved in the recent period through reducing its workforce and increasing productivity. This has also been due to the financial help allowed by a decree known as 'Salva-Rai' (Save-RAI) which has been re-enacted more than once.

Notwithstanding the fact that Italians have pronounced in favour of RAI privatisation as a result of a referendum, IRI still owns 99.55 per cent of RAI which now has a new management: Enzo Siciliano (President) and Franco Iseppi (Chief Executive). Power struggles between the two offices ended with the appointment of this new administration board. Apparently, there are no privatisation plans in view for the near future.

Turning now to the pay-TV sector we find currently a monopoly, with TELEPIÙ (owned by CANALPLUS 90 per cent and MEDIASET 10 per cent) holding three national channels with an additional eight satellite channels and twenty music channels. The launch of 'Hot Bird 2' (the new Eutelsat satellite in November 1996) represented the latest step towards digital satellite broadcasting in Italy. In this way the chief broadcasters in the television sector (and the main users of Hot Bird 2: RAI, MEDIASET, TELEPIÙ, and STREAM—part of the Stet Group) are moving into digital TV using the new opportunities that this advanced technology offers. This represents a real challenge for TELEPIÙ, which is the first broadcaster in Italy to have already started the so-called digital revolution. Since September 1997, the 0.8 million 'analogue' TELEPIÙ subscribers have been followed by just 0.13 million 'digital' subscribers. The new subscribers' growth seems to be less than 500 consumers per day so that the digital business may remain 'the not to be TV', the actual yearly budget on programmes being globally around £13 million. The last year was a commercial flop; however, monthly basic subscriptions will rise to £10 (plus £5 for renting the decoder), and new channels were added; Bloomberg TV (news with Ansa), Meteo (weather), Marco Polo (travels), Bet on jazz, and Match music (youth music). Classica (music), Disney Channel, and Ecclesia (produced by the Catholic Church Cei) will also be offered. Since October 1997 RAI has broadcast three unencoded channels (Raisat Ragazzi, Raisat Enciclopedia, Raisat Cultura) and is going to invest £10 million per year for each of them. In the near future a news and a sports channel will be added. Cecchi Gori Communications (TMC owner) is also working to develop a project for satellite Pay-TV. In Italy there is no important cable-TV business at the moment; however, Giunti Multimedia is currently planning to enter with a joint venture with STREAM (of the

Telecom Italia group) which will be used to transmit satellite broadcasting in city centres, thus avoiding antennae. Agreements on unified digital standards and infrastructure were formalised in November 1997 by TELEPIÙ, Telecom Italia, RAI, and TMC who participate in the *'piattaforma digitale'* under Italian control (60 per cent).

In 1996 the fastest growing TLC sectors are mobile telephony (47.7 per cent), services (31.4 per cent), and infrastructure (27.5 per cent), while transport, the biggest in added value, is lagging behind (4.8 per cent). In fixed telephony Telecom Italia was privatised in October 1997, in the light of a future globally deregulated EU telecom market. Italy is eighth in the world with a 10 per cent penetration of mobile phones (not far from the UK at 11 per cent): there are 7 million mobile phones; in the last three years the rate of growth has been around 30 per cent with a maximum of 46 per cent in 1996. We remain far behind north European countries; Sweden has 2.445 million mobile phones with a penetration greater than 27 per cent (Norway, Finland, and Denmark follow quite closely). TIM is the public incumbent: it is the biggest and most profitable in Europe with 6 million customers and profits of £340 million. Omnitel, the private competitor, is sixteen months old, has one million customers and bears losses of £214 million mostly for reasons of development. It was selected by auction with an entry tax payment and this has caused debates and controversies with the European Commission. Following the European Commission's decisions, as compensation TIM will have to pay back to Omnitel £22 million.[9]

However, though the EU deemed the entry tax to be anti-competitive, the Italian model has led to a very effective competition in terms of tariffs. For instance, as Table 3.3 shows, pre-paid tariffs are much lower than those set by Vodafone in the UK—a very competitive market.

Another major problem with mobile telephony that is to be tackled by the TLC Ministry (and later by the new Authority) is access pricing, which was reduced by 30 per cent on 6 June 1997 with four months of retroactive effect (appealed against by Telecom at TAR del Lazio). The connection charge to the fixed network remains around 170 per cent of the European average (ie £0.05 instead of £0.03 per minute).

2 REGULATION AND OTHER MEDIA POLICIES

In Italy media and communication issues have been historically under the responsibility of central government (mainly the TCL Ministry) and

---

[9] This decision 95/489/EC, taken 4 Oct 1995, may be found in the UGEC L280 of 23 Nov 1995. This solution is going to be implemented, after repeated attempts by the Italian Minister and EC intervention. TIM requires all concessionaires to be allowed to use (from

Table 3.3: Mobile telephone tariffs

Pre-pay Tariffs	Low	Usage Average	Intensive
Omnitel	8.73	102.85	242.19
TIM	8.76	103.34	243.40
Vodafone	25.50	148.90	287.16

Low = 25 mins (5 of high tariff)
Average = 140 mins (110 of high tariff)
Intensive = 300 mins (270 of high tariff)

the Parliament. However, the greatest impact in the evolution of the rules has been made by the Constitutional Court and by EU directives. As shown by recent debates in the regulatory and political arena, the television sector is considered the most important one from economic and legal perspectives.

In section 2.1 we will examine the evolution towards a comprehensive piece of legislation, trying to explain possible future changes. As shown in section 2.2 below, in the past specific issues related to technological, economic, and social aspects of regulation have been dealt with in a rather chaotic way, and sometimes few changes have taken place inside the existing legal framework.[10] As far as the new media are concerned, issues relating to multimedia, the Internet, and networks have started to be dealt with only recently.

2.1 Types of regulation and other policies

Media laws have been in a process of constant revision, recently with a higher frequency, under constant pressures by the Constitutional Court and the EU. At times, after costly and painful political disputes, the legislator has been forced to ratify the status quo or to comply with court decisions and directives rather than truly attempting to regulate. In subsection 2.1.1 we sketch the historical evolution of the regulatory arrangements and the erosion of the State monopoly. This is necessary to gain a

1998 as expected in the EC agreement) the new system Dcs 1800 (the same used by the forthcoming third concessionaire) and to withdraw all pending legal actions.

[10] For instance, copyright and intellectual property rights are still based on the 1942 Civil Code. EC Directives (92/100 on Rental Right, 93/83 on Satellite and Cable, 93/98 on Terms of Protection, 95/46 on Data Protection, 96/19 on Database Protection) have been slowly transformed into internal legislation, or at times initially partially ignored. See Corasaniti, G, *Diritto dell'informazione* (Padua: CEDAM, 1995).

better understanding of what led towards a unified Authority with enlarged powers, examined in subsection 2.1.2. In the final subsection 2.1.3 we reconsider our constitutional framework in the light of EU norms outlining the next steps and proposals for changes in the legislative framework and regulatory instruments.

2.1.1 The evolution of the regulatory framework (structure and institutions)

In Italy all communication services started under State monopoly after L. 33.06.1910 n. 395. On this basis the royal decree R.D. 08.02.1923 assigned the government the faculty to allocate radio-diffusion concessions. They were assigned exclusively to URI (Italian Radio Union), a private company, that gradually became public, with a large governmental presence in its management. It was renamed EIAR (Italian Enterprise for Radio Audition) first, and then RAI after the Second World War, becoming synonymous with radio and television broadcasting. Monopoly was reinforced with the L. 13.04.1933 n. 336 and the communication code RD 27.02.1936. During the republican era, governmental control on broadcasting was partly reformed with a decree 03.04.1947 n. 428 introducing: (i) a committee responsible for the broadcasting timetable and (ii) a parliamentary vigilance committee (*Commissione parlamentare di vigilanza*) to ensure political independence and information objectivity. RAI remained however firmly in the hands of the government, and only in 1960 were all political parties granted free access in two political programmes '*Tribuna politica*' and '*Tribuna elettorale*'. The radio-television monopoly (under direct government control) was declared not to be in conflict with article 21 of the Constitution (on freedom of communication). The Constitutional Court (CCS 13.07.1960 n. 59) justified this decision by the limited number of frequencies, invoking article 43 on public enterprises and the public interest more generally. This reasoning was the basis of a new communication code (the presidential decree DPR 29.03.1973 n. 156) whose article 195 established criminal liability for unauthorised private radio infrastructure and broadcasting. Other principles were: (i) uniformity of tariffs (articles 8 and 9), (ii) limited liability and (iii) assignment through administrative concession (article 184).

A subsequent Constitutional Court decision (10.07.1974 n. 225 and 226) defined more precisely the public interest and the guarantees of pluralism in the radio–television services and requested regulations (also for cable-TV) to prevent oligopoly. This led to a new arrangement under the L. 14.04.1975 n. 103. Greater pluralism and impartiality was ensured through the presence of three channels and by increasing the powers of a new parliamentary vigilance committee, which nominated ten (out of sixteen) managers (*consiglieri di amministrazione*) and formulated general TV guidelines. Advertising was limited to 5 per cent of the whole broadcasting, so as not to damage the periodical press.

Constitutional Court decision 28.07.1976 n. 202 abolished the public broadcasting monopoly at a local level, recognising the existence of a sufficient large number of frequencies and requiring procedures for assigning frequencies and authorisations. National channels (heavily financed by advertising) were created interconnecting local televisions in a network, and broadcasting the same programmes (including advertising and sponsorships) on a national scale, either at the same time or with a slight delay. The RAI tried to prevent these developments and the Constitutional Court was asked to pronounce again. Rizzoli was allowed to interconnect local channels functionally and the Parliament was explicitly asked to design a new regulatory framework to avoid monopolistic concentrations contrary both to pluralism and the rules of a democratic system (CCS 21.07.1981 n. 202), whilst, in the unregulated national market private broadcasters were quickly reduced to three (Rizzoli with Italia 1, Rusconi and Mondadori with RETE 4 and Berlusconi's Fininvest with Canale 5). Three years later, the Constitutional Court had explicitly to authorise private operation once more in the absence of any appropriate regulation (CCS 30.07.1984 n. 237). However, criminal courts proceeded to sequestrate private telecommunication infrastructures on the basis of article 195 of the communication code, as unauthorised private infrastructures. These developments led to a 'transitory discipline' (present in the unconverted DL 20.10.1984 and then in DL 6.12.1984 finally converted into L 4.02.1985 n. 10) authorising existing national networks, the only obligation being to devote at least 25 per cent of broadcasting to European productions. Subsequently, CCS 17.10.1985 n. 231 legalised advertising broadcasting by foreign channels in the national territory and recognised the need for setting some quantitative and qualitative limits to advertisements broadcast by private TV (to favour the press and consumers). The Court also urged a single regulatory and anti-trust regime for national channels (including incoming foreign channels) and stated that the 'transitory discipline' was not in conflict with the Constitution.[11]

Finally, a new legal and regulatory framework—the so-called 'Mammí Law' L 6.09.1990 n. 223 (named after the TLC Minister)—was approved in a fiercely divided political climate. It instituted an independent Authority—the *Garante per la radiodiffusione e l'editoria* (Watchdog for radio-broadcasting and the press)—implemented EUD 3.10.1989 n. 522 and started a *mixed regulatory regime*, examined in section 2.1.2.

The Mammí law was the object of many criticisms and has been seen as

---

[11] CCS 05.02.1986 n 35, 13.04.1987 n 153 and 14.07.1988 n 826.

the ratification of the existing duopoly in the television market system and a restraint on new opportunities brought by technological developments. The Constitutional Court stated that it was not in conflict with freedom of communication, and that anti-trust discipline and the *Garante*'s powers (being restricted by law) were legitimate (CCS 93/112). Later, the L 25.06.1993 n. 206—known as 'Professors' RAI Reform'—increased RAI's autonomy from politics and improved its budget. With this aim administrators are to be nominated by the presidents of the two Chambers (like the *Garante*).

Recently some events have led towards a rethinking. In 1994 Berlusconi's government raised the television ownership issue and the Constitutional Court decision CCS 1994 n. 420, by abrogating 4th comma article 15 of the Mammí law, limited to 20 per cent the share of a single operator (two out of twelve), to prevent a dominant position.[12] The following year, as a result of referenda (DPR 5.04.1995) Fininvest was able to maintain 1) the existing private television position (instead of reducing to one the national channels a private broadcaster could own) and 2) advertising during films. Italians also supported RAI's privatisation.

In relation to the TLC sector two Constitutional Court decisions[13] limited the TLC code principle of limited liability of the concessionaire leading to a rationalisation of the TLC sector. Law 29.01.1992 n. 58 tried to separate operational and regulatory activities, and assigned to a government committee CIPE (*Comitato Interministeriale per la Programmazione Economica*) the redesign of market working and the formulation of new tariffs (taking into account costs and EU patterns). Another step forward was the first EU service liberalisation—implemented through DLgs 17.03.1995 n. 103—and more generally the formulation of principles of competition and regulation in public utility services—law 14.11.1995 n. 481. However, since no new TLC authority was created, a new law was still required for these principles to become operative. Finally, law 23.12.1996 n. 650 implemented EUD 95/51 on cable-TV, EUD 95/62 on telephony and EUD 96/19 on competition in TLC; but with no reference to directives on mobile telephony.

A *Special Parliamentary Committee* (instituted on 14 December 1994) tried to answer the compelling request for reform by designing a new unified discipline.[14] The reform came in the new legislation following the presentation of two Government Bills on 17 July 1996 and on 25 July 1996, part of which have been approved after one year.

---

[12] See Bognetti, G, *Costituzione, televisione e legge antitrust* (Milan: Giuffrè, 1996). In relation to previous EU influences see Salvatore, V, *Concorrenza televisiva e diritto comunitario* (Padua: CEDAM, 1993).

[13] CCS 20.12.1988 n 1104 and CCS 28.02.1992 n 74.

[14] In its proposal (Atti della Camera 20.07.1995): i) the dominant position (including

2.1.2 Policy instruments and objectives in the mixed regulatory system

The Mammí Law, modified by a number of new laws (such as the L 17.12.1992 n. 408, the L 27.10.1993 n. 323 and finally the L 1.03.1994 n. 153), represents the most recent operating *regulatory regime*. One of its main innovative features was the institution of the *Garante* to stay in place for five years. It was given sanctioning powers and the tasks of 1) keeping the *Registro delle imprese televisive* (a national register of operators and owners, direct or indirect, with a quota larger than 2 per cent, and of advertising concessionaires and producers of radio–TV programmes), 2) keeping a record of and revising radio–television firms' budgets, and 3) proposing detailed regulation of sponsorship. It also institutes a *Consiglio consultivo degli utenti* (Consultative board of users) to guarantee consumers' interests as well as regional consultative and proposal-making authorities, the *Comitati regionali per i servizi radiotelevisivi*.

At present, with the partial approval of Government proposals, major legal and regulatory reforms are taking place. Given the different opinions in the majority coalition this initially seemed an unlikely outcome, as thousands of amendments were presented by the opposition. One novelty (present in the Maccanico law[15]) is the institution of a new kind of independent administrative Authority (inspired by the FCC) with enlarged powers—the *Autorità per le garanzie nelle comunicazioni*—composed of a) a Commission for regulating infrastructure and networks (*Commissione per le infrastrutture e le reti*), and b) a Commission for regulating services and products (*Commissione per i servizi e i prodotti*); and a general Council (*Consiglio*) (including both Commissions). The Senate and Chamber of the Parliament will appoint four commissioners (two for any Commission), while the President will be appointed by the Government (subject to parliamentary approval).

In particular, the Commission for regulating infrastructure and networks will mainly:

- give opinions (not binding) on the national frequencies' allocation plan set by the TLC Ministry
- draft plans for assigning frequencies
- define measures to prevent interference, and standards for decoders/ unscramblers
- keep a national register of operators in TLC, advertising, producers of radio–TV programmes, editors of newspapers and periodicals,

---

multimedia) was to be limited to 20% of national channels (as prescribed by the Constitutional Court) and to 25% of total resources, ii) a communication authority elected by Parliament should redesign the frequency plan, iii) a federal public channel was to be created (out of RAI 3) without advertising, and iv) EU Directives were to be fully implemented.

[15] L. 29.07.1997 n 650, L. 31.7.97 n 249.

and national press agencies, with a census of transmission infrastructures
- define criteria for interconnection and access to TLC infrastructures
- regulate relations between administrators/owners and users of infrastructures
- provide quick settlements in disputes on interconnection and access to infrastructures
- supervise interruptions of public services, giving general guidelines
- define, in compliance with EU legislation, uniform 'universal service' obligations
- single out other TLC services to be supplied uniformly
- promote international interconnections.

The Commission for services and products will:

- supervise all operators with concessions for the distribution of services and for advertising
- fix terms (starting from their first release) for the use of audio-visual products by different services
- enact regulations on advertising
- supervise the observance of the 'right to correction and reply', and protection of minors
- assure the enforceability of norms on political information
- propose terms of conventions with licensees and supervise their implementation
- watch over fairness in rating and correctness of methodology in opinion polls monitoring TV broadcasting.

The Council (ie the two Commissions together) has normative and sanctioning powers. Its main functions are to:

- suggest legislative intervention related to technological innovation
- ensure the correct application of norms on freedom of access to infrastructures
- promote research on new technology and multimedia services
- define general guidelines on concessions and authorisations, and supervise respect for the parliamentary commission guidelines
- audit accounts and balance sheets of licensees
- establish and ascertain the nature of 'dominant positions'
- assume all functions of the 'Guarantee for broadcasting and publishing'
- draw up a yearly Report to Parliament on the activity and plans of the Authority, with information and data on TLC, press, and other communications media
- authorise property transfers by corporations with concessions.

Before the new authority becomes operative, the TLC Ministry will assume all its functions apart from the ones attributed to the *Garante*.

The new Authority will co-operate closely with the TLC Ministry, the local public administration, and Financial Police. It is possible to appeal against the decisions of the new Authority, but only through the administrative courts: that is, first applying to the *Tribunale Amministrativo Regionale* (TAR) *del Lazio* and then to the *Consiglio di Stato*.

2.1.3 Criticisms and proposals for change in regulating the media

The Bill has been subject to severe criticisms on some specific points.[16] Let us start with a general one which leads us to re-examine the constitutional precepts and to formulate general proposals for change. The appointment procedure of the Authority and its President by the Government and the Parliament does not offer in itself sufficient quality assurance. Commissioners need only to satisfy the requirements of any member of an Authority for public utilities, although one of the main aims is to *guarantee* fundamental constitutional values; values such as secrecy and freedom in communication (C. art. 15), freedom of expression and pluralism in broadcasting (C. art. 21) and of private enterprises (C. art. 41). At the same time, references to European legislation and guidelines are not fully convincing; a prompt and complete implementation of EU directives would have simplified matters in most cases.

In TLC and audio-visual markets messages are to be protected both in their content (art. 21) and in their form if a communication is taking place (art. 15).[17] Consumers and suppliers (even firms) hold these constitutional rights, while network managers and service providers should ensure secrecy and freedom of what is transmitted. At the same time the freedom to offer TLC and broadcasting services may help implementing constitutional rights. This reinforces the provision of the 1st comma of article 41, which guarantees the freedom to exercise private enterprise, as long as basic values such as social welfare, security, liberty, and human dignity are not compromised. Finally, this supports service liberalisation when correctly interpreted along the lines of EU directives and guidelines, which in the Italian legislative structure lie at an intermediate level between constitutional and ordinary laws. Hence, in general, limits to private enterprise conflict with a constitutional principle (apart from EU

---

[16] eg the reform appeared to have as one of its main objectives preserving the status quo.

[17] More generally from art. 2 also follows the protection of reputation, personal identity, and privacy with many consequences (eg on data-banks EUD 24.10.1995 n 46 and L. 31.12.1996 n 675). As an example, whoever broadcasts a message from a national channel is protected by art. 21. If the same message is transmitted in a video on demand service art. 15 applies also as a communication takes place.

treaties). On the other hand article 43 (used in CCS 13.07.1960 n. 59 to support the state monopoly in broadcasting) seems to offer equal support to a state monopoly for essential services having a prominent general interest; but only when the law prescribes it. Therefore, given our international and EU obligations (C. art 10), article 43 should no longer apply to TLC and audio-visual markets.[18] Moreover the TLC code principle of assignment through administrative concession should be drastically limited according to EU directives and guidelines.[19] Concessions are based on the existence of a public power (for example the fiscal one), of a fiduciary element between the public administration and a firm, and affect its organisation: by conferring a specific office (or service), regulating its administration, and requiring particular behaviour (submission of operational plans, etc). But the creation of special or exclusive rights or of new faculties implicit in the administrative concession seems in itself not fully compatible with fair competition as required by the EU.

A general implication follows for changes. Clearly (once constitutional rights are protected, for example ensuring clear and specific licence rights and responsibilities) the only remaining public intervention should be an efficient economic (and administrative) regulation of frequencies and of the market. Accordingly, the new Authority should aim at facilitating the growth of competitive markets and regulating natural monopolies. In this light the introduction of licence auctioning—as currently done by the FCC—should be favoured, since establishing market values provides incentives for the most productive use of frequencies.[20] At the same time auctions may reduce the need for services regulation.

The consequent reduction in administrative powers leads to the criticism of the new Authority's far-reaching discretionary powers in a wide sector of the economy (all media and means of communication including electronic means). It has extensive power in deciding and changing the regulatory design. It will determine when MEDIASET (exceeding the 20 per cent limit) will abandon terrestrial frequencies with a channel. The same is true for the second pay-TV (only for the third is the deadline of 31 December 1997 fixed by law). Having relevant powers in the interconnection business it can decide how to model competition, that is, the opportunities for entry in a sector that has so far been a public monopoly. In the

---

[18] For more detailed discussions see Cassese, S, *La costituzione economica* (Bari: Laterza, 1995) and Cardarelli, F and Zeno-Zencovich, V, *Il diritto delle telecomunicazioni* (Bari: Laterza, 1997).

[19] Concessions should be substituted by authorisation or licences for already liberalised services, for 'alternative' networks, and from 1998 for TLC networks.

[20] Some complications arise from the EU directives. For instance when Italy (like Belgium, Spain, and Austria) received large licence fees from the winners of the second mobile phone tenders, to ensure a fair competition, the European Commission required charging the first licensee the same amount, or returning the licence fee.

audio-visual sector it can determine (through the frequency plans) the dimension and the format of the television system; like the FCC it can build or remove barriers between sectors. It will not only decide, like the referee in a football match, who violates the rules and what the penalties are, but also who participates in the game and to a large extent what the rules are.

Consequently we believe that on the economic–technical side more clear guidelines should be given limiting discretion and avoiding long-lasting judicial controversies. Luckily, there are European Directives and the Italian legislator tried to avoid judicial risks by (i) reducing the administrative process times by one half, and (ii) allowing administrative judges (*TAR del Lazio* and *Consiglio di Stato*) to define matters immediately, with shortened procedures when the suspension of the Authority decision is requested. However, the problems seem to lie at the origins and would be solved only by reducing administrative discretion and relying more on competitive market forces.

Regarding the technical regulatory role, the political composition of the Authority and the appointment of its President by the Government subject to the agreement of two-thirds of the competent parliamentary commissions do not seem to provide appropriate guarantees of impartiality and of technical competence (reference is made to article 2 of L. 14.11.1995 n. 481). The president is just a *primus inter pares* (accepted by parliamentary opposition) and directs a 'consensus-based' organism in which quite different positions and sometimes diverging visions are represented. In this way the reform acknowledges dissatisfaction with the 'Guarantee' figure as devised by the previous law, but then just proposes to merge it into one of the Commissions of the Authority. Moreover, the structure of this Authority appears to be too complex and intricate. A strange distinction between a 'technical' commission and a 'political' one creates some overlap in competencies and functions. Some of the functions of the Commission for services and products do not appear in line with the evolution of the telecommunications technology.

Hence, unlike similar European institutions characterised by just one head, there might be difficulties in taking quick, clear, and effective decisions and in providing technical guidelines. This should cause great concern, given that the Authority should be able to direct a crucial sector of the economy whose revenue is currently greater than £40 billion and is expected to grow quickly in the future. Accordingly, we believe that it could be useful to reinforce the presidency role and to base the organisational distinction instead upon the constitutional guarantee duties and the economic–technical regulatory role.

As far as the aim of preserving competition is concerned, the anti-trust powers attributed to this new Authority partly deprive the Anti-trust

Authority of its competence. This would imply a further weakening of the Anti-trust Authority, which has already lost competencies in the credit, financial, and insurance sectors. Also in this respect references to European standards appear rather weak.

An important part of the framework related to the *'public service'* in radio and television (as well as advertising regulation and the quota for Italian audio-visual) is still to be defined also, due to the recent crisis in the majority. In particular, the Bill 1138 (presented on 25 July 1996) proposes that *public services* should be effected by the Authority through a holding company with majority shares in corporations with national TV channels, national radio channels, cable and satellite channels, one radio channel for Parliamentary activity, and radio information for road-traffic. This holding company should receive public funds through a licence fee. These funds should be partially transferred (up to 50 per cent) to a different corporation (receiving also funds from regions but not from advertising) for local broadcasting, controlled by the holding company. The 'crowding index' (time per hour) of advertising on national channels of the public service concessionaire should be 20 per cent lower than that of private concessionaires. Moreover, there are (i) a peculiar definition of public service, referring to criteria of completeness and impartiality, and a 'global supply of general interest accounting for different opinions and political, social, cultural and religious trends', (ii) an obscure cross-reference to 'public interest', and (iii) an implicit connection of 'public service' to 'public holding'. Such important points need to be elucidated.

2.2 Topics and issues in media regulation

As in most western countries, the Italian media law system is a complex and evolving structure (whose lines have been examined in the previous section) aiming to affect media and communications technology, market structure, and content. In what follows, our aim is to gain a greater understanding of more specific issues related to technological aspects (section 2.2.1) and economic ones (section 2.2.2). Finally, we analyse social regulation, with particular attention to content and user protection (section 2.2.3). A general premise is that, since the system is in a transitional phase, current practices are likely to be modified once the Parliament passes new laws and the Authority starts working.

2.2.1 Technological regulation: infrastructure and standardisation

In Italy the technology side is under the control of the public administration; this is true for wireless and wired TLC. As with many other EU countries, Italy still needs huge infrastructure investments and is very much affected by public operators, for a number of reasons. The principal issue is that of the frequency spectrum and of satellites.[21] The right to reach the audience by cable connections is also becoming relevant. Concessions will be issued by the new Authority, which proposes the plan for frequencies and releases broadcasting concessions, distributing frequencies according to its own assignment plan. The latter will state the number of national and local programmes, according to (a) locality of transmission equipment, (b) radio-electric parameters of international standards, (c) numbers of programmes receivable without interference, (d) reserved frequencies for digital, satellite, and cable transmission, (e) reservations to local transmissions of one-third of programmes, (f) equal coverage of territory (at a national and local level), and (g) reservations benefiting linguistic minorities of channels for foreign or local broadcasters.

Concessions last six years and imply the payment of a fee. Any operator requesting concessions must be a corporation based in the EU (other nationalities are allowed on a parity basis). National concessions must reach at least 80 per cent of the population and all main towns. Local concessions imply the coverage of a 'catchment area'. All concessions will be supplemented by conventions with operators. For example, radio–TV concessions also set numbers of programmes that can be broadcast through assigned frequencies.

In the infrastructure field there is no real competition at the moment and governments seem to have no interest in it (favouring public incumbents). No major obstacles prevented Telecom Italia from entering the cable TV business, or RAI entering the satellite and digital TV business. So far there are large-scale telecommunications projects aiming to create a diffuse broadband network and work has already been started by SIRTI (part of the Telecom Italia group); however, major undertakings will take eight to ten years. Delays are mainly due to difficulties posed by intersecting competencies of different public administrations, and more specifically by local permissions (for example from councils).

In the near future, the cost of providing network access is expected to become a major issue.[22] In Italy a probable option lies in introducing competition for services and not for infrastructure. Both sectors require regulation for opposite reasons. Greater competition and innovation in services is expected, as has already been experienced with mobile telephony. Network innovation and investments will probably progress slowly, since incentives will be provided in any case by new technologies'

---

[21] In fact, the EUD 6.02.1997 on satellite TLC has been promptly applied through DLgs 11.02.1997 n 55. Moreover, incentives will be given to favour the sales of antennae and receivers.

[22] For an economic analysis of a possible solution see Vagliasindi, M and Waterson, M, *The Baumol-Willig rule under socially optimal non-linear pricing* (mimeo, Edinburgh, 1997).

by-pass opportunities. According to the Maccanico law corporations with concessions and authorisations must give clear separate accounts of costs for access and interconnection, 'universal services', installation, and management of infrastructures, demonstrating the absence of cross-subsidies and discriminatory practices.

The new Authority also has the power to limit access to networks for the protection of the technical integrity of the network, protection of data and persons, and for somewhat ambiguously defined 'general interest' and 'non-economic reasons'. Supply of universal services (including public security, national defence, justice, education) should be defined according to EU criteria. Financing of universal service will be provided through a common fund, receiving quotas of concession fees and interconnection tariffs, fixed as a proportion of corporate turnover. However, the lack of clarity in dividing universal service costs and the delays in liberalising TLC markets are the main reasons for Italy being included (together with Belgium, Denmark, Germany, Greece, Luxembourg, Portugal, and Spain) in the November 1997 'black list' of countries against which the Commission is opening procedures for violating telecommunications directives. This happened notwithstanding that the EU liberalisation directives were finally approved with DPR 19.9.1997 n. 318. The hesitation of the Commission in dealing with the issue (the average delay being around ten months) shows not only its difficulties in acting when strong German interests are at stake, but also the limited appreciation by EU countries of the need for a competitive TLC market, although the time-lag compared to the US damages firms' competitiveness and consumers' interests.

In 1991–93 new rules were introduced to regulate access to systems of public networks (L.58/1992), to regulate public infrastructures of telecommunications (DLG 519/92, in execution of EC Directive 91/263), and integrated services of digital networks (DLG 53/93, in execution of EC Directive 387/90). The new Authority is also concerned with standards and compatibility. Moreover, as in many other EU countries there are pieces of legislation and official standards bodies (i) to implement control through mandatory standards for electronic equipment, cabling, and so on, (ii) to protect the health and safety of consumers and workers (as well as TLC networks), and (iii) to provide technical quality, equipment interoperability, and compliance with international standards. However, for the new media, important areas should be regulated on a world-wide or at least on an EU perspective.

2.2.2 Economic regulation: Market structure, remuneration and finance

The Italian media law system right from the start aimed at influencing market structure, and governing concentration and ownership. After an

initial public monopoly, the Mammí laws represented the first step towards a systematic regulatory and anti-trust regime, mainly directed to
regulate free-to-air TV. Together with the TLC Ministry the *Garante* assumed an important role of control of the market and of ownership.[23] In
1994 an anti-trust limit of 20 per cent on the ownership of national channels (ie two out of the nine private ones) was imposed by the Constitutional Court and a new regulatory setting has been devised, as described
in section 2.1.2. Dominant positions (in TV, radio broadcasting, multimedia, the press) are forbidden. In particular concessions to a single operator
(or cross-controlled operators) should not exceed 20 per cent of broadcasting capacity at national level; moreover each specific radio or TV sector
has a 30 per cent limit on resources. In cases of dominant position the
Authority can exercise a direct power of intervention, either imposing
bans, or operating on the structure of firms (for example through divest-
ment). Concentrations and mergers are deemed null and void if not authorised. These operations must be communicated to the new Authority
when they concern operators in the telecommunications sector. Moreover,
the new Authority (i) regulates proceedings, (ii) establishes transitory
periods in which limits do not apply, and (iii) provides higher limits for
radio broadcasting.

Market and ownership are also subject to general laws governing trade
practices designed to prevent restrictive and monopoly trade practices
and to protect consumers.[24] The Anti-trust Authority (*Autorità garante per
la concorrenza ed il mercato*)—created in 1990 (L. 270/1990)—has deliber-
ated upon many controversies between new operators and existing
concessionaires in TLC, favouring market liberalisation. By comparison,
the intervention of ordinary justice (mainly by Appeal Courts) in these
matters has been limited and ineffective. No great relevance has been
given to the value of competition, article 41 of the Constitution, and EU
norms.[25] The administrative courts—which deliberate on the Authorities'
decisions—had a more positive attitude and will have a greater role, while
the Anti-trust Authority has been partly divested of its competence.

Another extensively regulated sector is print media. Regulation has
been at times so pervasive that a specimen Internet newspaper printed on
paper is required to comply with the current press rule. Satellite and cable

---

[23] It must be kept informed of all ownership transfers greater than 10% (2% if quoted in the
stock market). See section 2.1.2 for more details.

[24] New services are influenced by the previous media legislation where applicable by
analogy, or because the services are connected to traditional media. This is especially true for
on-line services or new media since no existing law is especially directed to them (eg
narrowcasting or subscription radio or Internet services).

[25] For instance on 30 May 1995 the Corte di Appello di Roma decided in favour of TIM
against OMNITEL. This decision was reversed on 4 October 1995 by the EU Commission
which found a disparity of treatment violating arts. 86 and 90 of the Rome Treaty.

communications are subject to specific control too. Recently DL 11.02.97 has implemented EU Directive 94/46 excluding radio-diffusion (ie the licensing of net services via satellite, for example BUSAT, SNG). Accordingly, there are only experimental licences awarded by the TLC Minister for the TV and other radio satellite services, as is the case for cable TV. In any case, commercial television licensees may not hold more than a minority share in satellite and pay-TV; this led Berlusconi to abandon the control of TELEPIÙ. Instead, public concessionaires (RAI and Telecom Italia) are taking advantage of the opportunity to participate in a common system of digital broadcasting; naturally open to the use of other operators according to the principles of transparency, competition, and non-discrimination, under the control of the new Authority.

The emerging issues related to the presence of independent service providers and bottlenecks in the new media market, are in part dealt with through separate accounts, the ban on cross-subsidies imposed on network owners, the design of codes of conduct, and control of the abuse of dominant position. Future regulation will be probably influenced by US rate of return and UK price cap regulatory experience.[26]

Regarding the protection of intellectual property rights, the main general source is the Italian Civil Code (1942); more specifically articles 2575–2583. These provisions define the object of copyright (creative intellectual works, in any medium), the time of acquisition of copyright (the moment of creation), the exclusiveness of publication by the author, reproduction of projects and compensation, rights of interpreters, actors, and executors, and transfers of rights. The Civil Code protects the 'right to name and image' (articles 6, 7, 10).

In Italy, copyright law is still governed by L. 22.4.1944, n. 633 (Copyright Act); it also deals with radio and television (articles 51–60 and 79). This remains the main source of copyright protection, and has been amended and integrated over time. It clearly defines protected intellectual works (it now includes, for instance, computer programs, when EC Directive 91/250 was implemented by DLG 29.12.1992, n. 518, art. 2; audio-visual aids and 'videograms' by L. 5.2.1992, n. 93; DLG 16.11.1994, n. 685 on EU Directive n. 92/100 on hiring and lending in connection with intellectual property rights; DLG 23.10.1996, n. 581 for broadcasting through satellite). The definition of protected works is detailed, inclusive, and can be applied to all media. The author of intellectual work is identified, together with his or her responsibility. Protection of copyright, its length (seventy years, fifty for discs), economic use, and the moral rights of the author are defined by the Copyright Act, which has intro-

---

[26] For a general theoretical reference see Vagliasindi, M and Vagliasindi, PA, *The economics of auctioning and related regulatory issues* (Edinburgh: mimeo, 1997).

duced a Government Office for literary, scientific, and artistic property, a Permanent Consultative Committee for copyright, and the Italian Society of Authors and Editors (SIAE), which receives payments for copyright and diffusion of protected works. However for PC software the 'aim of lucre' (*fini di lucro*, which envisages a connected and immediate monetary gain and is more restrictive than the general aim of profit) is a fundamental ingredient when judging whether duplication violates copyright; moreover duplication and fruition by connection is not even considered.

More recently L. 6.2.1996, n. 52 (implementing EU Directives 93/83 and 93/98) deals with copyright in satellite and cable broadcasting, in particular regarding payments to authors and for films, duration (seventy years), and management (only through a collective management corporation). The interests of the film industry are protected by specific laws such as 153/94 which prevents a film from being broadcast less than two years from release (one year for pay-TV, eight months for video release) and are also supported by public financing (through the Ministry of Culture). Protection is also provided to data banks by L. 23.12.1993 n. 547 in the form of copyright accorded by ordinary judicial decisions. For generic problems the norm against unfair competition (art. 2598 cc) remains a very useful instrument, for instance it should prevent mere imitation.

The new law imposes limits to the operators' revenues. Any operator is allowed to collect a maximum of 30 per cent of all resources of its sector in TV or radio broadcasting, cable and satellite TV. Resources include licence fees for public service, advertising, revenues from tele-sales and sponsorships, proceeds from conventions with public authorities, and any television supply of goods and services. Operators with participation in newspapers and periodicals are allowed up to 20 per cent of total resources of both sectors. Advertising concessionaires are permitted to collect economic resources up to the same ceiling. If an advertising concessionaire is owned by an operator it can collect advertising only for that operator. The limits do not apply to operators with a single national programme. Operators with more than two national concessions are to be allowed to transfer to cable or satellite one of the concessions, whilst one of the public service channels is to be divided into local broadcasting corporations, without advertising. The evolution of advertising regulation clearly shows how the legislator seems to be oriented towards restraints. From 1966 a Code for self-regulation in advertising tried to impose some basic guidelines concerning fairness, prohibition of misleading advertising, proper use of technical and scientific data in information, authenticity of evidence, verifiability of statements, clear identification of advertisements, respect for moral and religious convictions, protection of minors, and safeguarding health and security.[27] This Code prohibited some forms of advertising (imitative, indecent, defamatory, and comparative). In order to apply the principles stated in the Code a special Court (acting as a jury) and a Control Committee (acting as a prosecutor) were set up. The Code was drafted on a voluntary basis, against any kind of behaviour in advertising which might be deemed censurable, even if not strictly a criminal offence. The Court's decisions require corrective behaviour from condemned firms and persons. From 1990 misleading advertising received more attention with the institution of the Anti-trust Authority, which has been responsible for multiple interventions (with directives and administrative sanctions), and for limiting improper practices in commercial advertising (for example in 'indirect' advertising through product placement). Finally, the internal legislation was adapted to EC Directive 84/450, 1984, only by DLG 74/1992.

Temporarily the *Garante* remains responsible for advertising and sponsorship regulation. To protect the press, TV advertising has been restricted to 5 per cent of weekly broadcasting (with a maximum of 12 per cent per hour) for RAI and 15 per cent per week (with a maximum of 20 per cent per hour) for national channels. Current regulations—supported by a recent administrative court decision—assimilate advertising and sponsorship for radio and television and set qualitative criteria (see the EU Directive 552 2.10.1989), quantitative limits (advertising time is 4 per cent for RAI and 20 per cent for national private and 35 per cent local private stations), 'recognisability' criteria, and reserve local advertising for local channels. DM 13.07.1995 n. 385 allows only the presence of a reference to a sponsor in audiotex and videotex services. The inclusion of recognisable advertising messages in Internet services (not yet regulated) also poses a series of peculiar problems. For instance, they are costly for consumers since they require additional transmission time, so that consumers pay for something unwanted. Accordingly, they should at least be informed of cost incidence. Moreover, Internet being an international service, enforceability problems are posed for the DLgs 25.01.1992 n. 74 on the existence and efficiency of self-regulation systems and for the new Authority guidelines.

New electronic commerce is regulated by analogy to more traditional types of distance selling, even if it presents different features. For example, especially if order placement is provided by means of a host computer service, the geographic location becomes uncertain and so does the national law to be applied. This might also be an issue of international concern from a fiscal point of view when service providers are located

---

[27] See Vagliasindi, M, *Economia e tecnica della pubblicità* (Pisa: Tipografia Editrice Pisana, 1991).

abroad (and in particular outside the EU). Proposals to resolve the main issues have been formulated at a European level, including the suggestion of a 'bit tax' for the Internet which has been the subject of much criticism by the community of Internet users and by governments.

2.2.3 Social regulation: Content and user protection

There are complex sets of rules relating to social regulation covering a wide range of topics (including content standards and codes) relating to broadcasting, film, information services, and publications, whose principles apply to multimedia and aspects of on-line services. The existing laws impose a number of social obligations (for example news and information requirements, protection of minors, universal service, socially useful advertising, the reservation of 51 per cent of film programming for national and European works) and support for information services (for example for local channels). National radio and TV concessionaires have an obligation to broadcast news and information. To ensure impartiality of information, the current law declares as legally equivalent TV-news and newspapers. A Professional Order of Journalists has been established since 1925 (L. 2307) and is regulated by L. 69/1963. It consists of a national Council, with local Councils, that watches over respect for truth, the duty to publish corrections, and respect for professional secrecy, and is authorised to impose sanctions (censure, suspension, expulsion). The 1993 *Charter of Journalist's Duties* also determines a precise code of conduct. It fully acknowledges the 1993 *Resolution of the Council of Europe on Journalistic Ethics* with regard to the respect for privacy, personal responsibility of journalists, right to reply, correct citations of information sources, separation of advertising from information, and the protection of minors and vulnerable persons.

The new law draws a distinction between local commercial TV and local public service TV, and allows for different conventions. Some priority in frequency assignment is reserved for local operators broadcasting cultural, political, and religious programmes with less than 5 per cent of advertising time. Incentives will be provided for the joint use of production and broadcasting at local level, and for access to telecommunications markets. Whoever devotes at least 70 per cent of broadcasting at local level to socially useful broadcasting is also viewed with particular favour.

The Criminal Code (dating back to 1930 in its structure) provides rigorous criminal liability connected to media operations. Penal responsibility is provided for authors and directors omitting to exercise due control (art. 57) and is basically the same for the press and for radio–TV. It concerns (a) obscene publications and performances (arts. 528, 529), (b) defamation (arts. 595–596 *bis*) for which the 'right of criticism' and the 'right of chronicle' are important limits based on article 21 of the Constitution, (c) publication of false and exaggerated news contrary to 'public order' (art. 656), (d) 'crimes of opinion' such as public insult (art. 327), (e) inducement of, and apologia for crimes (art. 414), and (f) anti-national statements (art. 272).

Civil protection of information and privacy is provided with respect to secrecy in correspondence (arts. 616, 618), communications (art. 617 *bis/ ter*), industrial and commercial secrecy (art. 623), administrative secrecy (L. 241/1990), and secrecy relating to state security (arts. 256–263). While the professional secrecy of journalists is protected (art. 622), a strict safe- guard of court secrecy, for inquiry and investigations, and of classified acts of the courts is provided by the recent (1988) Code of Procedure in Criminal Courts (arts. 114, 115, 329). Audio-visual recording and direct TV broadcasting in courts are generally admitted only with the authorisa- tion of the court and the consent of the parties. Proper use of industrial and commercial information has been regulated by L. 157/1991 protecting financial markets from insider trading.

Advertising is prohibited in the case of medical services, products for smokers, and spirits. The law forbids broadcasts which may damage children, as well as violent, pornographic, racist, or sexist material. Films for those over fourteen can be broadcast only after 23.00 and before 07.00. National concessionaires also assume the obligation to accept principles for the protection of minors. The main commercial TV companies devised a classification system for films and programmes, distinguishing between (1) *green* programmes suitable for viewing by children, (2) *yellow* pro- grammes appropriate for children to watch under adult supervision, and (3) *red* programmes for adults only. Greater controls are being devised also for the Internet, starting from police and judicial investigation and ending with self-regulatory codes. This has followed the recent European trend against child pornography.

Starting with the L. 4.02.1985 n. 10 (the transitory discipline) private channels were obliged to devote at least 25 per cent of broadcasting to national or European productions. The limit is now set at 51 per cent. The electoral laws 276/93 and 277/93 set rules for news and broadcasters, in addition to imposing expenditure limits for political broadcasting during electoral campaigns. The principle of parity of access to information sources for all competing political parties during parliamentary elections was introduced with L. 515/93. Due to the alleged abuse of MEDIASET in the 1994 campaign, these measures were extended to European and local elections and referendums, and reinforced by the government in D. 83/95, known as *par condicio*, in order to guarantee equal treatment and impar- tiality for all competing political parties under *Garante* control, with strong pecuniary sanctions. A distinction between electoral *propaganda* (offered on a free basis and with equal time), *advertising* (fully regulated, permitted only up to thirty days before elections, and allowed only on private channels with requirements of equal treatment, a clear identification sign, and that it is not false, negative, denigratory, or misleading), and *information* (with impartiality, completeness, and fairness requirements) was introduced. This decree, though re-enacted many times, was never approved by Parliament. Accordingly, regional administrative judges suspended the effects of all sanctions and judgments until it could become law, which never happened.

In the past use of TLC services has been subjected to a number of conditions (based on a sort of fiscal privilege) by the concessionaire on behalf of the PA on the basis of the *regulation of service* approved by DM 8.09.1988 n. 484, while administrative decisions on tariffs were in practice delegated to the concessionaire with little transparency and control. The *regulation of service* has been only partially modified by DM 13.02.1995 n. 191, after some Constitutional Court pronouncements and ordinary judicial decisions argued, in line with CCS 17.03.1988 n. 479, that they should be organised following economic criteria and governed by private law, with a fair representation of interests. On both sides (consumers' rights and tariffs) the new Authority will face hard work dealing with non-competitive markets; accordingly competition and access-pricing regulation have a conspicuous consumer protection profile.

As regards extra-contractual responsibility, an important issue is the violation of personality rights in acquiring and diffusing personal data; that is, reputation (false and dishonourable data), personal identity (incorrect data which misrepresent a subject), and privacy.[28] From May 1997 an independent Administrative Authority for privacy protection (instituted by L. 31.12.1996 n. 675) has been set up under the direction of Professor Stefano Rodotà. It has taken over some powers of the older *Garante*, widening its own competence to protection of privacy (in particular of persons) from intrusiveness of other people, press, radio, and TV. From a general point of view its range of intervention appears wide and not clearly defined. It should protect individuals against intrusions into their privacy, even against the public administration, for example the Inland Revenue. The Government has been delegated to deal with Internet implications and a decree will appear by 1998.

3 CONCLUDING REMARKS

In what follows we provide an assessment of the present situation referring to the legislative framework (section 3.1), the market structure

---

[28] In TLC privacy was already ensured by L. 23.12.1993 n 547 (on information crime); later, following EUD 24.10.1995 on personal data treatment, the legislator also introduced L. 31.12.1996 n 675, obliging to rectify and also considering non-patrimonial damages.

(section 3.2), the regulatory instruments (section 3.3) and finally the problem of financing communication services (section 3.4).

3.1 The legislative framework

Recently, the European Commission has played a very important role in triggering legal responses to the evolution of the media, particularly in liberalising the radio-TV market. Many important directives will finally have been implemented without further delays by 1 January 1998, as everywhere in Europe.[29] These directives will require the liberalisation of telecommunication infrastructures and of cable TV networks, together with the removal of restrictions on use of third party infrastructures for the delivery of satellite and mobile communications and for provision of all terrestrial telecom services. Hence, also under pressure from public opinion (including through referenda), Italy is moving in the direction of a more competitive media market. A major debate on property rights in films was solved through a national referendum in 1995, implying the rejection of proposals aimed at banning advertising breaks within films.

As in Germany and Spain, the Constitutional Court also played a leading role. In many cases, the Italian legislation followed the lines of the Constitutional Court's decisions. The Constitutional Court has often pressed for reforms towards a mixed system.[30] Sometimes its decisions have been anticipated, as was the case in a decision declaring interconnection of local TV not to be in breach of the Constitution. Sometimes the legislation preceded even the general interventions of ordinary criminal courts.[31]

The Italian legislature never considered the idea of implementing anything similar to what the German Constitutional Court had devised in 1986, distinguishing between fundamental public service and subsidiary public service. The definition of 'public service' relating to radio–TV broadcasting has always been ambiguous and unsatisfactory. It refers, essentially, to *public ownership*, rather than to the characteristics of products. Equally undefined is the 'public interest', which, many times, appears to be more akin to political impartiality than to general utility. In fact the main characteristics of public service are found in ensuring equal access to private and public TV, and equal broadcasting and advertising time allo-

---

[29] We are referring in particular to Telecommunications Services Directive 90/388 and Open Network Provision Directive 90/387 EC.

[30] In particular, the state monopoly in radio–TV broadcasting, dating back to 1910 has been abolished. See L. 103/1975, L. 10/1985 and L. 206/1993.

[31] Initial responses were triggered by the practical impossibility of prohibiting Italian TV broadcasting from abroad (Monte Carlo, Switzerland, Yugoslavia).

cation to different channels. These principles, introduced for political broadcasting, have been progressively extended to other TV services.

However, the Italian legislation tended to understate technical problems in the evolving media. The nature of radio–TV services as public goods, from the point of view of the technology of consumption—that is access, externality, and non-rivalry in consumption—is generally recognised.[32] Possibilities of exclusion and rationing were introduced with pay-TV, but most characteristics of public goods are retained. The debate had some partial success in defining at least some ideas as products with properties of public goods and, as such, not to be encrypted.[33]

A different problem refers to the public good nature of telecommunications infrastructures and broadcasting systems. These seem to have, more properly, the nature of intermediate public goods, or public production goods, and therefore there is a case for advocating public monopoly (or a fully regulated firm).[34] This would allow easy access for private operators, since broadcasting infrastructures represent the highest barriers to entry into TV markets. Moreover, this solution would automatically regulate the efficient use of frequencies and prevent signal interference. Paradoxically the existence of a public productive factor in TLC was prevented by a joint public monopoly in services and infrastructures.

Some media activities may be considered meritorious and desirable goods, sometimes even against free consumer choices. Accordingly, they deserve periods of supported consumption, just to educate consumers and allow more responsible choices. This amounts to treating some products and structures of the media market as 'merit goods'. But it is not evident where the boundary between informational devices and political judgments lies. In fact, while information, cultural productions (as opposed to B-rated films), and news can be defined as merit goods (with limited objections), media seem not to be proper examples of merit goods.

3.2 Market structure

The emergence of very powerful interest groups has been a major cause of concern. In telecommunication markets *public interest groups* are very

[32] For an economic debate see among others, Minasian, JA, 'TV pricing and the theory of public goods', *Journal of Law and Economics*, Vol 7 (Oct 1964), 71–80 (and 'Reply' by Samuelson, PA, ibid, 81–3).

[33] This point was present in the draft of the recent Bill (25.7.96).

[34] A well-known specific reference related to the US experience is Noll, R, Peck, M and McGowan, J, *Economic Aspects of TV Regulation* (Washington, DC: Brookings Inst, 1973). The UK reader may be interested also in Beesley, ME (ed), *Markets and the Media*, (London: IEA, Reading 43, 1996). For some general reference see Beesley, ME (ed), *Regulating Utilities: A Time for Change?* (London: IEA, 1996), Reading 44.

strong and mainly concentrated in public radio–TV national bodies. A complementary typology of interest groups in the media market was the telecommunications state holding. Private interest groups also appear in private national TV: Fininvest (with interests in insurance, building, printing, and owning one national newspaper, ranked fifth in broadcasting) owns three TV channels and the Cecchi Gori Group (producer and distributor of films) owns TMC and TMC2. Pay-TV was concentrated in one group owning all national and satellite channels.

The present TV market can be described as an oligopoly characterised by a dominant duopoly. A classical point arising from the Pilkington Report is that a duopoly in TV can be even worse than a monopoly.[35] Monopolistic competition (due to the presence of many differentiated firms) would be preferable, at least from a theoretical point of view. The latter would ensure either (i) a public limited 'high-quality' production addressed to a qualified minority together with a wide set of commercial services or (ii) a public/private mix addressed to a wide audience, retaining some quality programmes, and directly subsidised or financed with advertising in other programmes. At the same time simple models have shown that in a fully liberalised market there would not be enough programmes to satisfy minority tastes.[36] Competition for audience share, especially when advertising is the only means of financing, would imply minimum differentiation and excessive similarity in programming. A monopolist able to discriminate would be able to satisfy more consumers and maximise welfare.

This traditional conclusion has been subject to some qualification, since its validity is restricted to situations of scarcity of available channels. When the assumption of technical scarcity is replaced by technological progress, duplication in programmes would not necessarily displace programmes addressed to minorities. Competition might satisfy more 'privileged' consumers, while monopoly might reach a wider audience. A regulated oligopoly characterised by a public–private mix as well as by mixed financing by licence fee and advertising would probably stay in between. In sum, it is the idea of audience-maximising broadcasters in the market for advertising and causing waste of resources (since advertising

---

[35] See, among others, Wiles, P, 'Pilkington and the theory of value', *Economic Journal*, Vol LXXIII (June 1963), 183–95.

[36] For a general reference with selected bibliography see Owen, B and Willdman, SS, *Videoeconomics* (Cambridge, Mass: MIT Press, 1992). See also Spence, M and Owen, B, 'Television programming, monopolistic competition and welfare', *Quarterly Journal of Economics*, Vol XCI (Feb 1977), 103–26; Beebe, JH, 'Institutional structure and program choices in TV market', *Quarterly Journal of Economics*, Vol XCI (Feb 1977), 15–37; Owen, B, Beebe, J and Manning, M, *Television Economics* (Lexington: Heath, 1974) and Steiner, PO, 'Monopoly and competition in TV: some policy issues', *Manchester School of Economics and Political Science*, Vol XXIX (May 1961), 103–31.

depends on audience size) that leads to conclusions in favour of monopoly or, at least, restricted oligopoly.[37]

However, this conclusion is not a final one, since developing competition and the rapid increase in the number of satellite/cable channels lead to further complications. An increase in programmes for minorities can be achieved by splitting the audience through enhancing competition and programme duplication, so that small audiences can attract advertising. Minority protection does not rely only on public funds and subsidies, but can be supplied by market competition. Reasoning based on the distribution of preference intensities and the presence of substitutes in programming lead to conclusions more favourable to competition than to monopoly.

The Italian legislation has some characteristics associated with the traditional view. Channel rationing has the practical justification of preventing the audience from being split, with negative effects on the supply of private advertising and financing opportunities. Artificial scarcity of concessions and limits to advertising time have ensured high profitability only through heavy investments in advertising. This favours big national operators, that is the public–private duopolist. Currently the audience is highly concentrated into two channels, one public (RAI 1) and one private (Canale 5). An additional intriguing problem concerns the role of the licence fee as a complementary financing means for public TV. Licence fees might be interpreted as a practical way to support concentration in advertising, which contributes to keeping advertising costs at high levels. Prices reflect the intensity of preferences only with direct payments, as in pay-TV or in pay-per-view TV. Licence fees and advertising—indirectly increasing the prices of advertised goods, but without a direct consciousness of this by consumers—are very poor substitutes for pricing, so that the phenomenon of market failure is unavoidably present. Legal analysis has not considered, so far, this kind of problem.

3.3 Regulatory instruments

Major limits to privatisation can explain many difficulties in achieving correct and timely responses in media legislation. Privatisation has always been considered an external imposition to comply with EC standards and financial needs induced by the budget constraint. A powerful incentive to privatisation was indisputably provided by the EC opposition

---

[37] For a different line of reasoning see Coase, RH, 'The market for ideas', *American Economic Review*, Vol LXIV (May 1974), 384–91. See also Owen, B, *Economics and Freedom of Expression: Media Structure and the First Amendment* (Cambridge, Mass: Ballinger, 1975) and Breton, A and Wintrobe, R, 'Freedom of speech vs. efficient regulation in markets for ideas', *Journal of Economic Behavior and Organization*, Vol 17 (Mar 1992), 217–39.

to transfers from state budget to public enterprises. Only recently has the Telecom Italia privatisation taken place. Privatisation is frequently accompanied by the use of 'golden shares', which is probably in conflict with articles 75b and 53 of the EC Treaty and has caused major concerns. Golden shares in privatised public bodies and corporations give the Government the right to appoint officials to the board of directors and to choose new shareholders up to the relevant quota of 5 per cent.[38] Moreover, they endow the Government with the right of veto over some proposals, such as mergers, break-ups, and voting trusts. In this way the Government retains the power to control changes in property and management.

No previous experience in US-style regulation existed, since public administration always relied on direct intervention. Some forms of 'regulation *without* privatisation' seem to have emerged as a result of recent legislation, so that the system appears oriented to 'mimic public administration in markets' rather than to 'mimic the market'. A special feature of this process can be seen in the legislative obsession with imposing ceilings, in percentage terms, on ownership, market share, circulation, number of concessions, etc. The same criteria which applied to newspapers has also been applied to TV, implying an artificial rationing of the national channels using VHF. National free-to-air channels are currently twelve in number, although the technical capacity would allow for over twenty channels. This implies a total number of concessions to a single private operator of no more than two channels. No regulatory scheme has been characterised by the use of clear economic criteria in defining tariffs or in controlling rates of return on capital or maximum profit rates. Price cap formulae for phone tariffs and water have been abandoned. The Antitrust Authority has became more and more concerned by the role played by administrative courts in challenging its regulatory actions. This attitude towards the activity of regulatory authorities risks becoming in the future a cheap but powerful tool to be used by private firms in order to deprive regulation of its real effectiveness.

TV licence fees, pay-TV fees and advertising taxes seem to be likely future components of TV pricing. Some form of price cap regulation might be employed to fix year by year the licence fee, with increases linked to the inflation rate. Consumers' licence fees in Italy became property taxes used to limit large-scale evasion. On economic grounds they are seen as special wealth taxes, though in legal terms they represent fees for use of public services. So far, alternative ways of TV financing have been discarded. Among those at least one deserves a brief mention. It proposes that public

---

[38] This is stated by L. 474/94 (art. 2).

service television should be financed with revenues collected from the already existing TV advertising taxes, with an additional special tax on advertising plus revenues from national and local operators' concessions. This proposal would have implied not only the abolition of licence fees, but also a new approach to general taxation of advertising expenditures in business accounts. These expenditures would have been only partially deductible and depreciated.

Legislation has, so far, missed an important point, that is the definition of efficient screening devices to allocate (artificially) scarce frequencies or future permits for cable and satellite to operators. No impartial mechanism, such as, for instance, an auction with competitive bids, has been devised. This would raise more money from concessions and efficiently ration scarce concessions. Strong public and private interests opposed to raising concession costs are against this solution. In this regard, the provisional definitions of the powers of the Authority as outlined by the 15.7.1996 Bill appear very obscure. The Authority appears to have discretionary powers excluding auctions and methods of impartial selection. As a consequence competition for a regulated oligopoly is not expected to come into effect in the near future.

3.4 Advertising

Changing media have of course strongly increased the market for advertising. Advertising has often been misrepresented. Theoretically it should be partly informational, rather than purely addressed to inducing new needs or manipulating tastes. This has caused restrictive public interventions, since advertising was often deemed to cause distortions and increased asymmetries in the information, politics, final goods, and services markets. Moreover, TV advertising was seen as an undesirable competitor to public service broadcasting. Limits to advertising were made in order to leave resources to newspapers. There are two basic points in the allocation of advertising revenues in the TV market. The first one is the distinction between advertising by producers and wholesalers, mainly addressed to national TV, and that by retail sellers, left for local TV. The other concerns the distinction, at national level, between advertising revenues of public TV, which have a complementary role to that of the licence fee, and advertising revenues for commercial, unencrypted, private TV, for which it represents the only source of financing. These distinctions have not been clearly taken into account by legislation, and in practice the result was to put beside the national duopoly in broadcasting a duopoly in the collection of advertising revenues. The role of the greatest private agency (Publitalia) has been much more comparable to that of the agency for the public networks (Sipra). Public TV has more limitations in the use of advertising time, the reason being that it can also raise finance through the licence fee. This caused more and more advertising by producers and wholesalers to be attracted to the private national networks, with the consequence of displacing financial resources from local TV operators, who strongly criticise the private agency. The proposed legislation is at least trying to break this duopoly in advertising.

Indirect and direct financing to cinemas and theatres developed perhaps as an unintended consequence of the increased markets for TV products. Film production by RAI and MEDIASET has considerably increased in recent times, and new legislation encourages the development, with a somewhat protectionist basis, of the direct production and broadcasting of EU products. The second national private group (TMC) is owned by a film producer and distributor; this may give some evidence of mutual advantages for film and TV with joint industrial and commercial management. Internal production of films for general circulation or exclusively for TV broadcasting has grown rapidly, whilst at the beginning the necessity of cost saving induced the purchase of cheap productions from the USA and Latin America. The same trend, on a reduced scale, seems to take place for theatre and music. The policy of advertisers appears to have given support to these positive results, but unfortunately the legislation is evolving only with some difficulties. Advertising is increasing revenues in sports programming, mainly for football clubs through pay-TV and pay-per-view. Unencrypted transmission, justified by public good or general utility reasoning, is partially guaranteed through VHF national networks with very high costs to the public and private networks as a result of competition in securing the right to broadcast football games.

The Italian legislation introduced limits on TV advertising, in order to ensure financial resources for the press. Joint ownership of TV stations and newspapers has been forbidden in the past and is now strongly limited, so that internal cross-financing opportunities are almost impossible. Political advertising is protected and considered a pure market for ideas, but the same does not apply to other types of advertising. The political ideology has progressively led to forms of repression of information, and ideas, through a system of licensing, authorising, selecting, and screening devices. Vested interests in the press are opposed to TV liberalisation, because this competition would erode advertising revenues.

Hence, economies of scale and scope (that is, the reduction in unit costs obtained by increasing production and by producing simultaneously two or more goods or services) for radio–TV and press seem quite strong. At the beginning of the 1980s three national publishers entered the market for private TV by launching three national channels, but in a short time they were obliged to withdraw, being unprofitable, and the major private group (now MEDIASET) was able to buy two national channels from those withdrawing.

4

The United Kingdom

STEFAAN VERHULST[1]

1 MEDIA DEVELOPMENT

1.1 The UK and the Information Society

One major characteristic of the UK is its gradualism; despite all predictions of revolution and profound change, UK media development is generally slow but continuous. A recent report published by the Department of Trade and Industry[2] (DTI) stated that the main characteristic of the so-called 'Information Society' is a general uncertainty about its shape. This uncertainty is only too obvious if the track records of other technologies are considered. Implementation of ISDN, EC-promoted unified telecoms, high definition television, UK cable television, a UK fibre-optic network, etc, has dragged on for years.[3] The former Minister for Information and Technology predicted in 1982 that 'by the end of the decade multi-channel cable television will be commonplace countrywide . . . TV will be used for armchair shopping, banking, calling emergency services and many other services'. In reality by the end of the 1980s, cable TV had reached 1 per cent penetration in the UK and the vision of armchair shopping has yet to be realised.[4]

However, although the Information Society is still an aspiration rather than a reality, according to the DTI the UK is far ahead of other countries—

- In 1995, UK cable companies alone invested more than £2bn in developing infrastructure
- BT announced a ten-year programme of work to install fibre-optic cable to bring interactive multimedia services into homes nationwide
- Nearly three million personal computers were sold in the UK

[1] The author gratefully acknowledges the assistance of Professor Tony Prosser, John Millar Professor of Law and David Goldberg, Senior Lecturer in Law, University of Glasgow.
[2] See *The Development of the Information Society: an International Analysis* (London: HMSO, 1996).
[3] See Cawkell, AE, 'The information superhighway: political realities and the time factor', *Journal of Information Science*, 21(1) 1995, 61–2.
[4] See Harrison, F, 'The Future of New Media', *Admap*, Nov 1996.

- More than two million people in the UK accessed the Internet in the year to August 1995.

The total market for information and communications technologies in the UK has been estimated at £48 billion per annum.[5] A recent survey stated that 'in many ways the UK is a microcosm of the battles for future media supremacy'.[6] Indeed, looking at the three converging sectors of telecommunications, media, and information technology, the UK scores very well, especially in the first two areas; thus 'the UK embarks upon the route towards the Information Society with considerable advantages compared with many other European Union members'.[7]

In telecommunications, the UK has a substantial lead over most of Europe in both technology and market structure, and a DTI report concluded that, 'Although never the most advanced in any one area, the UK is consistently a good second and does not lag significantly in any major respect, with no one country being a consistent first.'[8] This lead is generally considered a result of the Government's pioneering role in liberalisation and privatisation.

Besides the comparative advantage in telecommunications, the UK media strengths are software, creativity, and media packaging. The UK enjoys a significant wealth-creating asset through its talent in TV software production, music, computer games, publishing, advertising, animation, and film-making.[9] The former National Heritage Secretary stated that: 'It is clear that in regulatory, technological and commercial terms, Britain is the broadcasting heart of Europe . . . The UK is second only to the United States in the export of television programmes.'[10] Others suggest that the UK is better placed than any other country in Europe to benefit from growth and integration of global media and communication markets; 'Works in English circulate more easily than do works in other languages. And the large size and revenue base of the English language mean that there are high potential returns and, crucially, that costs of expensive and high quality works can be amortized in the English language market before being exported.'[11]

[5] *Information Society Initiative. Key Facts* (<http://www.isi.gov.uk/introisi/keyfacts.html>).

[6] See Snoddy, R, 'Alliances for a digital future', *Financial Times*, 11 Dec 1996.

[7] See Cave, M, 'Traffic Management on the Superhighway. Reforming Communications Regulation', in Collins, R and Purnell, J (eds), *Managing the Information Society* (London: IPPR, 1995), 20.

[8] The other countries were Sweden, US, Japan, Netherlands, Germany, and France. See DTI, *Study of the International Competitiveness of UK Telecommunications Infrastructure* (London: DTI, 1994), 76.

[9] See *Progress Through Partnership: 14 Leisure and Learning* (<http://www.dcs.ed.ac.uk/home/jhb/ost/docs/>).

[10] See *Britain is broadcasting heart of Europe* (London: Department of National Heritage, Press Release 210/96, 15 July 1996).

[11] Collins, R and Murroni, C, *New Media, New Policies* (Cambridge: Polity Press, 1996), 12.

The Advisory Committee on Film Finance aired another view, however, in a report concluding that the film industry was confronted with major structural, financial, and communications problems which lead to competitive obstacles.[12] Moreover, exports of TV programming indeed increased but imports rose as well from £69 million in 1983 to £228 million (real terms) in 1993.[13] It is expected that the growth of new channels and more broadcast hours will further increase imports.

Finally, the IT industry, the third major sector involved in convergence, is less competitive on a global scale than the UK telecom and media industry. A DTI statistical and comparative study ranked the UK fourteenth in competitiveness relative to the other forty major economies.[14] The UK is well positioned when comparing absolute values for GDP and IT production and consumption, but using the per capita figures the UK's ranking is significantly worse. IT production as a percentage of GDP is less significant since the leaders are the developing Pacific Rim countries. Moreover, UK IT productivity is also significantly worse than in the other G7 countries. These results must be seen as a European malaise. The chief executive of Intel claimed recently that Europe is falling behind the US and Asia in the use of information technology: 'The problem in Europe is an unenthusiastic approach to the use of IT in business'. This is putting the competiveness of European companies and the strength of its economies at risk, according to other executives of US high technology companies.[15]

1.2 Market participants and their responses

An intense degree of strategic corporate activity in the communications-related sectors can be seen partly as a reaction to the impact and the opportunities of the convergence of technologies on markets and services; everyone acts out of a wish not 'to miss the boat'.[16] This leads to restructuring both within and between industries, and to re-engineering to take advantage of the new technologies. Therefore, convergence is characterised in the UK as either a threat to, or an opportunity for, those in the current market. What follows gives a brief overview of the current composition of the UK media and telecoms industry, and considers the key strategic issues that most actors face as the industry develops.

---

[12] See The Advisory Committee on Film and Finance, *Report to the Secretary of State for National Heritage*, 1996.

[13] Figures from Central Statistical Office, Oct 1994.

[14] See *The World and UK Economies and IT Industry* (London: OST/DTI, 1996).

[15] See Kehoe, L, 'Europe is falling back in IT, US high-tech firms warn', *Financial Times*, 27 Jan 1996.

[16] See *Information Society Trends. Special Issue 1995* (Brussels: ISPO, 1996).

Print media

The major characteristic of the UK print media is the existence of a large newspaper sector. There are approximately 1,420 privately owned newspapers (not all are daily), of which twenty-one are national (including Sunday titles). The market is mainly polarised between weekday and Sunday titles, tabloids versus broadsheets, and nationals and locals.[17] The most widely read weekday national newspapers are the *Sun* and the *Daily Mirror* (tabloid) and the *Daily Telegraph* (broadsheet). The *News of the World* is the most widely read national Sunday newspaper. The national newspaper industry has experienced falling circulation; a price war between several prominent titles has failed to arrest this trend.[18] This has had a knock-on effect on revenues and regional titles.[19] The long-term decline in the (national) newspaper market has prompted many large media groups to pull out and concentrate their interests elsewhere. Thomson Corporation, Reed Elsevier, Emap, and Pearson have all sold their regional interests and have taken a more international and cross-media approach. These moves have left room for significant expansion by medium-sized companies such as Trinity International and Johnston Press. The magazine sector is large, and both the number of titles and circulation have been growing considerably in the past five years, but growth has been driven by increases in cover price.

Both newspaper and magazine publishers are investigating emerging opportunities to diversify revenue sources and extend their skills, content, and branding to other media, specifically on-line and Internet publishing, television (for example ITV companies and Channel 5), and, to a lesser extent, radio. This type of diversification can build on core competency while helping to protect the more mature print segment, making it 'future-proof'. In the long run, newspapers' expertise as content organisers will be pivotal. The former editor of *The Guardian* noted that: 'In the past newspapers were a manufacturing industry. Over the past 10 years there has been a shift to a realisation that we are news- and information-gatherers who currently happen to put out the result as newspapers. The real assets are in the newsgathering and processing, not production.'[20]

Broadcasting

Television is set to be by far the most dynamic sector in the UK media market and is still dominated by the BBC. There are now five free-to-air

[17] See Tunstall, J, 'The United Kingdom', in *The Media in Western Europe. The Euromedia Handbook* (London: Sage, 1997), 244–59.

[18] See Bell, E, 'The paper's problems are symptoms of a disease facing all nationals', *The Guardian*, 20 Apr 1996.

[19] See *The Future of the UK Media Industry* (London: FT Telecoms & Media Publishing, 1996).

[20] See Caulkin, S, 'Street of Shame', *Management Today*, Mar 1996, 31–5.

channels. The BBC supplies programming to two television channels (BBC1 and BBC2) and five radio networks, as well as to local radio. A new formula for increases over the next five years in the licence fee of the BBC is linked to the annual inflation rate, determined by the change in the Retail Price Index (RPI).[21] However, this core source of revenue is growing at a far slower rate than the revenues of its pay- and advertising-based competitors. The BBC has thus diversified its revenue base, developing complementary commercial interests, and intends to follow a similar strategy with television. However, such commercial endeavours can be controversial and provoke protests and resistance from competitors wary of misuse of licence fees and the BBC's ability to exploit its licence fee funded brands. The corporation must also guard against the possibility that in a fragmented environment its viewing share or reach may fall below a level where it becomes difficult to justify a universal licence fee. However, recent ratings show that BBC Television is increasing its share of the total British viewing audience in spite of increased competition from cable and satellite channels.[22] In May 1996 the BBC announced its plans for using digital technology to broaden its broadcasting activities.[23] This includes an extended BBC1 and BBC2 in widescreen; a 24-hour television news channel; more chances to see regional programmes; education services which take full advantage of digital technology's facility to promote interactive learning; and Europe's first digital radio service. In the meantime the BBC launched 'beeb', its commercial Web entertainment and information service.

The main national private channel is Channel 3 (known as ITV), which is operated by a number of regional television companies obliged to incorporate regional programmes into their schedules, with the exception of the breakfast-time franchise which broadcasts nationally. There have been some major mergers of the ITV companies during the last couple of years (such as the merger between MAI, and United News & Media) due to more liberal regulation, and it is expected that the ITV sector will consolidate further, with perhaps three broad groupings controlling the whole network, or even only one ITV company.[24] For the same reason, a restructuring, initiated by the three major companies Carlton, Granada, and United News has been announced. The ITV Association and its central commissioning body, the Network Centre, are being scrapped to create ITV Ltd.

---

[21] See Department of National Heritage Press Release DCMS 408/96, available on <http://www.worldserver.pipex.com/coi/depts/GHE/coi5213c.ok>

[22] See Snoddy, R, 'BBC lifts TV share despite competition', *Financial Times*, 15 Jan 1997.

[23] See 'Digital Decade', *The Economist*, 11 May 1996.

[24] See Ross, B, 'The Merger Mania', *Broadcast*, 15 Mar 1996; Horsman, M, 'Manifesto for a new media age', *New Statesman*, 15 Nov 1996, 18–21.

Channel 4 is a public service broadcaster, funded by advertising, operated by the Channel Four Television Corporation (in Wales, Channel 4 is replaced by Sianel Pedwar Cymur (S4C) which is a Welsh language channel). Finally, at the end of March 1997, Channel 5, a new national terrestrial channel was launched.

The UK launched Europe's first satellite service in 1982 (British Satellite Broadcasting); that later merged with a second non-domestic satellite service (Sky) to become British Sky Broadcasting (BSkyB, in which Rupert Murdoch's News Corporation holds a 40 per cent stake), which currently provides multichannel services all over Europe (such as Sky Movies, Sky News, Sky One, Sky Sports, Sky Travel, etc). More than 5.5 million homes in the UK and Ireland now subscribe and the numbers continue to rise gradually. In 1983 cable began in the UK with the awarding of eleven pilot franchises, and in the early 1990s was expanding rapidly with new franchises granted by the ITC for various parts of the country; by 1996 there were over 1.3 million cable households. There are now 114 operational cable franchises, operated by mostly North American owned companies. In recent years, however, a strong consolidation has taken place. In 1996, for instance, Nynex, Videotron, Bell Cablemedia, and Mercury Communications came together with Cable & Wireless to create the new Cable & Wireless Communications. There are now more than twenty English-speaking channels available by cable and satellite, with a growing number of cable-only channels such as Live TV (owned by The Mirror Group) and Channel One (owned by the Daily Mail & General Trust).

This will be followed by digital satellite (BSkyB) and cable services and the Independent Television Commission awarded in June 1997 licences for multiplexes (blocks of frequencies) for digital terrestrial television. A group of three licences was awarded to British Digital Broadcasting (BDB), a consortium which, at the time of the application, comprised Carlton Communications, the Granada Group, and BSkyB. However, the BDB application raised serious competition concerns and the licence was thus made conditional on BSkyB's withdrawal as a shareholder from the BDB consortium, though it would continue to supply programmes. The Commission also awarded the guaranteed multiplex for the existing Channels 3 and 4 to Digital 3 and 4 representing the existing broadcasters. All this will result in an increase in channels. It is expected that in the early years of channel expansion the average revenue per channel will fall and the need to differentiate channels and attract viewers will become more pressing. As a result there will be (even) more competition for rights to premium content (such as film and sport), and the cost of these particular rights will rise.

The funding model for the industry is changing, with pay-television by far the fastest-growing source of income.[25] Specialist subscription management and billing companies may enter the market, as they have done with magazines, in order to help the industry adapt and exploit this change. This will create specific bottlenecks and potential competition abuses. The new revenue will be leveraged by the industry to help fund new channels because advertising expenditure will not grow as quickly as channel availability. The television industry too will be able exploit its subscriber databases. Other important changes in television include a blurring of the traditional distinction between the terrestrial and non-terrestrial markets, the introduction of new broadcast services, such as near-video-on-demand (NVOD), the development of interactive television, and the packaging of television with other interactive services.[26] However, those services are still in their testing phase, with technology trials taking place in East Anglia (BT, Cambridge Cable), London (Westminster Cable), Peterborough (Bell Cablemedia), etc.[27] Those trials are characterised by a series of delays, while companies like Videotron and Two Way TV, offering elements of additional information superimposed on real-time broadcasts, are just at the beginning of a national roll-out programme.[28] Other services such as information retrieval (for example the Internet) are growing, with 579,000 Internet connections in the UK (July 1996) in comparision with 291,000 the year before, which makes the UK the country with the second highest connections.

The UK radio sector is undeveloped compared with that of, for example, France. However, radio has been the fastest-growing medium since 1993. There are 249 separate radio services of which three are national commercial radio stations (Independent National Radio or INR) and fourteen are satellite radio services. Radio is also set to go digital, and the market has already supported a dramatic growth in the number of broadcasters. Digital audio broadcasting (DAB) will result in even more competitors,[29] although the majority of radio services will remain local.

Telecommunications

The introduction of deregulation since the early 1980s, economic growth over much of that period, and the technological progress made over

---

[25] See Congdon, T *et al*, *Paying for Broadcasting. The Handbook* (London: Routledge, 1992).

[26] For instance, BSkyB plans to offer fast access to the Internet through conventional television sets when it launches its digital satellite television service. See Snoddy, R, 'BSkyB to offer Internet access through TV sets', *Financial Times*, 23 Aug 1996.

[27] For an overview see Quickbytes at <www.cia.co.uk/media/>

[28] See *The Future of Multimedia* (London: FT Telecoms and Media Publishing, 1996).

[29] Pilot digital broadcasts are now run on three test multiplexes in London. One is being

recent years have all contributed to a telecommunications market which is among the most advanced in the world. By 1996 more than 150 operators had received licences, in addition to those held by BT and Mercury from the Department of Trade and Industry (DTI) to provide telecommunication carriage in the UK. Several such licences permit the construction of national networks, both wire-based and wireless. Cable operators are also entitled to offer telephone services, and increasingly do so. In spite of the new entrants' attractive pricing strategies and lower charges, BT is still dominant among fixed telecommunication operators and has a huge lead over its main competitor in the local loop, the cable operators. However, entry by new players, like Energis and Ionica, together with number portability, may further stimulate competition at all levels of the UK telecom market and erode BT's dominance. Moreover, BT and Mercury may still neither convey nor provide broadcast entertainment services (that is, point to multipoint as defined in the Broadcasting Act 1990) under their main licences. This line of business exclusion has provoked strong objections from BT, and it is expected that the Labour Government will lift the ban. In the meantime, BT is already planning on the assumption that it will be able to offer a full range of interactive services by the year 2000.[30] It is currently undertaking technical interactive television marketing, and at the same time it is running a commercial experiment of video-on-demand involving 1,000 homes on a cable network in London. In March 1996 BT launched a mass-market Internet service which was followed by Mercury's (now Cable and Wireless) announcement of low-cost Internet access for existing customers of its residential phone service. Observers note that this is just the start of BT's Internet involvement, especially when Internet telephony will mushroom long-distance phone calls in the near future.[31] Due to the strong national competition, BT has also developed a global strategy with several plans for merger.

Conclusion

Consumer interactive services, which have come about through the convergence of media, telecoms, and IT have been prioritised in the business development plans of many telecom, cable, and media companies, which see them as an attractive, alternative source of revenues, in an area closely related to their core businesses and often requiring little additional invest-

operated by the BBC (running since September 1995), another by transmission specialist NTL (who simulcasts Kiss 100, 963 Liberty, Melody, Sunrise, Talk, and Virgin), and the third by its rival BT (home to GWR, LBC, News Direct, Classic FM, and the BBC's GLR). See Wood, D, 'DAB: the crest of an airwave', *Broadcast*, 24 Jan 1997.

[30] See Adonis, A, 'A long and winding road', *Financial Times*, Dec 1995.
[31] See O'Neill, B, 'It's good to talk on the cheap', *The Guardian*, 10 Jan 1996.

ment.[32] Most media companies involved in the creation of those services are now shifting the focus of their activities from CD-ROM publishing to developing new products for Internet users. The involvement of new non-media entrants, including small start-ups and major firms, such as Microsoft, will provide strong competition, and partnerships will become increasingly important. This is also the case in the emerging sector of Internet access services. Many Internet Service Providers (ISPs) are now struggling to survive against competition from the telephone companies (for example BT Internet) and big US providers. As a result consolidation is currently taking place in the UK with twelve major Internet providers in Britain.[33]

Interactive media offer companies the opportunity to derive revenues from their existing content and businesses. Although these markets will grow strongly, they will do so from a small base. The vast bulk of consumer media companies' revenues in the year 2000 will derive from existing core businesses. During this time, the new interactive media are likely to remain a supplementary activity buoyed by the traditional sectors. This explains the evolutionary aspect of these digital trends. It also explains the importance of the current regulation of the conventional media during the transition period to full interactive digital media. Most of the growth of the communications industry is likely to come through payments from consumers for cable connections and pay-television services. Pay-television will become a larger part of market value than free-to-air advertiser-funded channels.

Scale, co-operation, and alliances are becoming necessary in order to spread the risk of investment in new technological developments. Vertical integration can be seen as desirable by content providers, as it offers them access to distribution, while television channels, for example, gain a ready source of guaranteed content in a future where acquisition of rights may become increasingly competitive. The core concerns of the media companies, at least in the short to medium term, centre on maintaining and improving revenues and profits in their key traditional businesses.[34] However, more geographical expansion is also expected in order to develop a portfolio of related interests in various countries. Mirroring this trend, foreign companies are targeting the UK market as part of their own expansion plans.

[32] See *The Future of the UK Media Industry* (n 19 above).
[33] Figures prepared by *Internet* magazine show that a 'premier league' of Internet providers is starting to emerge. CompuServe outstrips all rivals at between 200,000 and 400,000 UK users, followed by AOL, Microsoft Network, and, among the non-proprietary networks, Demon Internet and UUNet Pipex. See 'Twelve ways to access the Net', *Financial Times*, 9 Dec 1996.
[34] See *The Future of the UK Media Industry* (n 19 above).

2 REGULATION AND OTHER MEDIA POLICIES

2.1 Structure and institutions

Policy-makers

Media and communications policy-making is divided mainly between two Government departments: the Department of Trade and Industry (DTI) and the Department For Culture, Media and Sport (DCMS, the former Department of National Heritage). The latter has overall responsibility for policy on broadcasting and the media. It is the 'sponsor of the audiovisual industry within Government, and aims to improve the international competitiveness of this sector'.[35] The Department is also exploring the impact of the Information Society on the cultural sector and is liaising with its sponsored bodies, other government departments, EU partners, the G7, and other bodies from both the public and private sectors.

The DTI's overall aim is to help UK business compete successfully, also the main rationale behind its media policy. It also aims, through the Office of Science and Technology (OST), to develop and co-ordinate Government policy on science, engineering, and technology (SET), including information technology. To this end the DTI has launched 'IT for all'[36] and the 'Information Society Initiative' (ISI) to 'encourage business to take full advantage of the explosion of new ways to access, use, and send information'.[37] Moreover, the 'The Thinking Ahead: Getting Ahead' programme[38] envisaged by the OST aims to make more approachable and comprehensible the full implications of the 'Technology Foresight' programme as it relates to the engineering and IT industries. Both Departments also negotiate international agreements for communications and the media.

Regulators

Broadcasting and telecommunications are regulated by several statutory and self-regulatory bodies.[39] The Broadcasting Act 1990 established the Independent Television Commission (ITC) and the Radio Authority. The ITC is responsible for regulation and licensing of commercial television, cable, and satellite services. The Radio Authority licenses and regulates

---

[35] See *The Work of the Department of National Heritage* (<http://www.heritage.gov.uk/WORK.HTM>).

[36] See 'Introduction to IT for all' at <http://www.itforall.gov.uk/>

[37] See 'Introduction to the Information Society Initiative' at <http://www.isi.gov.uk/>

[38] See 'Thinking Ahead: Getting Ahead' at <http://www.open.gov.uk/ost/foresigh/home.htm#anchor652977>

[39] For a more detailed overview see Collins, R and Murroni, C, *New Media, New Policies*, n 11 above, 199–212.

independent radio. The ITC Programme Code and the Radio Authority Programme Code set out rules on quality, taste and decency, portrayal of violence, privacy, and impartiality. Allegations of unfair treatment and invasion of privacy by radio and television programmes can now be made to the Broadcasting Standards Commission (BSC), replacing the former Broadcasting Complaints Commission and Broadcasting Standards Council; it also considers issues of the portrayal of violence and sexual conduct. The BBC is outside the remit of the ITC and the Radio Authority (but not the BSC) and is regulated by its own Board of Governors who are established under Royal Charter and are for legal purposes themselves the BBC. The Board has more recently been criticised by the Select Committee of National Heritage and a review is expected.[40]

Telecommunications is regulated by the Office of Telecommunications (Oftel) established by statute under the Telecommunications Act 1984. Its aim is to promote competition and to protect consumer interests (see below). Four self-regulatory bodies have been established by the industries. Complaints about the print media may be made to the Press Complaints Commission (PCC). The PCC replaced in 1991 the discredited Press Council, which was originally established in 1953 to remove the spectre of restrictive statutory regulation. The PCC is an independent body, funded by the print media. It has no legal powers, and thus cannot enforce judgments or ensure their publication. However, its adjudications will usually be published by the paper complained against, and often by rival papers. The Advertising Standards Authority (ASA) was set up in 1962, to make sure that non-broadcast advertisements appearing in the UK are 'legal, honest and truthful'. The ASA protects the public by ensuring that the rules in the British Codes of Advertising and Sales Promotion are followed by everyone who prepares and publishes advertisements. The British Board of Film Classification (BBFC), though a self-regulatory body, has statutory responsibility for video classification (under the Video Recordings Act 1984) and its film classifications are becoming increasingly important in television broadcasting regulation. Finally, the Independent Committee for the Supervision of Standards of Telephone Information Services (ICSTIS) supervises and handles complaints concerning promotion material and content of premium rate telephone services.

Yet more bodies discharge other regulatory functions. The Radiocommunications Agency allocates the radio frequency spectrum to both broadcasting and telecommunications. The Monopolies and Mergers Commission (MMC) and the Media Section within the Office of Fair Trading's (OFT) Competition Policy Division exercise jurisdiction over all the media and communications industries. Moreover the MMC has

---

[40] *The BBC and the Future of Broadcasting*, Fourth Report, HC 147, 1996–97.

special responsibilities for newspaper mergers under the Fair Trading Act 1973.

Depending on how one counts, at least fourteen statutory and self-regulatory bodies claim jurisdiction over matters of media and telecommunications in the UK. A major topic of debate, therefore, is whether there should be rationalisation whereby all those regulators (or some of them) would be merged into a single (and stronger?) regulator.[41] Moreover with the convergence of different communication sectors, a sector-specific regulator could become more or less obsolete. The Labour Party had plans to merge the powers of the ITC and Oftel into an 'Ofcom' to regulate the whole communications infrastructure and ensure fair competition, with a revamped ITC to regulate content.[42] The Chairman of the ITC has also called for the creation of a single broadcasting regulator.[43] And Don Cruikshank, DGT made clear that he 'consider[s] that the industry will be best served in the next century by a commission, not an individual regulator'.[44] However, the National Heritage Committee of the House of Commons concluded in its report that 'while the present system of regulation cannot be carved forever in stone . . . we are not persuaded that now is the time to change to a single regulator'.[45]

Interest groups

Part of the UK's approach to formulating communications policy involved the contribution of countless interest groups and individuals. The basic structure for this was the so-called 'COGs'—the Collaborative Open Groups managed under the auspices of the CCTA. Initiated in 1994 as a result of the CCTA conference on Information Superhighways, the Group's purpose was to discuss further the issues raised at the conference. The feedback conference on Information Superhighways—'The First Mile'—reaffirmed the value of Collaborative Open Groups as a mechanism for discussing issues and concerns, and for identifying opportunities and requirements for action.[46] However, with the launch of the Central IT Unit's (CITU) Green Paper 'Government Direct',[47] the CCTA found that the original objectives of the COGs were fulfilled and proposed to close them down. This proposal led to critical on-line discussion with as a result

[41] Murroni, C, Collins, R and Coote, A, *Converging Communications. Policies for the 21st Century* (London: Institute for Public Policy Research, 1996), 49–57.
[42] See *New Labour Manifesto, Information Superhighways* at <www.labour.org.uk/views/info-highway/index.html>
[43] See *The Case For a Single Regulator* (London: ITC, 11 Feb 1997).
[44] See *Don Cruickshank to Step Down as Telecom Regulator*, Oftel Press Release 62/97, 23 Sept 1997.
[45] See *The BBC and the Future of Broadcasting* (n 40 above).
[46] For a complete list, see <http://www.open.gov.uk/cogs/coglist.htm>
[47] See <http://www.ccta.gov.uk/citu/gdirect/ind1.htm>

the creation of a single COG group focusing on policy matters,[48] with further on-line debate concluding that a form of issue raising and debating facility was required. Since then, other on-line forums have been created such as Cyber Rights & Cyber Liberties,[49] the UK establishment of the Electronic Frontier Foundation,[50] Internet Freedom,[51] Digital Diversity,[52] CommUnity,[53] and others. Their main concerns and action areas are in free speech, intellectual property rights, privacy, and encryption of the Internet.

More input comes from, for example, the Global Highways Business Group (GHBG), the Federation of Electronics Industries (FEI), and the Computer Software and Services Association (CSSA). They form the National Information Infrastructure Task Force (NII-TF). The NII-TF was formed in November 1994 in response to a challenge by the then Minister for the Information and Communications Industries to devise initiatives to help 'UK plc' move into the digital age.[54] Unofficial input into the formulation of policy is also likely to be affected by other interest groups and associations such as the newly created Coalition on Public Information (CoPI),[55] the Telecommunications Managers Association (TMA),[56] the Information Technology Professionals Association (ITPA),[57] ISPA (Internet Service Providers Association), LINX (London Internet Exchange), and many others.

The media unions are of course also strongly interested in every aspect of media and communications policy and have all expressed their concern with an emphasis on the impact of digital technology on copyright.[58] The major media unions are the NUJ (National Union of Journalists), BECTU (Broadcast Entertainment Cinematograph and Theatre Union), GPMU (Graphical, Paper and Media Union), and the Chartered Institute of Journalists. There are also some organisations associated to those unions, who focus on a specific area of concern, such as CPBF (Campaign for Press and Broadcasting Freedom) and CCC (Creators' Copyright Coalition). More

---

[48] Added to the Open Government Website at <http://www.open.gov.uk/>

[49] The main idea behind this non-profit civil liberties organisation, founded on 10 Jan 1997, is to provide information related to every aspect of the law related to the Internet. See <http://www.leeds.ac.uk/law/pgs/yaman/yaman.htm>

[50] See <http://www.secure.eff.org/>

[51] See <http://www.netfreedom.org.uk.nofmain.html>

[52] See <http://www.diversity.org.uk/>

[53] CommUnity is the Computer Communicators' Association: an on-line activist group for Internet users which supports free speech. See <http://www.community.org.uk/>

[54] See <http://fm6.facility.pipex.com/niitf/nii/nii.htm>

[55] This and other interest groups can be found at: <http://www.dcs.gla.ac.uk/IIS/SIGS.html>

[56] See *About TMA* at <http://www.tma.org.uk/about/about.htm>

[57] See <http://www.msf.org.uk/legal.html>

[58] See for instance the paper *Copyright, Moral Rights and the Impact of Digital Technology* by the NUJ at <http://www.gn.apc.org/media/nuj.html>

influential perhaps is the National Consumer Council which is the independent voice of consumers in the UK. The Council was set up by Government in 1975 and is largely funded by the Department of Trade and Industry. It published a report in 1996 which recommended (not surprisingly) that 'the domestic consumer interest should be made a top priority by policy-makers, regulators and industry when formulating policies and developing networks and services'.[59] Various think-tanks have also published reports on the creation of the Information Society in the UK and Europe. Most of them have a specific political and ideological perspective on the topics. Examples are the Federal Trust,[60] the Institute for Public Policy Research (IPPR), the Policy Studies Institute, the Fabian Society, the John Wheatley Centre, the European Policy Forum, Demos, the Institute of Economic Affairs (IEA), and Scientists for Labour, amongst others.

2.2 Instruments of policy and their objectives

The roots of the UK new communications policy

The roots of the present communications policy date back to the early 1980s, when the Cabinet Office published the report of the Advisory Council for Applied Research and Development (ACARD) on information technology.[61] It recommended that a single minister and government department should be responsible for the development and promotion of IT and the regulation of communications and broadcasting, and that the Post Office should have a mandate to provide a world class UK communications network. In October 1980, Kenneth Baker MP was appointed the first Minister for Industry and Information Technology. This followed the creation of an IT Panel (ITAP) within the Department of Industry, later to become the Department of Trade and Industry, and the proclamation of 1982 as 'Information Technology Year'.[62]

However, from 1984, the integrated information technology approach was slowly abandoned and Government media policy rapidly shifted its emphasis away from those newer delivery systems to the restructuring of public service broadcasting and telecommunications. Thus it can be argued that the present media policy, which is focused on the 'information superhighway', 'multimedia', and 'convergence', is a reflection of the old

---

[59] See *The Information Society: Getting it Right For Consumers* (London: National Consumer Council, 1996), 4.

[60] See for instance *Network Europe and the Information Society* (London: Federal Trust, 1995).

[61] Saxby, S, 'A UK National Information Policy for the Electronic Age', *International Review of Law, Computers and Technology*, Vol 10, No 1, 1996, 105–35.

[62] For an overview of the policies and legislation considered during this period see Howkins, J, *New Technologies, New Policies?* (London: British Film Institute, 1982).

concerns and priorities of the early and mid 1980s: back to the future.[63] One feature of the current debate is the general lack of consideration of what lessons might be learned from the UK's first (and distinctly disappointing) dry run towards the interactive wired future.

Context of the UK Government's communications policy

There are a number of contexts within which the UK Government's media policy and regulation is formulated.

First, the UK is a member State of the European Union and the Council of Europe (see Chapter 5 below). Given its present political stance towards the EU, the UK is likely to judge results by the extent to which existing or planned domestic regulation finds favour within the EU as the basis for the latter's recommended way forward. The UK is also likely to take a pragmatic approach, namely that disharmony within Europe would hinder the UK information industry as much as its competitors. Potential conflicts may however arise in relation to the development of IPR and competition law, the creation of a trans-European public administration network, UK public information access policy, and the operation of the Citizen's Charter.[64] Finally, the commitment of the current Government to introduce legislation to incorporate the European Convention on Human Rights into United Kingdom law, which led to the introduction of the Human Rights Bill into Parliament, will give citizens and the media easier access to their Convention rights of the Council of Europe.

Second, the UK is also a member of the G7 group of countries. At the conference on the Information Society held in Brussels on 25 and 26 February 1995, the G7 countries jointly decided to take a leading role in the setting up of a global information network. The participants agreed that their future collaboration would be based on eight basic principles, two of which aim especially at encouraging competition and private investment. Within that framework, the UK Government has developed several Information Society Pilot Projects, including the government-on-line project (see below).[65]

Third, there was the specific political context of the Conservative Government's ideology, as advanced initially by Prime Minister Thatcher and later adopted by John Major, which dominated the political scene for almost two decades. Broadly, this was built on the themes of competitiveness, open markets, and the privatisation of public sector monopolies. This market orientation has already restructured the information industry substantially and remains the main perspective in the policy documents

---

[63] Goodwin, P, 'British media policy takes to the superhighway', *Media, Culture & Society*, Vol 17 (1995), 677–89.

[64] Saxby, S, 'A UK National Information Policy for the Electronic Age' (n 61 above).

[65] For an overview see <http://www.open.gov.uk/govoline/golintro.htm>

published so far; it remains to be seen how different the policies of the Labour Government will be.

Finally there is the political context of a constitutional framework, based on an unwritten constitution, that operates by custom and practice rather than by rights and duties. As a consequence, there is no formal protection for freedom of expression at the constitutional level and: 'The position in Britain is striking because of the complete absence of constitutional principles and the relative dearth of case-law.'[66] The official position of the UK Government is that there is a 'long tradition' of press freedom in the UK. The concomitant view is that self-regulation is preferable to statutory controls. This also means that the priorities and the implementation of the policies depend heavily upon the political party that governs the country.

Policy

It is important to distinguish policy-making for the communications sector from regulating it and from subsidising it. Policy-making involves setting the broad framework of policy towards the sector, including for example issues of ownership (public versus private), structural policy (free versus restricted entry), socio-political objectives (the extent of universal service obligations and the role of public broadcasting), and the broad framework of (positive and negative) content regulation. Regulation involves the detailed interpretation and implementation of policy. Beside regulation, government has also developed different state-financed programmes and financial advantages in order to stimulate initiatives to achieve the creation of an 'Information Society'. As will be seen from what follows, the UK Government is involved in each of these three areas of activity, and this will be discussed in general below.

The *leitmotiv* of the Conservative Government's policy was 'to encourage enterprise and ensure that markets operate efficiently through the promotion of competition, deregulation, privatisation and the opening of markets both at home and abroad'.[67] On the changing media and the Information Society, 'the Government is seeking to help develop these opportunities through liberalisation of telecommunications, better management of the radio spectrum, and expanding choice in broadcasting'.[68] This can also be considered as the summary of the aim of the policy documents issued by the Conservative Government, of which the major examples were: the DTI Command Paper 'Creating the Superhighways of the Future: Developing Broadband Communications in the UK',[69] DTI's

[66] Barendt, E, *Broadcasting Law* (Oxford: Clarendon Press, 1992), 10.
[67] *Competitiveness. Creating the Enterprise Centre of Europe* (London: HMSO, Cm 3300, 1996).
[68] ibid, para 8.2.
[69] DTI, *Creating the Superhighways for the Future: Developing Broadband Communications in*

White Paper on Spectrum Management[70] and the proposals of the Department of National Heritage introducing new rules for media ownership[71] and a framework for digital terrestrial broadcasting,[72] later incorporated in the Broadcasting Act 1996. The Labour Government, however, announced recently that 'Good regulation can benefit us all', at the launch of a new policy initiative 'Better Regulation, Not Deregulation'.[73] Thus, rather than simply deregulating, 'the Government's new regulatory policy will concentrate on ensuring that regulations are necessary, fair to all parties, properly costed, practical to enforce and straightforward to comply with.' How this will influence the regulation of media in particular and communications in general is not clear yet.

Of the regulators, the Office of Telecommunications (Oftel) can be considered the one which has produced the most substantial thinking about the future of the converging communications sector and how to regulate it. The Office has published several consultative documents dealing with these challenges.[74] *Beyond the Telephone, the Television and the PC,*[75] published in the summer of 1995, is regarded as the major force behind the wide-ranging debate about some key issues, such as broadband switched mass-market (BSM) services, set-top devices, and universal service. The key perspective of the document was to ensure the development of vibrant competition and the protection of customers' interests; some of the proposals are reflected in recent legislation on conditional access services, as described below.

Both the House of Lords and the House of Commons have examined the Information Society and media development. The House of Lords Select Committee on Science and Technology published its report, *Information Society: Agenda for Action in the UK*, in July 1996.[76] Recommendations include the setting up of an Information Society Task Force similar to that in the US; fundamental changes to the regulatory framework (such as the review of the restrictions on telecommunications companies either conveying or providing broadcast entertainment services in their own

---

the UK (London: HMSO, Cm 2734, 1994); and at: <ftp://ftp.open.gov.uk/pub/docs/dti/broadband_comms.txt>

[70] Department of Trade and Industry, *Spectrum Management: into the 21st Century* (London: HMSO, Cm 3252, 1996) and at <http://www.open.gov.uk/radiocom/rahome.htm>

[71] *Media Ownership: The Government's Proposals* (London: HMSO, Cm 2872, 1995).

[72] *Digital Terrestrial Broadcasting: The Government's Proposals* (London: HMSO, Cm 2946, 1995).

[73] Cabinet Office (Ops) Press Release of 3 July 1997, No 46/97.

[74] See <http://www.open.gov.uk/oftel/publicat.htm>

[75] *Beyond the Telephone, the Television and the PC, Consultative Document* (London: Oftel, 1995); or at <http://www.open.gov.uk/oftel/multi.htm>

[76] See Select Committee on Science and Technology, House of Lords, *Information Society: Agenda for Action in the UK* (HL 77, 1996); also at: <http//www.hmsoinfo.gov.uk/hmso/document/inforsoc.htm>

right, and a code of practice for the Internet Service Providers' Association); and the promotion of electronic publishing to facilitate widespread access to Government publications. The Committee also makes recommendations on the subjects of universal access including free use of the Internet by using terminals placed in public spaces such as libraries, post offices, etc, and special provision for education and healthcare. The former Government's response emphasised its actions and strategies within the framework of the Information Society Initiative but no real changes were proposed.[77]

The National Heritage Committee of the House of Commons recently issued a report on the BBC and the Future of Broadcasting.[78] One of the recommendations deals with the Board of Governors:

the BBC cannot survive if it is in the hands of a group of people nominated for various attributes not connected with broadcasting. We feel that the time has come for the BBC to be run by a single board comprising the executive chairman, nominated by the Secretary of State for National Heritage, the top management team, and a number of qualified non executive directors from different backgrounds. Overall regulation, particularly in terms of quality, taste, diversity and social responsibility, must be undertaken by an independent authority with the power of sanction, as in the case of Channel 4.[79]

The Committee was not persuaded that now is the time to change to a single (communications) regulator integrating tasks of the ITC and Oftel, but did recommend that the Government should lift completely in 2002 the restrictions on broadcasting by national telecommunications operators. Moreover, in November 1997 the Culture, Media and Sport Committee announced its intention to conduct an inquiry into the future regulation of television and radio in the light of convergence between broadcasting, telecommunications, and computer technologies.[80]

Regulatory framework

Regulation which affects the new communications services (such as the Internet, video-on-demand, and pay-TV) has mainly developed around traditional and separate telecommunications and broadcasting markets. Moreover, it will become clear below that UK regulation was not drafted with convergence in mind, and as a result the way in which existing rules apply to new communication services is something of an anachronism.

[77] See *Information Society: Agenda for Action in the UK. Government Response to the report by the House of Lords Select Committee on Science and Technology* (Nov 1996). At: <http://dtiinfo1.dti.gov.uk/hol/>
[78] See *The BBC and the Future of Broadcasting* (n 40 above).
[79] ibid, para 52.
[80] Culture, Media and Sport Committee Press Notice No 7 of Session 1997–98, 11 Nov 1997.

As mentioned above, deregulation was one of the former Government's priorities. The deregulation initiative 'Fewer, Better, Simpler' and the creation of a Task Force were just some examples of the Government's commitment.[81] However, despite the fact that deregulation has taken place within several industries in the UK, such as telecommunications, this is certainly not straightforwardly so for broadcasting. Moreover, broadcasting, and in particular private broadcasting, has been accorded a different legal regime to that governing other media: 'The irony that "deregulation" under the 1990 legislation means "more regulation" is a tribute to the perceived power of television to influence as well as to reflect ideas and social behaviour.'[82] It is also important in the context of new media that the UK has followed the Anglo-Saxon tradition of having no special body of press law. The general law (such as defamation) applies; this is also the case for the Internet.

Finally, as a result of deregulation and privatisation of different sectors and industries, competition policy and regulation have come more and more to the forefront. This is the case for the traditional media and will certainly be the case for the newer communications services, especially in the case of potential bottlenecks. Some (in particular 'New Right' commentators) predict that general competition policy makes the need for sector specific regulation obsolete; indeed, the blurring between sectors (and thus regulation) due to convergence requires an effective system of competition law, and this is likely to be reformed in the UK in the near future. Moreover, given the highly internationalised nature of the media, transnational attempts to preserve competitive markets will become crucial.[83]

Telecommunications

The main instrument of regulation is a Public Telecommunications Operator Licence, issued under section 7 of the Telecommunications Act 1984 ('the 1984 Act'). Under UK law there is no licensing requirement for the provision of telecoms services over a system; it is operating the underlying system which requires the licence. Broadly speaking, changes in policy in the sector have been achieved by granting new licences and by the modification and enforcement of existing licences.[84] The 1984 Act makes it a criminal offence to 'run' a 'telecommunications system' without a licence. The term 'telecommunications system' is defined in section 4(1) as:

[81] See *Task Force Report 1995/96—Government Response*, 1996 (<www.open.gov.uk>).

[82] Robertson, G and Nicol, A, *Media Law* (London: Penguin Books, 1992), 595.

[83] See Goldberg, D, Prosser, T and Verhulst, S, *The Impact of New Communications Technologies on Media Concentrations and Pluralism* (Strasbourg: Council of Europe, 1997), 60.

[84] The consent of the licensee is required to modify licences or they can be reviewed by the Monopolies and Mergers Commission under ss 12 and 13 of the 1984 Act.

. . . a system for the conveyance, through the agency of electric, magnetic, electro-magnetic, electro-chemical or electro-mechanical energy, of—

(a) speech, music and other sounds;
(b) visual images;
(c) signals serving for the importation (whether as between persons, and persons, things, and things or persons and things) of any matter otherwise than in the form of sounds or visual images; or
(d) signals serving for the actuation or control of machinery or apparatus.

It is thus defined so broadly that all apparatus which enables any type of communication whatsoever will require a licence. In this way, a mere service provider will most likely be running some form of telecoms system even if it is as minimal as a single switch or connection or terminal equipment.[85] A system such as the Internet, which is used for the conveyance of text, speech, music, and visual images falls within sub-clauses (a) to (c) of this definition.

The licences contain the operators' main social and commercial obligations (for instance the duties on BT to provide a service to all who request it, directory enquiry services, call boxes, low user schemes, etc); the price cap formula placed on BT; and the principal instruments for promoting competition (in particular the obligations placed on all service providers to permit interconnection to other service providers without discrimination) and now a general condition relating to fair trading (see below).

Broadcasting

Broadcasting is a highly regulated industry.[86] It is governed primarily by the Broadcasting Acts 1990 and 1996, although the legal framework of the BBC is established under its renewed Royal Charter.[87] In contrast with telecommunications regulation, broadcasting regulation in the UK is concerned with the licensing of services, and in particular the content of broadcast material. Moreover, broadcasting, and especially private broadcasting, has been accorded a different legal regime to that governing other media, initially because of spectrum scarcity but more recently through the trustee concept of broadcasting. Thus 'the trustee concept stemmed, among other things, from the effort to avoid "American conditions" in British broadcasting. The initial focus was on preventing chaos in the airwaves, which then gradually gave way to ensuring public responsibil-

---

[85] See Bannister, AD, *Telecommunication Regulation and the Internet* (London: Denton Hall, 1996).

[86] See Cave, M and Williamson, P, 'The Reregulation of British Broadcasting', in Bishop, M, Kay, J and Mayer, C (eds), *The Regulatory Challenge* (Oxford: Oxford University Press, 1995), 160–90.

[87] *BBC Royal Charter* (London: HMSO, Cm 3248, 1996).

ity for broadcasting.'[88] This rationale has dominated regulation for both public and private broadcasting, although the Broadcasting Act 1990 has led to a loosening of the public service commitments of private broadcasters without, however, fully departing from the public service concept as such. The legal requirements placed on the ITV companies have been even more detailed than those in force for the BBC, based on the assumption that a commercially financed broadcasting system would be especially tempted to side-step the traditional public service broadcasting commitments. Convergence and the creation of new communication services are questioning this rationale.

As described above, the ITC is entrusted with the licensing of television services[89] and the Radio Authority with radio licensing.[90] Channel 3 and Channel 5 licences were awarded by a process of competitive tender, after an assessment of whether the applicant was a 'fit and proper person' to hold a licence, and after application of the ownership rules, themselves revised by the Broadcasting Act 1996. Licences for satellite and cable programme services are awarded for any programme service which conforms to the requirement of the ITC Programme Code, and its codes for advertising and sponsorship. All licences are awarded for a ten-year period and may be revoked if there is a change of ownership of the applicant without the prior approval of the ITC. The Radio Authority's role is to ensure a diversity of national radio services, with at least one being devoted predominantly to the spoken word and one broadcasting 'music other than pop music', together with a range and diversity of local services.[91] Licences are granted for eight years to 'fit and proper' applicants (persons convicted for radio piracy offences in the preceding five years are excluded from this category) if the statutory duties relating to programming and the ownership rules are respected.

The Broadcasting Act 1996 also provides for licensing of multiplexes for digital terrestrial broadcasting, frequency bands on which several programme services and also data services can be combined. Six such multiplexes are licensed by the Independent Television Commission, the major criterion for selecting them being the promotion of digital terrestrial broadcasting. In order to safeguard existing public service broadcasting, each existing broadcaster is offered half a multiplex for each existing channel; digital cable companies are also required to carry the public service channels. This will pave the way for an eventual switch-off of existing analogue broadcasting. Part II of the Act makes similar

---

[88] See Hoffmann-Riem, W, *Regulating Media* (London, New York: Guildford Press, 1996), 78.
[89] Broadcasting Act 1990, ss 3, 4, and 5.
[90] ibid, ss 84 and 85.
[91] Broadcasting Act 1990, s 85.

arrangements for digital terrestrial radio, in this case licensed by the Radio Authority.

At first glance, it might seem odd that broadcasting regulation can apply to services such as the Internet.[92] However, the 1990 Act regulates 'licensable programme services' which include a service in which programmes may be received at different times in response to requests made by different users of the service.[93] It is clear that the section 46 licence can have a far reaching impact for Internet content providers. However, section 46(1) also specifies that a relevant programme must be a television programme (the latter is not defined in the Act). A clear response from the ITC on this issue has until now not been formulated.

Subsidy

In February 1996, the former Government launched its Information Society Initiative (ISI) which the Labour Government has promised to continue.[94] The ISI covers four major strands.[95] First, the ISI Programme for Business provides a comprehensive package of programmes and activities to help UK businesses, particularly SMEs, improve their competitiveness through use of the new technologies, based on a close partnership with industry.[96] Second, 'IT for All' is a four-year initiative designed to help people in all walks of life understand and exploit the benefits of new information and communication technologies (ICTs) in their everyday lives with a goal of increasing the proportion of the UK adult population confident in its use of a broad range of ICTs from the current estimate of 46 per cent to 60 per cent by August 2000.[97] Thirdly, the Department for Education and Employment (DfEE) launched the Superhighways For Education initiative at the beginning of 1995.[98] It includes twenty-four projects involving a variety of industry sponsors and education sectors to test out the potential of wideband and broadband technology to enrich the delivery and experience of education and to provide young people with the skills needed for lifelong learning. Finally, in November 1995 a small Central Information Technology Unit (CITU) was set up by the Deputy Prime Minister. Its mission is to devise a set of strategies and policies which will enable the Government to exploit the opportunities provided

---

[92] See Smith, GJH, *Internet Law and Regulation* (London: FT Law & Tax, 1996), 79.

[93] S 46.

[94] See House of Commons Debate on the Information Society, HC Debs, 11 July 1997, cols 1179–1245.

[95] See Tumilty, T, 'The Information Society Initiative', Paper given at Conference *Trading on Line*, Glasgow, 23 Jan 1997.

[96] See <http://www.isi.gov.uk/>

[97] See <http://www.itforall.gov.uk/>

[98] DfEE, *Superhighways for Education* (HMSO, 1995); at <http://www.hmsoinfo.gov.uk/hmso/document/supered/supered.html> and at <http://www.hmsoinfo.gov.uk/hmso/document/supered2/supered.html>

by information technology; it has been examining the use of IT to 're-engineer government'. In a broader context, the Government's Technology Foresight Programme brings together industry, academics, and government in a collaborative effort to identify opportunities in technologies and markets likely to emerge in the next twenty years. Fifteen Technology Foresight Panels have delivered reports on various sectors and the Programme offers funding for innovative industry/academic joint proposals.[99]

2.3 Technological regulation

Infrastructure regulation: wired

All countries need to make massive investments in telecommunications and cable infrastructure—the backbones of on-line and TV services—over the next few years, including the UK. The problem they face is how to get the large investments necessary from private sources whilst still operating—or moving towards operating—an open and competitive structure.[100] Some argue that competition may well speed developments.[101] Therefore the main objective of the former UK Government has been to provide benefits to customers from a policy of encouraging local loop infrastructure competition.[102] In 1991, the BT–Mercury duopoly in telecoms was reviewed. The Government decided that the market should be opened for national infrastructure competition and the requirement on cable operators to provide voice telephony services only in conjunction with BT or Mercury was lifted. This allowed cable operators to 'switch' their own traffic and marked the end of BT's monopoly in the local telephone loop. In addition, operators of adjacent cable franchises were allowed to link their systems together directly and 'national operators', primarily BT, were barred from *carrying* entertainment services over the existing infrastructure for ten years, although there was provision for this position to be reviewed after seven years, that is from 1998. However, BT was barred from *providing* entertainment services nationally in its own right for at least ten years. It has already been suggested that this ban will probably be lifted.

Another controversial issue arising from the duopoly review has been the question of interconnection of the potential new entrants to BT's

---

[99] See *Progress Through Partnership/Technology Foresight Panel on IT & Electronics* (London: Office of Science & Technology, 1996).

[100] See Venables, D, *Legal, Political and Social Issues of the Internet, 1996*, at <http://www.pavilion.co.uk/legal/issues.htm>

[101] See *The UK National Information Infrastructure. Report from the Parliamentary Office of Science and Technology (POST)*, May 1995.

[102] ibid.

network (Condition 13 of BT's licence), and its relation to BT's tariff structure.[103] BT claimed that it incurs a large loss in providing network access to consumers. The DGT however took the view that the access deficit poses no serious problems to BT's profitability until competition becomes sufficiently strong (that is until BT's market share had fallen below 85 per cent). He was also influenced by the incumbent advantages that BT enjoys over entrants, notably those arising from the inability of customers to keep their phone number if they switch to a competitor, and from economies of scale.[104]

It is interesting to note from this that the UK, in contrast to other countries, has opted for network competition with several operators building infrastructure, instead of the more traditional option of competition for services (mainly followed by the European Union) initiated in 1987 with the publication by the Commission of the Green Paper on the development of the common market for telecommunications services and equipment.[105] In such a regime innovation in services is likely to be slower but innovation and investment in networks faster and fuller.[106] New measures to promote competition in services over telecoms networks have also been published recently.[107] The measures include a new classification of the distinction between BT's basic network services and the enhanced services it offers, which underpins the prices BT charges itself for use of its own network.

Infrastructure regulation: wireless

Central to any communication policy is the question of allocation and control of two related resources: the radio frequency spectrum and the orbital positions in which communication satellites can be 'parked'. The use of wireless telegraphy, otherwise radio communications or spectrum, is regulated mainly under the Wireless Telegraphy Act 1949, the Telecommunications Act 1984, and the Broadcasting Act 1990. It is important to stress that radio communications is an area which, if only because of the disrepect of the medium for national frontiers, calls for international co-operation, rule-making, and standardisation. It is the International Telecommunication Union (ITU) and its agencies (for example ITU-R) who co-ordinate the orbit/spectrum resource at an international level. However, as in all other countries which are members of the ITU, the UK Government undertakes the task of overall radio spectrum manage-

---

[103] See Armstrong, M and Vickers, J, 'Regulation in Telecommunications', in Bishop, M, Kay, J and Mayer, C, *The Regulatory Challenge* (n 86 above).
[104] ibid, 304.
[105] COM (87), 290 final, 30 June 1987.
[106] Collins, R and Murroni, C, *New Media, New Policies* (n 11 above), 22–3.
[107] See *Promoting Competition in Services over Telecommunications Networks: Statement* (London: Oftel, Feb 1997).

ment, including frequency allocation through the Radiocommunications Agency (RA). The RA also represents the UK in ITU discussion of radio. Use and licensing of radio is categorised by service (for example mobile, fixed networks, satellite services, broadcasting, etc). The Wireless Telegraphy Act 1949 licenses and specifies the frequency assigned[108] to the licensee, location, antenna height (if applicable), and transmission power. Allocation decisions are still predominantly made on technological grounds and by using a 'first come, first served' rule. However, the introduction of market forces to spectrum allocation through administrative pricing and auctions[109] is proposed in the Wireless Telegraphy Bill 1997 (before the House of Commons at the time of writing).

Standards and interoperability

Standardisation is again an international issue and national initiatives are more or less limited to the implementation of international rules. Moreover, standards are also developed in different unofficial forums, for example the European Broadcasting Union. However, looking at standardisation of communications equipment in the UK, for instance, five main Acts have been passed in the area: the Wireless Telegraphy Acts of 1949 and 1967, the Telecommunications Act 1984, the Broadcasting Act 1990, and the Marine, Etc, Broadcasting (Offences) Act 1967. A number of statutory instruments have been made under these Acts covering control of interference, control of sales of unapproved apparatus, control of the content of transmissions, setting of licence fees, and exempting certain apparatus from licensing requirements.[110]

The Electromagnetic Compatibility (EMC) regulations,[111] made under the European Communities Act 1972, are also important. They affect all electrical and electronic apparatus, including communications equipment, and set out the approval regime for certifying that the apparatus complies with standards of immunity to interference both to and from apparatus. Enforcement of the EMC regulations is carried out by weights and measures authorities in Great Britain and by the Department of Economic Development in Northern Ireland. These authorities have powers to purchase and test apparatus as well as to search for, seize, and detain apparatus.[112]

---

[108] Assignment is the authorisation given to an individual user to use a specified frequency under specific conditions.

[109] See Verhulst, S and Goldberg, D, 'Spectrum Management Reform in the United Kingdom: the Wireless Telegraphy Bill 1997', *Mediaforum*, Sept 1996, 128–32.

[110] See *UK Legislation and British Standards Relevant to Radiocommunications* (London: Radiocommunications Agency, Feb 1997).

[111] SI 2372/1992.

[112] See Long, CD, *Telecommunications Law and Practice* (London: Sweet & Maxwell, 1995), 125.

2.4 Economic regulation

2.4.1 Market structure: Competition policy, concentration and ownership rules

Media

The media industry is in general subject to competition law in the same way as other industry sectors; for example, it may be subject to merger control under the Fair Trading Act 1973. Responsibility for non-newspaper mergers lies with the Director-General of Fair Trading (DGFT) in the first instance, who advises the Secretary of State for Trade and Industry about whether or not qualifying mergers should be referred to the Monopolies and Mergers Commission (MMC) for further investigation. However, in contrast to the treatment of mergers in industry at large, the Fair Trading Act 1973 contains specific provisions for cases of concentrations in the newspaper sector.[113] However, this 'will be at best a mild deterrent, to rein in further shifts in an already extremely high level of concentration. . . . The overwhelming impression . . . is that the MMC judgements had little impact on diversity.'[114]

Diversity of view is also the public policy objective that is used for special regulation of media ownership in the UK. This is reinforced by the role of the media as a source of information in a democratic society. The Broadcasting Act 1996 clarifies the notion of 'control' of a company, leaving more discretion to the regulator in determining this. The limit of two regional Channel 3 licences is abolished and replaced by a limit of 15 per cent of total television audience. The restriction of newspaper holdings to 20 per cent in television licence holders has also been abolished; newspaper groups with 20 per cent or more of national circulation may not have more than a 20 per cent holding in Channel 3 or Channel 5 licensees, but other newspapers are free to own any broadcasting licences subject to their passing a public interest test administered by the ITC and involving examination of the effects of the holding on diversity of information sources and on competition. Further provisions apply to local newspapers and radio.[115] Enforcement is for the Radio Authority and the ITC.

Telecommunications

Oftel's objectives include the promotion of competition (both in networks and in services) and securing fair trading in the telecommunications market. To achieve these objectives, Oftel believes that it is necessary to have a condition in licences modelled on Articles 85 and 86 of the European

---

[113] Ss 59–62.
[114] See Beesley, ME (ed), *Markets and the Media. Competition, Regulation and the Interests of Consumers* (London: IEA, 1996), 16–18.
[115] S 73, sch 2.

Community Treaty to prohibit anti-competitive behaviour, and this Fair Trading Condition was incorporated into BT's licence on 1 October 1996, effective from 31 December 1996; it has also been incorporated into other licences. The Condition prohibits abuse of a dominant market position and anti-competitive agreements where the behaviour or agreement has an appreciable effect on competition and no countervailing benefits to the consumer and to efficiency. It applies to activities which are carried out when running a telecommunication system or providing telecommunication services and is in the form of a general prohibition of such activities where they have, or are likely to have, the object or effect of preventing, restricting, or distorting competition. By the end of November 1997, the Fair Trading Condition was already included in more than 350 telecoms companies' licences.[116]

Independent service providers

Independent service providers, namely, those who do not themselves own telecommunications networks but provide services over networks belonging to others, have complained to Oftel that BT's position as both network operator and service provider places it at a competitive advantage. Specifically they argue that BT unfairly cross-subsidises its own new services from its other activities, overcharges for access to its network, and abuses its dominant position as a network operator to obtain disproportionate benefits as a provider of services. Oftel has taken these complaints seriously and in March 1996 published a consultation paper on the competitive position of independent service providers of fixed (not mobile) telecommunications services.[117] After a year's consultation, measures designed to bring about more effective competition in those services over telecoms networks were published.[118] They aim to improve competition at all levels of services, from provision of the access network through to delivery of basic and enhanced services over that network. Oftel also plans to set up an Independent Service Provider Forum, which independent service providers can use to highlight emerging issues.

Bottlenecks

The risk of anti-competitive behaviour is especially the case in the area of the so-called 'bottlenecks' such as conditional access systems, subscription management systems, and electronic programme guides. The latter have been the subject of recent Regulations developed by the DTI as

---

[116] See Oftel Press release 84/97, 28 Nov 1997.

[117] See *Promoting Competition in Services over Telecommunications Networks. Consultative Document* (London: Oftel, Mar 1996) at <http://www.open.uk.gov/oftel/oftelhm.htm>

[118] See *Promoting Competition in Services over Telecommunications Networks. Statement* (London: Oftel, Mar 1997) at <http://www.open.uk.gov/oftel/oftelhm.htm>

implementation of the EU Advanced Television Standards Directive.[119] The Advanced Television Standards Regulations[120] came into force on 7 January 1997, and have three main objectives. First, to ensure that the licensing of industrial property rights for the use of conditional access technology is carried out in a way which is fair and non-discriminatory. Second, to ensure that conditional access operators offer broadcasters technical conditional access services on a fair, reasonable, and non-discriminatory basis. Finally, to ensure that cable operators have the ability to use their own conditional access systems and associated services such as electronic programme guides.

The ITC has also issued a draft code of conduct on licensing (analogue and digital) electronic programme guides.[121] The Broadcasting Act 1990 requires the ITC to discharge its functions in the manner which it considers best calculated to ensure that a wide range of services is available throughout the UK, and to ensure fair and effective competition in the provision of licensed services and services connected to them.[122] The purpose of this Code is to implement this duty in relation to EPG services. Finally, Oftel, responsible for regulating conditional access services for digital television, also published guidelines[123] and a consultation document concerning the pricing of conditional access services for digital television.[124]

Pay-TV: Review of BSkyB's position in the wholesale pay-TV market

The Director General of Fair Trading published a review of BSkyB's position in the wholesale pay-TV market.[125] Since 1990, when BSB merged with Sky, the resulting company, BSkyB, has become both the dominant supplier of direct-to-home television services to UK customers and the dominant supplier of programming to UK cable companies. BSkyB also, through its sister company, NewsDatacom, owns the UK pay-TV industry's standard encryption technology—Videocrypt—access to which is generally essential for companies wishing to transmit programming as part of a pay-TV system. Cable companies and satellite channel operators have agreed that it is very difficult for them to gain access to the UK

---

[119] Directive 95/47/EC, OJ No L 2281/5.
[120] SI 1996/3151.
[121] *Draft ITC Code of Conduct on Electronic Programme Guides* (London: ITC, Jan 1997).
[122] S 2(2).
[123] *The Regulation of Conditional Access for Digital Television Services* (London: Oftel, Mar 1997).
[124] See *The Pricing of Conditional Access Services for Digital Television. Consultative Document*, (London, Oftel, Oct 1997) at <http://www.oftel.gov.uk/broadcast/ca1097.htm>
[125] See *Director General Publishes Report Of BSkyB Review*, Office Of Fair Trading Press Release No 57/96, 19 Dec 1996.

market without entering into some form of commercial arrangement with BSkyB and have accused it of abusing its dominant position in the pay-TV market—both in the supply of programming and Videocrypt technology—to force unfair commercial terms upon them. The DGFT found that although BSkyB's market position did cause competition concerns, BSkyB was not itself acting anti-competitively.[126] Consequently, he decided to accept new undertakings from BSkyB rather than ordering an MMC enquiry—a decision clearly influenced by the conflicting desires to reassure concerns of cable companies whilst not penalising BSkyB's commercial success.

In the meantime, the ITC also extended its investigation into the practice of premium channel bundling in the pay-TV market. A specific complaint had been made by the Cable Communications Association against the Disney Channel and its terms of supply will be looked at within the investigation. The focus of ITC's inquiry will be on the effects of bundling on competition at the retail level, with particular reference to the availability of premium channels to viewers of both cable television and direct-to-home satellite services.[127]

2.4.2 Remuneration and finance

Intellectual property rights

One of the major debates surrounding the concept of the information superhighway has been the extent to which existing concepts of 'Intellectual Property Rights' can serve a useful purpose in the common digital environment.[128] However given its adherence to various international conventions, there is only limited scope for the UK to differ from its neighbours on the principles of the regime concerning intellectual property rights, although there may be some difference in their application.[129] Subject to these constraints, UK communications policy is again driven by a desire to provide the infrastructure for a competitive business environment. The former UK Government made clear that:

the international provision of adequate intellectual property protection is extremely important to competitiveness, but difficult to enforce . . . Intellectual property issues associated with the development of the information superhighway,

---

[126] See *Director General's Review of BSkyB's Position in the Wholesale Pay TV Market* (London: Office of Fair Trading, Dec 1996).

[127] See *Competition Investigation into Premium Channel Bundling in the Pay TV. Consultation Document* (London: ITC, Dec 1996).

[128] See Charlesworth, A, 'Theft by Many Other Names', *Times Higher Education Supplement*, 12 Jan 1996.

[129] Saxby, S, 'A UK National Information Policy for the Electronic Age' (n 61 above).

multimedia systems and biotechnology are a major concern. The Government will seek to ensure that EU legislation on these aspects promotes the competitiveness of UK industry.[130]

Copyright is the first type of IPR which springs to mind as it deals with so many of the issues relating to the handling of content on the Internet, although patent law is something which cannot be ignored as trade marks and branding are a vital aspect of Internet trading.

Copyright law in the UK is currently contained in the Copyright, Designs and Patents Act 1988 ('the CDPA'). The Act does not deal specifically with 'multimedia' or even CD-ROM publishing, on-line distribution, or video-on-demand as separate concepts. In some ways, this can be helpful, as technology-specific legislation would be outdated before it reaches the statute books. On the other hand, this approach can create difficulties in interpreting the practical implications of the Act for new media technologies. Section 1 of the CDPA defines copyright as subsisting in:

(a) original literary, dramatic, musical or artistic works
(b) sound recordings, films, broadcasts or cable programmes, and
(c) the typographical arrangement of a published edition.

This list of works is exclusive—there are no other categories; however, although there is no specific mention of Internet works in the Act, such works are capable of falling into several of these categories. What is less clear is the situation regarding an individual who simply places material on a Web server where it can be copied by others. Much turns upon the word 'distributes'.[131] A broad interpretatation would appear to cover virtually all situations where infringing material is placed on an open access Web server, a narrow interpretation would require that the individual placing the material on the open-access Web server perform some action other than to simply provide a facility for illicit copying. It is clear that some areas of the CDPA are ambiguous and have yet to be tested in a law court.[132] Moreover, arguments can be raised as to where the accessing act takes place and which jurisdiction applies. The Berne Convention and the Universal Copyright Convention state here that local law of the database must apply, since this is where the release of the information occurs.[133]

The *Shetland Times* case could be considered as such a test case which has received widespread, and often ill-informed, comment in the

---

[130] *Competitiveness: Forging Ahead*, Cm 2867, 995, paras 15.37, 15.39.

[131] See Charlesworth, A (n 128 above).

[132] See Crown, G, 'Copyright and the Internet', *Computer Law & Practice*, Vol 11, No 6, 1995, 169–72.

[133] See Nicholson, K, 'Understanding Copyright and the Legal Issues Related to the Internet', Conference Paper, IIR, 23 May 1995.

press.[134] The pursuers published, in traditional form, a local newspaper, *The Shetland Times*. In February 1996 they launched an Internet web site. The second defenders provide an Internet-based news and reporting service under the name *The Shetland News* ('the *News*'). In October 1996 the *News* reproduced, verbatim, a number of headlines that appeared in the on-line edition of *The Shetland Times*. They included hypertext links to *The Shetland Times*, so that, by clicking on one of the headlines in the *News* the user gained immediate access to the relevent text in *The Shetland Times*, bypassing its front page and advertisements. The pursuers argued that the headlines made available by them on their web site were cable programmes within the meaning of section 7, CDPA 1988, as they consisted of sending information over a telecommunications system, although certain interactive services are excluded from the section. They also maintained that the facility made available by the defenders on their web site was a cable programme service so that, by including copies of headlines from *The Shetland Times* in their service, the *News* infringed copyright under section 20 of the Act. Granting an interim interdict, Lord Hamilton held that the pursuers' contention that the service provided by them involved the sending of information was prima facie well-founded and that, whilst in a sense the information sat passively awaiting access by callers, that did not preclude the notion that, on such access, the information was conveyed to and received by the caller. The case however was finally settled out of court on 11 November 1997, which means that no real precedent has been set.

Another trademark and branding issue which arises with the Internet is the issue of domain names. In a recent UK case Harrods of Knightsbridge brought an action in the High Court to force defendents to give up the 'Harrods.com' domain name they had obtained from the NSI in America. Pre-1995 the NSI had operated on a 'first come, first served' basis for domain names, so that a person did not have to prove that they 'owned a name' in order to obtain a domain name registration for it. Harrods alleged registered trade mark infringement, passing off, and conspiracy in the United Kingdom, and was successful. However, later the Vice-Chancellor set a precedent for allowing anyone to obtain any domain name that has not already been registered by another party.[135] Procedures for the registration of domain names have been tightened up in the UK in the last year and a domain name system (DNS) has been created. Nominet UK is responsible for the registration and maintenance of all .uk domain names on the Internet, and from 1 August 1996 operates a computerised

---

[134] *Shetland Times Ltd v Jonathan Wills and Anor*. Before Lord Hamilton Outer House [1997] FSR 604, 1997 SLT 669, 24 Oct 1996.

[135] *Pitman Training Ltd & anor v Nominet UK & anor*, Ch 1997 F 1984, Royal Courts of Justice, 22 May 1997 <http://www.open.gov.uk/lcd/scott.htm>

register of the user of the registered name, and of the addressing information associated with it.[136]

Advertising

Advertising is of central importance in this area given the reliance on advertising revenue by most audio-visual media, including the newer services. The Advertising Standards Authority (ASA) was set up in 1962, as a self-regulatory body, to make sure that non-broadcast advertisements appearing in the UK are 'legal, honest and truthful' through the operation of the British Codes of Advertising and Sales Promotion. The ASA has also launched its own initiative with respect to self-regulation of Internet adverts, arguing that its philosophy of self-regulation reflects the nature of the Internet itself as a network which no one body controls. The ASA has established an alliance—the European Advertising Standards Alliance—for the purposes of providing a cross-border complaints procedure. Self-regulating bodies throughout Europe intend to collaborate to ensure that complaints from one jurisdiction can be efficiently referred to and dealt with in the jurisdiction where the advert originated.[137]

The Broadcasting Acts 1990 and 1996 also require the ITC to draw up and enforce a Code of Advertising Standards and Practice, and the ITC has a duty under the Control of Misleading Advertisements Regulations 1988 to consider complaints about television advertisements which are alleged to be misleading.[138] Similar rules apply to radio, developed by the Radio Authority. As mentioned earlier, the 1990 Broadcasting Act includes broad definitions of what sort of electronic services should be subject to licences from the ITC and the Radio Authority, covering programmes conveyed by means of telecommunications systems for simultaneous reception or at different times in response to requests made by different users of the service. It has been suggested that the Act covers video-on-demand and possibly also Internet services.[139] Therefore, broadcasting regulations, including the advertising and sponsorship codes, could apply to those newer communications.

It is important to note that there are also criminal sanctions which govern false or misleading descriptions, as set out in the Trade Descriptions Act 1968, as well as civil sanctions for breach of the provisions contained in the Sale of Goods Act 1979 and the Misrepresentation Act 1967. Other relevant legislation is the Consumer Credit Act 1974, the Prices Act 1974, the Unsolicited Goods and Services Act 1971, the Con-

---

[136] See <http://www.nic.uk/nominet/>
[137] See Allan, G, *Electronic Trade: Contractual Niceties In Hyperspace* (London: Baker & McKenzie, 1996).
[138] See *Advertising & Sponsorship on Commercial Television* (London: ITC, Mar 1996).
[139] See 'ITC Monitors Moving Images on the Internet', *Financial Times*, 15 Mar 1996.

sumer Protection Act 1987, the Control of Misleading Advertisements Regulations 1988, and the Trade Marks Act 1994 (particularly with respect to comparative advertising).

Electronic commerce

Electronic commerce can in several ways be considered as a variant of distance selling, which, in the form of mail order, has been a feature of commercial life and legal consideration for generations. Much will depend on how the UK implements the Directive on Distance Selling.[140] It will certainly apply to sales concluded over the Internet and expressly includes communication by email. The main provisions of the Directive require the provision of information to consumers in writing, a right to withdraw, and a duty to execute the contract within thirty days.

Tax

There are basically three features of the Internet, at least in its commercial application, that are of considerable importance from a tax point of view.[141] First, its international nature; secondly, providers of services may be able to do so without any physical presence in the country where the end user is located; and, thirdly, a transaction effected via the Internet is different in nature from its equivalent outside the Net. This was already illustrated when discussing electronic commerce with the difference in approach between computer software on file or electronic transfer. This difference is very often reflected in a difference in tax treatment, especially in the field of indirect tax or VAT. The introduction of changes affecting the VAT treatment of telecom services (including the provision of Internet access) has recently been announced, and European Commission proposals will be included in the chapter on European regulation below.

Pricing

In the UK, price cap regulation was first introduced in 1984, to regulate the newly privatised BT facing competition by the new entrant Mercury Communications. By means of price cap regulation, increases in the average price of telecommunications services are limited to no more than the increase in an inflation index minus a specified amount referred to as the 'x' factor, the 'RPI − x' formula.[142] The rationale behind this system of price regulation is that it provides a simple scheme which ensures that customers share in the gains from cost reduction attained by the firm.

---

[140] Directive 97/7EC, OJL 144.
[141] See Smith, GJH, *Internet Law and Regulation* (London: FT Law and Tax, 1996), 137–46.
[142] RPI = Retail Price Index (annual rate of inflation).

Price cap regulation has also provided the regulated firm with more price flexibility than, for example, cost-plus rate of return regulation. However, it has been a common practice to limit the regulated firm's pricing flexibility through the use of separate price caps on each of several 'sub-baskets' of services. Regulation has sought to impose such constraints on overall pricing flexibility to reduce the ability of the regulated firm to cross-subsidise competitive services through price increases in non-competitive services.

2.5 Content regulation

Obscenity

The UK obscenity legislation has more recently been amended by the Criminal Justice and Public Order Act 1994 ('CJPOA 1994').[143] This was mainly because of the fear of child pornography and in particular to bring the UK laws up to date with technological changes. The Obscene Publications Acts 1959 & 1964 (for England and Wales) and the Civic Government (Scotland) Act 1982 constitute the major legislation to combat porno-graphic material of any kind in the UK. Much more stringent controls apply to sexual material which portrays children.[144] Child pornography cases on the Internet have also recently led to the establishment of a self-regulation code and hotline, Internet watch. There is no ban as such on the trade in goods which portray adults and are merely 'indecent'. However, section 42 of the Customs and Consolidation Act 1876 prohibits the impor-tation into the UK of indecent or obscene prints, paintings, photographs, books, lithographic cards or other engravings, or any other indecent or obscene articles. Moreover, section 43 of the Telecommunications Act 1984 makes it an offence to send 'by means of a public telecommunica-tions system, a message or other matter that is grossly offensive or of an indecent, obscene or menacing character'. In addition to dealing with indecent, obscene, or offensive telephone calls, the Act also covers the transmission of obscene materials through the telephone systems by elec-tronic means. For the purposes of the Act, a public telecommunications system is any telecommunications system designated by the Secretary of State and is not confined to that of British Telecom. However, the offence is not committed where a telecommunications system located outside the jurisdiction is used to send obscene materials into the UK, and the Act itself does not penalise the act of procuring a message to be sent. The 1984

---

[143] For a detailed and comparative overview of the UK obscenity laws, see Akdeniz, Y, 'Computer Pornography: a Comparative Study of the US and UK Obscenity Laws and Child Pornography Laws in Relation to the Internet', *International Review of Law, Computers & Technology*, Vol 10, No 2, 1996, 235–61.

[144] Indecency with Children Act 1960, s 1(1); Protection of Children Act 1978.

Act will also not apply to cases where the data is transmitted by using a local area network unless part of the transmission is routed through a public telecommunications system. The use of leased lines, for example by universities, would also not be caught by the Act. Therefore in some circumstances the Act may not cover obscene materials transferred by using telecommunication systems. It is also an offence to distribute indecent material through the postal system.[145]

Child pornography

Child pornography has been the most controversial topic arising from the use of the Internet in recent years. Its availability on the Internet has caused a 'moral panic' among the government, law enforcement bodies such as the police, prosecutors, and judges, together with the media in general. There is no settled definition of pornography in a multi-national environment such as the Internet and cultural, moral, and legal variations all around the world make it difficult to define 'pornographic content' in a global society.[146] The Protection of Children Act 1978 covers the use of children in pornographic photography even where no other form of abuse had occurred.[147] Section 84 of the CJPOA 1994 extends its coverage to so-called 'pseudo-photographs' of children created by computer software by using more than one picture. It is an offence for a person to have any indecent photograph or pseudo-photograph of a child in his possession, and this provision was used in the 'Birmingham University Case'.[148] The defendants faced a total of eighteen charges under the Protection of Children Act 1978 and the Obscene Publications Act 1959. During the trial they had argued that because pictures were stored on a computer hard disk they could not be regarded as photographs and could not be covered by obscene publications legislation. The judge ruled that the computerised images could be legally regarded as photographs; a pornographic computer image was, in law, the same as a photograph.

Self-regulation of content

The Internet Service Providers Association (ISPA) was formed in 1995, and established a Code of Practice after a meeting with the Home Office in January 1996. The former Science and Technology Minister stated at this

---

[145] Post Office Act 1953, s 11.

[146] See Akdeniz, Y, 'The Regulation of Pornography and Child Pornography on the Internet', *Journal of Information, Law and Technology (JILT)*, 1997 (1); also at <http://elj.warwick.ac.uk/jilt/internet/97_1akdz/>

[147] See Akdeniz, A, *Regulation of Child Pornography on the Internet. Cases and Materials related to Child Pornography on the Internet* at <http://www.leeds.ac.uk/law/pgs/yaman/child.htm>

[148] See *R v Fellows, R v Arnold* [1997] 2 All ER 548 (CA) 41.

meeting that the UK Government's 'position is that we would want to encourage the industry to develop a system of self-regulation which might address these areas of concern, rather than considering statutory options. UK ISPs must devise a Code of Practice to control access to illegal and unsuitable material or face increasing political pressure for curbing legislation.' Moreover, on 14 August 1996 the DTI issued a press release in which it was suggested that the ISPA should 'co-operate in developing services' which can make use of features such as PICS (Platform for Internet Content Selection) which makes it possible to rate every web page according to its content.[149] Subsequently, the Metropolitan Police wrote to all Internet Service Providers (ISPs) in the UK, concerning about 130 Newsgroups it believed to contain pornographic material. The letter concludes 'We trust that with your co-operation and self regulation it will not be necessary for us to move to an enforcement policy.'[150]

Acceptable use policies on the part of some organisations were already in place and Demon Internet, a major UK Service Provider, had (as a reaction to a newspaper article) developed a specific self-censorship policy using the new PICS standard. Finally, following a seminar organised by the Internet Developers Association, the 'Internet Watch Foundation' was created.[151] It is an independent organisation to implement the proposals jointly agreed by the government, the police, and the two major UK service provider trade associations, ISPA and LINX. It aims to enhance the enormous potential of the Internet 'to inform, educate, entertain and conduct business' by hindering the use of the Internet to transmit illegal material, particularly child pornography, and encouraging the classification of legal material on the Net in order to enable users to customise the nature of their experience of the Net to their own requirements. In its first full month of operation thirty-four calls were received. Of those only half referred to material which was actually illegal; six of the calls, all involving child pornography, were reported to the police. None had originated in the UK. However, not all of the UK ISPs are members.

Defamation

Current discussion in the UK on defamation is especially focused on the Internet. Almost all commercial bodies which operate any form of interactive service on the Internet are seeking ways in which to protect themselves from liability for defamation. At the time of writing there has been no real test case as to whether publication on the Internet would be libel

---

[149] See DTI Press Release P/96/636, 14 Aug 1996.
[150] See <http://www.community.org.uk/met-let.htm>
[151] The original *R3 Safety-Net* proposals can be seen in full at <http://www.ispa.org.uk/safetynet.shtml> See also Internet Watch Foundation <http:www.iwf.org.uk/>

or slander (a distinction only made in England), slander being defamatory material of a transitory nature, and libel having an enduring quality. However, in September 1997 two companies in the Norwich Union Group paid an estimated £450,000 and issued an apology to a rival company, Western Provident Association Ltd, for libellous comments sent by its staff by internal electronic mail. Members of its staff had spread rumours that Western Provident was close to insolvency. Thus, most legal opinion considers that defamation on the Internet would consist of libel rather than slander.[152]

The Defamation Act 1996 attempts to deal with electronic media including the Internet.[153] Section 1 seeks to offer a new defence of what is called 'innocent dissemination' to service providers and operators of bulletin boards who were unaware that their services were being used to publish defamatory material. The defence is available if a person (including a company) is able to show:

(1) that he or she was not the author, editor, or publisher of the statement complained of;
(2) that he or she took reasonable care in relation to its publication; and
(3) that he or she did not know and had no reason to believe that what they did caused or contributed to the publication of a defamatory statement.

So far as the Internet is concerned, service providers will not be treated as an author, editor, or publisher.[154] However, to gain effective protection the other requirements must also be met, and if a service provider does nothing to monitor its services it may not have taken reasonable care in relation to its publication, particularly if the author of a defamatory statement was a repeat offender and notice had been given previously.

Another aspect of defamation is how to determine which jurisdiction applies; the borderless character of the Internet could lead to 'forum shopping'. Jurisdiction is normally governed by the Civil Jurisdiction and Judgments Act 1982, schedule 4, but in the case of email or other Internet communication, a problem of interpretation can easily occur. Help can be found in the leading recent case of *Shevill and Others v Presse Alliance SA*,[155] in which the European Court of Justice (ECJ) was asked by the House of Lords to make an authoritative ruling on the interpretation of the wording of article 5(3) of the Brussels Convention, on which paragraph 5(3) of schedule 4 of the 1982 Act is closely modelled. An issue of the newspaper *France Soir* had been published by a French company containing an article

---

[152] See Freeman, DJ, *Law and the Internet*, at: <http://www.cygnet.co.uk/DJFreeman/>
[153] See Aslan, S, 'Libel and the Internet', *Communications Law*, Vol 1, No 6, 1996, 222–6.
[154] S 1(3)(e).
[155] [1995] 2 WLR 499.

with defamatory comments about an individual resident in England, a company registered in Yorkshire, a company registered in France, and one registered in Belgium. The ECJ made it plain that the plaintiff always has the option of bringing the entire claim, for damages arising in any country, before the courts of either the defendant's domicile or the place where the publisher of the defamatory material is established (these would normally coincide). This would overcome the disadvantage of having different courts ruling on different parts of the dispute. It was at the discretion of the victim, then, if he or she wished to bring an action where the defendant was established in respect of all the harm that occurred, or in each contracting State for the harm which occurred in that particular State.

Moral rights

The Copyright, Designs and Patents Act 1988 gave certain moral rights to authors (including directors of films). These include the right to be identified as the author or director whenever their work is commercially published, publicly performed, or broadcast (the 'paternity' right); the right not to have a work subject to derogatory treatment (the 'integrity' right); and the right not to have a work falsely attributed to them. Multimedia products often involve the work of joint authors. In these cases, each author has the right to be identified provided he/she has asserted his/her right. Moral rights can however be waived by the author in writing. The first two rights do not apply, among other things, to any copyright work produced for publication in a newspaper, magazine, yearbook, or other collective reference work if it was specifically created for that purpose. Moreover, they also do not apply to a computer program or computer-generated work.

Since copyright works need adaptation to transform them into, for example, multimedia products, the integrity right is an important one. However, derogatory treatment is less wide in definition than the words would at first sight suggest. Treatment is defined as 'any addition to, deletion from or alteration to or adaptation of the work, other than (i) a translation of a literary or dramatic work, or (ii) an arrangement or transcription of a musical work involving no more than a change of key or register'.[156] Treatment will be derogatory if 'distortion or mutilation of the work is otherwise prejudicial to the honour or reputation of the author or director'. Besides those three traditional moral rights, anyone who has commissioned a photograph or a film for private and domestic purposes has the right to prevent the work being issued to the public. Committing any of these acts—or authorising them—is an infringement of moral

---

[156] S 80(2).

rights. Producers of multimedia or Internet works should therefore ensure that the source of any still photographs or film clips used in them has been verified.

Data protection

Data protection in the UK is currently regulated by the Data Protection Act 1984.[157] It was designed to allow the UK to ratify the Council of Europe 'Convention for the Protection of Individuals with regard to Automatic Processing of Personal Data'.[158] The Convention has two objectives: to protect individuals in circumstances where information about them is processed automatically, and to facilitate a common international standard of protection for individuals, such that the free flow of information across international boundaries can proceed properly. The Act is therefore concerned with information about individuals which is processed by computer (personal data). It introduced significant new rights for individuals to whom that information relates and established the independent Data Protection Registrar reporting directly to Parliament. The Registrar is charged with administering the Act and supervising its operation. His decisions are subject to the supervision of the Courts and the Data Protection Tribunal, also established by the Act.

The new European data protection Directive[159] necessitates the reform of existing UK data protection law, and the Government published at the end of July 1997 its proposals for implementation.[160] The Act will have to be amended to contain strict conditions for the processing of sensitive, for example medical, data; to require those controlling the personal data to give individuals certain information when data about them is collected; to give individuals the right to object to their information being used for direct marketing; and to bring certain manually-held data within the ambit of the Act.

Encryption

Another Government concern related to data protection is the need to define an encryption policy. This must balance the needs of national security with those of participants in the information market. A new consultation paper was issued by the DTI in March 1997, now including the use of encryption services for protecting stored data.[161] The proposals

---

[157] For a detailed overview see Raab, C, 'Implementing data protection in Britain', *International Review of Administrative Sciences*, Vol 62, 1996, 493–511.

[158] Convention number 108, Council of Europe, 1981.

[159] Directive 95/46/EC of 24 October OJL, 23 November 1995 OJ L281, 31 and at: <http://www2.echo.lu/legal/en/dataprot/directiv/directiv.html>

[160] *Data Protection. The Government's Proposals*, at: <http://www.homeoffice.go.uk/datap1.htm>

[161] *Licensing of Trusted Third Parties for the Provision of Encryption Services. Public Consultation Paper* (London; DTI, Mar 1997).

involve licensing Trusted Third Parties[162] who offer encryption services to the public in order to facilitate the development of electronic commerce, to protect consumers, and to preserve the ability of the intelligence and law enforcement agencies to fight serious crime and terrorism, and protect economic well-being and national security, by requiring disclosure of encryption keys under safeguards similar to those which already exist for warranted interception under the Interception of Communications Act. How the current Government will implement those proposals remains to be seen.

2.6 Universal service

At the end of 1995 Oftel published an initial consultation document on Universal Service. It stated that:

in order to develop a more effective policy for securing universal service in the UK as we move towards the 21st century, it is necessary to define a basic minimum level of service that should be available to all customers, or to defined classes of customers everywhere, at the same price—Universal Service. It is also necessary to set out a methodology for quantifying any legitimate additional costs incurred by commercial operators in delivering universal service and establish mechanisms for sharing these costs fairly across the industry. And all this must fit into a competitive market.[163]

It proposed (a) a levy on all telecoms operators to finance a Universal Service Fund and (b) different levels of Universal Service for different categories of customer groups (including, in particular, a higher level of service for schools, public libraries, and public access points). However, this ran into difficulties. First, the cable companies argued that, while the idea of installing higher bandwidth connections to schools might be desirable, it could not be regarded as part of universal service. Second, the European Commission argued that such differential treatment would be in conflict with European telecommunications liberalisation provisions. As a result Oftel announced in June 1996 that it was establishing a separate 'Education and Public Access Points Task Force'.[164] In February 1997, the Task Force published its first report, stressing that affordable and predictable charges for high-speed telecoms network links (ISDN or

---

[162] Trusted Third Parties (TTPs) are trustworthy commercial organisations that can provide various information security-related services to enable transactions to be conducted securely. Typical services are management of cryptographic keys, time stamping of electronic documents, and arbitration of repudiation claims regarding the origin, receipt, delivery, and submission of electronic documents.

[163] See *Universal Telecommunication Services. Proposed Arrangements for Universal Service in the UK from 1997* (London: Oftel, Dec 1995), para 1.3.

[164] *Improving Access to the Information Society for Education and Public Access Points. Statement* (London: Oftel, 27 June 1996).

equivalent) were the key. Moreover, it said that improving access for schools is vitally important, and that primary schools were a 'top priority'. In the meantime a battle broke out between the cable industry and BT over who could offer the best and most cost-effective Internet access to schools.[165] Oftel has approved plans by BT to provide all of Britain's 32,000 schools with high-speed digital access to the Internet by the year 2000; at present, only 6,000 schools have access to the Internet. As for the Government, it has pledged to invest 140 million Ecu in updating computers and software in UK schools as part of its plans to establish by 2002 the National Grid for Learning, a nationwide network connecting all schools, universities, and libraries, and providing teaching material and teacher aid.

Universal Service in broadcasting in the UK is provided by two public sector operators (BBC and Channel 4, see above) and by positive content requirements imposed on commercial operators in exchange for spectrum. All terrestrial broadcasting services are also universally accessible and free at the point of use. However, protection is afforded for the public service broadcasters in the new digital environment by guaranteeing them multiplexes for digital terrestrial television, and a system of listed events has been retained, under which key national and sporting events cannot be shown only on subscription or pay-per-view services.[166]

2.7 Public access and the political process

Government oversight of the development of a new communications and Internet policy for the public sector is the responsibility of the CCTA, the Central Computer and Telecommunications Agency (or the Government Centre of Information Systems).[167] In November 1995 a small Central Information Technology Unit (CITU) was set up by the Deputy Prime Minister. Its mission is to devise a set of strategies and policies which will enable Government to exploit the opportunities provided by information technology. A Green Paper on the use of IT to improve the delivery of Government's services to the public and business was published in November 1996.[168] The purpose of this Green Paper was to explain the Government's vision of what is possible and to start a debate. The Government claimed that its strategy would provide electronic services which are cost effective and affordable, and which conform to the principles of

---

[165] See Snoddy, R, 'Cheap Internet deal for Schools', *The Financial Times*, 9 Jan 1997.

[166] Broadcasting Act 1996, ss 28–31 and 97–105.

[167] *Information Superhighways—Opportunities for Public Sector Applications in the UK. A Government Consultative Report* (London: CCTA, May 1994, Updated July 1995).

[168] See *Government Direct. A Prospectus for the Delivery of Government Services* (London: Cabinet Office, Nov 1996), at: <http://www.open.gov.uk/>

choice, confidence, accessibility, efficiency, rationalisation, open information, and fraud prevention.

Repeated calls for freedom of information legislation were answered in part by the publication of a code of practice on access to government information in 1994. The Labour Party promised in its election manifesto to introduce such legislation, but this has been delayed until at least the next session of Parliament; meanwhile, a Freedom of Information White Paper will be published, which will 'change the culture of government and how information is handled'.[169]

As regards participation in the political process, UK Citizens Online Democracy (UKCOD) is Britain's first national on-line democracy service. The Cabinet Office supports UK Citizens Online Democracy and has confirmed that it may approach all Government departments about the use of their material, and that UKCOD is 'congruent with the Government's aims under the Citizen's Charter of facilitating the dissemination and accessibility of Government information to the public and enhancing the effectiveness of UK democracy'.[170]

Several local authorities have also set up sites, not only to inform people of what is going on in their areas but also to stimulate political interaction.[171] By late 1996 around 200 of the 500 local authorities were making information available electronically via the Internet.[172] Leisure and tourism was the most prolific area, then economic development and 'council information'.

3 CONCLUDING REMARKS

This chapter commenced by suggesting that the UK had a number of advantages in relation to the development of the so-called 'information society', especially through its liberalised infrastructure. The UK has certainly taken a lead in Europe in promoting privatisation and investment in communications infrastructure but, despite these advantages, the process of convergence has been a gradual one and optimistic proposals about the growth of multimedia have often not been met. The role of the 'old' media, and especially public service broadcasting, remains central and it is important that new regulatory developments do not act on the assumption that they are a thing of the past.

The future of the media industries is also somewhat uncertain, but there

---

[169] Cabinet Office Press Release 111/97, 29 Oct 1997.

[170] See <http://www.democracy.org.uk/about/index.html>

[171] For a detailed directory of Local Government Web Sites, see <http//www.tagish.co.uk/tagish/links/localgov.htm>

[172] See *The State Of Local Government on the Internet* (Tagish, Summer 1996), at: <http//www.tagish.co.uk/tagish/pubs/lawebreview.html>

are moves towards consolidation and these make competition law important for the future. The UK has a working system of competition law, but one which has been heavily criticised; it remains to be seen how effective imminent reforms will be in responding to these criticisms. Much of the consolidation is international, making once more the point that international, especially European Community, scrutiny of competition is of the utmost importance.

The regulatory response to convergence has been nothing short of chaotic in the UK. In part this is inevitable given the historic difference in the nature of technologies; however, the plethora of different regulatory bodies cannot be justified in modern conditions and the existence of uncertainty about regulators' powers, regulatory discretion and the lack of accountability should be tackled. Therefore proposals for regulatory consolidation need rapid implementation. Having said this, the performance of individual regulatory bodies has been impressive and Oftel in particular has skilfully anticipated trends and has organised very sophisticated consultations on the emerging issues. However there remains a duplication of regulation. Several actors are still subject to multiple and overlapping regulation, not guided by a clear and explicit organising principle.

What is striking by its absence in the UK is a determining role for the courts. A few individual decisions have been mentioned in this report, but they have been concerned with very specific applications of traditional legal doctrines; the courts have not had a general constitutional role which has set the parameters of the developing media scene, as has occurred in the USA, Germany, or Italy. However, the lack of activity of courts does not mean an absence of law. Apart from the detailed legal provisions discussed here, an important trend is that of 'enforced self-reglation', for example in relation to the Internet, by which private actors are required to set up legal regimes of their own in response to threats of more formal legal intervention.[173] We shall return to this theme in our overall conclusion.

Finally, a lot will depend upon the media policy of the Labour Government and how it intervenes in this field. However, media legislation has until now reflected a high degree of consensus between Labour and the Conservatives, and therefore a major change is not expected. In the past UK media policy has been ineffective with regard to new media technology. Satellite and cable had a very slow uptake in comparison with other European countries, despite the UK Government's obsession with high technology at that time. It remains to be seen if this contradictory result will continue in the digital period.

---

[173] See Ayres, I and Braithwaite, J, *Responsive Regulation: Transcending the Deregulation Debate* (Oxford: Oxford University Press, 1992).

5

The European Institutions

STEFAAN VERHULST AND DAVID GOLDBERG

This chapter looks at legal responses to regulating the changing media in a European context, focusing on the two main intergovernmental organisations: the European Community and Union and the older, more inclusive Council of Europe. Apart from being of European importance, they are two of the main global drivers of policy and standards for the changing media. The Community's overall approach alternates between treating the sector as a cultural good or as an economic commodity. The Council is rather less ambivalent: the media are simultaneously both the means for realising the human right of freedom of expression and a principal condition for consolidating democracy or bringing it about in certain areas of the European audio-visual area. Generally, the Council's activities build a cumulative normative framework for media and communications based on certain, specific values. Indeed, as early as 1968, the Parliamentary Assembly of the Council held a seminar on the effect of the new communications technologies on human rights.[1] Virtually all of today's concerns were referred to during that meeting in the context of the media of the day. An important contemporary strand of activity concerns the impact of the new communication and information technologies on democracy, culture, and human rights. There are, of course, non-governmental organisations which some claim to be even more effective frameworks for co-operation and co-ordination, such as the European Broadcasting Union (EBU) and the Association of Commercial Television, the 'commercial' counterpart to the EBU. Each organisation is, inevitably, moving from dealing only or mainly with traditional or electronic audio-visual media to reacting to the evolution of new communications technologies (NCTs). The shift already affects European policy, law, and regulation—and will do so all the more in the future.

---

[1] Symposium on 'Human Rights and Mass Communication 5 (Brussels: Council of Europe, 1968).

1 STRUCTURE AND INSTITUTIONS

The European Community

The Community's media and communications policy is certainly not the product of a single and unified Community vision of the sector. Instead it must be regarded as the result of a hard won compromise between both Member States and rival power centres within the institutions. The EC Treaty established the Community institutions, notably the Council of Ministers, the European Parliament (EP), the Commission, and the Court of Justice of the European Communities.[2] It confers legislative, executive, and judicial powers in prescribed fields upon these institutions. The European Community has, however, a very powerful executive but a weak legislative process. Under the European Union Treaty, the EP has made some limited progress, partly due to the introduction of the co-decision procedure which is used for media and communications legislation. However, unlike the legislatures of Community Member States, the power of the peripatetic EP remains weak. The Council of Ministers, the final decision-making body,[3] is the institution where the priorities of the different Member States are best reflected.

The European Parliament is not only weak in legislative power but its Committee on Youth, Culture, Education, the Media and Sport is generally regarded as having low status and little influence.[4] Nonetheless, Community media policy was and is more frequently initiated by the Parliament than by the Commission or the Council. The Parliament's interest differs, however, from those two power blocks, being mainly based on the promotion of European integration with an emphasis on cultural as well as the market aspects. Recent important examples are the Resolution on the broadcasting of sports events[5] (which considers that exclusive broadcasting rights for certain sports events which are of general interest must be granted to channels which broadcast in non-encrypted form), and the report concerning the promotion and protection of public service broadcasting which was adopted by the Parliament during September 1996 (the Tongue Report).[6] On information society issues the European Parliament is far from leading the discussion, except for some limited actions such as discussion on the use of standards.

[2] EC Treaty, Art 4.
[3] The Council of Ministers is the most powerful of the EC institutions and wields the real decision-making power. Legislation is initiated by the Commission, but is adapted (or not) by the Council.
[4] Collins, R, *Broadcasting and Audio-Visual Policy in the European Single Market* (London: John Libbey, 1994), 31.
[5] OJ No C 166: 10 June 1996, 109–11.
[6] See, *EP News*, Sept 1996, 4.

The Commission, the executive arm of the EC, tends to view the communications sector as an industry and to apply the principles of market liberalisation to it. It is, however, divided by inter-institutional rivalry. Within the Commission at least six of the twenty-four Directorates-General are concerned with communications-related aspects, but each from a different perspective:

- DGI (present Commissioner Leon Brittan), responsible for external (economic) relations, is the representative at G7 and World Trade Organisation (WTO) meetings, which recently have dealt with the convergence of the communications sector, intellectual property rights, and the liberalisation of communication services.
- DGIII (present Commissioner Martin Bangemann), previously responsible for the internal market and now for Industry, originally produced the Green Paper *Television Without Frontiers*[7] which set the scene for the passing of the corresponding major directives in the field of the audio-visual industry (see below).
- DGIV (present Commissioner Karel Van Miert) is responsible for competition policy, and plays an important role in the prevention of anti-competitive behaviour (Article 85) and of abuse of dominant position (Article 86) through cartels, monopolies, or mergers.
- DGX (present Commissioner Marcelino Oreja), responsible for Information, Communication, Culture, and Audio-visual media, intervenes in the media in order to provide external protection and industrial support to the programme industry.[8]
- DGXIII (present Commissioner Martin Bangemann), responsible for Telecommunications, Information Market, and Exploitation of Research, has embraced the information society. Its main interest is to promote and standardise new technologies (for example HDTV, satellite, etc).
- DGXV (present Commissioner Mario Monti), responsible since 1993 for the internal market and financial services, wishes to harmonise national regulations in order to create an internal market. Liberalisation of the audio-visual market is its main rationale.

A study of the audio-visual policy in the European Community identifies DG III (whose responsibilities are now under DGXV which shares the same orientation as the former DG) and DGIV as having a 'markedly more liberal, market orientation' than the other Directorates 'which have advocated political intervention in the market'.[9] The struggle between 'liberals'

---

[7] COM (84) 300 final.
[8] The MEDIA I and II programmes (see below).
[9] Collins, R (n 4 above), 18–20.

and 'dirigistes' is thus not only conducted beyond but also within the Commission.

DG XIII has recently suggested the creation of a regulatory authority for telecommunications at the level of the European Union. A study commissioned by DG XII stated that convergence of telecommunications, audiovisual, publishing, and information technology may create pressures for a European Regulatory Authority and/or new approaches to its role. However the study also shows that there are a range of practical problems that need to be resolved and any attempt to create a new regulatory body with a policy function or an appellate role would require a Treaty amendment, though it would be possible under the present Treaty to create a body with an essentially 'managerial' or 'operational' role. The study concludes that 'the creation of a regulatory body for telecommunications at the level of the European Union is likely to be an organic process, with regulatory functions added to a new body as the need to do so becomes clearer'.[10]

The Court of Justice (CJEC) is the final interpreter of the Treaties and secondary legislation. As discussed below, the CJEC has played a key role in the development of an EC media policy since it has produced case law that cleared a path for the Community's involvement in broadcasting and media policy-making by establishing its regulatory competence. In its function as authoritative interpreter of EC law, the Court has also made some important judgments on the implementation of the Directive *Television Without Frontiers* and other audio-visual matters.[11]

The Treaties also create three other bodies: the Economic and Social Committee (ECOSOC), the Committee of the Regions, and the European Court of Auditors. The latter examines accounts of Community institutions and is thus not directly involved in policy-making. ECOSOC is an advisory board which consists of 222 members representing the interests of employers, trade unions, and consumers and has produced opinions on almost every policy proposal and legislation relating to media and communications policy. Although having a purely advisory role, its expertise has made it fairly influential. The Committee of the Regions and Local Authorities was established in 1993. Article 198a of the Treaty specifies

---

[10] See *Issues Associated with the Creation of a European Regulatory Authority for Telecommunications*, (NERA and Denton Hall, Mar 1996).

[11] The Court's judgment of 10 Sept 1996 in *Commission v Kingdom of Belgium* held that a member state is not authorised to control television broadcasts from another member state (Case C-11/95). A judgment of that same date in *Commission v United Kingdom* clarified from where a member state has jurisdiction over a television broadcaster, and held that it is the country in which the broadcaster is established and not necessarily when the broadcaster uplinks its programming that is determinative (Case C-222/94). More recently (29 May 1997) the CEJC released two preliminary rulings (both concerning Belgian cases) along the same lines drawn in the previous cases (Case C-56/96 and C-14/96).

that the Committee is to be consulted by the Council and the Commission on issues such as new proposals for cohesion, trans-European networks, and education and training. The Committee has recently underlined the cultural importance of the audio-visual industry as safeguarding and promoting the diversity of national and regional cultures.[12] The importance of regions was also reflected in the Inter-Regional Information Society Initiative (IRISI). The six participating regions[13] had to outline a strategy on the information society bringing together all the relevant regional actors. The innovative nature of the IRISI approach rests on partnership between all key players in a region; its success has convinced the Commission to continue in that direction with a new generation of innovative actions under Article 10 of the ERDF and Article 6 of the ESF.

The debate on information society issues is highly influenced by expert groups and forums initiated by the European Community, such as the High Level Expert Group (HLEG) on the Social and Societal Aspects of the information society, which published its Final Report 'Building the European information society for us all', in April 1997. It focuses on the following themes: employment and job creation; social and democratic values; culture and the future of new services and the media; universal access and consumer protection and support; sustainability in an information society; public services: bringing administration closer to citizens; and lifelong learning. The Information Society Forum—another advisory group—is composed of around 130 members from six main fields: users of new technologies, social groups, content and services providers, network operators, equipment manufacturers, and institutions. The Forum argued in its first annual report in June 1996 along similar and complementary lines as the HLEG. Finally, the Information Society Forum with Central and Eastern Europe was first held in Prague, in June 1995, and a follow-up meeting of the Forum took place in September 1996 in order to develop a workplan.

European policy in the field of media and communications is also affected by a whole range of non-governmental organisations at a regional level. A list of the major ones includes: the European Conference of Postal and Telecommunications Administrations (CEPT), the European Telecommunications and Professional Electronics Industry (ECTEL), European Information Technology Industry Round Table (EITIRT), European Multimedia Forum (EMF), European Telecommunications

---

[12] Opinion on the Commission's Green Paper on strategic options to strengthen the European programme industry in the context of the audio-visual policy of the European Union. OJ No C 210: 41, 18 Aug 1995.

[13] North West of England (UK), Nord Pas-de-Calais (F), Valencia (E), Central Macedonia (GR) and Piemonte (I).

Standards Institute (ETSI), European Public Telecommunications Network Operators' Association (ETNO), European Telecommunications Satellite Organisation (EUTELSAT), European Broadcasting Union (EBU),
Association of Commercial Televisions (ACT), International Telecommunications Users Group (INTUG), Union of Industrial and Employers'
Confederations of Europe (UNICE), and many others.

Council of Europe

Fritz Hondius has described the Declaration on the Freedom of Expression and Information, adopted by the Committee of Ministers on 29 April
1982, taken together with Article 10 of the Convention on Human Rights
and Fundamental Freedoms, as a 'veritable European media charter.'[14]
The most significant institutions are the decision-making Committee of
Ministers and the judicial European Court of Human Rights whose judgments interpret the conformity of national administrative measures, laws,
decisions and procedures with Article 10 (see below).[15] The Court has said
that Article 10 '. . . does not apply solely to certain types of information or
ideas or forms of expression',[16] so its relevance in principle for new communications technologies (NCTs) is clear.

The Committee is composed of the Ministers for foreign affairs of each
Member State; it meets twice yearly and adopts an annual Intergovernmental Programme of Activities, incorporating activities relating to the
media and communications. The Committee meets monthly when constituted by the Ministers' Deputies (the Permanent Representatives) who
draw up the Intergovernmental Programme of Activities, adopt the 1,300
million FF budget, and decide the follow-up to Parliamentary Assembly
proposals and the decisions of the Conferences of Specialised Ministers
(for example of Ministers responsible for Mass Media Policy) which held
its fifth session during December 1997. The Committee of Ministers' decisions may be Declarations, Recommendations, or Resolutions.[17] Finally,
there are the periodic meetings known as Summits—meetings of Heads of
State and Government—which produce agenda-setting Final Communi-
ques. The second such Summit (October 1997) considered developing a
Europe-wide approach to the use of new media technologies. It had before

---

[14] See Hondius, F, 'Regulating Transfrontier Television—the Strasbourg Option', 1988
Yearbook of European Law, Vol 8, 141, at 146.
[15] See generally *Case-law Concerning Article 10 of ECHR*, Council of Europe Document DH-
MM (97) 6.
[16] *Markt Intern Verlag GmBH and Klaus Beerman v Germany*, Series A No 165, para 26.
[17] See the Council of Europe Glossary for definitions at: <http://www.coe.fr/eng/std/
glosseng.htm>

it a Special Document on the 'New Information Technologies'.[18] The Summit's Action Plan, under the heading 'Democratic Values and Cultural Diversity', commits the Council to developing a '. . . European policy for the application of the new information technologies, with a view to ensuring respect for human rights and cultural diversity, fostering freedom of expression and information and maximising the educational and cultural potential of these technologies'. The value of and need to co-ordinate and co-operate in this sector is recognised, and the Heads of Government '. . . invite the Council of Europe to seek, in this respect, suitable partnership arrangements'.[19]

The deliberative Parliamentary Assembly of the Council meets either in Plenary Session or in Committees (standing or ad-hoc) or Sub-Committees, for example the Sub-Committee on Media of the Committee on Culture and Education. The Assembly adopts Texts on the basis of Reports from various Committees. It then passes Recommendations—for example Recommendation 1215 (1993)1 on the ethics of journalism, or Resolutions (on the same topic, Resolution 1003 (1993)1 on the ethics of journalism)—or adopts Orders. Its deliberations are recommendations to the Committee of Ministers, which may either make a response or simply 'take note' of them, as in the case of Order No 531 (1997), for example, on the impact of the new communication and information technologies on democracy.

Assisting these bodies is the International Secretariat. Within the Secretariat, media activities are co-ordinated by the Steering Committee on the Mass Media (CDMM). It was created in 1976, as a unit within the Directorate of Public Law. It relocated to the Directorate of Human Rights in 1981 and operates out of Division 2. Under its general auspices, various specialist, expert committees are created from time to time. Some relevant recent and current examples are: the Group of Specialists on Media in a Pan-European Perspective (MM-S-EP) which is concerned with elaborating guidelines for the guarantee of independent public service broadcasting; MM-S-NT which is the Group of Specialists on the impact of new communications technologies on human rights and democratic values; the Committee of Experts on Media Concentrations and Pluralism (MM-CM) which informs itself about national developments with a view to promulgating measures to protect and promote pluralism; the Group of Specialists on access to official information (MM-S-AC); and the Group of Specialists on media law and human rights (MM-S-HR).

[18] See <http://www.coe.fr/summit/enewinfotech.htm>
[19] See <http://www.coe.fr/summit/edeclplan.htm#ActionPlan>

2 SOURCES OF INSTITUTIONAL COMPETENCE

The EC Treaty and its relevance for media

The legal framework and the competencies of the European Community are determined by the *Treaty of Rome* ('the EC Treaty') as amended, which is, in effect, the constitution of the European Community. The principal treaties amending the EC Treaty are the *Single European Act*, the *Treaty on European Union* (Maastricht Treaty), and the *Treaty of Amsterdam*. The European Community can only act when, and if, there is a sufficient legal basis for action contained in the Treaties. Although the Treaty of Rome dates from 1957, it is only recently that the relevance of the Treaty to media and communications has been established. Despite the fact that the EC Treaty does not contain any explicit rules on media policy,[20] there are some Articles that can be applied to media and especially to broadcasting (see below). The Court of Justice has made clear in its judgments, such as in the *Saachi*[21] (1974), *Coditel*[22] (1980), *Debauve*[23] (1980), and *Dutch Advertisers*[24] (1989) cases that the principles of the Treaty are relevant to media, including broadcasting. This case law has formed the background to, and has given the impetus to, further legislation on media related issues, discussed in more detail below. The case law and the legislation, such as the EC Directive *Television Without Frontiers* 1989, sought at least to co-ordinate, if not actually to harmonise, national rules.

The Council of Europe

The Council's two most legally significant sources are (a) Conventions promulgated and opened for signature by states and (b) judgments of the Court. The latter scrutinise media and communications laws and regulations in national states in case they breach the protection of the applicant's human rights and decide using the (well-known) tests of legitimacy of aim; legality; necessity for democratic society; and proportionality. Relevant Conventions include the fundamental Convention for the Protection of Human Rights and Fundamental Freedoms,[25] Article 10 of which states that 'Everyone has the right to freedom of expression. This right

[20] However, in Article 128 of the EU treaty an explicit competence in the area of culture is dealt with and a protocol on Public Service Broadcasting is included in the Treaty of Amsterdam.

[21] Case 155/73, *Italy v Saachi* [1974] ECR 409.

[22] Case 62/79, *Coditel v Cine Vog Films* [1980] ECR 881.

[23] Case 52/79, *Procureur du roi v Debauve* [1980] ECR 833.

[24] Case 352/85, *Bond van Adverteerders (Dutch Advertisers' Association) and Ors v The State (Netherlands)*, [1988] ECR 2085.

[25] European Treaty Series (ETS), No 5.

shall include freedom to hold opinions and to receive and impart information and ideas without interference by public authority and regardless of frontiers.' As regards radio, there are two main treaties: the European Agreement for the Prevention of Broadcasts transmitted from Stations outside National Territories, and the European Convention relating to questions on Copyright Law and Neighbouring Rights in the Framework of Transfrontier Broadcasting by Satellite.[26] For television, the relevant treaties are the European Agreement concerning Programme Exchanges by means of Television Films; the European Agreement on the Protection of Television Broadcasts; the Third Additional Protocol to the Protocol to the European Agreement on the Protection of Television Broadcasts; and the European Convention on Transfrontier Television.[27] An important aspect of this Treaty are the Opinions and Recommendation (one so far) which are adopted by the Standing Committee on Transfrontier Television (T-TT).[28] The Opinions cover the time frame for the broadcasting of cinematographic works co-produced by the broadcaster; the notion of 'retransmission'; the notion of 'broadcaster'; certain provisions relating to advertising and sponsorship; the freedom of reception and retransmission; the legal framework for 'infomercials'; and the application of the Convention to advertising transmitted via teletext services. The Recommendation is on the use of virtual images in news and current affairs programmes.

Reference has already been made to the significance and role of Article 10 of the European Convention on Human Rights and Fundamental Freedoms as an element of European media law.[29] As Voorhoof notes,[30] 'Over the years and especially since 1990, a substantial body of case law has been established by the European Court with regard to Article 10 ECHR.[31] In the legal order of the Council of Europe and its Member States, media law (whether the traditional printed press or cinematographic films), broadcasting regulations and rules on journalistic freedoms are [to be] developed and applied on this basis and within this framework . . .'

---

[26] ETS Nos 53, 153.

[27] ETS Nos 27, 34, 131, and 132.

[28] T-TT (97) Inf 1 (Council of Europe).

[29] See, Janis, M, Kay, R and Bradley, A, *European Human Rights Law* (Oxford: Clarendon Press, 1995), especially ch 6, 'Freedom of Expression' and the survey in *IRIS 1995: Legal developments in the Audio-visual Sector*, 'Article 10 of the European Convention on Human Rights: the Foundation of media law in the Council of Europe and its Member States', (Strasbourg: European Audiovisual Observatory, 1995).

[30] See *IRIS 1995*, ibid, 'Article 10 of the European Convention on Human Rights: the Foundation of media law in the Council of Europe and its Member States'; a fuller version can be found in Voorhoof, D, *Critical Perspectives on the Scope and Interpretation of Article 10 of the European Convention on Human Rights* (Strasbourg: Council of Europe, Mass Media Files No 10, 1995).

[31] See 'Case-Law Concerning Article 10 of the ECHR' (n 15 above).

Of persuasive moral-political influence are Declarations of the Committee of Ministers, for example the already mentioned fundamental European Declaration on Freedom of Expression and Information (1982), and Recommendations. A number of the latter concern the media and communications, for example on sound and audio-visual piracy; media transparency; television advertising; the legal protection of encrypted television services; protection of rightsholders; exclusive rights for the broadcasting of major events; the production, marketing, and distribution of European audio-visual works; and the distribution of videograms of a violent, brutal, or pornographic nature. During October 1997 the Committee of Ministers adopted three further Recommendations on the portrayal of violence in the electronic media (Recommendation R(97)19); 'hate speech' (Recommendation R(97) 20); and the media and the promotion of a culture of tolerance (Recommendation R(97)21).

3 THE SINGLE EUROPEAN MARKET, HARMONISATION, AND THE MEDIA

The harmonisation of laws is a method by which the objectives of the Community can be achieved. Directives and regulations serve as tools to enhance and support the fundamental pillars of the Community: the free movement of goods, persons, services, and capital and the creation of a Single European Market. Therefore, the harmonisation of national rules on media, broadcasting, and telecommunications by directives serves mainly internal market objectives, since the actions undertaken within the European Community are determined by those fundamental principles. Moreover, one of the rationales behind European communications policy is based upon the lowering of market barriers within Europe, so that European commercial interests will benefit from expanded markets and the economies of scale they bring.[32] The latter was, and remains, one of the main advantages of US producers which enables them to offer developed products on world markets at 'bargain basement prices'. Therefore, DG III, responsible initially for the internal market, staked much on the promise that, once legal barriers were removed, European Member States would satisfy their escalating demand for programmes by increases in European production and intra-European exchanges, rather than by increasing dependence on US imports.

---

[32] Humphreys, PJ, *Mass media and media policy in Western Europe* (Manchester: Manchester University Press, 1996), 257–96.

General telecommunications policy[33]

In the 1987 Green Paper on the development of the common market for telecommunications services and equipment,[34] the Commission proposed the introduction of more competition in the telecommunications market combined with a greater degree of harmonisation in order to enjoy to a maximum extent the opportunities offered by a single EC market, in particular in terms of economies of scale. The Green Paper proposals received broad general support from the market actors and the Commission prepared a programme of action which was supported by Council[35] and the European Parliament, as well as by the Economic and Social Committee. This programme included the following actions:

- rapid full opening of the terminal equipment market to competition (section III.A.1);
- full mutual recognition of type-approval for terminal equipment (section III.H);
- progressive opening of telecommunications markets to competition (section III.A);
- clear separation of regulatory and operational activities in the Member States to conform with the EC Treaty competition rules (section III.A.2);
- establishment of open access conditions to networks and services through the Open Network Provision (ONP) programme (section III.B);
- establishment of the European Telecommunications Standards Institute (ETSI), in order to stimulate European standardisation (which happened in 1988);
- full application of Community competition rules to the sector (section II.C).

These actions have subsequently been implemented to a large extent through the adoption of a series of legislative measures. The common theme of the policy mix which has emerged is the evolving balance to be struck between liberalisation and harmonisation, competition and public service. This balance has resulted from the commonly called 1989

---

[33] For a comprehensive and detailed description see 'Status Report On European Union Telecommunications Policy', Brussels, 7 May 1997, DGXIII/A/1, and for a good general account Hunt, A, 'Regulation of Telecommunications: the Developing EU Regulatory Framework and its Impact on the United Kingdom', [1997] 3 *European Public Law*, 93–115.

[34] 'Towards a dynamic European economy: Green Paper on the development of the common market for telecommunications services and equipment', COM(87) 290 final, 30 June 1987.

[35] Council Resolution of 30 June 1988 on the development of the common market for telecommunications services and equipment up to 1992 (88/C 257/01; OJ C257/1, Oct 1988).

'compromise' reached between the EC institutions, and was firstly reflected by the joint adoption in 1990 of two Directives introducing competition in the telecommunications services market (notably for value-added services and data networks[36]) and establishing a framework for harmonisation at Community level[37] (see sections III.A.2 and III.B.1). In terms of practical results, the most important is that Member States must fully liberalise public voice telephony by 1 January 1998.[38]

Audio-visual policy

As distinct from telecommunications as a point-to-point communication, audio-visual media are defined within the European Community as mass media in the sense of point-to-multipoint communication. Although the border between both fields is beginning to shift, the mass media have so far been a separate field of legislative activities. Responsibility for policy, as described above, in this area belongs to DG X, the Directorate General for Information, Communication, Culture and Audio-visual. The development of an audio-visual policy by the European Union has a twofold objective: to establish and ensure the functioning of a true European space for audio-visual services, and to contribute to developing a strong, forward-looking programme industry that can compete on world markets and help European culture to flourish and create jobs in Europe.[39] Two major regulatory instruments are used: support systems for the audio-visual industry, and legal norms.

Support systems for the audio-visual industry

Anxious to promote a stronger and more competitive audio-visual industry and to support mechanisms which complement Member States' actions in this field, the EC has devised a strategy based on encouraging training for professionals, supporting the production and distribution of European audio-visual works, and ensuring that there are no internal frontiers within the Union to the distribution of broadcasts from within any Member State. The MEDIA[40] programme is the major initiative which

[36] Commission Directive of 16 May 1988 on competition in the markets in telecommunications equipment (88/301/EEC; OJ L131/73, 27 May 1988).

[37] Council Directive of 28 June 1990 on the establishment of the internal market for telecommunications services through the implementation of open network provision (90/387/EEC; OJ L192/1, 24 July 1990).

[38] Directive 96/16/EC, [1996] OJ L74/13; certain States may benefit from derogations for a limited period.

[39] In addition to these objectives, the Commission monitors closely the emergence and development of new audio-visual and information services, with emphasis on their impact on job creation, communication and fundamental rights.

[40] *Mesures d'encouragement pour le Dévelopement de l'Industrie Audiovisuelle.*

provides and streamlines funding and other support to develop the European audio-visual industry. From the beginning of 1996, Media II will spend ECU 45 million over five years in support of training of audio-visual professionals, and ECU 265 million over five years on development, production, and distribution of audio-visual projects and products, supplemented by a European Guarantee Fund to mobilise investment in the programme industry. The Action Plan for the introduction of advanced television services in Europe has provided financial support to cover part of the additional cost involved in adjusting new and existing programmes technically for 16:9 format so extending the shelf-life of European catalogues. In addition, the free circulation of broadcasting services, as organised by the *Television Without Frontiers* Directive contributes, through the promotion of production and distribution of European works, to the reinforcement of the programme industry.

Legal norms

The Treaty contains a large number of articles relevant to the audio-visual policy including 9, 12, 30, and 31 (free movement of goods) and 48 to 66 (freedom of movement of workers, right of establishment, and freedom to provide services). In addition, article 127 provides for professional training projects, article 128 for promoting culture, and article 130 for industrial policy initiatives. Competition rules and common commercial policy also play a significant role in this sector. Finally, the Treaty of Amsterdam contains a new protocol on Public Service Broadcasting which aims at securing the right of Member States to continue funding such broadcasting.

The *Television Without Frontiers* Directive[41] implements the free circulation of services principle in broadcasting thus creating the basis of a true European audio-visual area. Adopted in 1989 and amended in 1997, this directive provides for a minimum set of common rules concerning advertising, protection of minors, events of major importance to the public (particularly sports), right of reply, and promotion of European works. Member States shall ensure that broadcasters under their jurisdiction respect those rules and refrain from any restriction on reception of broadcasts coming from other Member States.

Turning now briefly to the Council of Europe, the Council's Intergovernmental Action Plan states that the European Convention on Transfrontier Television[42] will, throughout 1997, remain the key reference point in this field of constant technological change. The Convention's standing committee has been particularly involved in monitoring the

---

[41] Council Directive (EEC) 89/552 of 3 Oct 1989, OJ L298, 17 Oct 1989.
[42] <http://www.coe.fr/eng/legaltxt/132e.htm>

progress of the revision of the EC *Television Without Frontiers* Directive, 'with a view to examining any amendments which should be made to the Convention in order to maintain a coherence between the two instruments'.

The Information Society

Since 1994, all the media and telecom related topics have been overshadowed by the 'information society'.[43] The idea is not new and has been heralded before by the European Community. It has received renewed attention under the influence of recent technological and market developments which lead towards the convergence of telecommunications, media, and information technology.

It was the White Paper on Growth, Competitiveness and Employment, published in 1993, which first emphasised the significance of the information society for the future of Europe. It linked the creation of a common European information infrastructure to the creation of new markets and jobs and to European economic growth and competitiveness. Following the proposals, the Council asked for a high-level group of experts to present a report on the information society which would suggest concrete measures for its implementation. The group, chaired by Commissioner Martin Bangemann, submitted its report to the European Council in Corfu in June 1994. It emphasised the urgency of Community action to ensure that European enterprises remain competitive internationally, and highlighted the need to speed up the process of liberalisation whilst, at the same time, consolidating universal service. The report also specified that financing information infrastructure should be left to the private sector, the task of the public sector being to assume an enabling and catalytic function. Therefore, a list of ten initiatives aimed at demonstrating the feasibility and usefulness of new telematic applications and a coherent statutory framework to avoid the circulation of information being impeded by different national regulations was proposed.

In 1994 the Commission presented a Communication, 'Europe's Way to the Information Society. An Action Plan'.[44] It constitutes a general framework within which actions in different fields relating to the information society must be structured and mutually consolidated. Since then four main lines of action have been followed, covering: adaptation of the statutory and legal framework (notably liberalisation of infrastructure); encouragement of initiatives in trans-European networks, services, appli-

---

[43] See Schoof, H and Watson Brown, A, 'Information Highways and media policies in the European Union', *Telecommunications Policy*, 1995, Vol 19, No 4, 325–38.
[44] COM (94) 347, 19 July 1994.

cations, and content; social and cultural issues; and promotion of the information society.[45]

The main policy objectives in the field of the so-called information society were updated and outlined in 1996 by the EC Communication 'Europe at the Forefront of the Global Information Society: Rolling Action Plan', in which four new priority areas were identified. Firstly, improving the business environment through the efficient and coherent implementation of the liberalised telecommunications environment, the thorough application of the internal market principles, and promoting the introduction of new technologies into daily business activities. Secondly, the Florence Summit gave impetus to the educational dimension of the information society strategy by asking the Commission to adopt an initiative, 'Learning in the information society', which now needs to be implemented. However, adapting educational structures and the learning process is mainly a responsibility of the Member States. Thirdly, for European businesses to keep abreast of the fast pace of global technology change often requires substantial investment at a relatively early stage of market development, and the Action Plan refers in particular to the Commission's Fifth Framework Programme which is partly devoted to the promoting of the development of a user-friendly information society. Finally, the Commission will establish a number of actions to address the key issues relating to the implications of the information society for the citizen. At the same time, the process of using the advantages of the information society in the context of regional policy to promote European cohesion will be addressed. Another important element in this context is the protection of fundamental rights and freedoms, such as the right to privacy, in the information society. While the initial Action Plan did not fully reflect the importance of global co-operation, it is now clear that setting global rules is an essential element of the information society. Global rules concern market access, intellectual property rights, privacy and data protection, harmful and illegal on-line content, tax issues, information security, frequencies, interoperability, and standards. In this context, Commissioner Bangemann launched a call to governments, regulators, and industry to work together to establish a new global framework for communications for the next millenium during speeches in Geneva[46] and Venice.[47]

Within the framework described above, there are more than 400

[45] For a complete overview of all the steps undertaken until 1 April 1996, see *Europe's Way to the Information Society, Update of the Action Plan, Status of 1st of April 1996*, at <http://www.ispo.cec.be/infosoc/legreg/actionla.html>

[46] See <http://www.ispo.cec.be/infosoc/promo/speech/geneva.html>

[47] See <http://www.ispo.cec.be/infosoc/promo/speech/venice.html>

forthcoming, accomplished, pending, and ongoing actions. In order to co-ordinate all those actions and the actions taken by its Member States, the Communication concerning regulatory transparency in the internal market for information society services[48] addresses the concern that the regulatory activity for which the ground is being prepared in the Member States might, if it is not monitored, jeopardise attainment of the Internal Market objective.[49] Re-fragmentation and overregulation are cited as possible consequences of the lack of transparency. The Commission proposes tackling this by such means as including a binding legal instrument, a prior information procedure, and a consultation procedure. A political agreement was reached on a Common Position concerning a subsequent Directive based on the proposal on 27 November 1997.[50]

Finally, on 3 December 1997, a long awaited Green Paper on the convergence of the telecommunications, media, and information technology (IT) sectors was published. The Green Paper launched a Europe-wide debate on how this new generation of electronic media should be regulated in the next century. It avoids pre-packaged answers but asks open questions about the future, particularly about the extent and speed of change. One key message is that convergence should not lead to additional regulation. Current rules should be reviewed to check whether they will still be relevant in the light of convergence.[51]

The EC has developed within the context of the newer communications services numerous funding and research programmes. Examples are the ACTS Programme (Advanced Communications Technologies and Services); RACE, a collaborative European research programme aimed at the introduction of Integrated Broadband Communication; ESPRIT, an initiative of DG III for technological support; the telematics application programme; INFO2000, a programme aiming to stimulate the European multimedia content industry and to encourage the use of multimedia content in the information society; Multilingual Information Society (MLIS), a programme promoting the linguistic diversity of the EU in the information society; and Trans-European Telecommunications Networks (TEN-TELECOM), a programme promoting implementation of the trans-European services and applications of the information society, based on the use of telecommunication infrastructures. Finally, the 5th Framework Programme (1998–2002) includes a user-friendly information society as one of its major themes.

---

[48] COM (96) 392 final, 30 Aug 1996.
[49] ibid, 23.
[50] See Press Release IP/97/1054, 28 Nov 1997.
[51] *Green Paper on the Convergence of Telecommunications, Media and Information Technologies*, Commission of the European Communities, COM (97) 623, 3 Dec 1997.

Turning once more to the Council of Europe, the 5th European Ministerial Conference on Mass Media Policy (December 1997) had as its general theme, 'The information society: a challenge for Europe'.[52] The sub-themes were (a) the impact of new communications technologies on human rights and democratic values[53] and (b) re-thinking the regulatory framework for the media.[54] The Final Communique concluded that it was necessary to: enhance the general public's awareness, and use, of new communications technologies; prevent 'misuse' of services; encourage 'self-regulation at European and International levels'; and emphasise the 'Universal Community Service' principle to prevent an unequal information society. Finally, the ministers undertook to monitor the implications for human rights of the emerging communications technologies and to adapt national regulatory regimes to the new technological developments.

4 TECHNOLOGICAL REGULATION

Infrastructure

Wired

The development of the Information Society depends upon an efficient and highly developed telecommunications network being in place, capable of carrying the full range of newer applications. The European Commission recognised in its 1992 telecommunications review[55] that this could not be obtained so long as Europe's telecom industry remained in the hands of state controlled monopolies. Therefore the ultimate goal of the EU's information society policy is the liberalisation of the telecommunications infrastructure and the development of a set of interconnected networks owned and operated by many different organisations, following a common set of conventions, seamlessly interworking, and giving the appearance of a single system. The general telecommunications policy has been described earlier, but it is worth discussing briefly two communications which started the process. First, the Green Paper on the 'Liberalisation of telecom infrastructure and cable TV networks: principles and timetable'[56] established the general principle of the free choice of infrastructure to deliver services already open to competition. It proposed immediate limited action and linked full competition to the 1998 date for services liberalisation. Second, the Green Paper on the 'Liberalisation of telecom infrastructure and cable TV networks: implementation

---

[52] MCM (97) 14.   [53] MCM (97) 1.   [54] MCM (97) 2 and MCM (97) 3.
[55] COM (93) 159.   [56] COM (94) 440, 17 Nov 1994.

measures'[57] launched a consultation on the issues raised by allowing competition in infrastructure for the basic telephone service and the relevant safeguards. It set out future policy on infrastructure liberalisation and initiated public debate on the issues. Both Green Papers were followed by numerous legal instruments, such as the Directive amending Commission Directive 90/388/EEC of 23 July 1990 regarding the abolition of the restrictions on the use of cable TV networks for the provision of telecom services.[58] This measure provided for the use of cable television networks to deliver such services from 1996. Finally in May 1997 the Communication on the implementation of the telecommunications regulatory package was issued.[59] The communication assessed the steps taken by Member States to implement the provisions of the 1998 telecommunications liberalisation package, including measures already adopted and those still pending at the time the report was finalised. Measures have also been taken to stimulate the building of the necessary infrastructure for the information society.

Wireless (mobile and satellite)

The mobile and satellite communications market is considered by the European Union as having a huge potential for growth and consequently for job creation. In order to capitalise fully on this potential the Commission has published communications and subsequently adopted several directives, liberalising the market.

A Communication on the further development of mobile and wireless communications was published on 29 May 1997.[60] It presents an overview of the developments in the mobile and wireless markets within the EU and seeks to contribute to the debate on the future evolution of mobile communications towards a Universal Mobile Telecommunications System (UMTS) as a key component of the 'wireless information society'. The Directive amending Commission Directive 90/388/EEC of 23 July 1990 regarding mobile and personal communications[61] already requires the Member States to abolish exclusive and special rights granted to incumbent operators in the area of mobile communications, and to establish licensing procedures for new entrants to the market. The measure fully opens the market for mobile communications to competition as foreseen in the 1994 Mobile Green Paper. It provides for self-provision of infrastructure or use of third party infrastructure and from 1998 allows direct interconnection between mobile networks.

---

[57] COM (94) 682, 13 June 1995.   [58] Directive 95/51/EC, OJ L256/49.
[59] COM (97) 236, 29 May 1997.   [60] COM (97) 217, 29 May 1997.
[61] Directive 96/2/EC, OJ L20, 26 Jan 1996.

In the satellite field,[62] the Community adopted several directives to foster a harmonised and liberalised market. The 1988 Terminal Equipment Directive required Member States to eliminate the licensing of consumer reception antennae. The 1994 Satellite Services Directive[63] provided for an open market in the use of satellite telecommunications facilities, including uplink stations used to transport broadcast signals.[64] Finally, the April 1997 Licensing Directive was adopted to provide a common structure for licensing all telecommunications facilities, again including satellite facilities and services, but not the activity of providing broadcast programming to consumers, which is regulated in the *Television Without Frontiers* Directive.

It is important to underline that the European Community considers a strong and coherent satellite communications industry and services sector to be of high economic and political importance. Therefore the Commission decided in a recent Communication[65] on Satellite Communication to take a more proactive and consistent approach in this area. It aims to focus the European industrial potential on the new generation of global satellite systems, advanced services, and innovative applications which meet key user requirements in the global information society; namely, personal mobility, fast response times, global connectivity, and access to the broadband evolution of the Internet.

Standardisation

Standards determine the technology that will implement the information society and, consequently, the way in which industry, users, consumers, and administrations will benefit from it. This formed the underlying rationale for several communications on the issues; for example, the July 1996 Communication on 'Standardisation and the Global Information Society: The European Approach'.[66] At the time of writing a Communication on a European standardisation initiative for electronic commerce is also expected, which will analyse Europe's position in standardisation for electronic commerce, identify technical barriers to electronic commerce services, and submit proposals on the dissemination of standards. Finally, the role of public authorities in the standardisation process for

[62] See White, S, Bate, S and Johnson, T, *Satellite Communications in Europe: Law and Regulation* (London: FT Law & Tax, 1996).
[63] Directive 94/46/EC.
[64] For a comprehensive overview see Le Goueff, S, *Satellite Services: The European Regulatory Framework*, 5 June 1996, <http://www2.echo.lu/LAB>
[65] Communication on EU Action Plan on Satellite Communications in the Information Society, COM (97) 91 final.
[66] COM (96) 359.

electronic commerce will be elaborated. The Directive on the use of TV-standards[67] is one of the main legal steps in the area of standardisation of the newer communications. The Directive provides a regulatory framework for advanced TV (16:9, digital, HDTV), including standards, and deals with the issue of conditional access to digital pay-television, following the outcome of an industry-wide consultation (within the Digital Video Broadcasting group[68]) on this topic.

The Commission launched at the end of 1995 a set of six projects addressing market needs in a number of domains and intended to provide contributions to the work of standardsation bodies, drawing on the active participation of industrial manufacturers and users. They are called ISIS—Information Society Initiatives in support of Standardisation. The objective of the action is, by means of 50 per cent co-funded, multinational-consortium-based projects, to support work of an application, validation, or demonstration nature focused on the standards—or contributions to potential new standards—underpinning information society related domains of high economic and social impact. Special attention is paid to identifying user requirements for standards and/or acceptance of new draft standards, as well as contributing to interoperability and validation of critical interfaces necessary for the proper interworking of services and applications.

5 ECONOMIC REGULATION

Market structure

Interconnection of competing systems and open network provision

The issue of interconnection is considered crucial for the development of the Information Society. In 1995 the Commission presented a proposal[69] applying the Open Network Principles (see below) to interconnection and interoperability. This proposal aimed to ensure open access to networks and services, and to guarantee the rights of new market entrants to obtain interconnection, with infrastructure belonging to other operators. The Draft Communication on the application of the competition rules to access agreements in the telecommunications sector,[70] published in December 1996, aimed to clarify the role competition rules will play in resolving access agreements in the telecoms sector. It does not establish new princi-

---

[67] Directive 95/47/EC, OJ L281/5, 23 Nov 1995.

[68] DVB is a consortium of more than 140 European manufacturers, broadcasters, and programme makers.

[69] OJ C237, Sept 1995.

[70] COM (96) 649, OJ C76.

ples of competition law, but demonstrates how the principles existing in current case law of the Commission and of the Court of Justice will be applied to a new type of problem occurring in the context of the liberalisation of the telecoms sector. It sets out access principles stemming from EU competition law, defines and clarifies the relationship between competition law and sector specific legislation, and explains how competition rules will be applied in a consistent way across the converging sectors involved in the provision of new multimedia services, especially to access issues and gateways.

Perhaps even more important was the Council decision on the multilateral negotiations on basic telecommunications services in the context of the World Trade Organisation (WTO), adopted 15 July 1997. The agreement, to enter into force on 1 January 1998, was signed by sixty-nine countries on 15 February 1997. It commits all signatories to important measures, in particular most-favoured nation (MFN) treatment which bans discriminatory measures on a bilateral basis, as well as legally binding commitments regarding market access and national treatment. In addition, fifty-four countries agreed on a common set of regulatory principles aimed at securing more effective access and national treatment, in particular transparency, fairness, and non-discrimination in key areas such as interconnection, licensing, tariffs, universal service provisions, technical standards, and frequencies. This also includes a ban on anti-competitive practices such as cross-subsidising and disguised barriers to market access. The Commission negotiated on behalf of the European Union and its Member States.

The initial Community reforms in the telecom sector only involved the liberalisation of services, not infrastructure. However, the Community admitted that service liberalisation alone would not be sufficient to attract new entrants and stimulate competition. Therefore, it adopted parallel 'harmonisation' measures, to ensure open and efficient access to networks and services. The concept of Open Network Provision (ONP) was first presented in a Green Paper in 1987.[71] In 1990 the Community adopted an ONP Framework Directive[72] which established general principles relating to the provision and use of networks and services, tariff principles, and technical interfaces of network connections. This was followed by a series of measures implementing ONP. In December 1995 the Directive on the application of ONP (Open Network Provision) to voice telephony[73] was adopted. Its three fundamental objectives are:

- determining the rights of the users of voice telephony services in their relations with telecommunications bodies

---

[71] COM (87) 290, June 1987.   [72] Directive 90/387/EEC, OJ L192, 24 July 1990.
[73] Directive 95/62/EC, OJ L321/6.

- improving access for all users, including the providers of services, to the fixed infrastructure of public telephone networks (the Directive does not apply to mobile telephones)
- encouraging the provision of voice telephony services at Community level.

Concentration and media ownership

The emergence of large media companies and increased economic pressures have led to increased media concentrations and cross-ownership.[74] A certain degree of strength through size may well be desirable in some respects, but there is also a danger that further vertical and horizontal integration will force out competitors and lead to a lack of pluralism. The device used so far to try to counteract these forces has been competition law.[75] Articles 85, 86, and 90 of the EC Treaty provide a basis for action to eliminate anti-competitive behaviour. Article 85 is concerned with agreements that prevent, restrict, or distort competition, while Article 86 prohibits abuse of dominant position in the market. Both Articles are applied to the public sector by Article 90. Since the Merger Regulation (1989)[76] DG IV has powers to vet (and to block) certain mergers. For instance, the Dutch TV joint venture Holland Media Group (a venture between RTL 4, Veronica, and Endemol) was blocked.[77] The Commission concluded in this case that the HMG joint venture would lead to the creation of a dominant position on the Dutch market in TV advertising and would strengthen Endemol's already existing dominant position on the TV production market in the Netherlands.

However, since the late 1980s concerns have been expressed within the Community that competition policy fails to control media concentrations due to problems of market definition and issues of pluralism. Even DG IV identified the media sector as one which may require specific legislation.[78] At the end of 1992 the European Commission published a Green Paper[79] which analysed the issue of concentration in the media

---

[74] For a detailed description see Sanchez-Taberno, A, *Media Concentration in Europe. Commercial Enterprise and the Public Interest* (Dusseldorf: European Institute for the Media, 1993, Media Monograph No 16).

[75] For a discussion on the role of competition policy in the regulation of (new) media concentrations see Goldberg, D, Prosser, T and Verhulst, S, *The Impact of New Communications Technologies on Media Concentrations and Pluralism* (Strasbourg: Council of Europe, MM-CM (96) 3 1997), 60–6.

[76] Council Regulation (EEC) 4064/89 on the control of concentrations between undertakings, OJ 1989 L395/1.

[77] Decision of the European Commission in *Holland Media Groep (HMG)* (Case IV/M.553), 20 Sept 1995.

[78] See Harcourt, AJ, 'Regulating for Media Concentration: the Emerging Policy of the European Union', *Utilities Law Review*, Vol 7, Oct 1996, 202–10.

[79] Pluralism and Media Concentration in the Internal Market: An Assessment of the Need for Community Action, COM (92) 480 final, 23 Dec 1992.

and the need for action, and suggested possible courses of action.[80]
The Green Paper launched a wide consultation process, which culminated
in the 1994 follow-up Commission Communication,[81] and the Commissioner promised a proposal for a Directive by early 1996.[82] He also indicated at a meeting of the European Parliament's Committee on culture,
youth, and sports in September 1995, that he was in favour of harmonising
national media ownership rules.[83] However, an agreement on the proposal to be contained in a draft Directive has still not been reached; it is
expected that a proposal would use the UK and Germany as regulatory
models.

The problem of media and cross-media ownership, the appropriate
regulatory responses of Member States, and the implications for media
pluralism and diversity of opinion has also been of concern within the
Council of Europe for many years. The special committee of experts on
media concentrations and pluralism is considering a report on the impact
of new technologies on media ownership and pluralism with a view to
making recommendations for issues which could be the subject of policy
or legal instruments. In the field of television broadcasting, the Court has
struck down Austria's public monopoly, arguing that 'the far-reaching
character of the restrictions which a public monopoly imposes on freedom
of expression means that they can only be justified if they correspond to a
pressing need'.[84] Recommendation R(94)13 was adopted to propose strategies for guaranteeing transparency in the ownership of media organisations.

Licensing and spectrum allocation

With regard to licensing, the directive on a common framework for general authorisations and individual licences in the field of telecommunication services was adopted in April 1997.[85] The directive lays down
common rules to be applied by Member States as regards the procedures
and conditions for providing telecoms services. This is an essential feature
of the regulatory framework to be introduced at EU level with a view to
a fully liberalised sector from 1998. It will facilitate freedom to provide

[80] Option one was that no specific action should be taken at Community level; Option two
proposed co-operative action to ensure greater transparency of media ownership and control; Option three proposed to eliminate differences (harmonisation) between national
restrictions on media ownership. For an overview of the responses, see Hitchens, LP, 'Media
Ownership and Control: A European Approach', (1994) 57 MLR, 585–601.
[81] *Follow up of the Green Paper Pluralism and Media Concentration in the Internal Market: An
Assessment of the Need for Community Action*, COM (94) 353 final, Oct 1994.
[82] Several other deadlines were promised, but the Commission failed each time to reach
them. See <http://europa.eu.int/en/comm/dg15/pluralis.html>
[83] See *IRIS*, Oct 1995, Vol I, No 9, 12.
[84] DH (97) 6, para 49.
[85] OJ L117.

telecom services in the EU and the entry of new operators into the market, and must be implemented by Member States by 1 January 1998.

Licensing TV services still takes place on a country-by-country basis and depends upon the licensing regime of the Member State. However the primary objective of the *Television Without Frontiers* Directive is to harmonise and liberalise the provision of broadcast signals across European boundaries. Several decisions of the European Court of Justice have made clear that this directive requires each Member State to regulate and license broadcasts from its territory. A problem in the past was the determination of jurisdiction for licensing. The revised directive explains more clearly under which Member State's jurisdiction television broadcasters fall; the place of establishment, which is determined mainly by where their central administration is located and where management decisions concerning programming are taken, is used as the basis of jurisdiction.

The European Radiocommunications Office (ERO) is the permanent body for European spectrum management. The functions of the ERO are defined in the ERO Convention and include a role in the long-term planning of the radio spectrum, liaison with national frequency management authorities, co-ordination of research studies, and consultation with interested parties on specific topics or parts of the frequency spectrum. In addition the ERO assists the European Radiocommunications Committee (ERC) in carrying out its numerous activities. The ERC is one of three committees that form the European Conference of Postal and Telecommunications Administrations (CEPT), the regional regulatory telecommunication organisation for Europe. As of 1 January 1996, forty-three European countries were members of the CEPT. The ERC is concerned with the development of policy on radiocommunications issues, which includes the co-ordination of frequencies, and administrative and technical matters relating to the regulation of radio in Europe. The ERC is also responsible for preparing the European proposals and positions for conferences of the International Telecommunication Union (ITU) dealing with radiocommunications.

In the Council of Europe, Article 10(1), paragraph 2 of the European Convention on Human Rights expressly legitimises states' requiring the licensing of broadcasting, television, or cinema enterprises. However, the Commission on Human Rights has stated that '. . . a licensing system not respecting the requirements of pluralism, tolerance and broadmindedness without which there is no democratic society would thereby infringe Article 10 paragraph 1 . . .'[86] In 1965, the European Agreement for the Prevention of Broadcasts Transmitted From Stations Outside National

---

[86] *Verein Aslternatives Lokalradio Bern and Verein Radio Dreyeckland Basel v Switzerland*, DR 49, 126.

Territories was opened for signature, whereby States agree to make it a punishable offence to establish, operate, or support broadcasting stations which 'are installed or maintained on board ships, aircraft, or any other floating or airborne objects and which, outside national territories, transmit broadcasts intended for reception or capable of being received, wholly or in part, within the territory of any Contracting Party, or which cause harmful interference to any radio-communication service operating under the authority of a Contracting Party in accordance with the Radio Regulations.'[87]

6 REMUNERATION AND FINANCE

Intellectual property

With the development of the information society, a coherent regulatory framework at national, Community, and international level is required to address the impact that new technologies will have on copyright and related rights. Five copyright directives and a Green Paper have so far emerged.

One of the first Directives relevant to the media, was adopted by the European Community Council in November 1992.[88] It provides exclusive rental rights and a non-transferable right of reasonable compensation in favour of the author, performing artists, phonogram, and first film recording producers, along with some conditions of ownership. In October 1993 a Directive[89] was published whose aim was the harmonisation of the term of protection of copyright. A month later, the Council adopted the so-called 'Satellite and Cable Directive',[90] regulating the rebroadcasting of television programmes. Finally, in 1996 a Directive providing copyright protection on the computerised and manual databases was approved.[91] The Directive creates a new exclusive 'sui generis' right (which will last fifteen years after completion) for database creators and harmonises copyright law applicable to structures of databases. Along with the Green Paper on Copyright and Related Rights in the Information Society,[92] the

[87] Art 1.
[88] Council Directive of 19 Nov 1992 on rental and lending rights related to copyright in the field of intellectual property. OJ L346, 27 Nov 1992.
[89] Council Directive of 29 Oct 1993 harmonising the term of protection of copyright and certain related rights. OJ L290, 24 Nov 1993.
[90] Council Directive of 27 Sept 1993 on the co-ordination of certain rules concerning copyright and rights related to copyright applicable to satellite broadcasting and cable retransmission. OJ L248, 6 Oct 1993.
[91] Directive 96/9/EC of 11 Mar 1996 concerning the legal protection of databases. OJ L77: 20.
[92] COM (95) 382, 19 July 1995.

Directive is particularly important for the creation of new communications services. The Green Paper, published in July 1995, identifies in detail those issues in the field of copyright where initiatives may be needed with respect to the IPRs exploited for the new electronic services. After consultation, a Communication on the follow-up to the Green Paper on Copyright and Related Rights in the Information Society was published on 20 November 1996 announcing the Commission's internal market policy in the area of copyrights and related rights in the information society. In July 1997 the Council Decision[93] was adopted on the WIPO Copyrights Treaty and the WIPO Performances and Phonograms Treaty. Some months earlier the WIPO Diplomatic Conference in Geneva had adopted two new treaties on the protection of literary and artistic works, and on the protection of the rights of performers and producers of phonograms; these had been adopted by the Council on behalf of the Union. The two treaties provide for appropriate international response to the challenges facing intellectual property protection in the digital age. In December 1997, a proposal for a Directive harmonising aspects of rules on copyright and related rights in the Information Society has been presented by the European Commission which reflects consultations based on the 1995 Green Paper and international developments in this area.[94]

As regards the Council of Europe, the European Convention Relating to Questions on Copyright Law and Neighbouring Rights in the Framework of Transfrontier Broadcasting by Satellite (1994) covers the use of satellites to transmit radio and television programmes for the general public by means of dish aerials. It defines clear criteria for identifying the territory where broadcasting takes place, in order to pinpoint the applicable law for the clearance of rights. Building on existing international conventions, it also establishes a minimum harmonisation of the level of protection of the various categories of rights holders (authors, composers, audio-visual producers, performers, phonogram producers, and broadcasters). The aim of the Convention is to avoid differences in legal systems which could prejudice artistic creativity and expression.[95]

Commercial communications

The phrase 'commercial communication' is Euro-speak for advertising, direct marketing, public relations, and sales promotions, and is one of the less-known but none the less vital topics in this field given the reliance by

---

[93] COM (97) 193.
[94] <http://europa.eu.int/comm/dg15/en/intprop/intprop/1100.htm>
[95] For further arrangements in relation to television see the European Agreement on the Protection of Television Broadcasts (1960) and the Third Additional Protocol to the Protocol to the European Agreement on the Protection of Television Broadcasts (1989).

most audio-visual media and newer services on income generated by these activities for their existence. The future regulatory framework is set out in the Commission's Green Paper on Commercial Communications.[96] This will be relevant for transfrontier broadcasting and new information services, for example on-line services. The Commission acknowledges that national restrictions may be justifiable on public health and consumer protection grounds. A communication on an internal market framework for commercial communications based on home country control and mutual recognition is expected by the end of 1997. This Communication will be a follow-up to the consultations held in the framework of the Green Paper. Television advertising is regulated by the *Television Without Frontiers* Directive (see above).

For the Council of Europe, Chapter III ('Advertising') of the European Convention on Transfrontier Television deals with the issues of general standards and duration, form and presentation, insertion and advertising of particular products as well as advertising directed specifically at a single party. The general principle adopted by the Commission and Court on Human Rights is that commercial speech is not outwith the protection of Article 10, although there are dicta to the effect that the strictness of its protection is less than for political speech. Of course, as with most rights, there are circumstances where banning it would not be a breach of the applicant's right of freedom of expression.

Electronic commerce

The Communication on a European Initiative on Electronic Commerce[97] identifies four key areas where action must be taken by the year 2000: affordable access to infrastructure, products, and services; a coherent regulatory structure at EU level; a favourable business environment; a compatible and coherent regulatory framework at global level. The Communication complements issues already dealt with in the Directive on Distance Selling.[98] The latter clearly applies to sales concluded over the Internet, applying generally to contracts which are concluded 'without the simultaneous physical presence of the supplier and the consumer' by means of 'communication at a distance', expressly including communication by email. The main provisions of the Directive are to the effect that 'in good time, prior to the conclusion of any distance contract', the consumer must be provided with information including the identity of the supplier, delivery costs, the main characteristics of the goods and services, the

[96] COM (96) 192 final. See also: <http://www.cec.lu/en/record/green/gp006/en/index.html>
[97] COM (97) 157, 16 Apr 1997.
[98] Directive 97/7EC, OJ L144/19, 4 June 1997.

period for which the supplier's prices remain valid and, most importantly, the customer must be alerted to the fact that he/she has a right to withdraw from the contract. This must be provided 'in writing or another durable medium' at some point during the contractual process. The Directive will have a major impact on doing business over the Internet.

Financing

On pricing of the newer services the Directive on the legal protection of conditional access services is of considerable importance. The Directive was adopted in July 1997 by the Commission as a follow-up to the Green Paper on the legal protection of encrypted services adopted on 6 March 1996 and the EP Resolution of 13 May 1997.[99] It addresses the legal protection of TV and radio broadcasting and information society services offered to the public at a distance where access is subject to payment. Such services include pay-TV, video-on-demand, music-on-demand, electronic publishing, etc.

7 SOCIAL REGULATION

Content regulation

Two major actions have been undertaken by the Commission dealing with content and the newer services. Firstly, a Communication on harmful and illegal content on the Internet was issued in November 1996.[100] The Communication refers to the legal and regulatory challenges posed by content circulating on the Internet, giving particular emphasis to the issue of harmful and illegal content. It proposes options for short term action to combat or control such content, such as self-regulation, technical protection, improved international co-operation, education, and awareness. Secondly, the Green Paper on the Protection of Minors and Human Dignity in Audio-visual and Information Services initiated a medium to long term reflection on these issues.[101] Following consultations on these communications, the European Commission has firstly adopted an Action Plan[102] for 1998 to 2001 on promoting the safe use of the Internet which identifies key areas where measures are needed and could be supported by the European Union. This concerns in particular a hot-line on which Internet users could report apparently illegal content, industry-led self-regulation,

---

[99] <http://www2.echo.lu/legal/en/converge/condaccess.html>
[100] COM (96) 487.
[101] COM (96) 483.
[102] <http://www2.echo.lu/legal/en/internet/actplan.html>

content-monitoring schemes, internationally compatible and inter-operable rating, and filtering systems. Secondly, the Commission also adopted a draft Council Recommendation on the protection of minors and of human dignity in audiovisual services. The underlying idea is that self-regulation schemes at national level are the most appropriate answer as regards both television and the Internet.

Council of Europe Recommendations have been adopted on the following topics: distribution of videograms of a violent, brutal, or pornographic nature; violence in the electronic media; promoting a culture of tolerance through the media; and hate speech. The Court has considered cases dealing with issues such as defamation,[103] blasphemy, and obscenity. As regards the political process, the Parliamentary Assembly adopted Resolution 1120 (1997),[104] on the impact of the new communication and information technologies on democracy. An attempt is being made to understand and avoid the risks to democracy posed by the NCITs ('a reduction in political choice, the manipulation of consciences, the commercialisation and fragmentation of political messages, a surfeit of opinion polls, the marginalisation of parliamentary procedures, social discrimination, the monitoring of citizens and the danger of an instantaneous but devalued form of democracy') whilst rising to the challenge of the opportunity NCITs represent: 'developing interactivity as a remedy for the passiveness characterising those who merely observe events. The NCITs provide an opportunity to create a new type of two-way communication and develop a new concept, "electronic citizenship".' The competent committees may now take steps to draw up a European code of electronic commerce and distinguish between the law on information and the law on the means to convey it.[105]

User protection

Security

The Green Paper on the legal protection of encrypted services[106] (which was followed by the Directive on conditional access (see above)) aimed to identify, in the light of the Internal Market principles, the measures needed to safeguard the legal protection of encrypted services at an equal level throughout the Community. It was closely related to IPR protection

---

[103] <http://www.dhcour.coe.fr/eng/PRESS/EJUNE.97.html#>
JUDGMENT IN THE CASE OF OBERSCHLICK (no. 2) v AUSTRIA; <http://www.dhcour.coe.fr/eng/WINGROVE.html>
[104] <http://www.coe.fr/cm/d97/s3.a1.html>
[105] ORDER No. 531 (1997) on the impact of the new communication and information technologies on democracy <http://stars.coe.fr/ta/ta97/edir0531.htm>
[106] COM (96) 76.

(see above), to media policy, and to the Directive on satellite and cable broadcasting of 1993. A Communication on secure transactions was published in 1997, including digital signatures in electronic commerce initiatives in order to set the necessary frame for commercial transactions via the networks.[107]

Privacy

The Directive on the protection of individuals with regard to the processing of personal data and on the free movement of such data, adopted in November 1995, is the major measure in this field.[108] The Directive provides for a number of rights for the data subject, and of obligations on the controller of data processing (fair processing, quality of data, lawfulness of processing, notification of certain processing), and is designed to ensure a high level of protection for individuals, whilst creating a level playing field for the free circulation of personal data in the Community. The principles of the Directive apply to all areas of the information society and will constitute the basis for specific rules in the telecommunications field. A Directive concerning the processing of personal data and the protection of privacy in the telecommunications sector—in particular in the Integrated Services Digital Networks and in the public digital mobile networks—was expected to be adopted soon at the time of writing.

The Council of Europe was a pioneer in drawing up a Convention prescribing the confidentiality of data concerning persons which was processed automatically: the Convention for the Protection of Individuals with regard to Automatic Processing of Personal Data.[109] Other relevant Resolutions in the field concern protection of the privacy of individuals *vis-à-vis* electronic data and the protection of personal data in the area of telecommunication services. An important contribution was the 1989 study prepared by the Committee of Experts on Data Protection (for the European Committee on Legal Co-operation) on 'New Technologies: a Challenge to Privacy Protection?' which focuses specifically on telemetry, interactive media, and electronic mail systems.[110] The European Court ruled unanimously in a case brought by a police officer that there had been violations of Articles 8 and 13 of the European Convention on Human Rights in respect of the officer's complaints that telephone calls made from her office in Merseyside Police Headquarters had been intercepted and that she had not had available to her any effective remedy for this complaint.[111]

[107] The document is available on-line: <http://www.ispo.cec.be/eif/policy/>
[108] Directive 95/46/EC, OJ L281/31, 23 Nov 1995.
[109] ETS No 108.
[110] Council of Europe. Strasbourg. 1989.
[111] *Halford v The United Kingdom*, <http://www.dhcour.coe.fr/eng/PRESS/EJUNE.97.html#>

Universal service

It is generally accepted at a European level that in a liberalised telecommunications market, all citizens should be able to access a minimum level of service at an affordable cost. This principle of universal service was set out in the Communication on Universal Service in Telecommunications adopted in March 1996.[112] Building on the consensus established around the infrastructure Green Paper, the Commission presented a survey of the level and availability of universal service within the EU. It also drew together the elements of the 1998 package relating to universal service to propose a strengthening of the concept for voice telephony services, in particular with regard to affordability and quality of service. It also examined the impact of universal service on regional and social cohesion, criteria for its evolution over time, and the relationship between universal service and the information society. The latter was followed in November 1996 by the Communication on the assessment criteria for national schemes for the costing and financing of universal service and guidelines for the Member States on the operation of such schemes.[113] In order to assist Member States in preparing national reforms in advance of full liberalisation of telecoms in 1998, this Communication identifies the principal elements that the Commission will assess in looking at national universal service schemes which must be notified to the Commission by the end of 1996. It also provides detailed guidelines, building on the existing principles within Community law, which are designed to develop best practice in national approaches to the costing and financing of universal service.

The Directive on interconnection in the context of ONP and universal service, published in June 1997 provides not only a common framework for interconnection between the organisations operating public telecommunications networks in order to ensure 'any to any' services throughout the Community, but it also sets principles for the costing and financing of universal service. Finally the Directive on the application of open network provision (ONP) to voice telephony and on universal service for telecommunications in a competitive environment revises and replaces the existing Directive on the application of ONP to voice telephony (see above). It describes the scope of universal service for telecommunications which must be available to all users in the EU and requires Member States to ensure that this service is affordable, taking into account national situations. The Directive also sets out harmonised conditions for the provision of fixed public telephone networks and publicly available telephone services in the EU.

In its Recommendation on the independence of public service

---

[112] COM (96) 73.   [113] COM (96) 608.

broadcasting,[114] the Council of Europe has reaffirmed 'the vital role of public service broadcasting as an essential factor of pluralistic communication which is accessible to everyone at both national and regional levels, through the provision of a basic comprehensive programme service comprising information, education, culture and entertainment'.

8 CONCLUSIONS

There has clearly been a massive amount of action by the European Institutions, both those of the European Community and those of the Council of Europe. The latter has succeeded to a considerable degree in setting out some basic principles relating to such issues as freedom of expression and privacy; indeed, the Council and the Court of Human Rights have played a similar role to that of constitutional courts in some of the national jurisdictions. The issues addressed at the 5th Ministerial Conference show that the Council is aware of, and is trying to bring to bear on the NCTs, the same principles that it has already applied to the more traditional media and means of communications.[115] At the Community level, there is a lack of coherence in the overall picture; as we noted earlier, different DGs have markedly different approaches and the mass of activity described falls some way short of a clear strategy to deal with the new media. However, the Community, and in particular the Commission, must be given considerable credit for some of their achievements. The most notable is the very rapid progress made to telecommunications liberalisation; another is an early grasping of the nettle of the implications of the information society. In the field of broadcasting, however, progress has been slower, and has been bogged down by cultural concerns which have not fitted easily into the development of new market structures. Nevertheless, the progress described here suggests that international regulation can play an enormously important role in relation to the new media. Of course, the European Community and Union is a very peculiar and advanced form of international organisation and it is difficult to generalise from its experience. What it does prove, however, is that international action may be considerably more effective in addressing the changing media environment than leaving matters to national governments.

[114] <http://www.coe.fr/cm/96r10.html>
[115] <http://www.dhdirhr.coe.fr/media/home.htm>

6

Hungary

ILDIKO KOVATS[1]

1 MEDIA DEVELOPMENT

1.1 General trends

The key events currently taking place in the Hungarian media are:

- *criticism of the exclusive concession* granted to the Hungarian Telecom company Matav following the ending of the state monopoly telephone service in 1993;
- *fierce competition, mergers and strategic alliances* as industry prepares for deregulation of telecommunications within the European Union;
- recognition of the *need for an integrated telecom infrastructure* and a fight for dominance of such a structure between telephone, cable, and broadcasting companies;
- the emergence of *commercial radio and television stations* and a *proliferation of channels,* most recently pay-TV and a satellite channel following the establishment of the legal preconditions for independent broadcasting; and
- the emergence of *commercial Internet services.*

Convergence on a technological and content level (in 'multimedia' services) is mirrored in commercial concentration, as privatisation and media deregulation at both national and European levels allow:

- the expansion of Hungarian service providers outside their traditional areas of activity; and
- the absorption of local media companies by large Western interests.

Privatisation

Hungary opened its borders in 1989 and the first free elections were held in 1990. Privatisation was a key aim of the government, with the twin aims of political pluralism and the development of a market economy. Because of the aim of integration into the world economy and the lack of domestic capital, foreign capital had to be heavily involved in Hungarian media privatisation. In the year following the 1990 elections, the state printed

[1] The editorial assistance of David Attwood is gratefully acknowledged.

media were privatised and most of the shares in Matav were sold off by 1995.

New private ventures and concessions in telecom services (for example mobile services and paging) have followed and the preconditions for private commercial radio and TV programme provision are now in place. A key event in 1997 was the publishing of tenders for two national commercial TV channels and two radio channels.

Internationalisation

Another aim of privatisation is to support internationalisation of the media sector and build up Hungary as a regional centre and transit country in telecommunication, whilst at the same time ensuring the survival of the Hungarian telecom industry. Commercial and technological development in Hungary is closely linked to internationalisation, as it is dependent on the injection of foreign capital.

Liberalisation of the European media market and relaxation of media ownership rules have made Hungary attractive to western investors, but there is a risk that the interests of foreign investors may overrule the national or consumer interest. Their purchase of shares in privatised Hungarian media companies has in turn led to both horizontal and vertical integration. The most significant foreign media interest is the ownership of 67.1 per cent of Matav by Deutsch Telecom and Ameritech International. Most of the printed press and large parts of the other media are foreign-owned. The nationality of foreign owners is varied, the most significant being the German and US involvement in the media business. There is a strong German presence in the print media, as well as in commercial television and telecommunications, and a US presence in the cable and computer business and also now in commercial radio.

As a relatively small country, Hungary is for the most part a buyer rather than a seller in international media markets, but it is making efforts to increase international co-operation. For example, Hungary is playing a major role in the East-Central satellite TV programme, due to start at the end of 1997 and involving fifteen countries. Alfa Television is a Hungary-based multilingual cultural television channel for the East Central European region.

Hungary is increasingly taking part in international regulation and standard-setting activity in the communications sector. It became an associated member of the European Union in 1992, and harmonisation of the legal system with the EU's norms is a high priority; the Hungarian telecommunications and media industries also benefit from different forms of EU development or aid projects.

Convergence

Media convergence in Hungary has been much discussed, but so far there has been only limited progress because the key requirements have been lacking and there have been conflicts between different types of media.[2]

On a commercial level, convergence has allowed companies in the small Hungarian market to re-use market information, exploit the infrastructure better, and diversify. For example, telecom and cable companies are competing to provide Internet and cable TV services. With demand for voice telephony levelling off, Matav is expanding into cable TV and value-added network services, while the Hungarian Broadcasting Company is developing very small aperture terminal (VSAT) services.

Specific examples of multimedia developments in Hungary are the electronic versions of Hungarian newspapers available on the Internet and on CD, the Reuters news and Internet services provided by GSM mobile phone networks, and the Teledatacast system connected to Hungarian Television's Channel One.

Information superhighway

This had its origin in the academic and research computer network. Over thirty operators, including the main telecom and cable companies, provide Internet services; Hungarnet, an academic and research network is well established, and with Matav has joined the TEN-34 superhighway project. Matav has a large and increasing system of broadband optical fibre ISDN lines, while VSAT business data communications have been available since 1992.

Narrowcasting

The most characteristic type of narrowcasting in Hungary is the local radio and television services, serving one small area. The trend towards the provision of more specialised content to smaller audiences is again represented by Internet services and also by the growth of specialist TV channels, such as those for minority language groups.

Horizontal and vertical concentration

The processes described above are accompanied by concentration of ownership and the development of different types of cross-ownership. Matav has joined a consortium providing commercial television services, and

---

[2] See Arlandis, J, 'Understanding convergence', in Chamoux, JP (ed), *Regulating Regulators? Communication policies for the 90's* (Amsterdam: IOS Press, Oxford, Washington, Tokyo, 1991), 91–5.

also has a third of the Internet market. Local telephone service providers are also becoming involved in cable TV. Matav has nearly twenty-five subsidiary companies and has been accused by other operators of abusing its dominant position through cross-subsidy of its services. Small Hungarian companies in the computer software business have been bought by international companies which value their local experience and contacts. Vertical integration of publishing, printing, and distribution has taken place in the largely foreign owned newspaper industry and this has resulted in local monopolies and the decline of alternative information resources.

1.2 Developments in new services

During the last five years a mass of new telecommunications and content provision services and a mass of service providers have made their appearance in the consumer and business markets. The development is driven mainly by the supply of the competing large international companies but limited by local demand, the user capabilities, and the inadequacy of the system environment.

For residential users some spectacular examples of new service developments in Hungary are the multichoice programme packages of cable TV companies, the 24-hour shopping channel which commenced in February 1997, the electronic versions of newspapers, radio, and television programmes available on the Internet and/or on CD, the trials of Internet shopping, the teledatacasting of the Hungarian Television, and different telephone based additional services—among them recently homebanking, the Reuters news and Internet services provided by GSM mobile phone system, and paging. In the business sphere various communication services, computer system management services, network services, software and databank supply, consulting services, amongst others, are on offer.

1.3 Market participants

Fixed telephone services

Matav has exclusive rights to provide long distance and international voice telephone services until 2002. In recent years it has been the first or second largest Hungarian company. The majority (67.2 per cent) of the shares now belong to Magyarcom, a concessionaire company, composed equally of Deutsch Bundepost Telekom and Ameritech International. Twenty-five per cent +1 of the shares belong to the Hungarian state.

Matav has 75 per cent of the Hungarian market, with 2.1 million lines in 1997; the remainder is divided between thirteen concessionaire companies (with mainly foreign shareholders). Digitalisation of services is between 50–100 per cent, depending on service area.

Mobile telephone services

The three players in the mobile telephone market are Westel 450, Westel 900, and Pannon GSM. Pannon GSM is a 26 per cent Hungarian, 74 per cent Scandinavian company; Westel 900 is a joint venture of Matav and US West who already provide analogue mobile services. Together Westel and Pannon cover 95 per cent of Hungary, with market shares as follows: Westel GSM 54 per cent; Pannon GSM 33 per cent; Westel 450 13 per cent. GSM penetration is about 6 per cent but growing rapidly, with the help of added value services.

Radio and television programme distribution

Terrestrial radio and television broadcasting is controlled by the Hungarian Broadcasting Company, Antenna Hungaria, which is 100 per cent state owned and has exclusive rights to broadcast national and regional programmes. But the company's monopoly was broken following the establishment of local radio and television stations which are free to transmit their own programmes or turn to other companies. In the future only 50 per cent +1 of the shares is expected to remain in the state's hands, but privatisation has been hindered by political considerations.

Antenna Hungaria entered the satellite market jointly with Israel Aircraft Industry Ltd. The MagyarSat project is backed by the Hungarian Government, guaranteeing use of four channels on CERES (Central European Regional Satellite). Antenna Hungaria also developed digital television services which are distributed by satellite to cable TV systems.

The East-Central European satellite television programme is planned to start by the end of 1997. More than fifteen countries are taking part in the venture, which is supported by the Hungarian Government. Programmes will be made in Budapest but edited and translated by national editors for other countries.

There are an estimated 2,500–3,000 cable TV systems in Hungary (some of them illegal), ranging from small community systems to those serving several hundred thousand households. Of Hungary's 3.2 million households, more than 1.4 million are connected to some kind of cable system. Networking is permitted, with an upper limit for a system set at one-sixth of the Hungarian population, that is 1.7 million people. Technical differences between cable systems are a barrier to the development of new services.

A major player is Kabelkom, a joint venture between Time Warner Inc and United Communications International, offering the HBO film channel, documentary, and music channels. In 1997 Kabelkom had over 250,000 connections in Hungary.

Pre-recorded videocassettes are sold and loaned everywhere and receive attention only when issues such as illegal copying or pornography arise.

Internet, IT, and business communications

Both Government and academic institutions have played an important part in the development of a national computer and data network, HBONE. Hungarnet is an association of the users and developers of HBONE and participants in the National Information Infrastructure Development Project. In 1996 nearly 900 institutions took part in this project, now part of the TEN-34 superhighway project. By 1996 an estimated 44,000 computers were attached to the Internet, with up to 80,000 people accessing the Internet every day.[3] In 1997 there were over twenty-five Internet service providers. The two leading companies each control 30 per cent of the market, the third and fourth 15 per cent each.

The business communications and IT markets in Hungary are hard to define and rapidly changing. Many businesses are small local ventures, but international hardware and software companies also have a presence. Universities and academic institutions often form joint ventures with commercial companies. The government is a major IT client, forming up to 40 per cent of the Hungarian IT market in 1995. So too are banks and social services.

Matav is active in data communication services, which are not regulated in Hungary. Its size and existing network allow it to dominate the market, and competitors have accused it of anti-competitive practices such as cross-financing, complaints which have been upheld by the Economic Competition Office. Matav is also ahead of others in having a relatively large system of ISDN lines. The whole of the Matav service area will have ISDN capability by the end of 1997.

The VSAT data communication system serves banks, insurance companies, social services, and other organisations with large networks. Four companies compete in the satellite data communication service area.

Radio and television companies offer value-added services using surplus channel capacity. The Teledatacast service is provided by the Hungarian Television MTV1 channel, and teletext services are also available.

---

[3] Expert study to the Governmental strategy of realisation of the information society in Hungary. Manuscript for the Governmental Commission on Telecommunications and Informatics, Sept 1997.

Content providers

The main Hungarian newspapers have daily editions on the Internet, and Hungarian Radio has a presence too. There is also a special Internet journal, the InterNetto.

In 1996 there were in Hungary about 150,000 to 200,000 computers with a CD-ROM drive. There are currently six CD-ROM publishers and ten to fifteen CD-ROM publications. The Hungarian Association of Data Base Suppliers represents the interests of around 200 content providers; the libraries and the state bureaucracy are the major database owners.

All the large international software companies have a presence in Hungary. Software piracy is a significant problem with an estimated 75 to 80 per cent of software being in use illegally.

Radio and TV programme provision

The Hungarian broadcasting system has three levels: national, regional, and local. Under the Media Law, the national ones are to cover more than half the country, the regional ones at least 100,000 people. Local stations may have an audience of less than 1,000.

There are three national public service providers, owned and controlled by three public foundations. Hungarian Radio offers three national programmes, covering over 90 per cent of the country, with daily reaches of 41, 25, and 3 per cent. Hungarian Television offers two national programmes, one terrestrial and one satellite. The terrestrial channel has a coverage of over 90 per cent. Duna Television is a satellite service serving expatriate Hungarians in neighbouring countries. Both Hungarian Radio and Hungarian Television have regional programmes, but the future of these is not clear as a result of contradictions in media law.

Two national commercial television channels started in October 1997, and two national commercial radio channels are planned for the end of 1998. The national television concessions are for ten years, and for radio seven years. The successful bidders for the television channels were Magyar RTL (a consortium from Hungary, Germany, Luxembourg, the US, and the UK) and the Hungarian/Scandinavian consortium MTM-SBS. The awards were the subject of legal challenge questioning the impartiality of the Hungarian Radio and Television Board; this is slowly proceding but the channels are on the air and the losing bidder purchased three important regional stations.

There are three commercial TV services on a regional scale, available on cable or satellite. Recently KabelKom also became available on satellite.

The fate of about 180 local radio and television stations has seemed uncertain since the award of licences for terrestrial or cable distribution in 1993. They too have experienced problems caused by contradictions in regulatory policy, but are trying to survive through networking and joint selling of advertising time.

Printed media

There is a relatively large printed press in Hungary, with over ten national daily newspapers and twenty regional dailies. Competition is fierce, with aggressive marketing, technical modernisation, and cross-media initiatives. While general interest titles are declining, the market for special interest and entertainment magazines is stable.

The advertising market

Although there are more than 100 advertising agencies, 1993 estimates suggested that at least 75 per cent of Hungarian advertising was controlled by large multinational companies such as Saatchi & Saatchi, Young & Rubicam, and Ogilvy & Mather. The market—worth around $383m in 1995—is aggressive and poorly regulated. The growth of commercial broadcasting is likely to alter the market significantly.

All the above discussion should be subject to a caveat relating to the difficulty in obtaining information. It is very difficult in Hungary to obtain information about the telecom and media industry. Previous methods of data collection have been rendered ineffective by the rapid pace of mergers, alliances, and reorganisations. Deregulation has resulted in less surveillance and control of the industry, while fierce competition means that companies are reluctant to make commercially sensitive information available.

2 REGULATION AND OTHER MEDIA POLICIES

2.1 Regulation and other policies

2.1.1 *Structure and institutions*

There was no single high-level agency responsible for overall media policy in Hungary, and no comprehensive long term plan for the information society, until Spring 1997 when the *Government Commission on Information and Telecommunications* was established. The reaction to forty years of state planning has led to a climate which is reluctant to control centrally and actively economic processes through strategic planning or forecasting. Nor is there universal agreement on the main aims of society outside the very general triad of ideals: democracy, a market economy, and joining Europe. The forces of political and economic change have pushed IT issues into the background. This problem has been noted by Bangemann: 'The path to the information society is not simple in Eastern and Central

European countries, because structural reorganisations connected to political and economic change have priority.'[4] There have always been tensions between political/cultural will and economic forces in regulating the mass media. Increasingly, global technological convergence and market forces overrule national political aims.

The Telecommunication Act of 1992 gave the government the task of developing policy statements for telecom and broadcasting, though the OECD noted in 1996 the lack of progress in this area,[5] and attempts to develop them were not officially accepted by the government.[6] However, subsequent media convergence has made it illogical to develop separate policies in telecommunications, broadcasting, and information technology, though no sign of a comprehensive strategy emerged until 1997. Meanwhile there has been a rapid growth of different intellectual, professional, and political special interest groups intended to support and legitimate the state's programme.

2.1.2 Key strategies

Draft Programmes on Government Telecommunications Strategy made by the Ministry of Transport, Telecommunications and Water Management between 1994 and 1996

These programmes reflect an industrial policy approach to the development of telecommunications and the information society. To begin with, the government's communications policy was based on responses to technological change, but following the OECD experts' report,[7] it became one of liberalisation and competition, and the adaptation of the Hungarian market to the enormous changes European deregulation of the sector would bring about. This involved harmonisation with European regulatory norms, a new Telecommunications Act, and the introduction of new services. It was stressed that financing of the infrastructure cannot be fulfilled without further capital. The task of the government is to guarantee a friendly environment for investors and to decrease the risk factor. Services must be self-financing and demand-led, with price regulation to guarantee returns on investments. A further point was that policy

---

[4] Bangemann, M, *The path of the Eastern and Central European countries to the information society*, Session of the ECE-EU special committee, Bled, Slovenia, 7–8 Mar 1996.

[5] *Review of Telecommunications policy: Hungary*, OECD Examiners' Report, 29th Session of the Committee for Information, Computer and Communications Policy, CCET/DSTI(96)32 (1996).

[6] Borsos, K, *Hírközlés-politika—a fejlesztési koncepciókról (Communications policy: to the concepts of development)* Budapest: Magyar Távközlés, 1996), No 9; Csapodi, Cs, *Távközléspolitika Magyarországon (Telecommunications policy in Hungary)* (Budapest: Hiradástechnika, 1993), No 6; *Gondolatok a hírközléspolitikai koncepcióhoz (Comments on the communications policy conception)* (Budapest: Magyar Távközlés, 1996), No 7; Jutasi, I, *Gondolatok az OECD vizsgálati jelentéséről (Comments on the OECD Report)* (Budapest: Magyar Távközlés, 1996), No 7.

[7] n 5 above.

must have input from participants in information society development projects.

The National Strategy on Development of Information Technology

This strategy was made and published by a mixed group of professionals and intellectuals in 1995 as a result of discontent with the Government's passivity in this field. It formulates information technology goals in the context of overall national planning.[8] Based on technological convergence and global access to information, its key goals are:

- the development of the sciences and education
- the development of democracy and the elimination of bureaucracy
- the maintenance and support of national culture
- to become the telecommunication, financial, commercial, and industrial centre of the region
- to spread the positive effects of information technology through all levels of society.

It is based on private enterprise, the state's role being to co-ordinate, while civil organisations can expect interested, informed participation.

According to the strategy, the state has a responsibility to build up a legal environment in line with Europe, supporting freedom of information, data protection, and copyright laws.

The National Information Infrastructure Development Project

This project, which started in 1995,[9] originated in scientific and educational circles and is financed by state organisations and such agencies as the World Bank, the PHARE project, the National Committee of Scientific and Technical Development, and the Academy of Sciences. Its starting point is that the development of the electronic infrastructure is more and more a precondition for the effective functioning of the economy, the public administration, and indeed the whole of society. It is based on the academic computer network already mentioned, which forms the basis of Internet development in Hungary. Participants—from academic and public service institutions and state administration—have a role in developing IT applications and disseminating them to a wider circle of potential users.

First draft of Governmental Strategy on Realisation of the Information Society in Hungary

This study, ordered by the Governmental Commission on Information and Telecommunications, was completed in September 1997 and has not

---

[8] n 5 above.
[9] Bálint, L, *A Nemzeti Információs Infrastruktúra Fejlesztési Program körvonalai (The Frames of the National Information Infrastructure Development Project)*, Networkshop '95, Gödöllô, 19–21 Apr 1995.

yet been debated. It was made by a mixed group of professional and state administration experts and proposed a broad and active role for the Government and the realisation of the following goals:

- sustainable and competitive economic development;
- a well-developed society at a European level, including electronic administration and democracy;
- a higher level of social integration through access to information technology, culture, and entertainment;
- a knowledge-oriented society through education, research, and electronic literacy;
- regional centres of infrastructure provision through a well-developed telecommunication infrastructure; and
- active participation in global processes, such as EU harmonisation.

The Government's means to achieve these goals are to be regulation (legal, standardisation, agreements), projects (initiated or supported by the state), financial support (basis of competitive bidding), and co-ordination through active participation in the activity of international organisations.

2.1.3 Regulatory bodies

The highest forum where all the different issues of media policy and essential principles of regulation are drawn together is the Parliament, in the form of legal regulations and hearings in different parliamentary commissions. The fact that certain laws regulating information and communications issues (for example, the main elements of media and data protection laws) need a two-thirds majority in parliament to be carried, has made them dependent on the current state of political power relationships.

At the same time there are several other regulatory bodies, which control and affect the development of the media. Among them the most important are the Constitutional Court, the Economic Competition Office, the General Inspectorate of Consumer Protection, the State Property and Holding Agency, the National Committee on Scientific and Technical Development, and the National Office of Standardisation. All but the last two are the result of the change of regime and the move to a state based on the rule of law and to a market economy.

The *Constitutional Court*—which is modelled on the German Constitutional Court—has an important role, especially in connection with human rights, freedom of expression, and privacy issues related to the media. It is particularly a key player because of the lack of a new and comprehensive constitution and the mixture of new and old laws. Since 1990 it has repeatedly come under attack from both political wings on the ground that it has allegedly taken too active a role in policy-making.

The *Interdepartmental Committee on Information Technology*, established in 1992, has the role of co-ordinating the state administration's information technology development. It has an important role in regulation as the state administration makes up 35 to 40 per cent of the IT market.

The next level of policy making and regulating are the *ministries*—especially the *Ministry of Transport and Water Management*, which has responsibility for telecommunications policy issues and the development of the telecommunications infrastructure. Roles include the granting of concessions, quality control, technical requirements, and price regulation. This work is led by a Deputy State Secretary for Communication.

The *Ministry of National Defence* has responsibility for use of the frequency spectrum for non-civil purposes. The *Industry Ministry* covers IT issues, mainly through the *National Commission of Scientific and Technological Development*. The *Ministry of Culture and Education* became heavily involved in information and communication issues following the decision to introduce the Internet in Hungarian secondary schools in 1997. This Ministry also oversees copyright.

In 1997 the *Governmental Commission on Information and Telecommunications* was established at ministry level to co-ordinate government decision making in this area and to work out a national strategy for information technology.

The *General Communication Inspectorate* implements operational regulation of telecommunicaitons (including broadcasting). Its key roles are licensing the establishment of private networks, and use of equipment and network-based services, regulation of civil use of frequency spectrum, and economic regulation of telecommunications.

In 1996 the OECD[10] found the ministry's strategic policy making and the Inspectorate's economic analysis weak, while on the other hand technical regulation was too bureaucratic.

The regulation and control of radio and television programme provision and distribution belongs to an independent body, the *National Radio and Television Board* (NRTB), which is publicly financed and reports to a special parliamentary commission. The Board's main functions are to protect and support freedom of expression and the independence of programme makers. Board members cannot be MPs, in high state or party positions, or owners or employees in the media sphere. They are elected by the Parliament for four years. The president is nominated by the Prime Minister and the President of the Republic, with other members nominated by the parliamentary parties.

The NRTB has established an independent Complaints Committee to deal with complaints related to issues of balance. If the complaint is

---

[10] n 5 above.

upheld, the broadcaster must publish the findings of the Committee. In the case of more severe or repeated violations a fine may be imposed.

Under the Data Protection Act, Parliament appoints an ombudsman, supported by the *Bureau of Data Protection*, to oversee the functioning of the Act. He has the right to investigate data records, including politically or commercially sensitive information.

There are also many non-governmental special interest and lobbying organisations. Some are established by law, and at least partly financed from public money. Three types may be distinguished:

- independent professional advisory bodies, generally attached to a state authority, policy making, or regulating organisation. The most important is the *National Advisory Body on Communications and Information Technology*;
- forums of 'interest reconciliation', in areas such as communications and information technology. These forums are made up from service providers, regulatory bodies and user groups; and
- public foundations, founded and financed mainly by the state and increasingly taking over the functions of state bodies. They deal with issues such as copyright and intellectual property.

There are also many *trade associations*, such as the Association of Cable Operators and the Association of Information Service Providers, which represent their members' interests and lobby on their behalf, and *professional associations* (for example the Hungarian Journalists Association, the Hungarian Public Relations Association, etc). In the civil sphere, too, groups such as the Press Freedom Club and the Publicity or Openness Club aim to shape public opinion. The ethical committees of these bodies play a growing role in self-regulation.

Some powerful *private companies*, dissatisfied with the actions of official regulatory bodies, have formed their own regulatory and enforcement organisations. In the field of copyright there is the ASVA, a non-profit organisation financed by its members for the protection of audio-visual works, and the Business Software Alliance for the protection of software copyright. The BSA has achieved a significant decrease in the illegal sale and use of software.

2.1.4 Key media legislation

The *Telecommunications Act*[11] aimed to meet the demand for telecommunication services by supporting privatisation and competition, the state's task being to regulate the market and participate in the work of international regulatory organisations. The Act established the conditions needed for privatisation and liberalised infrastructure regulation. The aim

---

[11] Law 1992: LXXXII.

was nevertheless to ensure infrastructure development and the fulfilment of the former state monopoly's obligations to provide a universal service. Apart from fixed and mobile voice telephone services and paging, which operate on a concession basis, other telecom services were declared open to competition, needing only approval linked to technical requirements. Interconnectivity of systems is a priority, with equal opportunities for access for all service providers.

The *Frequency Management Act*[12] declares the state's exclusive right to manage and license frequency spectrum, taking into account social and economic requirements and international agreements. A key factor is the fee for frequency allocation and use.

The *Media Act*[13] aimed to realign the radio and television services with the changed political, cultural, technological, and economic environment and to harmonise media regulation with European norms. Key elements are guarantees of independence for the media, self-financing, and redefinition of the public service function. Advertising is regulated by the *Economic Advertising Act*.[14]

The *Copyright Act*[15] is based on the Berne Convention and asserts the material and moral rights of the author. This act is due to be amended again to take account of developments in IT as they affect intellectual property rights.

The *Data Protection Act*[16] had an indirect but significant effect on the development of the media sector. The Act is built on broad concepts of privacy and information autonomy. The Constitutional Court has also been active in the past on privacy issues, for example personal identification numbers.

The *Concession Act*[17] and concession agreement regulations cover the conditions under which state-owned institutions are privatised, for example guaranteeing that universal service obligations are met. They also control misuse of a company's monopoly, cross-financing of services and competition. However, in practice, revenue implications for the state play a significant role in determining the outcome of concession bids.

2.2 Regulation: topics and issues

The OECD report noted that there is no explicit statement of media regulatory policy in Hungary.[18] Despite the many drafts discussed above, a clear and accepted policy still does not exist at the end of 1997.

The main aims in Hungary's regulation of social and economic processes are now to:

---

[12] Law 1993: LXII.   [13] Law 1996: I.   [14] Law 1997: XVIII.
[15] Law 1969: III, last amended 1994.   [16] Law 1992: LXIII.   [17] Law 1991: XVI.
[18] n 5 above.

- reduce state intervention and have less regulation in general;
- separate regulation and policy making, and especially to detach it from party politics;
- harmonise Hungarian regulation with international and especially EU norms;
- promote desired ends through incentives and voluntary agreements rather than prohibition;
- encourage self-regulation;
- include more transparency and involvement of regulated bodies in shaping regulation;
- take the specific social needs of communities as a starting point, rather than provision of universal public service; and
- include consumer consultation when regulating the quality of products and services, and take consumer protection into account.

The aims as they specifically affect communications and information regulations are to:

- separate regulation from specific communication technologies, basing it as much as possible on general issues such as human rights, copyright, and the safety of electronic communications;
- have less regulation of individual service providers, and more regulation of the way they interact; and
- have as little content regulation as possible.

Here again may be mentioned the key goals of the National Strategy on Development of Information Technology (see above, section 2.1.2).

2.2.1 Technological regulation

The aim here is to:

- support technical development in the sector;
- encourage compatibility between equipment and interconnectibility of networks;
- ensure that international standards are complied with through mutual recognition (if technical standards are proved by a proper authority in an EU country, no further control is needed in Hungary); and
- ensure that systems do not harm the environment, or present health and safety risks to employees or consumers.

However, rapid changes in technology and convergence make regulation of technical standards very difficult.

In 1996 the OECD found that, for a variety of reasons (for example the political situation prior to 1990 and the low priority attached to economic performance in the telecom sector), technical regulation of telecommunications in Hungary was excessive and over-bureaucratic. In principle, technical regulation is now intended to be self-financing.

The Frequency Management Act put special emphasis on the creation of a National Table of Frequency Allocation. Geopolitical factors (a small country sharing its border with seven others) and potential EMC problems mean that international co-operation is especially important for Hungary.

The Telecommunications Act laid down technical preconditions for a unified telecommunication network and prescribed how systems standards might be developed. However, these have been only partly worked out, and given the shifts of emphasis in regulatory policy away from regulation of networks and towards that of interfaces and to guaranteeing quality of service, it seems unlikely that further work will be done in this area.

Both the Telecommunications and Media Acts provide strict measures to control the technical standards of cable TV networks until telecom liberalisation in 2002. Although the 1996 Media Act foresaw a separate cable bill, this now seems unlikely, technical convergence meaning that telecommunication and cable networks need a common regulatory framework.

Privatisation is seen as a means of accelerating technical development, and concession agreements set high technical standards.

2.2.2 *Economic regulation*

The state's withdrawal from the telecom and media spheres has led to the appearance of entrepreneurs and commercialisation of services. Public service and universal service provision now appear in a different perspective. The main principles of economic regulation are that the sector should be self-financing and use resources efficiently, and to speed up the development of new services.

In recent years a priority has been to draw up terms for privatisation and concession agreements. While a minimum state share has in the past been laid down by law, this is now less common. A 25 per cent +1 share is usual, except for broadcasting, where the state wishes to keep a 50 per cent +1 share because of the perceived political significance of the service. In the case of the telephone service, a state monopoly has become virtually a private monopoly, with 80 per cent of the voice telephone market under the control of Matav.

The most important part of a concession agreement is whether the concession is exclusive or not, and if not, how many other players are allowed to enter the market. Matav's exclusive concession until 2002 in long distance and international voice telephony is now in question because of EU liberalisation in 1998.

The concession fee is another important factor, because it influences the price of the service. Because decision makers are interested primarily in maximising the state's revenue they try to raise concession fees, which can result in expensive or unsatisfactory services to consumers. This was the case with the fixed and mobile telephone concessions. However, when bids for television concessions were considered, non-economic factors were given greater weight, and CME failed to win a concession despite a bid 50 per cent higher than that of its competitor.

Cross-subsidy is permitted to finance universal service provision, but is strictly prohibited for services in the free competition area. However, accounting methods and the interests of network owners make it impossible to separate them completely. Cross-subsidy in the telecom sector partly results from the fact that local calls have historically been cheaper than long-distance calls which new technology has made cheaper to provide. Harmonisation of costs and prices is the subject of regulation.

Tariffs are regulated through a price cap, indexed to the general producer's price index, but varying according to sector. The subscription fee, local usage charges, and long distance and international usage charges are subject to regulation. More detailed price control would require in-depth economic analysis by the regulator, and (as the OECD report stated) the analytical capabilities of Hungarian regulators are inadequate, especially compared to those of the owners' own economists and accountants.

The subscription fee for the radio and television service (effectively a tax on TV set owners) is set by Parliament and shared between the different radio and TV service providers according to the Media Act. There is an extremely high VAT rate of 25 per cent imposed on telecommunication services.

The intended purpose of public funds (from concession fees and other payments) is to support special development targets in telecom and media, and ease the conflicts of universal service provision and market forces. However, there is always a risk of these funds being retained by Parliament to balance the state budget—as happened with the Telecommunications Fund. The situation is different in the case of the media, where funding is separate from government and at the disposal of the National Radio and Television Board.

Ownership regulation

Privatisation has made ownership regulation increasingly important in Hungary, raising issues of monopoly, concentration, competition, market entry and access. Also important are copyright problems related to ownership of information (see below). The complexity of ownership (for example cross- and multi-ownership and internationalisation) makes regulation more difficult.

A key issue is the level of state ownership. There are legal restrictions in different media on what the state's share must be or could be, from 100 per cent state ownership to zero. The tendency is for the state to withdraw from ownership (though the Broadcasting Company was an exception, where the state's minimum share was increased by subsequent legislation). As already noted, the minimum state share is 25 per cent +1 share in Matav, and 50 per cent +1 share in the Hungarian Broadcasting and Radiocommunications Company. State ownership rights in Hungary are separate from regulation, the Hungarian State Property and Holding Agency involving itself in management together with the other shareholders.

State ownership originally served as a guarantee that public service obligations would be fulfilled by a private company, but other means are now employed to achieve the desired aims, such as the terms of concession agreements, a 'golden share' ensuring a right of veto in a company's decision making, or special requirements for the composition of boards of directors.

Ownership regulation is further complicated by the existence of concessions. A concession to provide a service can be linked to privatisation (for example the telephone business); to establishing an infrastructure (for example mobile telephony); or simply a licence (exclusive or not) to provide a service (for example radio and TV programme provision). Applicants for radio and TV concessions must meet requirements of Hungarian residence or registration within the Hungarian Republic, and their voting share in a joint company must not be less than 26 per cent. The case of Matav should be mentioned here: due to a gap in the regulations, they were able in negotiating their concession agreement to achieve a greater say in management than their share should allow. No shareholder can hold a majority of shares in a TV programme concession: there must be at least three partners, and the position in Matav where one consortium has over 67 per cent of the shares has been called into question recently.

To ensure the independence of national public service radio and television provision, ownership rights of Hungarian Radio and Hungarian Television (previously owned by the state) and Duna Television passed to three public foundations. These have boards of trustees (partly elected by Parliament and partly drawn from social and cultural bodies) which report to Parliament. The foundations' shares cannot be sold.

The National Information Infrastructure is owned by the member institutions (universities, public institutions, schools) of HUNGARNET. Ownership of telecom service-providing companies is regulated, while the ownership of the network, or of equipment providers, is not. In both telecom services and broadcasting or programme distribution, ownership is regulated by the terms of the concession, which limit the owners' powers to dispose of or make changes in the ownership structure of the country. Ownership is also controlled by general competition law.

Ownership regulation in the field of radio and television programme provision is linked to political rather than economic factors. Its aims are:

- to prevent a monopoly of programme service provision by political power holders, controlling bodies, and the main competitors in the field. National and local political leaders, MPs, members of the courts, the Competition Office, the State Property and Holding Agency, the National Bank, and media regulatory bodies, are all excluded from bidding for concessions, as are organisations directly or indirectly owned by the above;
- to prevent monopoly ownership in a given territory (the Hungarian voting system is partly based on regional representation). Area of coverage is taken into consideration when examining cross-ownership issues; and
- to prevent the development of market dominance in programme provision; an owner may provide no more than one national programme, or two regional and four local programmes, or twelve local programmes.

However, the radio and TV ownership regulations avoid the question of whether independence and pluralism can survive if service providers are so restricted in scale as to limit their economic viability.

Competition and competition regulation

Competition in Hungary is intensifying as market players seek to gain advantageous positions prior to deregulation of the EU telecom market, while hardware and software convergence in different communication fields creates new problems for regulators.

Although the media is covered by general competition law[19] the telecommunication and media markets also require special regulation. Under the Telecommunications Act, operators of fixed and mobile telephone services, paging services and regional and national broadcasting and distribution services are granted concessions for which the contract lays down quality and quantity parameters and conditions of co-operation with other service providers. Establishment of a network, or connection of the public network with corporate, closed, or special purpose networks needs the permission of the General Communication Inspectorate. Co-operation with foreign corporate or closed network operators and service providers is prohibited.

[19] Law 1996: LVII.

Mobile services are regulated in the same way as fixed services, but here concessions are not exclusive. As the two players in the GSM market began operation at the same time with equal opportunities, competition is healthy, with positive effects for service development and for consumers.

There is a major imbalance in the telecom market, linked to the overwhelming market dominance of one player, which directly or indirectly affects all telephone services and the free market area of Value Added Network Services too. Matav is over fifty times larger than any other local concessionaire company in fixed telephony, and small companies are dependent on Matav's backbone network because of its exclusive concession to provide long distance and international calls. It has not been possible to prevent Matav acting anti-competitively.

A further issue is that telephone companies are allowed to supply other kinds of services, while other service providers are prohibited from offering telephone services. In particular, the telephone companies can move into programme distribution while cable companies cannot start telephone services (the reverse of the situation in the UK, incidentally). Despite a ban on cross-subsidy, and requirements for separated accounting, equal treatment, standard tariffs, and Competition Office rulings, these imbalances seriously affect other players in the market.

Radio and TV broadcasting presents special problems: programmes are subject to both economic and political forces which have conflicting criteria. The Media Act stresses that political factors must be balanced against economic ones.

In practice there is no competition in the field of broadcasting, although local programme service providers are free to decide how to distribute their programmes. The strategic importance of the Hungarian Broadcasting Company meant that policy makers could not agree on privatisation and concession terms. Public service radio and television programmes are government subsidised, and it is unacceptable for government (and the state budget) to depend too much on a private broadcasting company in a monopoly situation. One possibility would be to make the company more efficient through diversification and to allow programme providers (under the auspices of the NRTB) to have a say in the running of the company—perhaps as shareholders—after privatisation.

There are also problems with the television programme market, due to the appearance of pay channels, the technical inability of cable systems to meet the need for conditional access systems, and the must-carry obligations of cable operators. As already noted above, the separate cable bill prescribed by the 1996 Media Act now seems unlikely, technical convergence meaning that telecommunication and cable networks need a new common regulatory framework.

Public services and universal service provision are important issues in a competitive market, but in principle such services should be self-financing. Thus public service radio and TV programmes are financed by commercial broadcasting as well as by subscriptions and state subsidy.

Intellectual property

Market changes since 1990, a new influx of foreign programming, and the spread of new information services have all made copyright and intellectual property issues more important, complex, and difficult. Penalties for video and software piracy have been toughened, as have the enforcement activities of international copyright controlling bodies (for example the ASVA). Video and software piracy and illegal use of pay-TV decoders are covered by criminal law.

As already mentioned (see section 2.1.4 above), amendment of copyright law is on the agenda (following international regulatory trends) covering, for example, Internet related issues, pay-TV decoders, and library loan of videos and CD-ROMs.

2.2.3 Social regulation

Content regulation

Freedom of information was one of the key tenets of the change of regime at the end of the 1980s. This led to a policy of having as little regulation as possible. However, Hungary, as a 'new democracy' wishing to join Europe, could not and did not wish to ignore international regulations. Where possible, liberal solutions were chosen, with emphasis on freedom and privacy issues. Indeed, the Hungarian Constitution provides protection for, and limits to, freedom of expression and of the press, reinforced by provisions of criminal law which prohibit defamation, unlawful handling of private data, threatening public danger, and a number of other widely defined offences. The 1986 law on the press is still in force, and also covers radio and television.[20] This law both gives positive support to the media, for example by stating rights of journalists, and imposes negative restrictions, such as prohibiting the media from harming public morale or inciting crime. Like the Media Law, it also requires advertising to be clearly separated from other content, and identified as such. The 1996 Media Law (see above) also sets out limits to free speech based on the Hungarian Constitution, and emphasises the need for impartiality, objectivity, and diversity in programming. It prohibits excessive violence and sexually explicit material. However, matters which have traditionally been regulated by law, such as pornography, remain the subject of provisions dispersed throughout Hungarian legislation.

[20] Law 1986: II.

There is a quota system to support independent producers and Hungarian output, and positive discrimination in favour of certain minority groups on public service channels. The proportion of European programmes is regulated by the Media Law for public service channels and by the concession conditions for commercial channels, the latter favouring a higher proportion of public service and Hungarian programmes.

Programme providers (either commercial or public service) can apply to the Programme Service Provision Foundation for funds for public service programming. This is funded from concession fees and other payments. But overall programme provision must be self-financing.

More advertising is allowed on commercial channels than on subsidised public service channels. In some cases regulation is lighter than that of the EU, in the interests of stimulating economic development.

In addition to the legal controls, a Compliance Committee—established by law—has the responsibility of ensuring that public service and commercial channels are impartial as prescribed by the Media Law. Citizens have established pressure groups to influence decision makers on various issues; for example the advertising industry was very active in lobbying for more liberal solutions in the law on advertising.

User protection

Historically Hungarians have expected a relatively high level of public service provision which can prove hard to sustain in a market economy with an international trend towards deregulation. Fulfilment of the state's public and universal service obligations by private companies are covered by concession agreements; for example, in the case of telephone services, there are obligations to fulfil demand for services within specified times. In addition, the Media Law implements support for the handicapped and requires special attention to be paid to childrens' programmes and advertising.

Protection of privacy is also important, but ethical and professional standards of accountability are higher in the public sector than in the private sector where competition encourages risk-taking. The protection of private data is afforded by law.[21] For example data can be used exclusively for the original purpose of data collection, and as a result the Constitutional Court declared unlawful the use of an all-purpose personal identity number.[22] The same law also requires public bodies to make official information available, with judicial remedies if they fail to do so. However, legal provisions for access to public records have so far been used very rarely. A law on consumer protection is being prepared as a comprehensive statement of the subject, currently contained in various

---

[21] Law 1992: LXIV.   [22] Decision 15/1991.

different statutes. The Ministry of Culture and Education also intends to support schools in teaching use of the Internet.

3 CONCLUDING REMARKS

In conclusion, a better title for this report might be 'The challenges posed by the changing media to legal regulation'—at least in the case of Hungary, as legal responses to the challenges of a changing media seem scarcely adequate. A lack of regulation, and delays in regulation, have had a greater effect on the media market than laws actually in force.

The most acute problems in Hungary relate to cable regulation, new media copyright problems, competition in network services and the contradictions inherent in political and economic regulation of the media. Cable regulation is particularly complex, with competition and convergence issues and the need to harmonise media, telecom, and IT regulations.

An overview of the situation leads to the conclusion that legal means of media regulation have serious limitations: there are difficulties in unambiguously defining regulatory issues and in enforcement, and as a result the use of legal norms is decreasing in importance when compared to other types of regulation. Legal regulations take a long-term view and so are often overtaken by rapid changes in technology or markets. While new communications technology can to some extent be regulated by extending the interpretation of existing legislation, this simply delays new legislation and can hinder new developments.

Regulation has to be seen in an international context, but what is suitable for one country, society, or economy may not be for another. The demand for harmonisation of the Hungarian legal system with EU norms means that proper Hungarian regulation often has to wait for EU regulation; this is the case for example with copyright issues for new media. At the same time, delays in framing regulation in less developed countries can lead to a regulatory vacuum which may then be exploited by companies from countries where regulation is stricter.

7

The United States

PETER JOHNSON

INTRODUCTION

The last decade in the US has been one of increasing technological convergence in the face of continuing regulatory Balkanization. Under the regulatory regime that existed prior to 1996, neither broadcast TV stations nor telephone companies (telcos) could offer cable TV in their local markets. Likewise, cable companies were prohibited from offering telephony. Except in some major markets, nobody but the local telco could offer local phone service, but the telco itself could not supply long-distance phone service or manufacture telephone equipment. Power companies could offer neither phone nor TV service. By the early 1990s, however, it was evident that communications technologies had so many points of similarity that artificially keeping them apart made no sense. The Telecommunications Act of 1996, which removes or phases out most market entry barriers, is an attempt to recognize this technological convergence. Where a company could formerly be either a telco, a long-distance company, a cable operator, or a broadcaster, the new law allows all media to converge under the umbrella of single 'Communications Companies' that offer all services.

1 MEDIA DEVELOPMENT

Like Gaul, US media divides into three parts: mass media (broadcast, cable and satellite TV, and radio), telephony (wired and wireless), and interactive computer services (America Online, CompuServe, and the Internet). Virtually every US household has at least one TV and one telephone. Seventy-five per cent have videocassette recorders (VCRs). A smaller percentage (40 per cent) have personal computers, but per capita computer use increases dramatically with the addition of computers used at work. An estimated 15 per cent of the people uses the Internet, at home or work or both.

Apart from over-the-air broadcasting, the US employs a two-wire system for media access. The telephone infrastructure consists of an increasingly fibre-optic backbone, with connection to individual users via paired copper wires, while cable TV uses a combination of fibre and coaxial cable. Most Internet modem connections are through the telephone. This duopoly is being nibbled at the fringes by cable and satellite modems and satellite TV, but fibre, wire-coax remains the basic structure.

1.1 General trends in media development

Convergence

The dream of convergence fixes on the image of an all-media 'compuphonavision'[1] machine that will roll into one the functions of a telephone, TV, and computer. That the compuphonavision has not yet arrived may be due to characteristics that make the three media *di*vergent rather than *con*vergent. TV, telephone, and computer speak to three different human behaviours: TV to the need for passive entertainment; telephone to the need for two-way active oral and aural communication; computers to the need for active (sometimes interactive) creative work and play.[2] The difficulties with technological convergence reflect the difficulties in force-fitting these three very different human functions into one machine.

For instance, several years ago interactive TV seemed the hope of the future, a combination of telephony and TV that would use telephone lines to order movies, video games, and home shopping. Congress and the Federal Communications Commission ('FCC') hoped that something called Video Dial Tone (VDT) would allow telephone companies to act as video common carriers, uploading and downloading 500 or more channels and allowing consumers to tailor and exchange their own video programming.[3] In 1993–94, encouraged by the VDT option and by court decisions[4] that allowed local phone companies to offer video to their customers, several phone companies started interactive video ventures. By 1997, however, both Time Warner and Bell Atlantic had ended their interactive TV experiments in Orlando, Florida and Toms River, New Jersey. Tele-TV, a joint venture formed in 1994 by Bell Atlantic, Nynex, and Pac Tel to offer a digital TV distribution system that would compete with cable, has yet to enter the programming market and has recently lost

[1] Maney, K, *Megamedia Shakeout* (New York: J. Wiley, 1995), 33.
[2] See Negroponte, N, 'Tangible Bits', *Wired*, May 1997, 232 (suggesting that computers will not become truly interactive until they satisfy a greater sensorium than the current touch, point, and click).
[3] See 'Report and Order In the Matter of Telephone Company-Cable Television Cross Ownership Rules', FCC Report No 95–20 20 Jan 1995.
[4] See, eg, *US West Inc v United States*, 855 F Supp 1184 (1994), aff'd 48 F 3d 1092 (9th Cir 1994), vacated and remanded, 116 S Ct 1037 (1996).

its chairman and half its work force.[5] Video Dial Tone has vanished, replaced in the new Telecommunications Act by Open Video System (OVS). However, nobody seems any more certain now than two years ago what a VDT or an OVS system would actually look like.[6]

Lately, talk of convergence has turned from video-telephone toward video-computer. The FCC's 1997 High Definition Television (HDTV) order establishes a timetable that will make fully-digital, high-definition TV the standard shortly after the millennium, giving the TV many of the characteristics of a computer. The new TV will be able to store viewer preferences and scan on-line schedules for viewing options; it will enable downloading of movies and games and facilitate on-line shopping; it will allow simultaneous access both to a TV programme and to a webpage keyed to the TV programme. Speculation about digital TV's future involves built-in videophones and holographic 3-dimensional video games. Still, parochial concerns bog convergence down. A conflict between computer and TV manufacturers over the HDTV scanning format, thus far at least, augurs a future of conflict, rather than convergence, between the two media.

Still, full technological convergence hovers near. Web-TV, which places a converter box atop a standard TV and connects it to the Internet via a phone line, represents a bet that there is a market for people who want the Internet but have no other computer interest. There are growing experiments in Internet telephone, radio, and TV, with some thoughts that interactive Internet TV will replace the 500-channel cable universe dreamt of a few years ago. Users routinely jury-rig their computers with sound and video cards to open a video window on the screen or play CDs. Add a microphone and telephone software, and a rudimentary compuphonavision emerges. Compaq and Thompson have introduced a PC home theatre, capable of showing TV programmes or prerecorded movies as well as incorporating interactive functions such as the Internet, computer games, or email.[7] Finally, several experiments combine cable and the Internet. There is, for instance an MSNBC cable channel and an msnbc.com website, a joint venture of Microsoft (computing) and NBC (broadcasting). So far, however, it is more a matter of shared content than full technological convergence, much as a book and a TV show might be offered as companion pieces. MSNBC programming does not run on msnbc.com, nor is the cable channel interactive like the website.

---

[5] Carter, B, 'Former CBS President Quits Troubled Tele-TV Venture' *New York Times*, 7 Apr 1997, D5.

[6] See Cunard, J, 'One Last Wheeze for VDT', *Cable TV & New Media*, August 1996.

[7] Brinkley, J, 'Compaq Plans to Show First Home PC Theater', *New York Times*, 28 Apr 1997, D5.

Convergence allows content providers to select one or many from a menu of media. Most national newspapers and magazines now have electronic editions. Telephone calls arrive by wire and air; TV by cable, air, and satellite. An enterprising service now offers to send distant radio signals via telephone to play on one's speakerphone.[8] News arrives by TV, computer, Internet, and even by portable pager.[9]

Information superhighways

In September 1993 the Clinton Administration's Information Infrastructure Task Force published *The National Information Infrastructure: Agenda for Action*, which foresaw 'a seamless web of communications networks, computers, databases, and consumer electronics that will put vast amounts of information at users' fingertips'. The notion of a single Information Superhighway, however, is misleading. The US seems headed toward an information system as various as the road system that carries motor traffic, a combination of all wired and wireless media: broadcast, cable, satellite, cellular, and copper-wire.

Wired versus wireless

Nicholas Negroponte[10] has noted that it is an historical accident and a waste of resources for TV to be wireless and telephone to be wired. The proper balance is wired TV and wireless telephony, since the 6MHz bandwidth necessary for a single TV channel could accommodate myriad phone calls. For a few years it appeared that this imbalance was about to be righted, with the pervasiveness of cable TV and the increasing penetration of cellular telephony. Now that future is unsure, since US Internet connections predominantly use hard-wired telephone lines, and satellite TV seems to have got at least a foothold, though cable operators still controlled 89 per cent of the multichannel market as of September 1996.[11]

Broadband

Long-distance companies such as MCI, Sprint, and Wiltel have installed huge amounts of fibre-optic cable over the last fifteen years, providing the essential backbone. Fibre-to-the-home, however, is a distant prospect, since the hard-wire telephone infrastructure, created by the AT&T monopoly under a regime that pegged its rates at a certain percentage above

---

[8] *Infinity Broadcasting Corp v Wayne Kirkwood*, No 96 Civ 0885, slip op at 1 (SDNY 6 June 1997).

[9] See *National Basketball Assn v Motorola*, 105 F 3d 841, 843 (2d Cir 1997).

[10] See Negroponte, N, *Being Digital* (New York: Alfred Knopf, 1996), 24.

[11] Kaut, D, 'FCC Reports Highlight Continued Cable Video Dominance, Telecom Revenue Rise', *BNA Electronic Info. Pol'y & L Rep*, 10 Jan 1997, 51.

costs, is 'gold-plated' and not deteriorating fast enough to warrant re-placement. Though computer modems now operate primarily through copper phone wires, there is some penetration both by ISDN lines and by cable and satellite modems. As of 1996, 25 per cent of users accessed the Internet via ISDN lines, 15 per cent used cable modems, and some 50 per cent connected through ordinary telephone lines.[12]

Off-line

The Video Cassette Recorder (VCR), used in 75 per cent of US households, is the off-line medium of choice. It has emerged as a home theatre, with people renting and buying videos at an ever-increasing pace. Though its demise is predicted annually, replaced by pay-per-view TV, digital video disc (DVD), and the like, it is not happening yet.

Broadcasting versus narrowcasting

The sheer number of cable channels and websites available has inevitably led to the growth of niche cable channels and specialized websites. As cable channels proliferated and viewership on the major commercial networks declined from 90 per cent in 1970 to 60 per cent in 1990, it became no longer necessary for a TV programme to appeal to a mass audience. The standard 75-channel cable system now includes separate channels dedicated to food, history, home shopping, sports, music, foreign language programming, science fiction, science, comedy, feminism, children, news, business, and sex. The World Wide Web's 22 million sites cater naturally to even narrower tastes. Even print has become more specialized. While local newspapers decline, niche magazines abound. In 1982 there were 1,800 magazines nationally; in 1997, over 3,000 divide the national readership into ever-finer slices.[13] On the Internet, PointCast, Inc has pioneered 'push' technology, which delivers individually tailored news and ads to subscribers' PC screens, as a screensaver. Inevitably, this has led to people knowing something about a few things and not much about everything. The loss of shared, common knowledge and values is widely lamented.[14]

Concentration

The Telecommunications Act of 1996, by removing many barriers to market entry and to mergers and acquisitions, accelerated a trend toward

[12] Maney, K, 'Moving to Fast Lanes on the Net', *USA Today*, 31 Oct 1996, 1B.
[13] Shenk, D, *Data Smog: Surviving the Information Glut* (London: Abacus, 1997), 111 (note).
[14] See eg, Hirsch, Jr, Ed, *Cultural Literacy: What Every American Needs To Know* (Pat Mulcahy, ed, Boston: Houghton Mifflin, 1988); Bennett, W, *Book of Virtues: A Treasury Of The World's Great Moral Stories* (New York: Simon and Schuster, 1993).

concentrated ownership of all media. For the moment, most discrete services are offered by discrete companies. The bills for long-distance calls, local phone service, Internet access, cable TV, electricity, gas, and water each arrive in separate envelopes. The future, by contrast, is one of one-stop-shopping, with a half-dozen 'communications companies' offering all services.

Ownership concentration extends past the media to embrace much of the nation's industry, leading to accusations that a 'National Entertainment State' has emerged under the control of four giant corporations—General Electric, Time Warner, Disney/Capital Cities, and Westinghouse.[15] Since these corporations not only control the mass media but have interests in all manner of diverse enterprises, the fear is that their control of the media will make it captive to their corporate interests. Briefly,

- *General Electric*, which owns NBC, has subsidiaries such as GE Transportation (trains), GE Power Generation (turbines), GE Americom (satellites) and Capital Communications (long-distance telephony), GE Information Services (software), GE Plastics, GE Appliances and Lighting, GE Aircraft Engines, and interests in insurance, medical systems, and financial asset management. Through NBC it owns nine TV stations, NBC Radio, CNBC (cable news), msnbc, and has interests in at least ten other cable stations. The Microsoft–NBC joint venture into cable and Internet (MSNBC, msnbc.com) joins the Microsoft software empire with GE.
- *Time Warner*, which now owns Turner Broadcasting, publishes books, music and two dozen magazines; operates over 100 Warner Bros retail stores; produces motion pictures, home video, and TV programming; has ownership interests in half a dozen cable channels; and owns cable franchises that reach 12 million subscribers. It also has investments in liquor, utilities, and finance. Through Turner Broadcasting it now owns professional sports teams, several production companies, and the Turner cable empire that includes the TBS superstation, three other cable channels, and the worldwide CNN news operation, including CNN International, Headline News and Airport News.
- *Disney/Capital Cities*, owner of ABC, owns five motion picture studios, several cable channels and TV production companies, worldwide theme parks, resorts and hotels, record production companies, over 400 Disney retail stores, several magazines, and a dozen newspapers. It also controls two professional sports teams and has interests as diverse as petroleum production and insurance. Through ABC it owns ten TV

---

[15] Miller, M and Biden, J, 'The National Entertainment State', *The Nation*, 3 June 1996, 23.

stations and has interests in others that cover 25 per cent of US households; ABC Radio, covering 24 per cent of US households; and ABC Network News, which produces over thirty hours of news and information programming each week.

- *Westinghouse*, owner of CBS, designs nuclear and electric power plants, communications and security systems, and mobile refrigeration units. It has interests in waste disposal, insurance, pension management, mutual funds, and investment banking. Through CBS it owns fourteen TV and thirty-nine radio stations and three cable channels as well as CBS Network News. CBS also has recently acquired Infinity Broadcasting, the nation's largest radio broadcaster.

In addition to the local stations they own outright, GE, Disney/Cap Cities, and Westinghouse have affiliated stations in virtually every market. The same content appears on both owned and affiliated stations.

This concentration raises fears that corporate interests control, not just the financing and the flow of information, but its content as well. They demand that attention be paid only to profitability, suppressing or manipulating news that is unfavorable to advertisers, to the corporate owners or to corporate culture in general. Supposed instances of such corporate censorship include ABC's and CBS's waffling on stories about the tobacco industry (whose non-tobacco affiliates such as Kraft Foods and Miller Beer are major TV advertisers), NBC's failure to report on nuclear energy in deference to parent GE's interests,[16] and the general failure of US news operations to report anything beyond the local, mundane, trivial, and sensational.

Similar concentrations affect other aspects of the media industry. Where just five years ago there were literally hundreds of small cable systems scattered through US communities, the landscape is now dominated by a score of multiple system operators (MSOs), such as Cablevision, Time Warner, and Tele-Communications, Inc, which control virtually every cable system in America. Mergers by Nynex and Bell Atlantic, Pacific Telesis and SBC, and the acquisition by US West of Continental Cablevision show the concentration in the telephone industry and the increasing convergence of cable and telephony under single corporate structures. Recently, AT&T and SBC have announced merger plans, converging local and long-distance phone services.

This concentration points the way toward one-stop communications shopping. Cablevision, for instance, a New York-based cable TV company, is offering local phone service and cable modems. Southern New England Telephone (SNET) is offering cable TV service in selected areas of Connecticut, in competition with Cablevision. In Maine, the electric

---

[16] ibid, 10, 22.

power company is rolling out fibre-optic wires to offer both telephony, cable, and Internet connections.

Public versus private ownership of information

According to Congress, the airwaves are public property licensed to broadcasters,[17] who, in exchange, are obliged to manage them as the public interest, convenience, and necessity demands. As one Supreme Court case put it, the contract favours the public: '[i]t is the right of the viewers and listeners, not the right of the broadcasters, which is paramount'.[18]

When the communications world was divided into broadcast and telephony, the contract seemed fairly straightforward. In telephony, the AT&T monopoly was obliged to provide service that was nondiscriminatory in terms of price or location—everybody was entitled to phone service at 'fair, just and reasonable prices'. As to content, that was up to the customers. As long as the communications were not obscene, harassing, or otherwise criminal, the government had no say. When pay telephony services arose, particularly erotic dial-in services, courts ruled that adults had the right to subscribe to them without government interference, provided that the content of the services was not obscene.[19]

Unlike telephony, which involves communications *between* members of the public, broadcasting involves communication *to* the public. Therefore, government has always taken a more active role in determining (a) what the public interest requires that broadcasters should *not* say, and (b) what the public interest demands that broadcasters *must* say (or must allow to be said over their licensed airwaves). In the first category, courts had ruled that, because broadcast radio and TV have a 'uniquely pervasive' presence in American life, Congress ('the public') may prevent them from broadcasting 'indecent' material during hours when children are likely to be watching or listening (the 'pervasiveness' rationale).[20] In the second category, courts have ruled that, because broadcasters consume a scarce resource, the radio spectrum, Congress ('the public') may require broadcasters to give a balanced presentation of political issues and candidates during election times (the 'scarcity' rationale).[21]

The rise of cable and satellite TV, of wireless telephony, and the

---

[17] The US distinguishes between 'broadcasting', which means free, over-the-air TV and radio, and 'cable', which means subscription TV delivered by coaxial cable. The definition of 'television broadcasting' in the European Commission's *Television Without Frontiers* Directive as 'transmission by wire or over the air, including that by satellite' is refined in US law.

[18] *Red Lion Broadcasting Co v FCC*, 395 US 367, 390 (1969) (rejecting a First Amendment challenge to FCC right of reply regulations).

[19] See *Sable Communications Inc v FCC*, 492 US 115 (1989).

[20] *FCC v Pacifica Fnd* 438 US 726 (1978).

[21] See *Red Lion Broadcasting Co v FCC*, 395 US 367 (1969).

Internet, have raised questions about the public interest obligations, not only of these new media, but of the old medium of broadcasting as well. A controversy over whether broadcasters should pay for radio and TV licences arose during the Communications Act debate, continued during the 1996 Presidential campaign, and continues now as a result of financing abuses during that campaign.

In 1993, when the FCC started making spectrum bands available to new personal communications services (PCS), Congress authorized auctions of the spectrum that had traditionally been given to licensees for free. Since the first 1993 auctions, more than $20 billion has been raised through spectrum auctions. Spectrum as a source of treasury funds made Congress look anew at the 6 MHz bands that TV broadcasters occupy for free, and, in particular, at a provision in the new Act that allowed the FCC to *give* existing television licensees second channels in order to develop High Definition TV (HDTV).[22] After considerable debate, the HDTV provision of the bill passed, with the understanding, later embodied in the FCC's HDTV decision, that, when HDTV is operational, the analog channels that broadcasters currently occupy will revert to the FCC for public auction.

Alongside the HDTV debate, a movement arose to ask broadcast stations voluntarily to give a nominal amount of free time to presidential candidates in the 1996 election.[23] When even so modest a plan proved unworkable, sentiment developed to make free political TV mandatory as a public interest obligation. This plan has gained force from the dawning public awareness that political campaigns require raising millions of dollars, that much of the money is raised from powerful groups with an interest in pending and future legislation, and that by far the greatest share of the millions so raised goes directly into TV advertising.

The debate about 'free TV for politicians' recircles to the argument over who owns the media and how much the public has a right to demand without infringing media operators' freedom of speech. The argument has two poles: 'no scarcity' and 'pervasiveness'. The 'no scarcity' argument holds that, while the radio spectrum is theoretically finite, there is no genuine scarcity of media voices. The proliferation of satellite, cable, and computer media have rendered scarcity notions quaint and archaic. With so many competing voices in the marketplace, the sensible choice is to constrain none of them, but to let the market do its work. If politicians balk at the ad prices charged by broadcast stations, let them advertise on cheaper cable outlets. Furthermore, broadcasting no longer represents a *'uniquely* pervasive presence' in American life, since all other media are

---

[22] 47 USC § 336.

[23] See, eg, Cronkite, W and Taylor, P, 'Election's Good Idea: Free TV For Candidates to Discuss Issues', *Philadelphia Inquirer*, 7 Nov 1996, A37.

equally pervasive.[24] Therefore it makes no sense to saddle broadcasting or any other medium with unique public interest obligations.

The 'pervasiveness' argument cuts the other way, asserting that broadcasting is no longer *'uniquely* pervasive' only because other media have become equally so. TV, radio, email, and the Internet are intrusive, and ubiquitous in American life, demanding 24-hour attention and consuming both the work and leisure time of the majority of Americans. In exchange for this pervasive, intrusive and dominating presence, the public has a right to demand that *all* electronic media act in the public interest by, among other things, quelling sexual speech,[25] offering educational programmes, and providing free time to the political process.

1.2 Market participants

The newest and fastest-growing market is the Internet and related technologies. Estimates of Internet penetration hover around 15 per cent of the population, with work-related usage accounting for about 75 per cent of that. Both the general and the work-related Internet percentage should increase dramatically with the introduction in the workplace of private Intranets—local networks that incorporate Internet technology while protecting local information behind firewalls.

Participants in the Internet market include both traditional media players and new entrants. They may roughly be divided into infrastructure providers, software and service providers, and content suppliers and aggregators.

Infrastructure

This includes providers of data networking equipment, both on the client (modem, ISDN, cable) and server (routers, modem pools, and call aggregators) side, by companies including US Robotics and Hayes modems. Also included are Internet security equipment and software providers and Internet service providers, such as 'Pure-plays' that simply offer access (such as Netcom) and Online Service Providers (OSPs) that offer Internet access through existing proprietary networks, such as America Online and CompuServe. Traditional telephone companies, including AT&T, MCI, Sprint, and several Baby Bells, offer Internet connections, as do cable companies, including Tele-Communications Inc's

---

[24] *Action for Children's Television v FCC,* 58 F 3d 654, 676 (1995), cert denied 116 S Ct 701 (1996).

[25] See *Alliance for Community Media v FCC,* 56 F 3d 105, 125 (DDC 1995), aff'd in part, rev'd in part sub nom *Denver Area Educational Telecomm Consortium v FCC,* 116 S Ct 2374 (1996) ('cable television is sufficiently pervasive and easily accessible to children to justify the government's attempts to regulate indecency on cable channels').

@Home and Time Warner's Road Runner. Telecommunications and related services are offered by long-distance companies including MCI,
which carries Internet traffic through an Internet backbone service, and
Sprint, whose SprintLink is strong in international connections. Cable
operators, who are potential competitors in the infrastructure market,
may lack the capital to enter the market. Other participants include telecommunications equipment providers, which will supply hybrid fibre-
coax to cable companies and digital cable for higher-speed PC Internet
connections.

Software and services

Application software is supplied by companies that preceded the Internet,
such as Microsoft and Adobe and by new, Internet-dedicated firms like
Netscape. The focus is on browsers, servers, and development tools as
well as enterprise and networking software from companies such as
Oracle. There is also a huge developing market for Internet consulting
and development.

Content and aggregation

New aggregators such as Yahoo and Infoseek are competing with established companies such as America OnLine and CompuServe for web
search sites that make the web navigable. For the moment, existing OSPs
have the advantage because they have been organizing on-line informa
tion for years. However, as users become more sophisticated, they may
rely less and less on OSPs to predigest information for them. As to content
providers, there are few pure information companies that are devoted to
the Internet. Content comes from pre-existing sources, both interactive
like Motley Fool and traditional like the *New York Times*. There is also a
growing need for transaction processing and financial services through
such innovations as DigiCash, CyberCash, and FirstVirtual, though the
whole structure of Internet commerce remains inchoate.

2 REGULATION AND OTHER MEDIA POLICIES

2.1 Types of regulation and other policies

Communications regulation in the US is shared by the Federal government and the fifty state governments. For instance, interstate and international telephony are the province of the Federal government, while
intrastate telephony is largely left to the states. While TV broadcast
licences are allocated by the Federal government, the government has
deferred to the states in awarding local cable franchises and regulating

cable rates. In addition, there are over 60,000 local municipal governments, some of which take an indirect role in communications matters
through franchising and zoning laws.[26] Three provisions of the US Constitution are of particular relevance to the interplay of these entities.

*   'The Congress shall have power . . . to regulate commerce with foreign
    nations and among the several states'[27] (the 'Commerce Clause').
*   'The Constitution and the laws of the United States which shall be
    made in pursuance thereof . . . shall be the supreme law of the land; . . .
    every state shall be bound thereby, any thing in the Constitution or
    laws of any state to the contrary notwithstanding'[28] (the 'Supremacy
    Clause').
*   'The powers not delegated to the United States by the Constitution, nor
    prohibited by it to the states, are reserved to the states respectively, or
    to the people.'[29]

These three provisions allow the Federal government to regulate national
matters and the states to regulate local matters, with federal laws
preempting state laws that conflict. Many clashes in communications
policy concern state *versus* Federal jurisdictional questions, including conflicts over rate regulation for local cable systems and telephone service,
and local zoning rules that obstruct federal policy.

2.1.1 *The Federal Communications Commission (FCC)*

Although states and municipalities have certain powers with regard to
telecommunications, by far the most potent entity is the Federal government, acting through the FCC. Under the authority of the Commerce
Clause, Federal regulation of radio began as early as 1910, when radio was
confined to maritime safety and military communications. By 1927 the
development of commercial radio required a body that would allocate
frequencies to prevent technical interference. The resultant Federal Radio
Commission became the Federal Communications Commission under the
Communications Act of 1934. Its responsibility, now far greater than the
mere allocation of frequencies, is 'regulating interstate and foreign commerce in communications by wire and radio so as to make available, so far
as possible, to all the people of the United States, a rapid, efficient, nationwide and world-wide wire and radio communication service with
adequate facilities at reasonable charges for the purpose of the national

---

[26] Local municipal laws are a matter of administrative convenience and may not conflict
with state or federal laws. See *Community Communications Co v City of Boulder*, 455 US 40
(1982) ('Ours is a *"dual"* system of government," which has no place for sovereign
cities')(citation omitted).
[27] US Const art I, § 8.
[28] US Const art VI.
[29] US Const amend X.

defense, for the purpose of promoting safety of life and property through the use of wire and radio communication . . . consistent with the public interest, convenience [and] necessity'.[30]

The FCC regulates interstate and foreign communications by radio, wire, television, satellite, and cable. The Commission comprises five members, appointed by the President with the advice and consent of the Senate. It has legislative powers through the adoption of regulations, executive power in the enforcement of rules, and judicial power in adjudicating disputes.

The FCC and broadcasting

Free, over-the-air reception of TV and radio broadcasts is a cornerstone of US media policy. The public pays no licence or subscription fee. Over 1,600 local TV broadcast stations and over 10,000 local radio stations provide such services, which the FCC licenses them to do through a competitive application process. Only a small administrative fee is charged for a broadcast licence, unlike the millions of dollars the FCC reaps through auctions for other uses of the spectrum, such as personal communications services (PCS).

In return for their virtually free licences, and under the theory that the radio spectrum is a 'scarce resource',[31] broadcasters are subject to content restrictions and public interest obligations that do not apply to other media. Among the content regulations are provisions that forbid broadcasters to air 'indecent' programming between the hours of 6 am and 10 pm.[32] Public interest obligations include the duty to devote at least three hours a week to children's programming.[33] Additionally, broadcasters are subject to equal-time-and-access rules for political candidates and may only charge such candidates 'the lowest unit charge' for paid advertising.[34] It has recently been proposed that, as part of their public interest obligations, broadcast stations be required to give entirely free time to candidates during political campaigns.

The FCC and cable TV

The FCC Mass Media Bureau also administers regulatory programmes for cable TV. Unlike broadcasting and common carrier licences, however, which are allocated by the FCC, cable TV franchises are awarded by local

---

[30] 47 USC §§ 151, 307.

[31] See generally, Franklin, M and Anderson, D, *Cases and Materials on Mass Media Law* (Foundation Press: Mineola, 4th edn, 1990), 790–885.

[32] See *Action For Children's Television v FCC*, 58 F 3d 654 (1995), cert. denied 116 S Ct 701 (1996).

[33] 'Report and Order in the Matter of Policies and Rules Concerning Children's Programming', FCC Report No 96-335 (8 Aug 1996).

[34] 47 USC § 315.

municipal governments, which also set, within FCC guidelines, terms and conditions for operating the franchise. This structure derives from cable TV's origin as community antenna TV (CATV), which involved simply erecting an antenna to bring distant broadcasts into remote communities. After a number of years of leaving cable TV virtually unregulated, Congress passed Cable Television Acts in 1984 and 1992, giving the FCC greater and greater control over cable TV matters.

In return for their local franchise, most cable systems are required to set aside a number of channels for public and leased access, for educational, and for government uses ('PEG' channels).[35] They also have obligations not to discriminate in prices or service among different sectors of the franchise area. Franchised cable operators must carry the signals of local broadcast TV stations that would be accessible over the air without cable. These 'must-carry' rules have twice been upheld by the Supreme Court under the theory that the cable TV 'bottleneck', through which 60 per cent of the nation receives TV signals, is a threat to the survival of free broadcast TV.[36] Franchised cable operators pay to local governments a franchise fee of up to 5 per cent of gross revenues.[37]

The FCC and telecommunications

The Common Carrier Bureau administers regulatory programmes for interstate and international common carrier communications by telephone and telegraph. The Wireless Telecommunications Bureau handles personal communications services (PCS), cellular, and paging. The International Bureau regulates satellite communications. Regulation is based on two premises. First, telecommunications, both local and long-distance, have natural monopoly characteristics that require regulation to control prices. Second, many telecom services use over-the-air transmission, like broadcasters, and so require central regulation to avoid electrical interference.

Though telecommunications carriers, both local and long-distance, are licensed by the FCC, local telephone rates are set by state Public Utility Commissions (PUCs). Traditionally, such regulation has been based on allowing telcos a certain rate of return (ROR) over costs. Since local telephone service has traditionally been a monopoly, such a pricing regime was thought necessary in order to prevent telcos from cross-subsidizing other services by raising prices on their local-phone-service monopoly. The recent trend is toward simply capping prices, which allows telcos to accumulate capital for new services as long as their rates, for a service or bundle of services, do not exceed a certain cap. As implemented by the

---

[35] See, eg, Va Code Ann § 15.1–23.1(D) (Michie 1996).
[36] See *Turner Broadcasting Sys, Inc v FCC*, 117 S Ct 1134 (1997).
[37] 47 USC § 542(b).

FCC, the new Telecommunications Act encourages PUCs to adopt price cap regimes.[38]

In the long-distance market, the FCC has long distinguished between 'dominant' and 'nondominant' carriers, subjecting only dominant carriers to full regulation, based on their ability to exert market power. AT&T was, for a long time, the only carrier classified as dominant. Now, recognizing the increasing competitiveness of the long-distance market, the FCC has classified *all* long-distance carriers as nondominant and, therefore, not subject to rate regulation. This includes AT&T, both domestically and internationally.

The FCC and the Internet

Section 502 of the Communications Decency Act ('CDA',[39] see below), authorized the FCC to promulgate regulations that identify 'reasonable, effective and appropriate' measures to keep offensive content off the Internet. At the time of the CDA's passage, some were worried that this would give the FCC a foot in the door to regulate the Internet, but in the wake of *Reno v ACLU* (see below) the FCC has taken no action in promulgating such rules. This forbearance is in keeping with the stated policy of the new Act 'to preserve the vibrant and competitive free market that presently exists for the Internet and other interactive computer services, unfettered by Federal or State regulation'.[40] None the less, Internet development in the US is shaped by government policy decisions. In particular, the FCC has determined that Internet service providers, though theoretically classifiable as long-distance phone carriers, are not subject to interstate access charges. Additionally, the states' regulatory requirements that local calls be available at flat monthly rates allow users unlimited Internet access for the cost of a single local phone call. Perhaps no other government policy has accounted equally for the spiralling growth of the Internet in the US.

In the absence of thoroughgoing FCC regulation, the Internet is regulated by analogy to laws affecting other media. Criminal activity, for instance, is the province of the states, which can lead to interesting anomalies: a California website operator is now jailed in Tennessee for making materials, which would not be considered obscene in California, available in Tennessee, where they are. As to other laws, copyright, defamation, false advertising, etc, apply equally on the Internet as anywhere. The interplay of state and Federal law on the Internet can be seen in the two recent cases that voided state statutes restricting Internet content on the

[38] See 'Report and Order In the Matter of Price Cap Performance Review', FCC Report No 97–158 (16 May 1997).
[39] 47 USC § 223(e)(6).
[40] ibid, § 230(b)(2).

grounds that (1) forbidding anonymous postings violates freedom of speech,[41] and (2) for a state to restrict Internet content imposes excessive burdens on interstate commerce.[42]

FCC rulemaking procedures and court challenges

The FCC does not pass laws, but rather implements, through rule-making procedures,[43] the laws that Congress passes. The process is one of fitting specific issues into existing regulatory and legal frameworks. Rule making is a three-step procedure that requires (1) *notice* of the proposed rule, including information about opportunities for public participation; (2) *participation* by interested parties, who comment on the proposed rule both by submitting written comments and through informal contacts; and (3) *a report and order*, issuing the rule and spelling out its basis and purpose. It is during the *participation* phase that interest groups, both public and private, have their voices heard. A proposed rule involving telco-cable cross-ownership, for instance, in addition to receiving opinions from telcos and cable companies, may elicit comments from municipal franchising agencies, from state PUCs, cable associations, broadcasters, the National League of Cities, the United States Conference of Mayors, as well as numerous consumer groups, landlord-and-tenant associations, and anyone else the rule might affect.

Once the rule is passed, it may be challenged in court, often by one of the interest groups who commented at the proposal stage. For instance, when the FCC passed a rule that required cable operators to 'ban or block' indecent programming on leased- and public-access channels, a court challenge was brought by, among others, the Denver Area Educational Telecommunications Consortium, Alliance for Community Media, Alliance for Communications Democracy, People for the American Way, and the American Civil Liberties Union.[44] An FCC rule banning indecent programming from broadcast stations between 6 am and 10 pm was challenged by, among others, Action for Children's Television, the Association of Independent Television Stations, the Motion Picture Association of America, the National Association of Broadcasters, the Reporters Committee for Freedom of the Press, and the Society of Professional Journalists.[45]

---

[41] *ACLU of Georgia v Miller*, 1:96-CV-2475–MHS, slip op, (ND Ga, 20 June 1997).
[42] *American Library Assn v Pataki*, 97 Civ 0222 (LAP), slip op (SDNY, 20 June 1997).
[43] Administrative Procedure Act, 5 USC § 553.
[44] See *Alliance for Community Media v FCC*, 56 F 3d 105 (DDC 1995), aff'd in part, rev'd in part sub nom *Denver Area Educational Telecomm Consortium v FCC*, 116 S Ct 2374 (1996) (upholding cable operators' right to ban indecent programmes on leased access but denying their right to segregate and scramble such programming if they do air it).
[45] *Action for Children's Television, Inc v FCC*, 58 F 3d 654 (DDC 1995), cert denied, 116 S Ct 701 (1996) (upholding ban on broadcast of indecent programming between 6 am and 10 pm).

The National Information Infrastructure

In 1993, the Clinton administration published *The National Information Infrastructure: An Agenda for Action*. It promised that, while the infrastructure itself ('a seamless web of communication networks') would be a private sector product, 'there remain essential roles for government in this process'. These roles include:

- promoting private sector investment through tax and regulatory policies;
- extending the 'universal service' concept to ensure that information resources are available to all at affordable prices;
- acting as a catalyst to promote technological innovation and new applications;
- promoting seamless, interactive user-driven operation of the NII by ensuring transferability of information across networks, as from TV to computer;
- ensuring information security and network reliability;
- improving management of the radio frequency spectrum;
- protecting intellectual property rights;
- co-ordinating with other levels of government and with other nations; and
- providing access to government information and improving government procurement.

Some of these plans have proved easier to implement than others. The primary organ of change is the Telecommunications Act of 1996.

2.1.2 The Telecommunications Act of 1996

The Act, the most sweeping overhaul of national communications law since the first Communications Act of 1934, touches every area of communication by wire and air, including radio, broadcast TV, cable TV, telephony and (for the first time) interactive services.

Broadcast radio and TV

Previous acts limited the number of TV and radio stations a single entity could own.[46] The new Act removes many limits on aggregate radio station ownership,[47] and provides only that a single entity may not own TV stations that reach more than 35 per cent of the nation's

---

[46] Before the new Act, a single entity was limited to ownership nationally of twelve TV stations, and twenty AM and twenty FM radio stations, with no new licence issued to an entity which already owned a broadcast station in the same or overlapping area. See 'Memorandum Opinion and Order In Re Revision of Radio Rules and Policies', 7 FCC Rcd 6387, 6388 (1992); see also Geller, H, 'Ownership Regulatory Policies in the US Telecom Sector', 13 Cardozo Arts & Ent LJ (1995), 727, 733.

[47] 47 CFR § 73.3555.

households.[48] Both the radio and TV ownership rules, however, constrain ownership of multiple stations in the same local market.[49] An antiquated,[50] but surviving, 1975 rule prevents newspaper-broadcast cross-ownership in local markets, though existing combinations were allowed to continue.[51] New rules extend the licence period to eight years (up from five for TV and seven for radio) and virtually guarantee renewal unless the broadcaster commits 'serious' violations of FCC rules or fails to serve the vaguely-defined public interest.[52]

The most controversial of the Act's broadcasting provisions empowers the FCC to grant each current TV broadcaster an additional channel for the development of High Definition Television (HDTV).[53] A further provision, which applies equally to cable and broadcast TV, requires producers of video programmes voluntarily to rate programmes for 'sexual, violent or other indecent material' or face an FCC-mandated rating system.[54] Viewers (parents of young children in particular) will be able to block this material by means of a rating-sensitive 'V-chip' (V for violence) that will be installed in all new TV sets.[55]

Cable TV

Prior to the Act, a cable TV system enjoyed a virtual monopoly on video programming services in its local service area. Though exclusive franchises were forbidden, and fledgling competition arose from Direct Broadcast Satellite (DBS), Multi-Channel Multipoint Distribution Services (MMDS), and Satellite Master Antenna TV (SMATV), such services still account for less than 10 per cent of the country's multichannel video offerings.[56] Meanwhile, local telephone companies (telcos), the likeliest competitors to local cable systems, were forbidden by law to offer video services in their own local markets. As a result, Congress chose to regulate cable rates as if cable were a monopoly.

---

[48] 47 CFR § 73.3555(e)(1). Note that a 'superstation' like WTBS in Atlanta, though it reaches more than 35% of the national audience, reaches only the Atlanta area by *broadcast*. It reaches the rest of the country by satellite and cable, to which the 35% rule does not apply.

[49] ibid, § 73.3555(a)–(c).

[50] See 'McCain bill would end crossownership ban', *Broadcasting & Cable*, 28 Apr 1997, 6 ('Senate Commerce Committee Chairman John McCain (R-Ariz) has introduced legislation that would lift the ban on ownership of a newspaper and either a radio or TV station in the same market . . . call[ing it] "one of the most archaic provisions in telecommunications law [that] dates from a day when there was a realistic fear that common control of both media in the same locale could result in the public's receiving only one point of view".').

[51] 47 CFR § 73.3555(d).

[52] 47 USC § 309(k)(1).

[53] ibid, § 336(a).

[54] ibid, § 303(w).

[55] ibid, § 303(x).

[56] Botein, M, 'Antitrust Issues in the Telecommunications and Software Industries', 25 *SUL Rev* (1996), 569, 596–7.

The new Act phases out cable rate regulation, to let cable companies accumulate capital to compete in the broader communications market, including offering cable modems and phone service. Commensurately, bowing to a series of recent court decisions,[57] the Act allows telcos to enter the local cable market, with the goal of controlling cable rates through competition rather than regulation. To ensure that lifting the telco-cable cross-ownership restriction does not simply result in telco-cable buyouts, mergers, and joint ventures, the Act prohibits these[58] and further provides that a telco can acquire only 10 per cent of a cable company in its own service area and vice versa.[59] After 1999, a cable company will be subject to rate regulation only if it does not face 'effective competition'[60] either from a competing cable system run by a telco, electric company, or other wire-based entity, or from a DBS or other satellite system.

Some surviving ownership restrictions recognize the continuing monopoly characteristics of cable systems. For instance, until a cable system is certified as subject to effective competition, it cannot offer a satellite TV service.[61]

In addition to the existing obligations to carry public, educational, and governmental ('PEG') programming and the must-carry rules, the new Act requires that cable programming, like broadcast, be rated for 'sexual, violent or other indecent material'[62] that can be blocked by a V-chip.

Telephony

In its most complicated provisions, the Act ends the court-enforced separation between long-distance (domestic and international) and local phone service. The separation was created by the 1982 consent decree[63] (the 'Modified Final Judgment' or 'MFJ') that broke up AT&T. Before the MFJ, AT&T operated almost as an autonomous PTT, with its monopoly over local phone service and a national monopoly over long-distance and equipment manufacturing. The MFJ divested AT&T of its local phone companies (telcos), divided the telcos into seven regional fiefs (the 'Baby Bells' or RBOCs) and kept AT&T out of local phone service and the telcos out of long-distance and equipment manufacturing. Combined with the exclusion from the video business, these 'line of business restrictions' effectively limited the telcos' communications offerings to phone service alone, though they could diversify into unrelated fields such as real estate.

[57] See eg, *US West Inc v United States*, 855 F Supp 1184 (1994), aff'd 48 F 3d 1092 (9th Cir 1994), vacated and remanded for consideration of mootness 116 S Ct 1037 (1996).
[58] 47 USC § 652(c).
[59] ibid, § 652(a)–(b).
[60] ibid, § 543(l)(1).
[61] ibid, § 533(a).
[62] ibid, § 303.
[63] *United States v American Tel & Tel Co*, 552 F Supp 131 (DDC 1982), aff'd sub nom, *Maryland v United States*, 460 US 1001 (1983).

Furthermore, the practical difficulty of duplicating the telcos' local loops and switches created insurmountable entry barriers to potential competitors, ensuring a perpetual local monopoly.

The new Act ends all this. In a section called 'Development of Competitive Markets' it lays out both a substantive and a procedural blueprint for the future of telephony.[64] The three basic questions the Act addresses are:

- how can the local telephone market be opened to competition?
- how can entry barriers be reduced in the long-distance market?
- how can universal service obligations be allocated among market participants?

The first, and key, duty for all telecommunications carriers under the new Act is interconnection—all carriers must let all other carriers interconnect with their equipment and cannot design their networks to prevent it.[65] Telcos must provide, at just and reasonable rates, interconnection 'at any feasible point' within the network to 'unbundled' elements thereof, allowing a competitor to combine network elements in any way it wants to offer a full telecommunications service.[66] Telcos must further allow competitors to buy and resell, at wholesale rates, any elements that they themselves offer to subscribers.[67] They must even allow firms seeking interconnection to locate their equipment on the telcos' premises (the 'physical collocation' requirement).[68] The Act also preempts state and local barriers to market entry.

Of these requirements, unbundled access is the most important. Assuming, for instance, that a cable TV operator, with its own coaxial lines into individual households, would not need the incumbent telco's local loop, unbundling allows it to pick operator and directory assistance services from the telco's remaining menu.[69]

In August 1996, the FCC implemented the interconnection requirement with its Interconnection Report and Order.[70] Though state PUCs will still set prices for individual unbundled elements, the FCC established the framework for the pricing methodology and the price ceiling. This preemption of state authority was immediately challenged by several PUCs in Federal court, which ultimately found that the FCC had exceeded its authority by setting such rules.[71] Though prices, whether set by the states or the FCC, would probably be the same, the court decision repre-

---

[64] 47 USC §§ 251–52.   [65] ibid, §§ 251(a)(1)–(2).   [66] ibid, § 251(c)(2), (3).
[67] ibid, § 251(c)(4).
[68] ibid, § 251(c)(6).
[69] See Cunard, J, 'Interconnection Order Seeks to End Local Telco Monopolies'. *Cable TV & New Media*, Aug 1996.
[70] Report and Order in the Matter of Implementation of the Local Competition Provisions of the Telecommunications Act of 1996, FCC Report No 96-325 (8 Aug 1996).
[71] *Iowa Utils Bd v FCC*, 120 F 3d 753 (8th Cir 1997).

sents the continuing Constitutional struggle between the states and the FCC over the management of local telephone policy.

In addition to allowing competitors into local phone service, interconnectivity is also the key to the second element of full competition: allowing telcos to offer long-distance service to its local subscribers. In order to get permission from the FCC to enter the long-distance market, a telco must be certified by its state PUC to have fulfilled its obligation to allow local competition.[72] The Act's 'competitive checklist' of criteria that a telco must meet consists largely of specific interconnection requirements.[73] The telco's fulfilment of the interconnection requirements must also undergo Department of Justice scrutiny.

A second barrier to entry into the long-distance market has been the tariffs that telcos have traditionally imposed on long-distance carriers for access to their local loop. This access charge has added as much as 40 per cent to the price of long-distance service, with the avowed purpose of subsidizing local phone rates. In keeping with the Congressional directive that competition replace regulation as the mechanism for keeping local prices low, the FCC in May 1997 issued a Report and Order reducing the access charge by up to 80 per cent over five years.[74]

The third great question in telephony is universal service. Though universal service has been a goal of US communications policy since its inception,[75] the new Act actually codifies it.[76] Traditionally, universal service has meant little more than subsidizing the provision of voice-grade dial tone to poor people and rural areas. The new Act not only defines universal service as providing 'advanced telecommunications and information services' to all areas and income levels, and makes all providers of telecommunications services contribute to it,[77] but defines universal service as 'an evolving level' of service to be determined 'periodically', depending on what services (a) have become essential to education, health, or safety, (b) are used by 'a substantial majority of residential customers'; and (c) are 'consistent with the public interest'.[78] Further, '[e]lementary and secondary schools and classrooms, health care providers, and libraries should have access to advanced telecommunications services.'[79]

---

[72] 47 USC § 252(e).

[73] ibid, § 271(c)(2).

[74] Report and Order in the Matter of Price Cap Performance Review For Local Exchange Carriers—Access Charge Reform, FCC Report No 97-159 (21 May 1997).

[75] 47 USC § 151 (one purpose of the FCC is 'to make available, so far as possible, to all the people of the United States . . . communication service with adequate facilities at reasonable charges').

[76] ibid, § 254.

[77] ibid, § 254(b).

[78] ibid, § 254(c)(1)(A)–(D).

[79] ibid, § 254(b)(6).

FCC implementation of universal service arrived in a May 1997 Report and Order.[80] The order establishes a Universal Service Fund of $4.65 billion to equip schools and libraries with high-speed Internet connections and rural health care centres with phone service, while continuing the existing subsidies of rural phone service. The money will come from a tax of 1–2 per cent on the total local and long-distance sales of all phone companies. Funds for schools and libraries will come from a tax on second phone lines for residential and business customers. The Universal Service Report and Order supplied the third instalment of the 'FCC Competition Trilogy', which, with the orders on interconnection and access charges, establishes the price of entry to the telephony market.

Internet

Though the Act does not deal with the Internet in detail, it does lay down three important policies that will have significant effect on the growth of on-line services. *First*, the Act makes it a criminal offence to use an 'interactive computer service' to make 'patently offensive' sexual material 'available' to minors.[81] This provision was overturned by the Supreme Court in *Reno v ACLU*.[82] *Second*, the Act provides that no on-line content provider shall be considered 'the publisher or speaker' of content provided by another,[83]and that efforts to police one's website for objectionable material do not subject one to publisher-type liability.[84] *Third*, the Act explicitly preempts state laws that are inconsistent with these policies.[85]

Policies embodied by the Act

While the Act is intricate in detail, its broad outlines balance three policies. *First*, and most important, the free market, rather than regulation, will determine prices and services. Thus, rate regulation, ownership quotas and line of business restrictions are either eliminated or phased out over a number of years. No attempts were made to interfere with the free market of the Internet. *Second*, counterbalancing the first, entry into markets is regulated to prevent anti-competitive advantages. Thus, telcos can offer long-distance only after being certified for interconnectivity; telcos and cable operators cannot engage in buy-outs, mergers, or joint ventures; telcos must conduct long-distance or equipment manufacturing under separate subsidiaries. *Third*, regulation survives in the form of certain

[80] Report and Order in the Matter of the Federal-State Joint Board on Universal Service, FCC Report No 97–157 (8 May 1997).
[81] 47 USC § 223(d).
[82] 117 S Ct 2329 (1997).
[83] ibid, § 230(c)(1).
[84] ibid, § 230(c)(2)(A).
[85] ibid, § 230(d)(3).

'pro-social cross-subsidies'[86] that ensure fair treatment of groups or areas with unequal political or economic power. Universal service is the most obvious of these, protecting poor and rural areas at the expense of richer, urban ones; less obvious are content restrictions that protect children at the expense of adults and must-carry rules that protect the broadcast industry at the expense of cable operators.

The Act represents an increase in power for the FCC over all communications media and a consequent diminution of the power of other Federal agencies and of state PUCs and local franchising agencies. However, such agencies' powers are not reduced to nil. Two recent mergers under the new Act, that of Nynex with Bell Atlantic and that of Time-Warner with Turner Broadcasting, demonstrate the continuing interplay of Federal agencies with each other and with local PUCs.

Nynex and Bell Atlantic are two of the Baby Bells that spun off from the break-up of AT&T, the former controlling local phone service from Maine to New York, the latter from New Jersey to Virginia. Under previous law, a merger between these two would have been unthinkable, a step toward reassembling the old AT&T colossus. The new Act, however, stripped away many of the philosophical and regulatory barriers to such a merger, allowing much more freewheeling than before. It also made such a merger attractive—since both companies could now, by passing the 'competitive checklist', offer long-distance in competition with AT&T, it makes more sense to offer such service as a united front than in competition.

Still, approval of the merger, which was announced on 19 April 1996, took a full year, until 25 April 1997, and involved fourteen state and two Federal agencies. First, each company had to get approval from the PUCs of the states they served. Some states simply waived jurisdiction, but others wrested concessions. New York, for instance, demanded that Nynex improve its local customer service and spend $1 billion over the next five years to upgrade its local network. It further demanded that the merged company's headquarters be located in New York City rather than Philadelphia, as proposed, and that it hire 750 to 1,000 New York workers by the end of the year.[87] Having acceded to these demands, the companies next had to face anti-trust scrutiny by the Justice Department, which determined that, since the merging companies do not and would not compete in the local phone market, the merger would not deprive either of a likely competitor.[88] Finally, FCC approval had to be sought. (For the

---

[86] Krattenmaker, T, 'The Telecommunications Act of 1996', 49 *Fed Comm LJ* (1996), 1, 9.

[87] '2 Bells Accept Terms of New York Merger', *New York Times*, 22 Mar 1997, B5.

[88] Landler, M, 'Merger of Nynex and Bell Atlantic Clears Hurdle', *New York Times*, 25 Apr 1997, A1.

interplay of Federal agencies in the Turner–Time Warner merger, see the section on *Concentration and Anti-trust Rules* below.)

2.2 Topics and issues

2.2.1 *Technological regulation*

As noted above, the FCC began as the Federal Radio Commission, charged essentially with allocating radio frequencies in order to prevent electrical interference. Though the FCC has evolved tremendously as a regulatory body, its origins in technological regulation still survive. For example, the new Act allows the FCC to preempt state and local laws that interfere with the public's ability to receive over-the-air signals.[89] The FCC has lately implemented this portion of the Act via a Report and Order that limits local regulation of antennae to considerations only of safety and historical preservation.[90]

The FCC's latest venture in technological regulation involves the stunning process that will lead to the establishment of High Definition TV (HDTV) as the standard for US TV shortly after the turn of the century.

High Definition Television ('HDTV')

The arrival of HDTV has been a ten-year process, initiated by the FCC in 1987 in reaction to Japanese technological advances. The FCC's Advanced Television Systems proceeding was, in effect, a competition among various industries to produce a computer-age television set, incorporating a digital signal and a high-resolution picture with twice as many lines as a standard picture (1,080 as opposed to 525 lines). Under FCC prodding,[91] the competition resulted in an agreement among the Broadcasters Caucus, the Consumer Electronics Manufacturers Association and the Computer Industry Coalition on Advanced Television Service, which was approved by the FCC in late 1996 and incorporated into an FCC order of 3 April 1997.

The Telecommunications Act gave a boost not only to the HDTV effort, but to the broadcast industry in particular, by providing that initially licences for 'advanced television services' may be issued only to existing TV broadcast licensees.[92] The FCC implemented the Act by an order of 3 April 1997[93] that gives each of the nation's 1,600 television stations a

---

[89] Cunard, J, 'FCC Watch', *Cable TV & New Media*, Sept 1996, 5, 8.

[90] Report and Order in the Matter of Preemption of Local Zoning Regulation, FCC Report No 96–328 (6 Aug 1996).

[91] See Gladwell, M, 'Just Ask for It: The Real Key to Technological Innovation', *The New Yorker*, 7 Apr 1997, 46.

[92] 47 USC § 336(a)(1).

[93] Advanced Television Systems and Their Impact Upon the Existing Television Broadcast Service, FCC Report No 97-115 (3 Apr 1997).

second channel to broadcast digital versions of what they are now broad-casting on analog channels. Each broadcaster will use the second channel to develop digital programming and, when the digital channel is completely operational, will return the analog spectrum to the FCC, which will auction it off. The FCC Order sets a timetable for HDTV roll-out. Major network affiliates in the top ten markets have until May 1999 to get a digital signal on the air; markets eleven to twenty have until November 1999; all other commercial stations have five years; non-commercial stations have six years. The FCC set the year 2006 as the target for ending the analog standard and switching completely to digital.

One effect of the HDTV ruling is to render obsolete all of the nation's TV sets by the year 2006 and to require their replacement with new high-definition digital sets, which will begin hitting the market by the end of 1998. However, the implications of HDTV for convergence remain to be seen, since there is so far no agreement on making the new digital signals computer-compatible. Omitted from the standard adopted by the FCC is any agreement on scanning format.[94] The broadcasters soon announced that they would transmit programmes in both interlaced and progressive scanning formats. However, computers—both the current PCs and the proposed big-screen PC theatre products—are equipped to handle only progressive scanning. Unless there is some agreement on scanning format, digital TV programming will not be translatable to computer screens.[95]

As noted above, the HDTV ruling has been attacked as an unfair giveaway to the broadcast industry. Congress and the FCC's answer is that public interest obligations can be demanded of the broadcast industry that cannot be demanded of others and that the Act itself specifies that the HDTV section 'shall [not] be construed as relieving a television broadcast station from its obligation to serve the public interest, convenience and necessity'.[96] However, what those public interest obligations will be, and whether they will be better-defined than existing ones, remains to be seen.

Spectrum auctions

One thing that has spurred debate about the 'giveaway' of HDTV channels to existing broadcasters is the FCC's new Congressionally-approved practice of auctioning-off portions of the broadcast spectrum. Before 1993, radio spectrum licences were allocated either through lottery or through comparative hearings that determined which applicant could best serve the public interest. Under the Budget Reconciliation Act of 1993, Congress

[94] Cunard, J, 'FCC Watch', *Cable TV & New Media*, Jan 1997, 8.
[95] Brinkley, J, 'No Narrowing of 2 Industries' Rift on Advanced TV', *New York Times*, 14 Apr 1997.
[96] 47 USC § 336(d).

instead authorized the FCC to use competitive bidding to auction-off licences for new wireless services. Since 1993, the spectrum auctions have raised over $20 billion,[97] with many of the early licences going to small businesses owned by women or minority groups under a 'Designated Entity' programme that gave them special concessions. Although a Supreme Court decision[98] subjecting race-and-minority-based concessions to strict constitutional scrutiny has forced the FCC to end the 'Designated Entity' programme for such groups (keeping it for small businesses), the auction process itself continues.

2.2.2 Economic regulation

Concentration and anti-trust rules

US anti-trust law is based on the Sherman and Clayton anti-trust acts and court decisions interpreting them, which confer on the Department of Justice (DOJ) and the Federal Trade Commission (FTC) the responsibility for policing uncompetitive behaviour. The new Act ratifies and, at least in theory, expands their authority. '[N]othing in this Act . . . shall be construed to modify, impair, or supersede the applicability of any of the antitrust laws.'[99] Furthermore, the Act repealed two provisions that allowed the FCC to confer anti-trust immunity on transactions it had approved, such as local telco mergers. According to the *Joint Explanatory Statement* that accompanied the bill:

Mergers [between telecommunications companies] should not be allowed to go through without a thorough antitrust review. . . . By returning review of mergers in a competitive industry to the D[epartment] O[f] J[ustice], this repeal would be consistent with one of the underlying themes of the bill—to get both agencies back to their proper roles. . . . The Commission should be carrying out the policies of the Communications Act, and the DOJ should be carrying out the policies of the antitrust laws.

This pro-anti-trust language, however, must be seen in the context of other provisions of the Act, which sharply delimit anti-trust authority. For instance, when a Bell Operating Company, by meeting the interconnection requirements, applies to the FCC to be permitted to offer long-distance, the FCC 'shall notify the Attorney General', who may give 'an evaluation of the application using any standard the Attorney General considers appropriate'. However, though the FCC 'shall give substantial weight' to the evaluation, it *'shall not have any preclusive effect on any Commission decision'*.[100]

---

[97] Cardilli, C, 'The Great Spectrum Shootout', *J of Comm*, 12 May 1997, 7A.

[98] *Adarand Constructors Inc v Pena*, 515 US 200 (1995).

[99] Telecommunications Act of 1996, § 551(b)(1), Pub L No 104-104, 110 Stat 56 (1996).

[100] 47 USC § 271(d)(2)(A) (emphasis added).

Furthermore, general US anti-trust policy, which has been extremely pro-merger for at least the last twenty years, has shown little inclination to block media mergers on anti-trust grounds. The Turner–Time Warner merger is a case in point. The $8.5 billion deal proposed to merge two of the largest content-providers in all media: Time Warner, which produces magazines, books, music, and films as well as the cable channels HBO, Cinemax, and E!; and Turner Broadcasting, which also produces books and movies as well as the Turner *oeuvre* of news and entertainment cable channels. The assemblage of two movie studios and a dozen cable channels under one corporate roof was further complicated by TeleCommunications, Inc, (TCI), the cable MSO, which owned 21 per cent of Turner. Under the merger plan, TCI would exchange its Turner shares for 9 per cent of Time Warner, with the resultant interlocking of the nation's two largest cable companies controlling 40 per cent of all cable subscribers. The deal thus involved both horizontal and vertical integration: horizontal, in linking up the cable operators and in expanding Time Warner's programming empire; vertical, in Time Warner's (and TCI's) acquisition of Turner, a main supplier of cable programming.

Approval of the merger was seen as a test of the theories of Federal Trade Commission chairman Robert Pitofsky, who has written that anti-trust policies should be applied not only to mergers involving tangible products, but to those involving ideas, particularly when they threaten to decrease the diversity of ideas in the marketplace.[101] The FTC consent decree that approved the merger, however, required only minimal concessions from the principals:

- TCI may not acquire more than 9 per cent of Time Warner, take an active role in running it, or carry Turner programming at discounted prices;
- Time Warner may not 'tie' its programming by, for example, requiring the purchase of other channels in order to get HBO;
- predatory pricing by Time Warner is prohibited;
- Time Warner may not acquire equity in cable programmers in return for carrying their content on Time Warner systems; and
- Time Warner must carry an all-news channel in addition to CNN.

Approval of the merger, though by a narrow margin, was in keeping with the current trend in anti-trust law, which has always been 'the handmaiden of social, economic, and political policy'.[102] Thirty years ago competition theory demanded anti-trust scrutiny, not only of whether merging companies *actually* compete, but whether they have the *potential*

---

[101] See Pitofsky, R, 'The Political Content of Antitrust', 127 *U Penn L Rev* (1979), 1051.
[102] Botein (note 56 above), 600.

to do so. Removing even a potential competitor from the marketplace was seen as anti-competitive.[103] The DOJ refused to apply this analysis in the Nynex–Bell Atlantic merger, ruling instead that, since Bell Atlantic and Nynex had no *present intent* to compete for local phone service in each other's markets, there was no threat to competition. Similarly, where market-share theory[104] might once have killed the Turner–Time Warner merger, a 40 per cent control by the merged entity of the nation's cable subscribers was, in 1996, no deterrent.

Current anti-trust policy reduces everything to price, mainly the effect of a merger on consumer prices. The DOJ's merger guidelines, for instance, demand that any merger analysis take into account the existence of 'uncommitted entrants', who *would* enter the relevant product market within one year in response to a hypothetical price increase.[105] Therefore any analysis of a merger between two telcos would have to take into account the potential entry into the local telephone market of both cable and long-distance companies, who are freed up to do so by the new Act. Indeed, hard on the heels of approval of the Nynex–Bell Atlantic merger came the entry of AT&T to the Nynex local phone market, a development which promised to supply the local competition that the merger threatened to stifle. Similarly, the safeguards built into the FTC's Turner–Time Warner consent decree are largely designed, not with any market philosophy in mind, but simply to protect consumers against price increases by the merged companies.

2.2.3 *Remuneration and finance: intellectual property*

Copyright

The Copyright Act of 1976 anticipated the information revolution in a number of ways. In particular, the Act was written to be media-neutral, defining the beginning of copyright protection as the fixation of a work in 'any tangible medium of expression now known or later developed', without limiting the media in any way. As was pointed out as early as 1964:

[Y]ou can read the bill from beginning to end and you won't find in it any reference to computers, for example. Yet these are one of the coming instruments of communication in the future. We have tried to phrase the broad rights granted in such a way that they can be adapted as time goes on to each of the new advancing media.[106]

---

[103] See *FTC v Procter & Gamble Co*, 386 US 568 (1967) (disallowing soap manufacturer's acquisition of bleach manufacturer because soap manufacturer had the potential to enter the bleach market as a competitor of the acquired company).

[104] *Brown Shoe Co v US*, 370 US 294 (1961).

[105] Horizontal Merger Guidelines, 1992 FTC LEXIS 176, *27 (Dep't Justice 1992).

[106] *Copyright Law Revision: Hearings on HR 4347, 5680, 6831, 6835 Before Subcommittee No 3*

Further, 'it makes no difference what the form, manner, or medium of fixation may be—whether it is in words, numbers, notes, sounds, or any other graphic or symbolic indicia, whether embodied in a physical object in written, printed, photographic, sculptural, punched, magnetic, or any other stable form[.]'[107] Additionally, providing for perception 'with the aid of a machine or device', allows copyrighting of works fixed in microfilm, audio or video tape, film, CD-ROM, computer disk, digital video disc, and other encoded media. Finally, since the Act defines a machine or device as 'one now known or later developed',[108] works fixed in new media and communicated by as-yet-unimagined machines are also covered. The Act even protects live broadcasts by providing that such works are copyrightable 'if a fixation of the work is being made simultaneously with its transmission',[109] for instance, a simultaneous videotape.

The Copyright Act also facilitates the transmission of copyrighted material on new media by imposing compulsory licences on cable and satellite transmissions. The Audio Home Recording Act imposes a royalty on digital recorders and audio tape (DAT) reproduction.[110]

Though certain bills pending before Congress are designed to amend the Copyright Act to deal with the digital era, many controversies over digital media are being fought out in court. In 1993, for instance, a coalition of freelance writers sued the *New York Times* and other major publications for including their contributions in the electronic editions of the newspapers available on the Lexis-Nexis electronic research database. At issue was a specific provision of the Copyright Act[111] that allows the copyright holder of a newspaper, magazine, or other 'collective work' to reproduce a freelancer's contribution only 'as part of that particular collective work' or 'any revision' thereof. While the publications contended that an on-line edition constitutes 'that particular collective work', the freelancers argued that the digitization and coding, which allows individual articles to be downloaded separately from the publication as a whole, breaks up the collective work into its components and constitutes the sale of individual articles and, consequently, infringement. At issue, in a larger sense, was whether the current digital explosion was so far from Congress's mind when it wrote the Copyright Act as to constitute something beyond even the expansive scope of the statutory media 'now known or later developed'.

---

of the House Committee on the Judiciary, 89th Cong, 1st Sess 57 (1965) (testimony of George D Cary, deputy Register of Copyright).

[107] HR Rep No 1476, 89th Cong 2d Sess 52 (1976).
[108] 17 USC § 101.
[109] ibid.
[110] 17 USC § 1001 *et seq* (West 1997).
[111] 17 USC § 201(c).

In ruling in favour of the publications,[112] the court found that an electronic version of a periodical constitutes 'any revision' of that work within the meaning of the Copyright Act. It further observed that the publishers' 'right to revise their collective works', which at the time of the Copyright Act was 'perceived to have only limited economic value', had become, in the digital age, 'a right that time and technology have since made precious', constituting a potential 'windfall for publishers'. Nonetheless, the court concluded, it was not up to the courts but to Congress to rebalance whatever economic imbalance the new technologies might cause:[113]

If Congress agrees with plaintiffs that, in today's world of pricey electronic information systems, Section 201(c) no longer serves its intended purposes, Congress is of course free to revise that provision to achieve a more equitable result. Until and unless this happens, however, the courts must apply Section 201(c) according to its terms, and not on the basis of speculation as to how Congress might have done things differently had it known then what it does now.

Meanwhile, the real world of commerce has moved beyond the *Tasini* case: publishers now routinely acquire specific 'electronic rights' even when a writer's or photographer's contract already yields 'all rights'.

Another recent case involves website 'framing', a technology that allows a host site to link to other sites, while leaving the host site's frame on the user's screen. The user thus sees the linked site's page surrounded by the host's frame, on which the host sells ads unrelated to the linked site. In *The Washington Post Co, et al v Total News, Inc*[114] a coalition of six companies sued a framing website for, among other things, copyright infringement, alleging that the display of their sites 'surrounded and partially obscured by advertising and other material unrelated to the original content' violated 'several of the exclusive rights' of the copyright holders. The case had been settled, with no judicial resolution of the copyright issues.

Though providing that '[n]o provider or user of an interactive computer service shall be treated as the publisher or speaker of any information provided by another information content provider',[115] the new Act does not extend such publisher-immunity to intellectual property.[116] In the absence of any statutory directive, the question whether an on-line service provider ('OSP') is liable for copyright infringement for user postings has

[112] *Tasini v New York Times Co*, 972 F Supp 804 (SDNY 1997).
[113] ibid, 827.
[114] 97 Civ 1190 (PKL) (SDNY filed 20 Feb 1997).
[115] 47 USC § 230(c)(1).
[116] 'Nothing in this section shall be construed to limit or expand any law pertaining to intellectual property.' 47 USC § 230(d)(2).

been left to the courts and addressed in a number of cases. The evolving rule is that an on-line service provider that allows uploading of users' postings is analogous to a self-serve photocopying service and that direct infringement requires 'some element of volition or causation which is lacking where a defendant's system is merely used to create a copy by a third party'.[117] This knowledge-based standard for direct infringement became the basis for a settlement in *Frank Music Corp v CompuServe, Inc,* where the defendant OSP was absolved of liability for uploads and downloads by its users of plaintiffs' copyrighted music. However, where an OSP actively selects and alters the content of his site, for instance, by removing trademarks or adding advertising, he is liable for direct infringement.[118] It is insufficient, however, that an OSP merely 'knew infringing activity was occurring, and that he solicited others to upload' copyrighted material, unless it can be shown that he 'himself uploaded or downloaded the [copyrighted] files, or directly caused such uploading or downloading to occur'.[119] Such knowledge and solicitation, however, makes the OSP liable for contributory infringement.[120]

In September 1995 the Clinton Administration's working group on intellectual property rights published a White Paper recommending that the definition of distribution in the Copyright Act[121] be redefined to include a 'transmission' right that would be infringed by unauthorized computer transmission of copyrighted works. The proposed National Information Infrastructure Copyright Protection Act incorporates this recommendation, but also provides a 'safe harbour' of time for OSPs to remove copyrighted materials from their websites after receiving notice from the copyright holder. This legislation, on hold since April 1996, may resurface when Congress discusses ratifying and implementing the recent WIPO treaties on digital copyright and sound recordings.[122]

Trademark dilution: domain names

A thorny issue in US Internet law is the problem of domain names. The clearinghouse for domain name registration is Network Systems, Inc ('NSI'), which allocates domain names on a first-come-first-served basis, 'does not determine the legality of the domain name registration, or otherwise evaluate whether that registration or use may infringe upon

---

[117] *Religious Technology Center v Netcom On-Line Communications Service,* 907 F Supp 1361, 1370 (ND Cal 1995).

[118] *Playboy Enters v Frena,* 839 F Supp 1552 (MD Fla 1993).

[119] *Sega Enters v Maphia,* 948 F Supp 923, 932 (ND Cal 1996).

[120] ibid.

[121] 17 USC § 106.

[122] See Lucas, Jennifer B, 'Congress Awaits Administration Action on WIPO Treaty Ratification', *BNA Electronic Info Pol'y & L Rep,* 2 May 1997, 472.

the rights of a third party', and demands indemnity against any claims resulting from the registration.[123] Even holding a valid or federally-registered trademark in a name is no protection from infringing registration: the trademark holder must still win the domain name back through a cumbersome dispute resolution process. This policy has resulted in a tremendous black-market commerce in domain names, as entrepreneurs register famous names wholesale and retail them back to trademark holders.

A favourite legal device in establishing trademark holders' rights to domain names is the new Federal Dilution Act,[124] which protects 'famous' marks regardless of confusion. Enacted in part to fulfil US obligations under the international TRIPs agreement,[125] the Act has found its most efficacious early use as a bar to domestic domain name piracy. Barely a month after the Act's passage, for instance, Avon Products filed suit to regain the name avon.com under a Federal dilution theory.[126] Within the last year, the Act has been used by a children's toy company to regain the name candyland.com from an erotic website;[127] to strip a domain name trafficker of famous names;[128] and to prevent the name plannedparenthood.com from being used to promote anti-abortion literature.[129]

The Internet Society's International Ad Hoc Committee (IAHC) has recently proposed stripping NSI of its registration monopoly, transferring responsibility for domain name registration to two dozen new *Generic Registrars* of diverse nationality, and creating seven new domain name suffixes in addition to the familiar .com, .net, .org, and .edu.[130] It remains to be seen whether the proposed new system clarifies the chaos or simply adds more possible combinations for traffickers to exploit.

2.2.4 *Remuneration and finance: advertising*

Electronic commerce

Over $500 million was spent by US customers in the Internet retail market in 1996. Computers and computer-related products, including software,

---

[123] Network Solutions' Domain Name Dispute Resolution Policy, <http://rs.internic.net/presentations/dispute-pol>

[124] 15 USC §§ 1125, 1127.

[125] See HR Rep No 374, 104th Cong, 1st Sess 4 (1995).

[126] *Avon Products, Inc v Lew*, No 96 Civ 1213 (SAS) (SDNY filed 20 Feb 1996, settled in 1996).

[127] *Hasbro, Inc v Internet Entertainment Grp*, 1996 US Dist Lexis 11627 (WD Wash 5 Feb 1996).

[128] *Panavision Int'l, LP v Toeppen*, 945 F Supp 1296 (CD Cal 1996); *Intermatic Inc v Toeppen*, 947 F Supp 1227 (ND Ill, 1996).

[129] *Planned Parenthood v Bucci*, 1997 US Dist Lexis 3338 (SDNY 19 Mar 1997).

[130] IAHC Proposal, <http://info.internet.isi.edu:80/indrafts/files/draft-iahc-gtldspec-00.txt.> See, generally, Wells, A, 'Internet Domain Name System Is Poised for Change', 3 *Multimedia & Web Strategist*, No 3 (Jan 1997).

CDs, books, etc, still make up over half of on-line computer revenues. Other services are closely related to businesses that have long-term on-line presences, such as the stock market, whose financial information and daily quotes have long been available on-line. More than thirty discount brokers now offer on-line trades.

The key to electronic commerce in the US is to burst out of the technology market and into the general consumer market. As with most new media, sex is showing the way.[131] Erotic products are second in sales to computer-related products on-line, with an estimated one-tenth to one-third of retail sales.[132] Many retailers lament that sex is the only thing that sells on-line and seek to imitate the erotic sales model. Strategies include lavish promotions, free samples, and early entry into international markets.

Other on-line markets include travel (buying tickets, etc), retailing (on-line catalogue shopping), books, and music. Internet advertising is of two kinds: banners ads, which not only advertise products and services, but link to the advertiser's home site; and the home sites themselves, which act as both company store and help line. Advertising is slanted heavily toward technology, with the top ten advertisers including AT&T, IBM, Microsoft, Netscape, NYNEX, and MCI.[133] In 1996 Internet advertising revenues were $267 million, compared with $60 billion for TV and $10 billion for radio. Even though much Internet advertising results from barter arrangements that do not count as revenue, the grand total is still only a tiny fraction of the advertising on the mass media.

Advertising regulation: The Lanham Act

Media advertising is covered by both state and Federal law. The Trademark Act of 1946, also called the Lanham Act,[134] makes false advertising in interstate commerce a Federal cause of action, providing that 'any person who, on or in connection with any goods or services . . . misrepresents the nature, characteristics, qualities, or geographic origin of his or her or another person's goods, services or commercial activities, shall be liable in a civil action by any person who believes that he or she is likely to be damaged by such act.'[135] Most states have equivalent legislation. The effect of the laws is to remove the responsibility for enforcement from state and Federal agencies and place it in the hands of private litigants and law courts.

[131] See Johnson, Peter, 'Pornography Drives Technology: Why Not To Censor the Internet', 49 *Fed Comm LJ* (Nov 1996), 217.

[132] 'Tremble, everyone', *The Economist*, 10 May 1997, S10.

[133] That the best-seller from the on-line bookstore amazon.com is *How to Build Your Own Website* reflects the Web's technology-heavy demographics.

[134] 15 USC § 1051 *et seq.*

[135] 15 USC § 1125(a) (usually referred to as Lanham Act § 43(a)).

Under both Federal and state regimes, there is no necessity that the injured party be mentioned by name in the false advertisement. It is sufficient that he show that his business is likely to be injured by a competitor's false claims. For instance, a TV commercial that shows one soap cleaning faster than an anonymous second soap is vulnerable to suit by any soap that claims the advertisement is wrong.[136]

The Lanham Act applies as much to on-line advertising as to any other. One court has found that even the use of a website to solicit names for a mailing list constitutes an advertisement for its services and subjects it to a Lanham Act suit. 'Because Internet communications transmit instantaneously on a worldwide basis, there is little question that the "in commerce" requirement would be met in a typical Internet message, be it trademark infringement or false advertising.'[137]

Other media-related causes of action

State statutory and common law protects against violations of the _right of publicity_, that is, the unauthorized commercial use of a person's name, voice, photograph or other likeness for the purpose of advertising or selling products or services.[138] Even the use of look-alike models may violate the right of publicity,[139] as may imitations of characters created by performers,[140] or of their distinctive entertainment styles.[141] _Misappropriation_ is a state law doctrine that protects valuable news and information against free-riding. For instance, if one TV station has 'hot news' on a shipwreck that it has found through its own 'enterprise, organization, skill, labor and money', a competing station must cover the same shipwreck itself rather than scooping its rival by free-riding on the first station's reports.[142] A Federal appeals court recently overturned a lower court ruling that the use of a subscription-paging service to relay plays and scores of ongoing basketball games constituted misappropriation, while at the same time reaffirming the vitality of the misappropriation doctrine.[143]

[136] _L&F Products v Procter & Gamble_, 45 F 3d 709 (2d Cir, 1995).

[137] _Maritz, Inc v Cybergold, Inc_, 947 F Supp 1328, 1335–36 (ED Mo, 1996)(quoting Jerome Gilson, 1 _Trademark Protection and Practice_ § 5.11[2]).

[138] See, eg, Cal Civ Code § 3344 (prohibiting, without written permission, the use of a person's 'name, voice . . . photograph or likeness, in any manner, on or in products, merchandise, or goods, or for purposes of advertising or selling or soliciting purchases of, products, merchandise, goods or services').

[139] _Prudhomme v Procter & Gamble Co_, 800 F Supp 390 (ED La, 1992) (double for Chef Paul Prudhomme).

[140] See _McFarland v Miller_, 14 F 3d 912 (3d Cir, 1994)(right of publicity of George McFarland who played Spanky character on Little Rascals violated by restaurant called Spanky McFarland).

[141] _Lahr v Adell Chem Co_, 300 F 2d 256 (1st Cir, 1962) (actor Bert Lahr's distinctive voice).

[142] See _International News Service v Associated Press_, 248 US 215 (1918).

[143] _National Basketball assn v Motorola, et al_, 1997 US App Lexis 1527 (2d Cir, 30 Jan 1997).

2.3 Social regulation

2.3.1 Content regulation

The Communications Decency Act

The First Amendment to the US Constitution provides that 'Congress shall make no law . . . abridging the freedom of speech.' The Fourteenth Amendment applies this prohibition to the states and, by extension, to local governments as well. However, it has been clear for as long as the republic has existed that 'no law' does not mean 'no law' and that government may, in fact, regulate speech. The extent of the regulation depends on the medium. Different media have different First Amendment rights.[144]

Print enjoys the greatest freedom,[145] broadcast the least,[146] with cable falling somewhere in between.[147] Thus, the law can demand that broadcasters give politicians a 'right-of-reply' to political editorials, while it may not demand the same of newspapers.[148] Similarly, broadcasters may be completely forbidden from broadcasting 'indecent' material, while cable must be given a 'safe harbour'.[149]

Internet 'indecency'

The great question, therefore, that the new Telecommunications Act raised about the Internet was, under which of the three broad areas of First Amendment protection would it fall? The Act itself made sure the decision would not be long in coming. First, it contained the Communications Decency Act ('CDA'), part of which made it a criminal offence to 'make available' to minors on the Internet any material that was 'sexually indecent' or 'patently offensive'. Second, it provided for expedited review by a three-judge district court of the constitutionality of the CDA and allowed for direct appeal to the Supreme Court.[150]

On the day that the Act was passed, the American Civil Liberties Union ('ACLU') filed suit in a Federal District Court in Philadelphia. On 12 June 1996 the court ruled that the Internet more closely resembled speech and print than the more regulation-susceptible cable and broadcast media. Therefore, such terms as 'indecent' and 'patently offensive', as used in the

---

[144] *Kovacs v Cooper*, 336 US 77, 97 (1949) (Jackson, J, concurring) ('Each [medium] is a law unto itself'). See *FCC v Pacifica Fnd*, 438 US at 748 ('We have long recognized that each medium of expression presents special First Amendment problems').

[145] See, eg, *Miami Herald Publishing Co v Tornillo*, 418 US 241 (1974)

[146] See, eg, *FCC v League of Women Voters*, 468 US 364 (1984); *FCC v Pacifica Fnd*, 438 US 726 (1978).

[147] See *Denver Area Educational Telecommunications Inc v FCC*, 116 S Ct 2374 (1996).

[148] Compare, *Tornillo*, 418 US 241 with *Red Lion*, 395 US 367.

[149] See *Action for Children's Television v FCC*, 58 F 3d 654, 664 (DC Cir, 1995).

[150] Telecommunications Act of 1996, § 561(a)–(b), Pub L No 104-104, 110 Stat 56 (1996).

Act, are unconstitutionally vague. '[T]he Internet may fairly be regarded as a never-ending world-wide conversation. The government may not . . . interrupt that conversation. As the most participatory form of mass speech yet developed, the Internet deserves the highest protection from government intrusion.'[151]

The government appealed to the Supreme Court, which upheld the decision striking down the 'Internet indecency' law. Declaring the Internet 'the most participatory form of mass speech yet developed',[152] and unwilling to 'burn . . . the house to roast the pig', the Court found the law 'casting a . . . shadow over free speech, [that] threatens to torch a large segment of the Internet community'.

The Court also resolved what 'level of scrutiny' should apply to laws affecting the Internet, finding that there is 'no basis for qualifying the level of First Amendment scrutiny that should be applied to this medium'. The broadcast traits of invasiveness and scarcity are 'not present in cyberspace'. This dynamic, multifaceted category of communication includes not only traditional print and news services, but also audio, video, and still images, as well as interactive, real-time dialogue. Through the use of chat rooms, any person with a phone line can become a town crier with a voice that resonates farther than it could from any soapbox. Through the use of Web pages, mail exploders, and newsgroups, the same individual can become a pamphleteer.

The Administration's reaction, far from declaring the Internet a free speech zone, was to ask 'industry leaders . . . to join with us in developing a solution for the Internet as powerful for the computer as the V-chip will be for television, to protect children in ways that are consistent with the First Amendment'. The V-chip legislation has so far escaped Constitutional challenge by requiring only a 'voluntary' rating system that consumers may activate or not.

A subsequent White House meeting showed what such a voluntary solution for the Internet might look like, as industry leaders agreed to a scheme that would substitute private for public censorship and subject on-line speech to a variety of blocking and filtering technologies. Netscape, Microsoft, IBM, and CompuServe announced a uniform method of content rating. Operators of the largest Internet search engines discussed excluding unrated sites from their searches. A new legislative proposal called the 'Online Cooperative Publishing Act' threatened civil and criminal penalties for mis-rating websites.

The ACLU, victor in the 'Internet indecency' lawsuit was soon asking

---

[151] *ACLU v Reno*, 929 F Supp 824, 883 (ED Pa, 1996).
[152] *Reno v American Civil Liberties Union (ACLU)*, 117 S Ct 2329 (26 June 1997).

'Is Cyberspace Burning? How Rating and Blocking Proposals May Torch Free Speech on the the Internet',[153] and envisioning 'a scenario which in some respects has already been set in motion':

- First, a uniform method for content rating emerges.
- Next, a particular rating system becomes the de facto standard.
- Soon, the rating system is built into Internet software as a default, effectively blocking unrated speech.
- Search engines refuse to reveal unrated or unacceptably rated sites.
- Government makes self-rating mandatory and mis-rating a crime.

As the ACLU pointed out,

Despite the Supreme Court's strong rejection of a broadcast analogy for the Internet, government and industry leaders alike are now inching toward the dangerous and incorrect position that the Internet is like television, and should be rated and censored accordingly.

If the 'voluntary' rating system is embodied in legislation, it, along with the V-chip legislation, may provide the next grounds for a free speech challenge.

The CDA also resolved a question that had split the courts as to whether an on-line service provider who hosts other providers' content is to be treated as a 'publisher' or a 'distributor'.[154] If a publisher, the host would be liable for actionable content, such as defamation, posted by others; if a bookstore, there would be no such liability. The situation was complicated in the courts by the implication from the developing case law that the very act of policing one's website opened one to liability if the policing was inadequate, while failure to police created no liability at all. The Act's resolution of the problem was to provide that there was no publisher liability for others' content, nor did the act of policing make one liable. It further invalidated any state law that conflicted with these provisions.

The reach of these provisions was tested recently in *Zeran v America Online, Inc.*[155] In what the court described as a 'malicious hoax', an anonymous posting on America Online affixed the plaintiff's name and phone number to a series of advertisements for T-shirts and other items that glorified the 1995 bombing of a building in Oklahoma City. The plaintiff sued America Online under the state-law theory that it 'knew or had reason to know' of the offensive postings by virtue of the plaintiff's

---

[153] ACLU White Paper: 'Fahrenheit 451.2: Is Cyberspace Burning?' available at <http://www.aclu.org/issues/cyber/burning.html>

[154] Compare *Cubby Inc v CompuServe*, 776 F Supp 135 (SDNY 1991) (distributor) with *Stratton-Oakmont Inc v Prodigy Service Co*, 23 Media L Rep 1794 (Sup Ct NY Cty, 24 May 1995) (publisher).

[155] 958 F Supp 1124 (ED Va, 1997).

complaining about them and yet had failed to remove them.[156] The court, while ruling that the CDA had not entirely preempted the field of Internet regulation, none the less ruled that in this case there was a direct conflict between the Federal and state law, before which the state law had to yield. Thus it seems that state law causes of action for such things as 'negligent distribution of defamatory material' do not survive Federal preemption.

V-chip legislation

The new Act contains a two-pronged attack on TV violence. The first prong is a technological one, requiring that a 'V-chip'[157] (the V standing for violence) be installed on all new TV sets of screen size greater than 13 inches. When TV programmes are rating-encoded, parents will be able to decide whether to activate the V-chip on their home sets and block what-ever rated programmes they choose. The second prong is a substantive one, providing that, if 'distributors of video programming' do not estab-lish a voluntary rating system for 'sexual, violent, or other indecent mate-rial' within one year, the government will do it for them. Spurred by the threat of government action, network and cable executives delivered a ratings programme within the allotted year. The proposed rating system, however, rates programmes, not by content, but by age category. For instance, TV-Y is for all children, TV-Y7 for children aged seven and above, TV-G Suitable for all ages, TV-PG Parental Guidance Suggested, TV-14 Parents Strongly Cautioned, TV-M Mature Audiences Only.[158] Crit-ics have complained that this scheme does not meet the legislative man-date for content-based rating, and the FCC has established an interactive website for public comment on the rating system.

Perhaps the most startling aspect of the V-chip controversy is Con-gress's acceptance, in the text of the Act itself, of the 'violence hypothesis', that is, that viewing violent television programming in fact causes violent or aggressive behaviour, usually by children:[159]

[s]tudies have shown that children exposed to violent video programming at a young age have a higher tendency for violent and aggressive behavior later in life than children not so exposed, and that children exposed to violent video program-ming are prone to assume that acts of violence are acceptable behavior.[160]

---

[156] Under state tort laws, distributors of defamatory material are only liable if they 'knew or should have known' the material was of a defamatory character. *Cubby*, 776 F Supp 135, 141.

[157] The chip is described as 'a feature designed to enable viewers to block display of all programs with a common rating . . .' 47 USC § 551(c).

[158] Cooper, J, 'Is Everybody Happy?', *Cablevision*, 27 Jan 1997, 30.

[159] Krattenmaker, T and Powe, Jr, L, 'Televised Violence: First Amendment Principles and Social Science Theory', 64 *Va L Rev* (1978), 1123.

[160] 47 USC § 551(a)(4) (emphasis added).

Critics have assailed this acceptance and questioned the constitutionality of the V-chip provision.[161] As yet, however, no court case has challenged it.

2.3.2 Security

Encryption

One of the barriers to increased Internet commerce is the current stalemate on US encryption policy. Software manufacturers and other commercial Internet users favour the free use and export of encryption both in order to ensure the security and privacy in the transfer of electronic data and to allow the US software industry to compete in the global encryption market. The government, on the other hand, fears the use of encrypted messages by criminals. Under Commerce Department regulations issued at the end of last year, US manufacturers of the more powerful types of encryption software (that is, with keys exceeding 40 bits) can only export if they have in place a system that would give law enforcement authorities 'key escrow' access to the encrypted messages. Few companies have shown a willingness to do this.

The encryption stalemate pits two competing needs at loggerheads. One is the need of users, both individuals and companies, to transmit secure messages and data, free from intrusion by outside sources, including the government. The other is the law-enforcement needs of government, which requires access to potentially criminal uses of computer technology just as much as it requires access to criminal uses of the mails or the telephone. The key escrow system is the government's equivalent of a wiretap.

The reluctance to give the government key access derives from several sources. The most rudimentary is a distaste for government spying and a fear that, given any access at all, law enforcement agencies will abuse it to access private transactions. A greater fear, however, concerns, not the government's honesty, but its competence. Companies fear that a bumbling government will lose the key to their encrypted transactions, that others will gain access to their data, and that the government's misuse of the key will expose them to loss of data, compromise their trade secrets, and make them vulnerable to commercial espionage.

The four-year stalemate over encryption policy has had unfortunate consequences. Unable to export the same strong encryption they can market domestically, US software companies have had to develop a two-track encryption strategy, one for the domestic market, one for export. This lack of a unitary standard has inhibited the growth of a robust

---

[161] See Johnson, P, 'The Irrelevant V-Chip: An Alternative Theory of TV and Violence', 4 *UCLA Ent L Rev* (1997), 185.

encryption market and the ability of US encryption software to compete overseas. One result is that even government systems fail because of inadequate encryption. The Social Security webpage, designed to give people access to their social security records, proved to have so many leaks that the government shut it down. The inability of government systems adequately to encrypt themselves is symptomatic of the wider problem and prevents government systems from leading the way to new uses of the new technology.

Privacy

The Federal Trade Commission, in January 1997, released a staff report about protecting consumer privacy on-line, identifying four key elements to consumer protection:

- 'Notice' to consumers about how personal information collected on-line is used;
- 'Choice' for consumers about how and whether their personal information is released;
- 'Security' of personal information; and
- 'Access' of consumers to on-line information about themselves.

Two recent cases, *CompuServe Inc v Cyber Promotions Inc*,[162] and *America Online Inc v Cyber Promotions Inc*,[163] have considered the right of on-line subscribers to be free from junk email and, conversely, the right of advertisers to solicit business from large on-line mailing lists. In both cases, Cyber Promotions gained access to the OSP's mailing lists and bombarded subscribers with promotional material from its advertising clients. In the *America Online* case, the court rejected an argument that Cyber Promotions had a First Amendment (free speech) right to send email to America Online subscribers. In the second case, the court ruled that continued use of the CompuServe system for email marketing constituted common law trespass, harming CompuServe's on-line property in two ways. First, the volume of email put a tremendous strain on CompuServe's filtering and storage network, draining resources that would otherwise be available to subscribers. Second, the complaints spawned among subscribers by the unsolicited emails caused harm to its goodwill and business reputation, harming it still further. The Electronic Communications Privacy Act of 1986 prohibits unauthorized access to or use of stored email. However, recent court cases have held that employers are completely free to monitor their employees' email, under the theory that the email system is the employer's property.

---

[162] 25 Media L Rep 1545 (ED Ohio, 1997).
[163] 25 Media L Rep 1193 (ED Pa, 1996).

3 CONCLUDING REMARKS

One way to judge the current state of US communications policy is to balance the accomplishments of 1997 against some of the goals laid down in the 1993 *The National Information Infrastructure: Agenda for Action.*

Promote private sector investment

Removing the regulatory barriers to mergers and expansions has caused a boom in technology stocks (though cable TV stocks have plummeted). Though volatile, the technology market continues to attract new investors. There are more start-up, small-capitalization technology companies than any other type of start-up small business. Furthermore, the elimination of market-entry barriers has spurred new investment in more traditional communications companies as they enter previously forbidden markets.

Extend the 'Universal Service' concept

Extending new technology to poorly-served areas and classes remains more a hope than a reality. The information society, like other societies, is one of haves and have-nots. Beyond menial data-entry tasks, computer use in general, and Internet use in particular, is the province of the educated and the affluent. On the positive side, the FCC's Universal Service Order appeared only in the spring of 1997, with the specific goal of linking schools and libraries to the Internet. Any kind of government-assured universal access to advanced information technology lies far in the future. Even farther in the future lies the answer to the question whether, given universal *access*, otherwise disadvantaged people will have sufficient education to use it.

Promote technological innovation and new applications

The government-initiated programme to develop HDTV may be the most imaginative use of government resources since the space programme. Unlike the space programme, however, it has not put the government in the role of contracting for services with tax money, but rather as the arbiter/referee of a programme that allows the winner to market the winning product to the public. Thus the expenditure of minimal government funds has resulted in the development of a huge new technology that, with government blessing, will replace every TV in America in the next ten years.

Content control is always a deterrent to technological innovation. In this regard, both the 'Internet indecency' and 'V-chip' provisions of the new Act put potential brakes on the development of interactive and innovative computer and TV programming. Fortunately, unconstitutional restrictions imposed by the legislature and implemented by the executive can be removed by the judiciary. This has already been done to the 'Internet indecency' provisions. The V-chip legislation has proved more resistant to court challenge, which may arise as soon as the controversial TV-rating system has reached its final form. The Administration seems to have yielded on the content-regulation issue even before a Supreme Court ruling. A recent policy draft stated:

To the extent, then, that effective filtering technology is available, content regulations traditionally imposed on radio and television need not be extended to the Internet. In fact, unnecessary regulation or censorship could cripple the growth and diversity of the Internet.[164]

Preempting state and local laws is one way the new Act promotes innovation. As confirmed in the *Zeran* case, since Online Service Providers may not be treated as publishers of third party obscenity, indecency, or defamation under Federal law, all state law causes of action to the contrary are preempted. Similarly, the Act preempts local state and zoning laws that arbitrarily restrict or place high tariffs on the *impedimenta* of new technology, such as satellite dishes that threaten neither safety nor aesthetics.

Promote seamless, interactive, user-driven operation of the NII

The Internet derives from the government-owned Darpanet, which the government essentially turned over to private users. The best thing the government has done since then is to leave it alone and to resist temptations to over-legislate. Allowing all communications companies, including cable and satellite, to offer computer modems in competition with the phone companies similarly increases interconnectivity.

Ensure information security and network reliability

The greatest impediment to information security, according to many, is the absence of a robust encryption technology that has been caused by the four-year stalemate over key access. Though consumer transactions over the Internet are relatively secure, the kind of large international commerce that will make the Internet viable are inhibited by the lack of a secure, embedded encryption code.

Improve management of the radio frequency spectrum

'Spectrum management' has become a euphemism for spectrum auctions. The new auctions policy has raised over $20 billion and has led tax-shy legislators to cast a lustful eye at the free spectrum that is used by radio

---

[164] Broder, J, 'White House Is Set To Ease Its Stance on Internet Smut', *New York Times*, 16 June 1997, B9.

and TV licensees, the largest spectrum consumers. The rumblings in favour of making them pay for it, however, are unlikely to develop into a consensus. Rather the consensus is likely to be that, since free over-the-air radio and TV are woven into the American fabric, nothing that threatens it is in the public interest. What remains to be seen is whether Congress has the will, rather than charging over-the-air broadcasters for spectrum, to impose meaningful and enforceable affirmative public interest obligations on them instead.

Protect intellectual property rights

Thus far, the Copyright and Trademark Acts have proved resilient enough to accommodate the new media, and the courts have proved adequate forums for resolving the disputes that do arise. Furthermore, for copyright, publishers have taken automatically to including 'electronic rights' in publishing contracts, even when 'all rights' are already granted. Still, there is pressure on Congress, much of it from the Administration, to add 'transmission' to the bundle of exclusive rights of copyright, so that copyright owners may demand approval or licensing for any electronic display of their work.

Any accommodation of intellectual property interests to the new media should take into account that giving authors and inventors the exclusive right to their works is only the secondary goal of copyright policy. The primary goal, as stated in the Constitution, is to 'promote the progress of science and useful arts'. It follows that if science and the useful arts are flourishing, there is no need to fashion stricter patent and copyright laws. Such seems to be the case. The number of annual patent applications continues to grow exponentially. During the last decade, which roughly coincides with the computer revolution, the number of Americans who describe their profession as 'writer' has almost doubled, far outstripping the mean growth in other professions. Society is far better served by finding more and more incentives for writers and inventors to create, which the new media encourage, than by endlessly refining what constitutes a copy.

Provide access to government information and improve government procurement

One of the designs in the *Agenda for Action* is for the government to take the lead in using the new media both for the dissemination of information about government services and for interactive communication between citizens and the government. The theory is that if people get used to accessing government services through computers, they will also turn to interactive computers for other services.

The government has been successful in the information-dissemination half of the equation. Many US government departments have easily accessible and navigable websites, including the FCC, which has opened its website to public comments on pending rulemaking. Particularly successful is the Library of Congress's 'Thomas' website (named for Thomas Jefferson, whose collection started the Library of Congress), which has put millions of government publications on-line.

Less successful, however, have been attempts to let the public actually do business with the government on-line. Of the two government agencies that touch the most American lives—the Social Security Administration ('SSA') and the Internal Revenue Service ('IRS')—only the SSA has tried to establish an interactive web site, one that would give immediate information to taxpayers about the current status of their retirement funds. After a few weeks, it was forced to shut down the interactive part of the site because faulty encryption made it leak. For similar reasons, the IRS has made no attempt to initiate anything but the crudest and most cumbersome electronic filing of income tax returns.

Thus the government-imposed restraint on exporting strong encryption has returned to haunt the government. The government-bred failure of US software companies to develop a strong, embedded encryption programme has prevented the government itself from taking the lead role it envisions for itself in the new media.

Conclusion

The Telecommunications Act, like much legislation, contained something for everyone, leaving it up to the FCC to implement it. This reminded many observers of the agreement between God and the devil to bring peace to mankind—God would design it; all the devil asked was implementation rights.

So far, however, the devil has proved not to be in the details, as both the speed and the substance of the FCC orders have met general approval. Most notable are (a) the telephony 'Competition Trilogy' that implements the interconnectivity, access charge, and universal service provisions of the Act, and (b) the HDTV Order. The latter took many people by surprise, since HDTV was barely understood by the industry, let alone the general public. Now, however, digital TV has reached the mainstream consciousness, as both broadcasters and cable operations gear up to take advantage of the new technology. Furthermore, consumers show a dawning awareness that HDTV assures the obsolescence of their current TV sets. It will be interesting to watch how this awareness affects the market for conventional TV sets between now and the HDTV roll-out.

The main fault with current US media law is that it lacks a social conscience. Despite universal service, wiring schools and libraries, and increasing lip-service to public interest obligations, there is no real sense of social direction. For instance, though interactive systems have the capability of monitoring households for fire, crime, and health emergencies, there is no national thrust in that direction. Similarly, US policy is now to wire schools for the Internet, but not yet to provide computers or software to plug into the wiring.

The only content directives are not positive but negative, forbidding Internet indecency and discouraging TV violence. There is no national consensus or will to turn the new media toward positive social good or to bridge the growing gap between information haves and have-nots.

8

Australia

MARK ARMSTRONG, TREVOR JORDAN, MICHAEL HUDSON[1]

1 GENERAL TRENDS

The current trends in Australia are similar to those throughout the developed world. They include liberalisation, internationalisation, and increasing reliance on competition law to resolve communications, and information industry issues. The main features of the Australian environment are: a very pragmatic policy environment, free of expressed theories and ideologies; the role of distance, both within Australia and in communication with the rest of the globe; a strong emphasis on local media content and a stated reliance on market forces.

In the pragmatic Australian legislative environment, the policy issues have been addressed in relation to the emergence of specific services, such as subscription television and mobile telephony; not as part of a European-style holistic view. There have been official reports on the future of broadband services and the future of communications, but these have generally stopped short of proposing specific legal changes.

Whilst the official and parliamentary literature recognises the major changes in new and old media, the recent changes have been proposed within existing categories of legislation, such as telecommunications, broadcasting, radiocommunications, copyright, and obscenity. Thus, many of the legal developments relating to multimedia and on-line services are not to be found in reports or decisions directly affecting those topics. For that reason, this report focuses on the developing edges, and overlaps, of existing laws. There is no master plan such as the Malaysian 20-20 vision, or the Singapore Intelligent Island strategy.

Local content is well supported and popular in traditional areas such as film and television. Globalisation will not necessarily introduce profound changes in broadcasting systems in Australia, as they have always been relatively open to programmes imported from overseas. Ever since films were first distributed and since television was first broadcast, local programmes and films have always needed to win an audience alongside the full output of Hollywood and of every other international source of

---

[1] The authors are grateful to Helen Molnar and Jane Vaughan for their contributions to the interim report on this project.

English-language material. Thus, there is no prospect of the radical restructuring still occurring in Western and Eastern Europe, where media structures and laws limited US material until recently.

Whilst the technical capacity to transmit programmes directly from overseas via satellite or submarine cable is increasing, rights to most films and programmes of wide appeal are already held by enterprises with strong domestic distribution channels and audience loyalty. However, there are continuing efforts to encourage investment in locally-produced programmes, through a mixture of regulation and support for what has come to be described as 'creative infrastructure'.[2] Most of the policy-makers have said that the content of broadcasting, audiovisual, and on-line services is the key to future success. It is recognised that there is a special need to increase the volume of local content in on-line and audiovisual services, as the computer software industry has been dominated by US producers.

Many of the Australian policies are affected by population patterns. Most of the community live in five cities, with the rest of the population thinly spread across a large, arid land mass. This produces major differences in the cost of delivering telecommunications and audiovisual services. Many efforts have been made to offer reasonable quality communications to the remote areas. The positive side of the distance problem is that optic fibre and satellite offer the first opportunity in history for Australia to have immediate contact for trade and cultural exchange with its own Asia–Pacific region and the rest of the world. Until now, the main immediate contact has been via telephone, and that has been costly.

2 COMMUNICATIONS SYSTEMS AND DEVELOPMENTS

Before explaining the legal and policy issues, it is necessary to say something about recent developments in the delivery of media and communications services. In the pragmatic Australian policy environment, the actual developments are often more significant than the announced policy changes. In many cases, policy is made through the actual behaviour of major players, rather than through government planning.

It is unlikely that there will ever be a single, major policy initiative to address broadband and on-line services. Most of the issues, and the future structure of most aspects of Australian communications, are already being resolved incidentally, in the course of subscription television

---

[2] *Networking Australia's Future: Final Report of the Broadband Services Expert Group* (Canberra: Australian Government Publishing Service (AGPS), 1994), 73ff.

development. Subscription television, usually known as 'pay-TV' in the media, has been the battlefield for virtually all the convergence issues. Every sector of communications has been affected by the struggles for control and access.

Cable rollout

The most significant recent development has been the rapid rollout of cable. The two largest telecommunications carriers, Telstra and Optus, have spent the last three years building national broadband infrastructure based on hybrid fibre-coaxial cable to deliver telephony services, subscription television, and a range of interactive multimedia applications across Australia. The carriers planned to spend an aggregated amount of $A7 billion to roll cable past most metropolitan homes by the end of 1998. With cable continuing to be laid, actual expenditure reached about $A5 billion by mid 1997. It was estimated that Telstra interests had cabled past 2.1 million households (4 million originally planned) with Optus interests passing 2.2 million households (3 million originally planned). The broadband network for each services largely the same homes (85 per cent duplication).[3] Both carriers are reviewing their plans for further network development and Optus has experienced considerable difficulty with the implementation of its local telephony service over its cable network.

There were several reasons for these investments being committed, which explain much about the communications environment in Australia. The first reason was historical. A combination of laws and policies effectively banned cable television until 1992, so as to preserve the size of the free-to-air market. The absence of subscription cable television meant that most Australian homes and streets were cabled with only enough capacity to deliver telephone services using conventional technology. It also led to a high penetration of VCRs and an extensive network of commercial video libraries. Thus, it was possible to fund the upgrade to fibre and hybrid fibre/coaxial systems in a single step. The absence of cable also meant that there was no history, as in North America and Europe, of separating cable ownership from broadcasting ownership. The issue had simply not arisen. Even the Broadcasting Services Act 1992 made no provision for that separation, except in relation to satellites. Thus, there was nothing to stop the carriers and broadcasters combining their resources to fund and support new cable systems. Another reason was geographic. Australia is one of the most urbanised nations in the world, with nearly half of its population of 18 million people concentrated in and around two major metropolitan areas, Sydney and Melbourne. And the majority of the Australian market can be reached by cabling five major cities.

[3] Minister for Finance, Telstra Share Offer, Public Offer Document, Sept 1997, 45.

Lying behind those reasons is a mixture of regulatory and competitive issues. An auction system was used to introduce subscription television via DBS satellite and MDS. The excessive bids generated by the auction process deterred most experienced media corporations. Legal restrictions on expansion of ownership by existing media also drove those media towards cable television. For example, the cross-media and foreign ownership laws (summarised later) excluded News Corporation from controlling free-to-air television stations. With its Australian newspaper interests and its US film and television interests, including Fox, it had obvious motives to find an Australian outlet through which it was allowed to expand. The telcos were concerned about being isolated as mere carriers, so cable television gave them the opportunity for closer involvement in audiovisual content. The recent rollout of subscription television channels on new, high-capacity cables is one reason why debates over digital television are not yet as intense as in other developed countries. There is no immediate shortage of delivery channels.

Optus has been conducting a trial of cable modems for more than a year and Telstra launched a commercial service in May 1997 which provides a 10 Mbits/sec continuous Internet connection. With the increasing use of satellites for broadcast television, this may become an important source of revenue for cable operators.

Satellite communications, local and international

Access to satellite systems in the East Asian region has been possible in Australia for many years. However, use of the systems to receive television has been confined to a few hobbyists. That is because there is little compelling programming that is not already available, in a country which has always been open to imported programmes. The generation of satellites to be switched on within the next two years will make it easier for domestic consumers to receive foreign signals. No serious attempt has been made to regulate any aspect of international satellite reception.

For some years, satellites have had a major role in delivering communications to the remote, sparsely-populated areas which constitute most of Australia's land mass. Major systems serving Australia include the Optus domestic satellite system, Intelsat which has been the traditional international system, PanAmSat, and Palapa, the powerful Indonesian system.

Excluding Intelsat capacity because of the very large antennae required, there will be over eighty medium-to-high powered transponders with footprints, of varying strengths, over Australia. With digital compression conservatively estimated at four television channels per transponder, this implies over 300 potential channels. The numbers of satellite systems, footprints, and channels continues to rise.

On-line services and multimedia

On-line services are growing very rapidly. Australian geographic disper-
sion gives these services an obvious attraction. In mid 1997, it was estimated that there were 1.5 million Internet users in Australia, increasing at
the rate of 12 per cent per month, which would take the figure beyond 2
million by 1998.[4] By June 1997, there were around 400 Internet service
providers, giving Internet access to around 3.2 million people.[5] On a per
capita basis, Australia is the fourth largest user of the Internet after
Sweden, Finland, and the US, although some surveys place it second only
to the US. Currently, more than 14 per cent of the population regularly
connect to the Internet, mostly from work.[6] The recent traffic growth has
been around 500 per cent per annum. It is currently expected that Internet
traffic between Australia and North America will exceed telephone traffic
in 1998. This forecast date has advanced by two years over the last six
months.

The legal and policy picture of new on-line services and multimedia is
very different from that of established telecommunications and broadcasting, because reports and analyses are about enterprises and industries
which are only just emerging. It is not yet possible to project from the
existing media enterprises to new interactive enterprises, except to say
that obvious players include: the telecommunications carriers, the newspaper corporations (with their vast information resources including classified advertising), broadcasting corporations, and all the corporations
who are using subscription television to build experience with direct
provision of audiovisual material to households and businesses. The
efforts being made by governments and policy-makers are to generate
local content initiatives, and to avoid repeating the pattern of consumer
computer software, nearly all of which comes from the United States. The
efforts are directed at encouraging local content and carriage, in conjunction with whichever global corporations are interested.

Few of the traditional approaches to regulation of on-line services are
expected to have much impact, given that the services are networked
globally and are beyond the reach of any national policy-making body.
The issue of concentration of influence and market power is not addressed
through ideas about ownership, but rather through frequently-repeated
affirmation of the need to ensure access to emerging systems. In principle,
the access regime outlined later is capable of ensuring access to available

---

[4] *Report of the Senate Select Committee Inquiry into Community Standards Relevant to the
Provision of Services Utilising Electronic Technologies*, Apr 1997, 2.

[5] Estimates by Cutler & Company Pty Ltd, Melbourne, Mar 1997, and ABA, *Regulating the
Internet: A Comparison of Approaches in Four Countries* (Sydney, Oct 1997).

[6] Australian Bureau of Statistics, *Australian Demographic Statistics: December Quarter 1996*
(Canberra: AGPS, cat no 3101.0).

capacity for those who seek it. The emphasis is on 'available capacity' because the first-access issue is seen as ensuring that it is technically possible for the population to connect to on-line networks.[7]

Australian multimedia producers are small in size and number, but they do produce a range of games and educational products in their own names, or for distribution by the largely US-based distributors. The Federal government and State governments have a range of initiatives to support local multimedia development.[8] The likely trend in multimedia development is a large number of joint ventures with traditional media corporations or overseas software producers to support production of titles.

Current market research points to the continued strong demand for new and innovative technologies by Australians. At present, for example, multimedia enabling equipment in Australian households is estimated at: personal computers, 47 per cent; modems, 16 per cent; video game applications, 29 per cent; mobile telephony, around 25 per cent; home banking applications, 9 per cent; household fax capability, 17 per cent; VCRs, 86 per cent.

Internationalisation versus regionalisation

In recent years Australian firms have increasingly focused on the region and in particular Australia's proximity to Asian markets, for business and trade. The shared time-zone provides an opportunity for businesses to operate across the region. Assisting the engagement in Asian markets is the fact that an increasing proportion (now approaching 10 per cent) of the Australian population is of Asian origin. This has created a large multilingual skill base from which to build business and cultural links.[9]

Many media and telecommunications enterprises based in Australia have already expanded into Asia and the Northern hemisphere. Telstra, the largest carrier, has entered joint venture arrangements in Asian markets for switching and transmission technologies. Australian media (print, radio, and TV), both commercial and public service, have outlets or joint ventures in East Asian countries. At the formal level, the engagement with the rest of East Asia has been accelerated through the continuous interchanges through the Asia-Pacific Economic Co-operation (APEC) process.

---

[7] For example, *Networking Australia's Future: Final Report of the Broadband Services Expert Group* (Canberra: AGPS, 1994), 49–62.

[8] For example, *Creative Nation: Commonwealth Cultural Policy* (Canberra, 1994), commits around $80m over four years to supporting multimedia development, including the creation of the Australian Multimedia Enterprise which invests capital to support new projects.

[9] ibid.

Major players in media and communications

The nature of communications trends and markets can be explained by highlighting some of the major players. With a relatively small population base and limited advertising revenue, Australian electronic media have always relied on considerable cross-ownership to raise venture capital for new developments.

In free-to-air television, a large number of local, commercial stations have coalesced into three national networks, called Seven, Nine, and Ten. The national, non-commercial broadcaster, the Australian Broadcasting Corporation (ABC), has the fourth national channel; and the Special Broadcasting Service (SBS) provides multicultural services on the fifth channel.

The Nine Network has, over time, held the largest share of the commercial television audience. It is wholly owned by Publishing and Broadcasting Limited (PBL), which is ultimately controlled by interests associated with Mr Kerry Packer. PBL's other major interests include magazines and a number of equity investments in companies involved in pay-TV, film production, on-line services, leisure, entertainment, and newspapers. PBL holds an equal share with Microsoft in a joint venture known as 'ninemsn' which will provide a consumer on-line service business including Internet access. PBL's international interests include magazines throughout Asia–Pacific countries, and a 25 per cent stake in New Regency, a Hollywood film producer.

The large stakeholders in the Seven Network include Mr Kerry Stokes and News Ltd. Mr Stokes holds other broadcasting and newspaper interests. The Seven Network also controls Australia Television, the international TV channel started by the Australian Broadcasting Corporation. Seven shares control of MGM Studios with Mr Kirk Kerkorian. In Network Ten, the largest economic interest is held by the CanWest Global Communications group of Mr Izzy Asper, based in Canada. In subscription television, Foxtel is a joint venture in approximately equal shares between News Ltd (the largest newspaper group) and Telstra (the major telecommunications carrier). The system has over forty channels. Optus, the second largest telecommunications carrier, is the other main cable content provider, through its Optus Vision system, with over eighty channels. Australis Media Ltd includes satellite and MDS in its subscription TV delivery systems. In 1997, it was financially precarious, and likely to merge in some way with Foxtel.

Telstra, the largest telco, was originally the telecommunications section of the Postmaster-General's Department. It was corporatised in 1989, and operates on a commercial basis. One-third of its shares were sold to the public in 1997. The remaining two-thirds are still owned by the federal government. Optus Communications, the second general carrier, was formed in 1991. Its major shareholder is the UK-based Cable & Wireless. AAPT is the largest of several communications corporations which became carriers when limits on carrier numbers were removed in July 1997.

In radio, the two largest metropolitan players are Austereo and Australian Radio Network. The major interests in Austereo are held by the Village Roadshow, a large Australian film distribution, exhibition, and production group which also has theme park and leisure operations. The other major group, Australian Radio Network, is owned in equal shares by two media groups. The first is Australian Provincial Newspapers, controlled by the O'Reilly family, who have Irish associations. The second is Clear Channel Communications, one of the largest radio and TV groups in the US.

The public broadcasters, officially known as the national broadcasters, are the ABC and the SBS. They both have television and radio outlets, and both provide programmes for subscription television. The ABC is a major publisher of books and music, and provides many Internet services. Since 1932, a feature of the Australian broadcasting system has always been a clear division between commercial broadcasting and public broadcasting. The ABC may be loosely compared with other national broadcasters such as NHK in Japan, the CBC in Canada, and the BBC in the United Kingdom. The television service of the SBS is unlike the ABC in that it carries advertising. Its radio service does not. The SBS has three radio networks whereas the ABC has five.

With on-line services proliferating, print media are increasingly relevant to the new media, particularly because of classified advertising, which is already going on-line. News Ltd is the largest newspaper group, by a considerable margin. The major shareholding interests are a series of family trusts associated with the family of Mr Rupert Murdoch. News has major broadcasting, newspaper, and film interests around the globe, and a significant part of its senior management is Australian. John Fairfax Holdings Ltd is the second largest newspaper group.

Optus Communications, the second general carrier, was formed in 1991. It is owned by six major shareholder groups, four Australian and two overseas. The main shareholders are: Cable & Wireless (49 per cent), Mayne Nickless (25 per cent), AMP Society (10.3 per cent), National Mutual (6.1 per cent), and the AIDC Telecommunications Fund (9.6 per cent). The Australian groups control about 51 per cent of the shares. Optus Communications is expected to make a public issue in 1997, through which shareholding proportions may change; including the sale of the Mayne Nickless shares. BellSouth sold its 24.5 per cent shareholding to Cable & Wireless in 1997.

3 LEGISLATIVE AND POLICY ENVIRONMENT

The forms and symbols of Australian communications look similar to those of the Western world, and include influences from the United Kingdom and the United States. Communications policy is expressed in the same technical and economic jargon to be found elsewhere. The legislation frequently borrows and adapts overseas concepts. But there are significant differences, and it would be a mistake to be distracted by the forms. Official changes to the identity of regulatory bodies and legislation should not distract from the much slower rate of underlying change.

Within the Australian federation, most electronic communications and media issues are primarily the responsibility of the federal (Commonwealth) parliament, not the State parliaments. On the other hand, there are very limited federal powers over print media or information technology. UK and US ideas were the main influence on the drafting of the Australian constitution in the 1890s. For example the houses of the federal parliament are the House of Representatives and the Senate, as in the US. This affects communications law, because minority parties usually hold the balance of power in the Senate. Thus, it is rarely within the power of a federal government to enact whatever communications laws it chooses. The system of government accountability is based on the Westminster system, so that the governing party is responsible to the House of Representatives. The Minister responsible for communications, and his or her department, have had various titles in recent years. In 1997, information was added to the portfolio, so that the title became Minister for Communications, the Information Economy and the Arts.

Many of the developments in media and communications can be better understood against the background of broad trends toward deregulation and increased competition. The Broadcasting Services Act 1992 reduced the regulation of some aspects of broadcasting. For example, it introduced requirements for different sectors of broadcasting to devise their own codes of practice for content regulation. There are still some restrictions on the licensing of services, and new imposts on licences such as the auctioning of licences and spectrum rights.

In telecommunications, competition has been progressively increased since the Telecommunications Act 1989. New carriers commenced operations under the Telecommunications Act 1991 which also removed the restrictions on the resale of services. Under the Telecommunications Act 1997 there is no limit on the number of carriers, or on competition in other areas of telecommunications.

Whilst official policies focus on deregulation, in practice the trend is to substitute competition regulation for the previous regimes specifically addressing broadcasting and telecommunications. The effect of removing specific laws is to increase the jurisdiction of general regulators, such as the Australian Competition and Consumer Commission (ACCC), mentioned below. Overall, the volume of regulatory activity and regulatory instruments appears to increase as a result of 'deregulation' policies. New economic values and regulators appear to have replaced earlier social values. The main federal Acts which currently affect electronic communications and media are:

The *Broadcasting Services Act 1992*, which provides for the regulation of all broadcasting, including technical planning as well as licensing and programme rules. It also sets out limits on control of broadcasting. Through cross-media restrictions, it affects the structure of print media and some new communications services. It is administered by the Australian Broadcasting Authority (ABA). The Act extends well beyond conventional broadcasting, into narrowcasting and other new and specialised services. There is some discussion about extending the Act to cover the content of all electronic information services, including on-line services. However, no federal legislation applies expressly to on-line issues.

The *Telecommunications Act 1997* governs facilities and services which carry telecommunications. The Act is generally seen as a vehicle for economic and technical regulation of telecommunications, without regulating the content of services. The powers within the Act could possibly be used to control the content of on-line services, but there are no proposals to use it for those purposes. The Act is administered by the Australian Communications Authority (ACA).

The *Radiocommunications Act 1992* provides for regulation of technical and planning aspects of the radio frequency spectrum. Although the Act receives little attention, in fact it shapes the environment for new services. For example, it lays down the market-based system for allocating spectrum and frequencies. Like the Telecommunications Act, it is administered by the ACA.

The *Trade Practices Act 1974* has a significant effect on the structure and ownership of media and communications. It is administered by the ACCC. Until 1995, specific rules about broadcasting and telecommunications in their respective Acts left the ACCC with little scope to regulate electronic communications. The recent trend has been to avoid 'industry specific' competition rules for new media, by making the ACCC the universal industry regulator. In a compromise between general and specific regulation, two Parts of the Trade Practices Act have a special impact on telecommunications: Part XIB subjects telecommunications conduct to ACCC regulation; and Part XIC imposes the telecommunications access regime. The ACCC is the most powerful regulator of communications, except in relation to technical issues and communications content.

4 REGULATORS

The main regulators have already been mentioned, in relation to the Acts which involve them. The overall scheme is:

Competition regulator
  Australian Competition and Consumer Commission (ACCC)

Communications regulators
  Australian Communications Authority (ACA)
  Australian Broadcasting Authority (ABA)
  Minister and Department of Communications, the Information Economy and the Arts.

The Australian Broadcasting Authority[10]

The ABA is responsible for implementing most provisions of the Broadcasting Services Act. When it was created in 1992, the broadcast planning role of the Department of Transport and Communications was transferred to it, to add to the licensing and programme regulation roles which the ABA inherited from its predecessor, the Australian Broadcasting Tribunal. The planning role of the ABA works within those parts of the radio frequency spectrum allocated to broadcasting by the Minister under the Radiocommunications Act 1992. The ABA's other roles include 'responsibility for monitoring the broadcasting industry' (s 5(1)), and monitoring and investigation of complaints about all broadcasting sectors (s 158(1)). Other ABA functions involve the conduct or commissioning of research on community attitudes to issues relating to programmes (s 158(g)), and monitoring and advising government on technological advances and service trends in the broadcasting industry (s 158(m)).

To support its monitoring function, the ABA is given extensive investigative and enforcement powers. The normal method of ABA operation is intended to be conducted through information gathering and investigation, for which it is equipped with considerable powers (ss 170–180). It does not need to conduct a hearing or inquiry in order to require disclosure of information on oath or production of documents. The 1992 Act removed public hearing as a normal method of reaching broadcasting decisions but the Act does retain section 168(2) which requires the ABA,

---

[10] Armstrong, M (ed), *Communications Law and Policy in Australia* (Sydney: Butterworths, 1992), Vol 1, para 5000 *et seq*.

subject to any direction of the government, to inform itself in the manner which it considers will be 'the quickest and most economical in the circumstances'. This is less radical than the original legislative proposal that the hearing procedure be used 'only in exceptional circumstances'. There has been some criticism of the ABA's *modus operandi* from groups who believe its processes are not sufficiently public.

The Australian Communications Authority[11]

The ACA was created in 1997 out of components of two bodies: AUSTEL, which was the telecommunications regulator; and the Spectrum Management Agency, which planned and administered the radio frequency spectrum (other than the broadcast spectrum). The previous powers over economic regulation and telecommunications competition were removed from AUSTEL and given to the ACCC. The ACA provides specialist expertise to the ACCC in the consideration of competition issues for telecommunications.

The ACA is responsible for technical regulation of telecommunications, including carrier licensing, and for the radio spectrum, as well as the management of much of Australia's contribution to the setting of international standards. The functions of the ACA under the Telecommunications Act include: technical standards about customer equipment and customer cabling; technical standards for the interconnection of facilities; the issue of carrier and cabling licences; and the development and administration of the Australian numbering plan. The ACA may also conduct public inquiries, and investigations as well as gathering information from carriers, and service providers and specifying the records that they must keep.

The functions of the ACA under the Radiocommunications Act include: preparing spectrum, frequency, marketing, and conversion plans; administering spectrum, apparatus, and class licensing systems; administering the system of standards and technical regulation; settling interference disputes; conducting public inquiries; making advisory guidelines; administering an accreditation system; and determining charges for spectrum access and other purposes.

The role of the government

Whilst the statutory regulators of communications have a significant and visible role, the federal government retains very significant powers over the areas with which the regulators deal. For example, the regulators must perform their functions in accordance with policies notified by the

---

[11] Armstrong, M (ed), *Communications Law and Policy in Australia* (Sydney: Butterworths, 1992), Vol 1, para 40000 *et seq.*

government, and are subject to government directions on most matters, through the minister. Many directions must be 'only of a general nature' and must be published. Apart from the powers of direction, the government has various powers to regulate directly and make decisions about communications. The Telecommunications Act, in particular, is replete with specific powers of the government.

The Telecommunications Industry Ombudsman scheme[12]

The Telecommunications Industry Ombudsman (TIO) scheme was expanded under the 1997 Act, with membership of the scheme mandatory for all carriage service providers unless exempted. The definition of carriage service providers includes Internet service providers, giving the TIO significant interest in on-line services.

The TIO has a wide jurisdiction over consumer complaints relating to telecommunications services suppliers, from those offering basic telephony, to mobile communications and Internet access. It has power to investigate and arbitrate consumer complaints about the provision of carriage services, Internet issues, billing, faults, operator and directory services, and privacy. This is a potentially broad area of operation given the increasing range of services offered on-line. The TIO does not deal with industry complaints, referring these to more appropriate forums, such as the ACA or the ACCC.

5 ADVISORY BODIES

Whereas the old media, apart from newspapers, are subject to regulatory bodies, there are advisory bodies to suggest ways to develop the new media. There is little regulation of on-line services as such. Proposals for 'cyberlaws' to facilitate 'e-commerce' are mentioned below. Apart from one-off inquiries and reports, there are three federal advisory bodies.

National Office of the Information Economy

In October 1997, the federal government announced an expansion of the communications and arts portfolio by the addition of the National Office for the Information Economy (NOIE). The NOIE is headed by a full-time CEO, supported by a chairperson and project managers who together form the advisory board. The advisory board reports to a Ministerial Council consisting of the federal treasurer and attorney-general, and government ministers having responsibility for communications and the arts, trade, industry, science and tourism, finance, administrative services and

---

[12] Telecommunications Act 1997, Part 10.

justice. It is the responsibility of the NOIE to develop policy in key areas of Australia's information society, including:

- development of a national information and on-line services infrastructure and strategy;
- encouraging a sound framework for electronic commerce;
- the provision of on-line government service delivery; and
- promoting public awareness and education about on-line services.

The Information Policy Advisory Council[13]

In August 1996 the Minister for Communications and the Arts announced the establishment of the Information Policy Advisory Council (IPAC). IPAC contains a mix of industry, academic, and government experience, led by Dr Terry Cutler of Cutler & Co.[14] Its function is to advise government on the development of on-line information and communications services and technologies, particularly the Internet. IPAC has produced two major reports: *A National Policy Framework for Structural Adjustment within the new Commonwealth of Information*, released in July 1997;[15] and the report of the working party investigating the development of on-line infrastructure and services development in regional and rural Australia released in March 1997.[16]

The Information Industries Taskforce[17]

A parallel body to IPAC is the Information Industries Taskforce, established at the same time by the federal Industry Minister. It advises the government on development of a new national information industries strategy. The Taskforce consists of eight members drawn from a cross section of information industries, including developers, manufacturers and/or suppliers of computing, communications, and multimedia products and services. It is chaired by Professor Ashley Goldsworthy. In July 1997, the Task Force produced a report on Australia's future participation in the global information industry.[18]

6 STANDARDS AND TECHNICAL REGULATION

Technical regulation is in process of change. The emphasis of the new approach is increased self-regulation. The ACA is intended to provide a

---

[13] <http://www.ipac.gov.au/>
[14] <http://www.cutlerco.com.au>
[15] <http://www.ipac.gov.au/report2/index.html>
[16] <http://www.ipac.gov.au/report/ipac.htm>
[17] <http://www.dist.gov.au/itt/tskforce/index.html>
[18] Department of Industry Science and Tourism, Information Industries Taskforce, *The*

safeguard where self-regulation is inappropriate. Technical regulation of telecommunications and radiocommunications is intended to be harmonised. The telecommunications laws require carriers to submit industry development plans to support the equipment manufacturing industry. Planning and technical aspects of broadcasting are the separate responsibility of the Australian Broadcasting Authority. There are no proposed compulsory standards affecting technical aspects of multimedia or on-line services.

The Telecommunications Act and related Acts require mandatory standards on customer equipment and cabling to protect the health and safety of consumers and telecommunications employees, and to protect networks. Other standards are intended to address matters such as the ability to call emergency numbers and compatibility of the standard telephone service. Standards for customer equipment and customer cabling relate to areas such as: integrity of networks and the safety of people; interoperability of customer equipment and cabling; compliance with international standards about connecting equipment and cabling to networks; maintaining end-to-end technical quality; containing interference to radiocommunications; and immunity from electromagnetic disturbance.[19] Technical standards are made and administered by the ACA.

Part 4 of the Radiocommunications Act deals with standards and other technical issues. It aims to establish an efficient, flexible, and responsive system for technical regulation of equipment that uses, or is affected by, radio emissions. Technical regulation under the Act includes: prohibitions relating to non-standard devices (ss 157–61); standards for a wide range of devices (ss 162–5); technical licence specifications for apparatus licences (ss 179–81); labelling of devices to indicate compliance (ss 182–8); and prohibition of devices which would adversely affect radiocommunications (ss 189–91). The only technical area of communications not subject to the ACA is broadcasting. It is the role of the ABA to develop technical guidelines for the planning of individual services which use the broadcasting services bands as a means of delivery.[20]

7 MARKET STRUCTURE

Laws affect the structure of the media and communications environment through a variety of means. Telecommunications is subject to a very

---

Global Information Economy: The Way Ahead (Canberra: AGPS, 1997); also at <http://www.dist.gov.au/itt/golds/index.html>

[19] Telecommunications Act 1997, s 376.
[20] Broadcasting Services Act 1992, s 33.

complex scheme of controls and discretionary powers, all apparently intended to increase competition. Broadcasting is affected by specific limits on permitted levels of cross-ownership and foreign ownership. On top of these two different kinds of structural regulation, all media and communications players, new and old are affected by the Trade Practices Act and the Foreign Acquisitions and Takeovers Act.

Telecommunications structure and licensing

The current structure of telecommunications was created in 1997 as part of a process which continued throughout the 1990s. This explanation includes some references to the recent history of telecommunications liberalisation, because that history is an integral part of the status quo. Competition among carriers was introduced through the Telecommunications Act 1991. Two general carrier licences and three mobile carrier licences were issued under that Act. Telstra, the incumbent government-owned carrier, and the privately-owned Optus received both general and mobile licences, and Vodafone received a mobile licence. Carriers also had a general right of access to the services provided on each other's infrastructure; including access to services which were not provided commercially to other parties, and at prices which were not subject to the constraints on commercial tariffs.

There are around 10 million fixed access lines in Australia, nearly all of them provided by Telstra. Optic fibre rings installed by Optus are in the centres of the major capital cities, as are a small number of Optus local access services to businesses. Optus also intends to provide local access services on its cable TV network, which passes 3 million of the 6 million households in Australia. Access to the Optus long-distance telephone service is available to all customers by both dial code access and preselection from fixed services. There is no choice of long-distance carrier for mobile customers.

The 1991 Telecommunications Act removed restrictions on the resale of telecommunications services. Some resellers developed extensive networks using the transmission capabilities supplied by Telstra and Optus so as to develop services for supply to the public. Others simply resold services which were provided by the carriers, and operated on the margin provided by the carriers' high volume tariffs. Access to the service provider networks was originally by dial code, although preselection was introduced in 1997.

In their general carrier licences under the 1991 Act, Telstra and Optus had the exclusive right to install line links, which could be broadly described as transmission systems based on wireline or optic fibre bearers. There was no restriction on the installation of radio transmission systems (other than normal spectrum licensing) but there were restrictions on the purpose for which radio technology could be used. This was to protect the general carriers from extensive bypass by radio links. There was no restriction on a broadcaster installing a network to distribute its services, although there was a restriction on such a network also being used to provide telecommunications services.

A mobile carrier licence under the 1991 Act permitted a licensee to provide mobile services to the public. The three licensees were required to establish separate digital networks. The newer licensees, Optus and Vodafone, are not permitted to install analogue equipment and the GSM standard was mandated for digital networks. In order to introduce competition into the mobile market more quickly, both Optus and Vodafone were permitted to resell AMPS (analogue) services provided by Telstra. However only Optus chose to do so. The existing AMPS network operated by Telstra is to be closed down in the year 2000 as a matter of government policy.

There are approximately 5 million mobile services in Australia. About 2.4 million services are on the Telstra AMPS network, of which approximately one-third are services resold by Optus. There are about 2.6 million services in total on the Telstra, Optus, and Vodafone GSM networks.

The current Telecommunications Act 1997, and various related Acts, removed the distinction between mobile and general carriers. It also allowed for an unlimited number of carriers.[21] Subject to some limited restrictions, anyone may obtain a carrier licence. In general, any owner of transmission infrastructure must have a carrier licence in order to supply telecommunications services to the public over that infrastructure. However, the supply of services by resale from a licensed carrier does not require a licence. Resellers are subject to explicit obligations similar to, but less extensive than, those which apply to carriers. The current Telecommunications Act makes a distinction between carriage service providers and content service providers. The latter is a person who uses carriage services to provide a content service to the public. No special conditions apply to content service providers.[22] The standard service provider rules appear to have little bearing on the supply of content services.

The other important feature of the telecommunications structure is the access regime in Part XIC of the Trade Practices Act. It is so important to all sectors of communications that it is discussed later under a separate heading.

Control of radio and television

The rules about control of broadcasting have interacted with the actual market structures since the 1930s. The current rules are set out in the

[21] Telecommunications Act 1997, Part 3—'Carriers'.
[22] Telecommunications Act 1997, Part 4—'Service Providers'.

Broadcasting Services Act. Most of them are directed at free-to-air commercial television broadcasting. The rationale for this emphasis is that television is a more influential medium, with a higher impact on community, political, and family life. In brief summary, a person must not control:

- commercial television licences reaching more than 75 per cent of the Australian population. This means that a single network can effectively control the programming of a national channel, but not all of the outlets for that channel;
- more than one commercial television licence in the same geographic licence area;
- more than two commercial radio licences in the same area; or
- both a commercial television licence and a commercial radio licence or a major newspaper in the same area. Under this cross-media rule, a person can control only one of those three kinds of outlets in an area. For example, a major newspaper owner in Melbourne cannot control commercial radio or television in Melbourne, and a person who controls a Brisbane commercial radio station cannot control a Brisbane newspaper or commercial television station.

These rules operate in a commercial television environment where each major population centre has only three free-to-air licences, and, for a mixture of technical and policy reasons, there is little prospect of another becoming available. In 1997, the federal government proposed removing the cross-media rules. This produced some months of political upheavals and differences of view among media proprietors. The proposals were then abandoned.

Community broadcasting (non-commercial, with local or specialised programmes) is not subject to specific limits, but in licensing those services the ABA is required to avoid allowing one person to control more than one such service in an area. It is also to avoid control of community licences by governments and political parties. Furthermore, community broadcasters are required to represent the community interest for which their licences were originally granted.

There are no restrictions on control, ownership, or licence numbers for other kinds of broadcasting such as narrowcasting and subscription radio. However, they are subject to the general competition and merger restrictions in the Trade Practices Act, discussed below.

Control of print media

There are virtually no specific laws or policies dealing with concentration in control of print media. There is not even a parliament or government which claims responsibility for the area. Under the Constitution, the federal parliament has no specific powers in the area. In theory, the States might be responsible for policy. In practice, State regulation of national and international print enterprises would be difficult. However, print media ownership does not escape some forms of 'back door' regulation and influence. It is affected by three areas of federal law. First, competition laws in the Trade Practices Act affect mergers and acquisitions of press interests. Secondly, the broadcasting cross-ownership laws exclude radio and television proprietors from controlling major daily newspapers in their audience areas, and vice versa. Thirdly, the Foreign Acquisition and Takeovers Act allows the federal government to restrict foreign ownership of newspapers, and, in the course of doing so, to exert political influence on other aspects of newspapers.

In 1992 a federal parliamentary committee produced a major report on laws affecting newspaper ownership, called *News & Fair Facts: the Australian Print Media Industry.*[23] The inquiry investigated ownership concentration, and the adequacy of existing laws to encourage competition and diversity of ownership in the print media. *News & Fair Facts* recommended that the ACCC should be required to consider special factors, in addition to the usual competition criteria, in making a determination on whether a newspaper merger should be authorised on public benefit grounds. These included the impact of mergers on freedom of expression, the fair and accurate presentation of news, and the economic viability of the newspaper affected if a merger was banned. These recommendations were not implemented.

Foreign control

Foreign control of media is affected by the Broadcasting Services Act and the Foreign Acquisition and Takeovers Act 1975 ('the FATS Act'). The FATS Act does not lay down principles and procedures to be implemented in detail. It confers a broad discretion on the Treasurer, a minister in the federal government. Thus, foreign investment decisions are in practice a mixture of administrative and political judgment. The absence of definite rules has attracted much criticism. A document published by the Treasury, titled *Australia's Foreign Investment Policy: A Guide for Investors,*[24] says that the Government requires all investment proposals by foreign interests which relate to the media sector to be notified to the Foreign Investment Review Board (FIRB), a body which advises the Treasurer, regardless of the size of the investment. It emphasises a case-by-case

---

[23] Australia, Parliament, *News & Fair Facts: the Australian Print Media Industry: Report from the House of Representatives Select Committee on the Print Media* (Canberra: AGPS, 1992).

[24] Australia, Department of Treasury, *Australia's Foreign Investment Policy: A Guide for Investors* (Canberra: AGPS, 1992), 2–3.

approach. In 1993 the government announced a new policy for applications to the FIRB involving newspapers. The policy allows a shareholding of up to 25 per cent in a mass circulation newspaper by a single foreign investor, with a 30 per cent aggregate of all foreign interests in a newspaper.

In 1993, the Senate Select Committee on Certain Aspects of Foreign Ownership Decisions in Relation to the Print Media inquired into the origin and basis of decisions in 1991 and 1993 to increase the permissible percentage of foreign ownership of newspapers. Remarks in Conrad Black's autobiography were one of the reasons for the inquiry. He suggested that the then Prime Minister had agreed that Mr Black would be allowed to increase his investment in Fairfax if its political coverage of the 1993 federal election was 'balanced'. There were also concerns about FIRB processes leading up to foreign investment decisions. The committee was very critical of the foreign investment rules and procedures. It said, among other things, that recommendations about foreign investment decisions in key industry sectors should be made public.[25] This is a very controversial area, because governments of all persuasions have been reluctant to abandon the relatively unfettered power to pressure shareholders in newspapers.

The Broadcasting Services Act restricts interests held by 'foreign persons', who are essentially non-citizens or companies controlled by them, in free-to-air television. A foreign person must not have company interests exceeding 15 per cent in a licence, and the aggregate of foreign interests in a licensee must not exceed 20 per cent.

Competition law

Competition law, embodied in the Trade Practices Act 1974, plays the major role in determining the ownership and control of communications channels and content, as already mentioned. Its two main impacts are on mergers of communications enterprises and on access to communications facilities.

The main purpose of the Act, which is heavily influenced by US anti-trust law, is to control restrictive trade practices and monopolisation, and to protect consumers from unfair commercial practices.[26] Media and communications enterprises are often affected by section 50 of the Act, which prohibits mergers likely to have the effect of 'substantially lessening competition' in a market, and section 46 which deals with 'misuse of market power'. The aim of both is to promote economic efficiency through

[25] Australia, Parliament, *Percentage Players: The First Report of the Senate Select Committee on Certain Aspects of Foreign Ownership Decisions in Relation to the Print Media* (Canberra, 1994), p. xix.
[26] Australia, House of Representatives, *Parliamentary Debates*, 16 July 1974, 225.

ensuring that markets are competitive. The application of the sections does not depend on other public benefits or detriments. The basic questions are simply about levels of competition in a market. Communications is seen within the trade practices regime as a market like any other, and the market is the main solution for policy issues. There is no provision for 'old' media values such as social accountability and obligations to serve agreed community needs.

When an acquisition is considered under section 50, matters to be taken into consideration when deciding whether it is likely to substantially lessen competition include: the height of barriers to entry to the market, the level of concentration in the market, and the degree of countervailing power in the market. Even where an acquisition would contravene section 50 it may be authorised by the ACCC. The Commission will not authorise unless it is satisfied that in all the circumstances the proposed acquisition would be likely to result in such a benefit to the public that the acquisition should be allowed to take place. This 'public benefit' test does allow some values other than competition to be recognised by the ACCC on occasions. Section 50 differs from the broadcasting control and ownership rules in the Broadcasting Services Act in two main ways. It relies on the concept of substantial lessening of competition rather than any specific numerical limits; and it relies on a decision by the regulators, on a case-by-case basis, about what is the relevant 'market'.

There has been much controversy about the effectiveness of section 50, and the administration of the Trade Practices Act, in relation to communications. For example, there was criticism of the decision not to intervene in the takeover of the *Herald and Weekly Times* by News Limited in 1987. The takeover led to acquisition of around 65 per cent of capital city and national newspaper ownership by News Limited. In 1990, the predecessor of the ACCC refused to authorise the controllers of the Perth *West Australian* to take over the *Daily News*, Perth's only afternoon newspaper. In the absence of an alternative buyer, the *Daily News* closed. More recently, great controversy arose about a proposed merger of two of the subscription television content providers, Foxtel and Australis Media. In February 1996, the Chair of the ACCC issued a statement to the media on the Commission's 'consideration' of the proposed merger. The ACCC considered that the original merger proposal was likely to breach section 50 as it would be likely to lead to a substantial lessening of competition. That form of merger was abandoned. In late 1997, a later, and different, form of merger between the same two parties was challenged by the ACCC in proceedings which appeared likely to produce protracted litigation.

Control and ownership of commercial free-to-air broadcasting is addressed in Part V of the Broadcasting Services Act 1992. It was decided in

Austereo Ltd v Trade Practices Commission[27] that section 77 of the Broadcasting Services Act 1992, which says that the provisions of Part V of the Broadcasting Services Act 1992 'have effect notwithstanding the Trade Practices Act', was only 'concerned with preserving the full operation of Part V'. Accordingly, Part V does not preclude the operation of the Trade Practices Act. The practical effect of this decision is that ownership of broadcasting enterprises is subject to a dual regime: the specific broadcasting laws, and the general competition laws.

8 THE TELECOMMUNICATIONS ACCESS REGIME

One of the principal determinants of future economic structures is likely to be the new access regime forming part of the proposed telecommunications laws mentioned above. The effects of the regime go far beyond traditional telecommunications services, to affect virtually all electronic delivery systems.

The previous telecommunications access regime in the Telecommunications Act 1991 provided for all of the three carriers to have fairly broad access to the facilities of each other, such as ducts, radio towers, and buildings; to services of other carriers that were not supplied to the public, such as originating and terminating access in the switched telephone network; and to publicly available services at favourable prices. To support the duopoly/triopoly market structure, the access regime was exempt from the provisions of the Trade Practices Act 1974 with respect to the anti-competitive aspects of refusal to supply certain services to parties other than licensed carriers. The ability to supply services at less than tariffed prices was in contrast to the requirement in the Telecommunications Act 1991 that for most services supplied to the public, Telstra, as the dominant carrier, could not vary from its published tariffs.

In 1995, Part IIIA was introduced into the Trade Practices Act 1974 to provide a general regime for access to infrastructure. This regime provided two alternatives to the owners of significant infrastructure: they could either volunteer to provide access through having an access undertaking approved by the ACCC as administrator of the Trade Practices Act; or they could wait until an access seeker had the infrastructure 'declared', and then negotiate in private with the access seeker. The ACCC can arbitrate in the absence of agreement.

The current telecommunications access regime borrows from both these regimes. In July 1997 a new Part XIC was introduced into the Trade Practices Act. The structure of Part XIC is based on the general access regime in Part IIIA in that an infrastructure owner (carrier) may have an

---

[27] (1993) 115 ALR 14.

access undertaking approved by the ACCC, or wait until a service is declared by the ACCC in response to a request from an access seeker. The ACCC may also declare a service on its own initiative after conducting a public inquiry or on the recommendation of the Telecommunications Access Forum (TAF), which is a body representative of carriers and service providers. Carriers and service providers are then required to provide access to those declared services either in accordance with an Access Undertaking that they have given to the ACCC or by negotiation with the access seeker. The ACCC may arbitrate on access disputes to the extent that its determination is consistent with any Access Undertaking which it has previously accepted from the carrier or service provider.

The current telecommunications regime differs from the general access regime in relation to the standards applied for the declaration of a service. The major requirements of the general access regime are that: access to the facility would promote competition; it would be uneconomical to replicate the facility; and that the facility should be of national significance. By contrast, the requirements of the telecommunications access regime are that the access provider is capable of supplying the service, including supply to itself, and that the supply of the service would promote the long-term interests of end-users of carriage services or of services provided by means of carriage services.

The current regime applies to both carriers and service providers,[28] including content service providers, whereas the 1991 regime applied only to licensed carriers. It does however provide for exemption from the regime, either individually or by a specified class of carrier or service provider, if the exemption will promote the long-term interests of end-users. In those areas where it applies, the new telecommunications access regime effectively overrides the general access regime.

9 UNIVERSAL SERVICE

The only sector of communications which is subject to a definite universal service requirement to ensure community access is telecommunications. In broadcasting, the planning of services and broadcasting frequency allocations is expected to ensure relatively even coverage of the population by free-to-air services. Commercial broadcasters are also required to provide 'adequate and comprehensive service' in the content of broadcasts to the communities they are licensed to serve.[29] However, 'adequate and comprehensive service' has proved impossible to define in practice.

---

[28] In slightly different ways: access to services is the same for both carriers and service providers, but provisions exist for carriers to have access to the infrastructure of other carriers.

[29] Broadcasting Services Act 1992, Sch 2, Part 3, clause 7(2).

In addition, the free-to-air, non-commercial channels of the national broadcasters, the ABC and SBS, are intended to provide access to information, education, cultural, and multicultural broadcasting.

Origins of universal service in telecommunications

The term 'universal service' was first introduced into law in the Telecommunications Act 1991. Until carrier competition was introduced by that Act, planning and provision of universal services were part of the responsibility of the monopoly government carrier.

The current obligation embraces universality of access, affordability, and geography to a minimum level of telecommunications infrastructure and services. The scheme was created and operates in recognition of the importance of telecommunications in supporting the effective participation of Australians in society; particularly in a country where market forces would make communications for remote and isolated consumers prohibitively expensive. The attempted 'safety net' for consumers who would otherwise be disadvantaged by market forces is the complex scheme set out in Part 7 of the Telecommunications Act 1997. The idea behind the scheme is that all carriers should contribute to the extra costs of a carrier who provides defined uneconomic services to them. The government may declare one or more additional universal service providers (USPs), in other words providers of defined uneconomic services, at any time. It may also determine that the method of selecting USPs be opened up to tendering and competition, to see which carrier can provide such services at the lowest cost. Currently, Telstra bears the cost of the universal service obligation (USO) on a national basis and is entitled to contributions towards that cost from other participating carriers.

The exact method for calculating contributions had not been finally determined in late 1997, although contributions of each 'participating carrier' will be in proportion to their 'eligible revenue' (not yet defined). In June 1997, the government released a discussion paper calling for submissions on two main issues. The first was how 'eligible revenue' should be calculated. The second was the possible exemption of classes or types of carriers from the requirement to contribute to the cost of the USO; in other words, the definition of 'participating carrier'.

The legal structure of universal service

Section 137 of the Telecommunications Act 1997 sets out the basic requirements of the USO:

The main object of the universal service regime is to ensure that all people in Australia, wherever they reside or carry on business, should have reasonable access, on an equitable basis, to:

(a) standard telephone services; and
(b) payphones; and
(c) prescribed carriage services.

The more functional features of the USO are defined in section 149(2) which says that it is part of the USO:

(a) to supply standard telephone services to people in Australia on request;
(b) to supply, install and maintain payphones in Australia;
(c) to supply prescribed carriage services to people in Australia on request.

The USO requires the provision of a standard telephone service (STS) for all Australians, which means access, equipment, and service. Access to voice telephony is the most basic requirement but that also embodies equivalent services to the disabled so as to meet the requirements of the Disability Discrimination Act. Supply of a STS also incorporates a range of additional obligations which customers of a USP are entitled to obtain. These are dotted through the Act and include operator services,[30] directory assistance services,[31] and emergency call services.[32] Access must also be given to payphones. The government has power to direct that payphones be installed at particular locations.

The level of service required

One of the most far-reaching aspects of the USO relates to the capacity to provide the whole community with access to levels of service and capacity above simple voice telephony. In 1996, the government established the Standard Telephone Review Group to examine whether the definition of the standard telephone service applicable within the universal service obligation should be upgraded to take account of new technologies. The Group reported in December 1996.[33] A majority of the Group recommended that by 1 January 2000, the universal service obligation should include the provision of a digital data capability that is reasonably accessible to all Australians on an equitable basis wherever they reside or carry on business. It said:

The digital data capability should provide a platform for access to a range of services such as fax, email, access to the Internet, electronic commerce and educational applications. The functionality offered should be broadly comparable to that currently offered by ETSI ISDN services, although the particular ways of supplying the digital data capability may have different transmission and other

---

[30] Telecommunications Act 1997, Sch 2, Part 2.
[31] Telecommunications Act 1997, Sch 2, Part 3.
[32] Part 12, except where exempted.
[33] Standard Telephone Service Review Group, *Review of the Standard Telephone Service*, December 1996; <ftp://www.dca.gov.au/pub/docs/stsreport.doc>

characteristics from ISDN services. The focus should be on functions and capabilities, not particular technologies.

It recommended that where such a capacity was not met by the new competitive environment, it should be included in the universal obligation as a 'prescribed carrier service' (PCS) from mid-1998. The aim of incorporating it into the USO at that time is to allow sufficient time to have the capacity to provide the specified functional requirements brought to all Australians by 1 January 2000. 'Prescribed carriage services' do not yet have any definition in the new Act. However, the government is obliged to conduct a review by September 1998 in order to decide whether digital data services with a capacity of 64 Kbs should become part of the prescribed service from 1999 onwards. This is some recognition of the importance that on-line services may soon play in the context of standard telecommunications services.

10 CONTENT REGULATION

Content is regulated through a variety of different mechanisms. For broadcasting services, a system of mandatory standards and prohibitions has evolved into a system which relies on self-regulatory codes for many topics. There were State-based schemes for censorship of books, magazines, and some other printed material; another censorship scheme, largely based on federal legislation, governed films. During the 1990s, the diverse systems for censorship of non-broadcast material evolved into a co-operative and relatively uniform scheme, based on the powers of the federal and State parliaments. All restrictions on content may be affected by the implied constitutional right to freedom of communication. However, its main protection is confined to discussion of political and government issues. '

The implied constitutional right to free communication

The Australian Constitution has no express recognition or guarantee of freedom of speech. However, in a series of cases commencing in 1992 with *Australian Capital Television v The Commonwealth (No 2)*[34] the High Court has held that a limited form of such a right is necessarily implied in the structure and wording of the Constitution. That freedom may be truncated only by a law that complies with constitutional doctrine.

The *Australian Capital Television* case struck down amendments to the federal Broadcasting Act inserted by the Political Broadcasts and Political Disclosures Act 1991. The aim of the provisions was to establish a scheme

[34] (1992) 177 CLR 106.

for the regulation of political announcements, particularly during an election period, including a prohibition of the broadcasting of political advertisements. A majority of the court held that the Constitution contains an implied guarantee of freedom of communication, at least in relation to public and political discussion, which was contravened by the new provisions. That freedom was fundamentally important in the Australian system of representative government, although it was not to be regarded as a personal right but, rather, 'an immunity consequent on a limitation of legislative power'.[35]

On the same day, the court's decision in *Nationwide News v Wills*[36] dealt with similar issues in relation to the legislative suppression of any comment calculated to bring the Australian Industrial Relations Commission into disrepute. Again, the provisions were struck down, this time unanimously, on the basis that the suppression was so broad that the overreaching of the limitation on legislative power was manifest.

Later cases, *Theophanous v Herald & Weekly Times Ltd*[37] and *Stephens v West Australian Newspapers*,[38] further defined the nature and scope of these principles, and modified the law of defamation applying to the case of publications concerning government and political matters. In the *Theophanous* case, the court was asked to consider whether a letter published in a newspaper shortly before a federal election, criticising Dr Theophanous, a member of parliament, was defamatory. One of the defences was the implied freedom of speech on political matters established in the *Australian Capital Television* case. The majority formulated a test designed to make the law of defamation consistent with the implied freedom of communication.[39] The *Stephens* case also involved defamation. The action concerned articles published in Western Australia alleging that an overseas trip taken by certain members of the WA parliament was a 'mammoth junket'. The same majority as in the *Theophanous* case held that the freedom implied in the Constitution extends to public discussion of the performance, conduct, and fitness for office of members of a state legislature, as well as to federal issues.

These principles were re-examined in a 1997 decision of the High Court, *Lange v Australian Broadcasting Corporation*. It arose out of the publication of allegedly defamatory material about a member of the New Zealand parliament. The High Court reviewed the earlier cases and in a unanimous judgment clarified this difficult area. The principles that emerged from that re-examination are, in brief summary:

[35] Brennan J. A view with a later echo in *Lange v Australian Broadcasting Corporation*, High Court, 1997 <http://www.austlii.edu.au/>
[36] (1992) 177 CLR 1.
[37] (1994) 182 CLR 104.
[38] (1994) 182 CLR 211.
[39] Incorporated in the text of the orders made.

(1) 'Freedom of communication on matters of government and politics is an indispensable incident of that system of representative government which the Constitution creates by directing that the members of the House of Representatives and the Senate shall be "directly chosen by the people" of the Commonwealth and the States, respectively'.

(2) That freedom is not conferred on individuals but is manifest in the invalidation of laws. This consequently creates an area of immunity from legislative control at all times, and not merely during an election period. Hence, defamation laws or other laws restricting freedom of communication or speech will only be valid to the extent that they comply with the Constitution.

(3) Communications limited to government or politics at state, territory, or local level receive some protection whether or not they bear directly on federal issues.

(4) It will be a defence to a defamation action arising out of the publication of information on government and political matters for the publisher to establish that the publication was reasonable in the circumstances. A defendant's action will not be reasonable unless the defendant believed the information to be true, took steps to verify it, and sought and published a response from the person defamed where possible.

(5) The interest that each member of the Australian community has in disseminating and receiving information, opinion and argument about government and political matters extends the common law categories of qualified privilege over defamatory communications. Unlike absolute privilege, qualified privilege is lost if the communication is actuated by malice or made to an audience that was *unreasonably* broader than the occasion demanded.

Broadcasting standards and codes

There are three sources of rules which govern broadcast media content. First, there are some specific provisions in the Broadcasting Services Act 1992. Parts 2 to 7 of Schedule 2 operate as licence conditions on the different licensed services. These deal with areas such as cigarette and political advertising and sponsorship announcements. The ABA has a limited power to impose additional licence conditions, and a few conditions are also imposed in the body of the Act, rather than in the Schedule. Second, the ABA is required by the Act to determine standards that relate to programmes for children on community and commercial television, and for the Australian content of programmes for commercial television.[40] Detailed standards have been developed in each case.

The third, and most significant, source of regulation is through industry

---

[40] Broadcasting Services Act 1992, s 122.

codes of practice which are administered by the ABA. Separate codes have been developed and registered by the ABA applicable to commercial television, commercial radio (drafted by the Federation of Australia Radio Broadcasters), community broadcasting (drafted by the Community Broadcasting Association of Australia), subscription radio, and television and narrowcasting services (all drafted by the Australian Subscription Television and Radio Association). Once registered, codes are binding on the relevant sector and enforceable by the ABA. Except where specific reference is made, none of the regulatory schemes in the Broadcasting Services Act apply to the public broadcasters, the ABC and the SBS.[41] Both are governed by separate charters contained in their own legislation and both are required to develop their own codes.[42] The ABA plays a more limited role in this process. It is not involved in the development or formal registration of the public broadcasting codes, but it is given responsibility for the investigation of complaints and may make recommendations to the ABC or SBS and report to the Minister, who must in turn report to the Parliament.

The principal mechanism for review of licensees' broadcasts is by a complaints process which is built into each code and the Act. Complaints, which must first be made to the relevant broadcaster, are generally made by consumers. Where no satisfactory resolution is reached between the broadcaster and the complainant, the ABA is required to investigate. For the purposes of investigating and resolving complaints, the ABA can:

- recommend action by the licensee to remedy the breach;
- impose a condition on the relevant licensee requiring compliance with the existing code or with the National Classification Code (NCC);[43] or
- determine a standard of its own where there is convincing evidence that the relevant code is not providing adequate community safeguards.

The essence of this scheme is that, after remedies are exhausted, the ABA can convert a licensee's code obligation into a legally binding licence condition. Once an obligation becomes a licence condition, then the next step for the ABA would be to issue a notice requiring compliance with the condition. If the matter continues to the stage of prosecution, possible penalties for breach of a condition range up to $A2 million in the case of commercial television broadcasters. In practice, nearly all complaints are addressed by internal adjustments to licensees' operations and without

[41] Broadcasting Services Act 1992, s 13(5).

[42] Australian Broadcasting Corporation Act 1983 and Special Broadcasting Service Act 1991.

[43] Office of Film and Literature Classification and Film and Literature Board of Review, *Reports on Activities 1991–1992* (Canberra: AGPS, 1992), 63–4.

the need for the imposition of penalties. During 1996, there were 1,054 written complaints made to commercial television stations by viewers about programmes. From January to June 1997, there were 540.

The Commercial Television Industry Code of Practice, developed by the Federation of Australian Commercial Television Stations (the 'FACTS Code') is the most comprehensive code. It contains detailed provisions about all areas of television broadcasting, including provisions dealing with the content, classification, and scheduling of programmes. The FACTS Code draws heavily on the NCC described below and requires that *all* material (excepting news, current affairs, and live sporting programmes) is to be classified and broadcast only in the designated time zone.

Australian content

Based on standards developed by the ABA under the Broadcasting Services Act,[44] commercial free-to-air television broadcasters are required to meet a total score of points in any year for: new drama programmes, children's drama, and diversity of programme types. In addition, 55 per cent of programmes transmitted between 6.00 am and midnight must be Australian. Eighty per cent of advertisements broadcast during that period must be made in Australia. There are also requirements that each commercial station transmit a minimum of ten hours of Australian documentaries per year, and transmit Australian children's drama for thirty-two hours per year.

In subscription television broadcasting, the only Australian content requirement is that 10 per cent of the programme expenditure of any drama channel must be spent on Australian programmes. This may be raised to 20 per cent as services develop. In commercial radio broadcasting, a proportion of music (ranging from 5 per cent to 25 per cent) must be performed by Australians. Class-licensed services such as narrowcasting and subscription radio are not subject to any rules about Australian content.

In 1996, it was decided that the ABA Standard for Australian content in commercial television, which came into force in that year, breached the Closer Economic Relations (CER) trade treaty with New Zealand.[45] The Broadcasting Services Act specifies that the ABA is required to take international treaties into account in formulating its Standards. The CER requires New Zealand products and services to be treated 'no less favourably' than Australian ones. An appeal to the Full Federal Court was upheld, the majority holding that the obligations of the ABA to set an

---

[44] Section 123.
[45] *Project Blue Sky Inc v Australian Broadcasting Authority*, No NG807 of 1995, 19 July 1996.

Australian content standard and to comply with the provisions of the CER were mutually inconsistent. The consequence was that, the specific direction to implement an Australian standard prevailed over the general CER provision. The ABA standard was therefore valid. A decision by the High Court of Australia on the appeal from this decision was expected late in 1997.

Classification of print, film, and computer games

The National Classification Code (NCC), a schedule to the federal Classification (Publications, Films and Computer Games) Act 1995, is central to the national co-operative scheme which co-ordinates the classification of print media, films, and computer games, administered by the Office of Film and Literature Classification (OFLC). As a result of co-operative state and territory legislation, all material embodied in these media must be classified according to the NCC.

The classification spectrum stretches from 'G' films and television programmes, which are suitable for unsupervised children's viewing, to 'R' films which may not be broadcast and are restricted to viewing by persons aged 18 years or over, 'X' films, which cannot be shown publicly and are illegal to purchase on video in most states, and 'RC' material which is illegal. The classifications 'PG', 'M', and 'MA' apply to material which includes some or all of the following elements:

- violence
- sex and nudity
- offensive language
- references to or use of drugs
- references to suicide.

For broadcast content, the classification determines the time-zone in which a programme may be transmitted. Which of the three classifications is assigned to programmes containing material of this type depends on the amount and intensity of that material. Assessment of material is carried out by the content originators or networks themselves, by reference to the NCC and guidelines published in the federal Government Gazette from time to time, or else by direct consultation with the OFLC.

Because of their interactive nature, computer games that would attract a classification higher than MA are illegal to sell, exhibit, or distribute. Two additional restricted categories apply to print media, the application of which governs the circumstances of their sale. Depending on the intensity of the material, it may be confined to sale in sealed plastic covers or display only in a place to which entry is confined to persons aged 18 or over.

Regulation of on-line services

Government investigations and inquiries commencing in 1995 have made it apparent that some attempt will be made to control the content of material that is available over the Internet and other on-line services. In Australia, as in the rest of East Asia, few experts about on-line communication believe that any such regulatory scheme will be effective in practice. However, the political and community pressures for restricting offensive content are strong.

The most prominent of these was a 1996 report to the federal government by the ABA.[46] A further report of a Senate Select Committee was published in 1997.[47] Overall, the ABA recommended systems of voluntary codes, whereas the Senate Committee was more sympathetic to direct regulation. In formulating an approach to regulation, the ABA drew a distinction between traditional media, particularly broadcasting, and on-line services. The basis of the distinction was that on-line services were still essentially offered only on demand. As a consequence, it recommended that on-line services should not be governed by the same level of legislative restrictions as applies to broadcasting. However, the Senate Committee, by majority, found no justification for distinguishing between the two forms of communication, claiming that convergence was whittling away any proper grounds for distinction. Both the ABA and the Senate Committee recommended that essentially private on-line communications such as email should remain free of regulation. That position will not necessarily be adopted in legislation as email becomes an effective substitute for the publication of an expanding variety of compelling multimedia products.

Policy development has been sensitive to the international context. It has recognised that any prospect of effective regulation of Internet content, however remote, must involve international co-operation. The ABA has consulted with foreign regulatory and industry bodies in Asia, Europe, and the United States in attempts to formulate a consistently enforceable scheme for Internet regulation.[48]

---

[46] ABA, *Investigation into the Content of On-line Services: Report to the Minister for Communications and the Arts* (Sydney, July 1996), also at <http://www.dca.gov.au/pub/aba/olsfin.doc>

[47] *Senate Select Committee, inquiry into community standards relevant to the provision of services utilising electronic technologies* (Canberra, June 1997); at <http://www.aph.gov.au/senate/committee/comstand/online/contents.htm>

[48] The ABA produced reports for both UNESCO (involving the United Kingdom, Malaysia, Singapore, and Australia) and the OECD, and is a member of the Internet Content Rating Group, a coalition of representatives from Internetwatch (UK), the Recreational Software Advisory Council (USA), the ECO Forum (Germany), and Childnet International (UK and USA).

Announcements by the federal government have revealed the likely structure of legislation that is due to be released in draft form in 1998. Amendments to the Broadcasting Services Act are likely to constitute the ABA as the central administrative body of the on-line regulatory scheme. The Australian Internet Council ('AIC') has emerged as the national peak body representing the Internet community. It is likely to play a significant role in the development and implementation of a national scheme.

The ABA has been directed by the government to consult with industry groups with a view to establishing enforceable codes of practice. Each discretely identifiable industry group, and probably end users as well, will be bound by codes of practice registered by the ABA. In cases where no code has been formulated, the ABA will have power to substitute its own version. State legislation is likely to complement the changes to the federal Act, reflecting the constitutional division of power. Internet service providers fall within federal enforcement jurisdiction. Content providers and end users fall within state and territory power.

Where codes deal with the regulation of content, the NCC will probably have some role to play. However, it has been generally recognised that on-line media have unique features that are not necessarily best addressed by application of the scheme for off-line media. In particular, on-line content may contain features which fall within all existing categories of classification (print, film, and software) which may expose contradictions in classification. It has also been recognised that the most effective place to restrict access to material is at the point of the end user, probably with filtering devices or software.

One of the most important features of future codes of practice will be the complaints mechanism. A fax and/or email hotline to field consumer complaints and notifications of offensive material has been implemented overseas, and is likely to be introduced to Australia.[49] The ABA's role in the administration of complaints about broadcast content will probably be expanded along with power to enforce compliance with decisions. On-line service providers may be treated in the same fashion as carriage service providers in the Telecommunications Act, that is, as not responsible for the content of material transmitted unless they are involved in its creation or are otherwise involved in its content.

Although not binding, a number of on-line services bodies, including the West Australian Internet Association (WAIA), the Internet Industry Association of Australia (INTIAA, now merged into the AIC), and the

---

[49] The UK Internet Watch operates an email hotline that has led to hundreds of investigations into potentially illegal web sites; see ch 4, n 151 above.

Committee of Australian University Directors of Information Technology (CAUDIT) have been pro-active in establishing industry codes of practice.[50] It is uncertain if any of these ultimately will be accepted under any registration scheme.

Electoral and political laws

Broadcasting is the only area of electronic communications subject to any laws in the nature of 'equal time' or 'tele-democracy' requirements. Schedule 2 of the Broadcasting Services Act prescribes rules in relation to political broadcasts.[51] During an election period, a broadcaster must give reasonable opportunities for the broadcasting of election matter to all competing political parties (sch 2, clause 3(1)). This requirement is substantially the same as the law which has applied since 1956. The obligation to afford reasonable opportunities extends to elections for all Australian parliaments, and to state and territory local government authorities. The obligation is far from being a guarantee of free access to radio and television for political parties. The requirement has a number of limitations. It does not require a broadcaster to allow the time free of charge. It does not apply to a broadcaster who transmits no election matter at all; and it does not extend to parties which were not represented in either house of the federal parliament before a relevant federal election. The main practical effect of this obligation has been to prevent stations from actually banning material from candidates or parties whom they dislike.

The compulsory 'reasonable opportunities' requirement does not apply to the ABC or the SBS, which allocate free time to political parties under guidelines designed to reflect their current representation in the relevant house of parliament and the extent of community interest in their policies. The obligation to provide reasonable opportunities extends only to election matter broadcast during an election period.

11 FUNDING AND SUPPORT FOR LOCAL OUTPUT

Tax law

Investment in the Australian film industry may attract a deduction for capital expenditure incurred in acquiring an interest in the initial copyright of a new Australian film, under Division 10BA of the Income Tax Assessment Act 1936.

[50] Information about these organisations may be found at their homepages, at: <http://www.waia.asn.au> at: <http://www.intiaa.asn.au> and at: <http://www.caudit.edu.au/>
[51] Armstrong, MC (ed), *Communications Law and Policy in Australia* (Butterworths, Sydney, 1992), paras 9300 *et seq*.

Film industry funding

The Australian film industry is supported through federal and state government grant programmes, which provide funding assistance to new Australian film projects, including documentary, motion picture, telemovie, and series productions. A commercial television fund for Australian drama was established in 1995. The funding is administered by film bodies in each of the states as well as the federal body, the Australian Film Commission. Recently the Victorian film body, Film Victoria, became known as Cinemedia as it took on a new role in the area of multimedia as well as film development.[52] The Australian Film Commission has also taken on a role in multimedia project development. Multimedia products are likely to receive some benefits from the structures originally established to support film production.

Multimedia content

Strong support for the development of multimedia was expressed in *Creative Nation*, the last major arts policy statement of the previous federal government.[53] Combined funding of $A84 m over four years was allocated under this document. The funding initiatives included:

- establishment of the Australian Multimedia Enterprise (AME) ($A45 m) to provide financing for the development and commercialisation of interactive multimedia projects and services;
- the 'Australia on CD' programme ($A7.6 m over two years) for distribution to educational institutions and overseas markets;
- the national Multimedia Forums programme ($A3.9 m over four years);
- establishment of six Cooperative Multimedia Centres over two years to conduct research and development and facilitate education and industry collaboration ($A20.3 m over four years); and
- a series of specific measures to foster film agencies' involvement in interactive multimedia.

Some of the most radical initiatives to support multimedia and on-line content have originated in the State of Victoria. In 1995, the Victorian Government established what was thought to be the world's first Ministry for Multimedia, supported by a range of structures including a task force of industry leaders chaired by the Premier. Programmes to put all government services on-line, to provide ready access to the Internet for all citizens, and to attract investment are more advanced that in any other Australian State or Territory. Victoria has also been the State with the

[52] Skulley, M, *Australian Financial Review*, 9 July 1996.
[53] Department of Communications and the Arts, *Creative Nation: Commonwealth Cultural Policy* (Canberra, 1994).

most advanced proposals for cyberlaws and other structures to support e-commerce and electronically-distributed cultural activities.

12 COPYRIGHT

Copyright law is based on the federal Copyright Act 1968. The Act has proliferated in recent years, as a variety of new technologies, transmission systems, and media forms challenge the original ideas about reproduction on which it was based. The Act is generally regarded as overdue for reform.

The basic principles of the Act are that although there is no protection for mere ideas, protection is automatic once a work is reduced into some material form from which it may be reproduced, including an intangible form such as digital storage. There is no system of registration of copyright. The principal subjects of copyright are literary, artistic, musical, and dramatic works. Computer programs are defined as literary works for the purposes of the Act. To attract copyright protection, a work must satisfy a low threshold of originality involving the application of some independent knowledge, skill, or labour by the author. In theory, separate, identical works may be protected by copyright so long as they have been created without actual copying. The degree of similarity of a work that is claimed to infringe an original is an important factor for a court when inferring actual copying. For most copyright works, protection lasts for fifty years from the death of the author, although, depending on the exact type of work, that period may vary.[54] International Copyright treaties held with a majority of countries provide reciprocal protection for Australian and overseas works.

Consistent with European schemes, copyright does not confer a monopoly over the use of works but a set of exclusive rights to deal with the work, one of which is the right to reproduce it. In recent years, digital copying and electronic storage of copyright material has created new challenges for regulation in this area. Reform in Australia is now running in parallel with international initiatives. In response to the World Intellectual Property Organisation (WIPO) Copyright Treaty (WCT) and the WIPO Performances and Phonograms Treaty (WPPT), concluded in December 1996, the federal government issued a discussion paper in July 1997, entitled, Copyright Reform and the Digital Agenda. The aim of this consultation process was ultimately to introduce amendments to the Copyright Act to allow Australia to sign both treaties. Proposals have

---

[54] Copyright Act 1968, s 33.

already been framed in draft legislation and include the following new features:

- extension of the existing right of communication to the public in the Berne Convention to the transmission of literary and artistic works, ie, text and images, respectively;
- a right to equitable remuneration for producers of sound recordings and performers in relation to the broadcasting and communication to the public of their sound recordings and performances;
- a new exclusive right called the 'right of making available to the public' for works, performances, and sound recordings;
- a prohibition on the abuse of technological copyright protection measures (eg, 'locks' for computer programs); and
- a prohibition on the deliberate alteration or removal of electronic rights management information (including authorship and copyright ownership details) attached to copyright material.

The discussion paper was preceded by a report completed in 1994 by the Copyright Convergence Group (CCG), *Highways to Change: Copyright in the New Communications Environment*. The CCG recommended the introduction of a broadly-based technology-neutral transmission right to authorise transmissions to replace the diffusion right and encompass an expanded broadcast right. It also recommended that the broadcast right should be expanded to include wire and wireless broadcasts, consistently with the definition of 'broadcast' in broadcasting legislation. Those recommendations all had government support.

It is unclear what effect, if any, these amendments would have on the system for collection of copyright royalties from educational institutions. In the past, calculation of royalties has been a relatively simple matter, based on the number of photocopies of copyright works made on campus. The widely practised capacity for digital scanning, storage, and reproduction of copyright works has created difficult issues to be decided by the federal Copyright Tribunal in 1998.[55]

Copyright law has also been challenged by changes in the Australian telecommunications environment with the introduction of cable television in 1995. Cable operators took advantage of section 212 of the Broadcasting Services Act, which allows a person who is not a licensee to transmit free-to-air programmes which have already been broadcast. In 1995, Amalgamated Television Services argued in the Federal Court that the re-transmission was a breach of copyright.[56] However, it was held that

[55] *Copyright Agency Limited v University of Adelaide* (not yet heard).
[56] *Amalgamated Television Services Pty Ltd v Foxtel Digital Cable Television Pty Ltd* (1996) 136 ALR 319.

section 199(4) of the Copyright Act offers a defence to infringement of copyright where programmes broadcast on free-to-air television are re-transmitted to 'subscribers to a diffusion service'. Whether pay-TV opera-tors could properly be described as operating a 'diffusion service' was not argued. At the time the Copyright Act was written, diffusion service was regarded as a community television antenna system or an antenna distri-bution system for a multiple dwelling building.

13 PRIVACY LAWS

Australian privacy legislation

Australia has no general legal right to privacy. Instead, a clutch of issue-specific legislation has evolved which protects privacy interests in defined circumstances.[57] At both federal and state level, laws operate to maintain privacy in particular situations where it is seen to be threatened. Other instruments, such as the Australian Privacy Charter developed by the Australian Privacy Charter Council[58] are little more than policy state-ments although they illustrate the importance with which privacy is regarded as a social value.

The principal statute is the federal Privacy Act 1988 (the 'Privacy Act') which regulates the operations of all federal government departments on privacy issues, particularly in the handling of personal information. It enunciates eleven Information Privacy Principles (IPPs) which deal with the solicitation of personal information, its storage, rights of access, and amendment. The IPPs expand on the obligations accepted by Australia under article 17 of the International Covenant on Civil and Political Rights. They also correspond to OECD Guidelines concerning the protec-tion of privacy and individual liberties.

Only certain provisions of the Privacy Act are applicable to the private sector. These deal with the use of tax file numbers and consumer credit information. Similarly, the Crimes Act 1914 gives privacy rights in

[57] Telecommunications Interception Act 1979, s 7 (bugging and telephone tapping, see below); Privacy Act 1988, s 27 (general limits on the invasion of individual privacy by government agencies); Data Matching Program (Assistance and Tax) Act 1990 (data match-ing guidelines between agencies); National Health Act 1953, s 135AA (use of health informa-tion); Freedom of Information Act 1982, s 41 (nature of restrictions on access to government documents where there are privacy concerns); ASIO Act 1979, s 26 (Australian Security Investigation Organisation's powers); Australian Federal Police Act 1979, ss 12B–12L (offence and investigation powers); Customs Act 1901, ss 219A–219K (powers of customs officers in narcotics offences); Human Rights (Sexual Conduct) Act 1994 (liberties of consent-ing adults in private).

[58] The Australian Privacy Charter Council was established in December 1992, chaired by Kirby J, to develop a charter which would apply to all forms of privacy and surveillance in both public and private sector environments.

relation to spent convictions, no matter who is in a position to exploit them. In most cases, an individual also has the right to inspect personal data that relates to him or her and to correct any errors on the record.

The Office of the Privacy Commissioner is created by the Privacy Act, currently allied to the Human Rights and Equal Opportunity Commission. The Privacy Commissioner has an obligation to promote privacy, provide policy advice to the government, and monitor compliance with the Act. Individuals who believe that their privacy has been infringed by breaches of the statutory safeguards may complain to the Privacy Commissioner. If the complaint cannot be resolved following investigation and attempts at conciliation, the Commissioner has power to make binding orders, including orders for compensation. The Privacy Commissioner has monitoring roles under a variety of other Australian legislative schemes, including under the Data Matching Program (Assistance and Tax) Act 1990 which regulates the matching of data held by different federal departments and also in telecommunications.

Telecommunications privacy

The Telecommunications Act 1997 contains a range of references to privacy issues and the control of access to and use of personal information. These provisions have been implemented following a history of investigations into general and telecommunications privacy, one of which was a report in December 1992 by the Australian Telecommunications Authority (AUSTEL).[59] Focusing on the two telecommunications privacy issues of freedom from intrusion and control of personal data, AUSTEL recommended that:

- the level of data protection in the telecommunications industry be comparable to international standards;
- the framework to regulate telecommunications privacy issues focus on current and prospective services, rather than on the technologies that deliver those services;
- the capture and use of personal data by means of telecommunications services should, as far as possible, be consistent with general privacy principles or laws;
- telecommunications players and government agencies adopt a voluntary co-regulatory approach to regulation; and
- a Telecommunications Privacy Committee be responsible for maintaining adequate privacy levels by consultation with industry and consumers and development of codes of practice.

[59] AUSTEL (Australian Telecommunication Authority), *Telecommunications Privacy* (AGPS, 1992).

Other matters dealt with in the review included Calling Line Identification (CLI) based services, unsolicited telecommunications, and the use of Telephone Information Management Systems (TIMS).

The Telecommunications Privacy Committee

The Telecommunications Privacy Committee was established in 1994.[60] The Committee reports to the ACA in an advisory capacity, using the experience of its members drawn from industry, government, consumer, and user groups. The Minister originally requested the Committee to address the issues of customer personal information, in particular that of unlisted number customers, telemarketing, and Calling Number Display. Under the current Act, it has a role in advising the ACA on those parts of industry codes of conduct that relate to customer confidentiality and privacy.

The Privacy Commissioner

Part 13 of the Telecommunications Act deals with the protection of communications, administered by the Privacy Commissioner. This part provides that carriers, carriage service providers, number-database operators, and emergency call persons must protect the confidentiality of consumer information that comes to their knowledge or into their possession. Disclosure of any such information is an offence punishable by imprisonment for a term of up to two years.

Privacy protection in telecommunications is also contemplated in the creation of industry codes of practice. The Act provides for each sector of telecommunications to formulate a code of practice in consultation with the ACA. The creation, amendment, or revocation of any privacy standards must be submitted for consideration by the Privacy Commissioner before registration. Section 113 gives examples of matters for possible inclusion in industry codes and standards:

(i)   the protection of personal information;
(ii)   the intrusive use of telecommunications by carriers or service providers;
(iii) the monitoring or recording of communications;
(iv)   calling number display; and
(v)   the provision of directory products and services.

Privacy issues arise in other sections of the Telecommunications Act. Division 5 of Part 13 governs the keeping of records about disclosures of consumer information made by telecommunications players. Again, this Division is to be monitored by the Privacy Commissioner. Part 12 provides the ACA with power to make determinations consistent with the

---

[60] Now constituted under Australian Communications Authority Act 1997, s 51.

Privacy Act which bind carriers and carriage service providers in relation to information gained through the administration of emergency call services. Certain disclosures are permissible in the public interest when properly authorised in accordance with procedures established by the ACA and the Privacy Commissioner.[61] Even the details to be included in itemised bills for telecommunications are subject to the IPPs set out in the Privacy Act.[62]

Interception of communications

Provisions in the Privacy Act and the Telecommunications Act generally deal with the use which may be made of information disclosed to members of the telecommunications sector in the ordinary course of business. There is also federal protection for the privacy of communications passing over a telecommunications system under the Telecommunications (Interception) Act 1979. This Act prohibits the secret interception of communications over all networks, both public and private, except in certain prescribed circumstances concerning, for example, the issue of warrants for the prevention or combat of crime. This sort of safeguard has been a part of Australian telecommunications since 1960.[63] It is broad enough to apply to newer services such as email.

Private sector communications

One of the recommendations of the 1992 AUSTEL report was for consideration to be given to extending the scope of the Privacy Act 1988 to the collection, storage, and use of data by private companies. A number of groups, including the Australian Law Reform Commission, have criticised the absence of comprehensive privacy legislation applicable to the private sector, arguing that it should be a fundamental element of legislative reform.[64]

In 1993, the government established the Broadband Services Expert Group (BSEG) to examine the technical, economic, and commercial preconditions for widespread delivery of broadband services to homes, businesses, and schools in Australia.[65] It issued an interim report in 1994 recommending that the Privacy Act be broadened to apply to the private sector in conjunction with industry codes of conduct. It suggested that this 'self-regulatory' approach would offer sufficient flexibility of application to different industry groups so as not to impose blanket approaches

---

[61] Telecommunications Act 1997, s 282(7) and (8). See also s 309.

[62] Telecommunications Act 1997, Sch 2, clause 15.

[63] Telephonic Communications (Interception) Act 1960.

[64] Senate Economics Reference Committee, *Connecting You Now . . . Telecommunications Towards the year 2000* (Canberra, 1995).

[65] The Broadband Services Expert Group presented its Final Report, *Networking Australia's Future*, in 1994.

inappropriately. It also recommended a complaints process ultimately to be administered by the Privacy Commissioner. A Senate Economics Reference Committee Report of 1995 supported the BSEG recommendations, emphasising that the expansion of existing privacy principles was necessary to deal with privacy risks presented by technology convergence and new information delivery mechanisms. The Committee noted the importance of maintaining a balance between personal privacy and fundamental public interests such as effective law enforcement and national security.

In 1997, the federal government reversed an earlier commitment to extend privacy legislation to the private sector. It was concerned about compliance costs for businesses, large and small. Instead, the government directed the Privacy Commissioner to investigate the potential for self-regulation of the private sector. In August 1997, the Commissioner called for submissions on a proposed scheme with three tiers: principles for the handling of personal information; processes for business to 'sign on' to the scheme; and mechanisms for handling complaints and providing effective remedies. It remained possible that the government would modify its 1997 stance, in order to allow some minimal data protection laws for on-line transactions. Many e-commerce firms were concerned about loss of consumer confidence and trade if there was no statutory protection of electronic transmissions.

14 CONCLUDING REMARKS

Australia's greatest challenge in the communications and IT revolution is to make decisions quickly. It is not a legal challenge, nor really a policy challenge. It is simply a matter of making changes quickly enough to keep up with global developments. The resources to enliven economic and social life through new communications developments are all present, in the form of an educated population, good technical resources, and a history of rapid take-up of new technologies.

Australia is an egalitarian, democratic country in which power is very dispersed. For historical reasons, leadership in government and industry is difficult. The community is used to treating leadership and visionary ideas with suspicion. Public power is dispersed between national, State, and local government. In the last two decades national governments have rarely been able to command a majority in the Senate, the upper house of parliament.

For success in the Internet era, rapid changes to laws and policies are necessary. Yet community leaders have little experience in making rapid change. For example, the Australian Law Reform Commission drafted

Bills to reform defamation and privacy laws in 1979.[66] Strenuous efforts since then to reform these laws have produced no changes despite wide recognition that the laws are inappropriate. Copyright provides another example, as mentioned earlier. In late 1993 the federal government commissioned the Copyright Convergence Group to address the urgent need for reform of the Copyright Act to deal with the new communications environment, pending longer-term review. The Group was required to report quickly, so as to allow the law to be changed during 1994. However, the only government response since the report[67] in mid-1994 has been yet another discussion paper. On media ownership, the 1996 electoral platform of the Howard federal government included a promise to amend cross-media laws. However, the government announced in 1997 that reform was no longer a priority during its three-year term.

The obvious contrasts with Australia are its neighbours in the ASEAN group, which includes a number of the 'tiger economies'. The greater concentration of power in countries such as Malaysia and Singapore has enabled them to form and implement visionary policies to convert their economies to the on-line environment. They do not need to wait years for community attitudes to change, or for numerous different power-bases, including industry groups and trade unions, to be convinced of the need for change. The United States also has the competitive advantage of a less consensual society, where economic advancement is less retarded by concerns about injuring existing interests in the process of change. Although Australia is not culturally similar to Europe, it shares the European difficulty in changing laws and structures quickly. It has similarly complex processes of government.

In the last decade, Australian telecommunications laws have changed as radically as anywhere in the world, at least on paper. Since July 1997, all sectors of telecommunications have been fully open to competition. How can this happen in a country where change is difficult? The first answer is that the legal and structural revolutions of the 1990s were simply the culmination of a long process. Serious attempts to introduce competition resulted in the very comprehensive Davidson Report of 1982.[68] It is often said that a new idea takes about ten years to win acceptance. Telecommunications reform had fifteen years. There were compelling reasons for change. The Postmaster-General's Department was the largest enterprise in Australia, and the largest employer of labour, for most of Australia's

---

[66] Law Reform Commission, *Unfair Publication: Defamation and Privacy* (Canberra: AGPS, 1979).

[67] Copyright Convergence Group, *Highways to Change: Copyright in the New Communications Environment* (Sydney: AGPS, 1994).

[68] *Report of the Committee of Inquiry into Telecommunications Services in Australia* (Canberra: AGPS, 1982).

history as a single nation. With large distances between major population centres, telecommunications has always been a significant cost of production. Thus, it was impossible to ignore the need for ways to provide cheaper telecommunications.

The stresses of forcing the pace of change in telecommunications changes the legislation, which clearly pushes drafting and implementation skills to the limit; some experts believe they have gone beyond the limit, to the point where the laws are too complex to implement. For example, the legislation has grown increasingly long. The relevant laws contained only 114 sections in 1975. There were 185 sections in the 1989 rewrite, and 409 sections in the 1991 rewrite. The Telecommunications Act 1997 and related provisions contain 920 sections. As the legislators struggle to fuse competing values, they have come close to creating a legislative melt-down. Nobody can be entirely confident that the 1997 laws will work as intended. The legal and consulting professions have flourished in this environment, as clients make increasing investments in attempts to find some certainty about their future under the new laws.

Among the unresolved tensions are the balances between competition law and telecommunications law, and between specific rules and discretionary power. One focus involves the role of the ACCC (the general competition regulator), the ACA, and the self-regulation schemes in the Telecommunications Act. The ACCC, and not the ACA, is responsible for competition in telecommunications. On many issues, the competing players are expected to resolve their differences, with resort to the ACCC being available as a last resort. The ACCC also has considerable telecommunications 'conduct regulation' powers to intervene when it so decides.[69] In practice, although not in theory, the ACCC has become the major telecommunications policy-maker.

The new access regime[70] is a good example of the tensions in the Act. Effectively, it allows the ACCC to set the terms on which communications and media networks allow others to use their cables and systems. At one extreme, it could force carriers to provide carriage for competitors at bargain prices. At the other extreme, a very protective approach from the ACCC would force all new players to build their own separate networks in order to reach consumers. There are few definite criteria to limit or guide the ACCC in situations where the players do not agree. For example, the Act says that the ACCC is to have regard to the 'reasonably anticipated requirements'[71] of the carrier, existing users, or contracted future users. There are obviously many possible interpretations of that criterion.

[69] Trade Practices Act 1974, Part XIB.
[70] ibid, Part XIC.
[71] ibid, s 152AR.

The broadcasting sector has been subject to various legislative innovations, but less radical than those in telecommunications. That is because most broadcasting has always been in the private sector, which is better equipped than the public sector to defend itself against changes to the status quo. If telecommunications had been a private sector monopoly, it is unlikely that the rate of change would have been as rapid. The main impact of broadcasting changes has been on new services such as narrowcasting, subscription services, and the use of the radio frequency spectrum. Through a variety of auction-based allocation systems and fee structures, the opportunity to start new broadcasting services apart from commercial free-to-air services has been made almost entirely open. However, new players face auction processes in order to gain access to the spectrum. Alternatively, they need to purchase spectrum rights from those who have successfully bid for those rights. Subscription television broadcasters are inhibited by some direct restrictions, such as programme anti-siphoning rules giving free-to-air broadcasters priority.

There have been no recent attempts to recognise convergence by creating a legal regime addressing the whole communications sector as one. When telecommunications, broadcasting, and radiocommunications laws were rewritten in 1991 and 1992, the intention was that the separate regulators of those three sectors would be merged in future, to become a single Australian Communications Authority. In 1997, a body of that name was created, but not for the original purpose. The broadcasting regime remains separate, and the ACA is concerned only with some aspects of telecommunications and radiocommunications. The major change has been that competition issues are now the province of the ACCC. Apart from its specific telecommunications powers, it exercises general powers over all communications players, including broadcasters.

Mergers and anti-competitive conduct within communications and media are the province of the ACCC. This role has been controversial in the age of convergence. For example, the ACCC has treated subscription television as a separate market from free-to-air broadcasting; and it has treated newspapers as a separate market from other media. Yet the ACCC has intervened to prevent Foxtel, the largest of the three subscription television providers, from merging with Australis, the smallest provider which is reported to be in danger of financial collapse. There have been controversies over the failure of the trade practices laws to recognise convergence or globalisation; and over the lack of any recognition of Australian ownership. Some have argued that whilst media trends lead to ever-larger global corporations like Microsoft, the ACCC and its empowering laws devote their focus to preventing local enterprises from becoming large enough to compete internationally. These issues remain unresolved, and there are no policy initiatives aimed at resolving them.

Unless they are resolved, in a way which recognises convergence and globalisation, the growth of media in Australia will be retarded.

The traditional media and communications sectors may lack a holistic view, but at least they are recognised as economically and socially important. With on-line and multimedia services, the problem has been to convince decision-makers and law-makers that they are important. This is not to suggest that new media seek laws or policies to authorise their activities. Rather, they seek changes to laws addressing other subject-matters, written before the on-line world was significant, which have become obstacles to development.

The first category of obstacles are those often known as 'cyberlaws'. The cyberlaws list is similar to that in other countries: extension of copyright to recognise on-line transmissions; recognition of documents, signatures, and evidence in electronic form; recognition of encryption systems; data security laws; and small changes to criminal laws so as to outlaw interception and other interference with private electronic communication. Whilst some Federal and State laws do address the last two topics, most items in this list are yet to be addressed. In late 1997, the government of the State of Victoria had prepared a comprehensive package of these laws, but was awaiting further discussions with the federal government about a national legislative scheme, which would be preferable. Various policy reports had mentioned the need for these changes, but the essential problem was one of time, as mentioned earlier. Whilst the new laws were required immediately, the political process and the media were treating them as possibilities for the future, without any sense of urgency.

The second category of obstacles are those relating to consumer take-up of on-line and multimedia. The need is to increase the proportion of the community participating in the on-line world from current estimates of around 10 per cent to somewhere around 30 per cent, at which point the critical mass of users should be sufficient to draw in the rest of the community. No government or industry body has yet officially recognised any 30 per cent or any specific target. However, they do recognise the need for Australia to build a market base large enough to support the creation of local content. At the present state of development, the US dominates on-line content. If this trend continued, it would lead to an increasing trade imbalance, apart from obvious social and cultural alienation. Federal and State governments are actively attempting to put all of their operations on-line, with a view to being leading-edge users and exemplars. It is not difficult to persuade governments to make this change, because there is little opposition to such a move. Rightly or not, they believe that on-line delivery of government services will also save public funds. However, there are no national plans or targets to encourage the community to adopt on-line communication. With the appointment of a federal Minister for the Information Economy in September 1997 it is possible that definite national plans may be formulated.

The third, and most significant, obstacle is taxation. It is generally regarded as the most important. The Australian capital gains tax regime appears to have been enacted with industrial, mining, and property investments in mind. In practice, it penalises investments in multimedia, software, and on-line services which face high risk, but also produce a very high capital gain if a venture is successful. The impact of the tax system is much less severe on regular dividends from more traditional, less volatile, investments. There are innumerable examples of foreign investors rejecting Australian prospects because of the tax regime, and an equal number of examples of Australian enterprises which have been driven offshore by the tax regime. Whilst these problems have been officially recognised, there is no prospect of an early solution. Tax reform is not an issue which any Australian government will lightly adopt.

In conclusion, the prospects for Australian enterprise in old and new media, and for reform of the laws which support them, are good. If there were a national plan showing leadership in communications, with clear national goals, there would be every possibility of Australia's educational and economic advantages making it, in the words of Kenichi Ohmae, 'the brains trust of Asia'.[72] The reality may fall short of that, depending on the speed with which a very egalitarian country and its institutions can make decisions quickly.

[72] *Australian Financial Review*, 14 Oct 1997, 1.

9

Conclusions

DAVID GOLDBERG, TONY PROSSER, STEFAAN VERHULST

1 INTRODUCTION: UNIFORMITY THROUGH CONVERGENCE?

If anything is clear from the material in this study it is that national and cultural differences remain of enormous importance in shaping both the changing media and their regulation; there has been no straightforward move to uniformity under the pressure of technological change.[1] In this respect we would begin by echoing the point made recently by institutional approaches to politics and economics: namely, that approaches to policy development which see it as a process of resolving essentially technical tasks assumed to be similar in any market-oriented economy neglect the particular constraints of political and legal culture which may be of the utmost importance.[2] One point of particular relevance is that convergence is at radically different stages in each of the countries studied, and that this has been the result of a number of factors including differences in legal and political structures. One need only refer to the difficulties caused in Hungary by the absence of any clear regulatory framework for the new media, or the difficulties in the introduction of digital television in Germany. In the latter case, this has to a large degree been the result of problems with competition law, but the limited take-up of such services when they have been made available suggests that there may also be a degree of consumer resistance; as our US contributor has suggested, full convergence assumes a 'force-fitting' of very different human functions into one technology, so it is hardly surprising that consumers do not necessarily take up new opportunities. Other national peculiarities include the especially prominent role of the courts as determinants of policy in the United States, Germany, and Italy, the precarious nature of any political base for regulatory action in Italy and Hungary, the

---

[1] Herman and McChesney came to a similar conclusion and noted that 'nation states remain the most important political forces in communication and much else'. See Herman, ES and McChesney, RW, *The Global Media. The New Missionaries of Global Capital* (London and Washington: Cassell, 1997), 64.

[2] See eg, Hall, P, *Governing the Economy* (Cambridge: Cambridge University Press, 1986); Graham, C and Prosser, T, *Privatizing Public Enterprises* (Oxford: Clarendon Press, 1991).

geographical context of Australian communications; one could give many others.

Of course, much of this is very predictable and would not require detailed research to establish it. A further point which needs reiteration, however, is of great importance for regulatory policy-making. This is that the degree of convergence in services is not only highly varied but relatively slow in many cases, and a radically new media world dominated by the new services is far off, and indeed in some cases may never arrive. As noted earlier in this work, however, the inevitability of the so-called 'converged environment' is taken for granted, particularly at the European level.[3] One of the problems in much of the debate is the assumption that technological change is the only determinant of this growth. However, this not only assumes the unimportance of particular legal and regulatory cultures whose role is amply illustrated in this book, it also assumes that new technologies will always prove marketable and that different markets are shaped by technology, not by social or cultural factors. This is why the area is dogged by false predictions, as documented in several places in this book. The implication from the uncertainty of how far convergence should advance is that we should treat with caution suggestions that the brave new world of media abundance is imminent, and be slow to abandon the protections developed in the old world of a limited number of media outlets and services.

A further point of some importance is that there is no single new media form or market, and there is never likely to be such uniformity. Markets remain distinct; for example, there is still a clear distinction between television-type services and on-line services. Technological convergence may be imminent in the form of television Internet access (or Web TV) becoming cheaply available, but the cultures remain radically different. Indeed, in the context of television, it seems likely that, though delivery forms may change, the culture may not, and that new types of media may supplement rather than replace existing ones.[4] Again the message is one of caution before we scrap existing regulatory arrangements. Even in the area of the so-called information superhighway, the metaphor of such a single network is inappropriate; as our US chapter notes, instead a system as varied (complex, and in some cases congested) as the road system that carries motor traffic is more likely.

These radical differences between new forms of media market have contradictory implications for regulation. On the one hand, they lessen the likelihood of the sort of dull uniformity based on the broadcasting of

---

[3] Commission of the European Communities, *Green Paper on the Convergence of Telecommunications, Media and Information Technologies*, COM (97) 623 (1997).

[4] See, eg, 'US Entertainment and Information: Traditional Media Stay in Fast Lane', *Financial Times*, 29 July 1997.

similar, cheap programmes which has been feared in the context of the development of new television services and is referred to in our German and Italian chapters. The newer media will be much more complex than this and will have the *potential* to differentiate many markets more effectively than has been the case in the old media; in this sense the popular convergence model is misleading since it suggests narrowing, whereas what is happening is some degree of broadening through market differentiation. The implication could be drawn that the market can be successful in maintaining forms of diversity beyond the reach of regulatory controls. On the other hand, fragmentation of markets means that regulatory concerns will need to be addressed not across media markets, for example through controls on percentage ownership, but instead by concentrating on regulation of particular technological or economic instruments which might give control of each or several of the fragmented markets; an argument for behavioural rather than structural regulation to which we shall return later.[5]

One further point needs to be made in this connection. We have stressed that convergence has been unequal between different nations, has been slower than expected and will not break down distinctions between different markets as rapidly as is claimed. Nevertheless, the industry is behaving as if fundamental change is imminent. Again the implications are contradictory. On the one hand there has been a considerable degree of industrial diversification with the creation of new industries and sectors; key examples are those of Internet service providers, publishers, and content providers. At first this has appeared to be an example of the market creating and preserving diversity; after all, these have been industries in which entry barriers have been low and so small operators have emerged. Even here, however, there are signs that this is ending with a strong degree of consolidation and emerging dominance as exemplified, for example, by the sale of CompuServe during 1997 in a three-way deal with WorldCom and America Online; at the same time it was estimated that as many of 90 per cent of Internet service providers in the USA could disappear in the next five years.[6] Moreover, as documented in our national chapters, the large operators such as the telecommunications, entertainment, and information technology businesses have embarked on a wealth of acquisitions, joint ventures, and alliances; to cite just one example from many, the acquisition of MCI by WorldCom is, it is claimed, symptomatic of fundamental changes in the industry. The history of WorldCom also underlines the key role of US stock markets in reshaping the world's high-tech industry. They played an instrumental role in

[5] For an early statement of this theme see Graham, A, 'Exchange Rates and Gatekeepers' in Congden, T *et al* (eds), *The Cross Media Revolution* (London: John Libby, 1995), 38–49.
[6] For discussion of both issues see 'Survival of the Biggest', *Financial Times* 15 Sept 1997.

enabling a second-rank company such as WorldCom to become a global giant in a matter of a few years. Stock markets in Europe seem unlikely to play a similar role. This suggests that European companies may lack the structural capacity to grab new opportunities as rapidly as US ones and that they may come under yet increased pressure of aggressive, young, and fast-growing US companies such as WorldCom. There are also important implications for the Net itself:

The net began as a disorganised, decentralised network of networks. There is no owner, no central guiding force, just a collection of standards and some voluntary bodies to administer them. But recently a handful of big companies have built up powerful roles in providing access to the internet and carrying its data. . . . [T]here is a risk that the consolidation of the industry will transform the way the internet works . . . As individual participants get bigger, there is a growing temptation for the larger to discriminate against the smaller, charging them for access or refusing connections altogether. . . . The proposed merger unites two of the biggest participants in the emerging internet industry, together handling around 60 per cent of backbone traffic. It provides an ideal opportunity for an examination of the competition issues.[7]

The result of all this corporate restructuring is that the potential for market dominance, anti-competitive practices, and barriers to market entry are likely to increase, not decrease, in the changing media world.

2 WILL WE NEED REGULATION?

Of course, before we discuss the potential role of law as a regulatory device, we need to answer the preliminary question of whether any regulation will be required at all. The discussion above has already suggested that there will be a need for continuing regulation of competition aspects of the industry; this could of course simply be part of overall competition law and policy with no specific media constraints, and whether a special regime is needed in the future will be discussed below. Yet when commentators refer to media regulation this does not usually refer to competition policy and law; rather it refers to social control of content, special measures to secure diversity on democratic and public interest grounds, and the broad (and vague) concept of public service broadcasting.[8] As we noted in our introductory chapter, there are influential arguments to the effect that the days of these types of regulation are numbered with the ending of spectrum scarcity as a justification for regulation—although

---

[7] 'Internet Merger' *The Financial Times*, 12 Nov 1997 (leader).
[8] For a good brief survey of the traditional justifications for media regulation see Barendt, E, *Broadcasting Law: A Comparative Study* (Oxford: Clarendon Press, 1993), 3–10.

the European Commission's Green Paper on Convergence makes the point that '[f]requency remains a key, but finite resource even in the digital age'[9]—the ending of the uniquely pervasive and intrusive role of television in the household as it is supplemented by other media delivery systems, and with the promise of a diversity of content undreamt of in public service broadcasting with the arrival of multi-channel digital broadcasting.

We would suggest that these arguments for the withering away of regulation should also be treated with considerable caution. Firstly, as already described, it will be a long time before convergence has reached a stage in which the new media supplant the old, or, in key markets, offer effective competition to them. Secondly, it is very likely that the elimination of the scarcity of transmission frequencies will intensify new and other scarcities.[10] Scarcity of available media content and programme software is already a large problem. Moreover the problem becomes even bigger when considering the qualitative aspect of programming. Other major scarcity problems are concerned with user attention and shared knowledge, the latter dealing with the role of media in providing a 'cultural cohesion to the nation'.[11] As Hoffmann-Riem stated: '[s]carcity constellations of all kinds are at the same time power constellations. The crucial topic of regulation is the problem of use and abuse of power.' Concerning the newer media he concludes that 'the basic normative idea of necessary protection against the one-sided use of power, however, continues to apply, even if there is a shift in scarcity constellations and new abuse potentials become identifiable.'[12] Thirdly, there are other arguments which support the maintainance of a media sphere which is different from that which would be supposed by a market-based model, even should convergence develop much further. The argument has been made in the past convincingly in relation to the different treatment of the press and broadcasting industries, and has been summed up as justifying 'the divergent treatment of the two media on the ground that society is entitled to remedy the deficiencies of an unregulated press with a regulated broadcasting system. This may be preferable to attempting to regulate both sectors. Regulation poses the danger of government control, a danger which is reduced if one branch of the media is left free.'[13] This argument maintains its force even in conditions of growing diversity; to quote the leading proponent:

---

[9] op.cit. (n 3 above), 19.

[10] For a discussion see Hoffmann-Riem, W, 'New Challenges for European Multimedia Policy', *European Journal of Communication*, Vol 11 (3), 1996, 327–46.

[11] Negrine, R, *Politics and the Mass Media in Britain* (London: Routledge, 1994).

[12] Hoffmann-Riem (n 10 above), 333.

[13] Barendt (n 8 above), 8. This theory is particularly associated with the work of Lee

[E]ven though we may have the *opportunity* to acquire all relevant points of view, in the absence of agreed-upon structures or methods for deciding questions, we may very well end up with poorer decisions than we would otherwise have. It is important, therefore, that we recognise the following: public regulation requiring the media to grant access under certain conditions need not be thought of as designed only to correct structural defects in the market. . . . [W]e must therefore be careful not to make the mistake of thinking that public regulation hinges only on one possible rationale, and certainly not on the traditionally expressed rationale of market failure.[14]

An implication from this is that there may be justification for regulating *part* of the media whilst leaving other parts free in order to achieve true pluralism; regulation may be needed simply to ensure that the media landscape does not become too uniform and to guarantee access *somewhere* in the media to a range of different viewpoints; in Bollinger's phrase, 'partial regulation'.[15] This may require forms of regulation similar to those associated with public service broadcasting in the past to ensure that the best traditions of such broadcasting are preserved alongside new types of media.

If one accepts this argument, then, there may be good reason for regulating part of the media even where competitive markets can operate; regulation should not be limited to competition law. Apart from particular rationales for different types of regulation, already discussed in our introductory chapter and to be further developed below, there are at least two justifications at a macro-level for such partial regulation. Firstly, if regulatory action can preserve something qualitatively different from the outcome of unregulated markets, this has in itself the justification of creating real choice and real diversity for consumers. One example referred to in some of the national reports is that of the listed events by which national action (now supported by European Community facilitation) has been taken to protect universal free-to-air access to events of key national importance which would otherwise be priced outside the range of large numbers of consumers; another is that of the must-carry rules which require public service broadcasting to be included in subscription and cable systems, thus increasing their availability and hence consumer choice. In both cases the effect is to provide consumers with a broader range of programming than that which would be made available simply through specialist subscription channels, especially as the choice available

Bollinger; see his 'Freedom of the Press and Public Access' (1976) 75 Michigan L Rev, 1–42, and 'The Rationale of Public Regulation of the Media' in Lichtenberg, J (ed), *Democracy and the Mass Media* (Cambridge: Cambridge University Press, 1990), 355–67.

[14] Bollinger, 'The Rationale of Public Regulation of the Media' (n 13 above), 364 (emphasis retained).

[15] See Bollinger, 'Freedom of the Press and Public Access' (n 13 above), esp 17, 26–37.

to subscribers is anyway constrained through packaging by those who offer subscription services. Regulation here can also support the availability of a common culture in the same way as public service broadcasting has done in the past. Finally, some of the regulatory action described in the national reports designed to limit the bundling of programming packages and rights can be seen as, amongst other justifications, serving to maximise consumer choice, in this instance by attempting to prevent companies using a powerful market position to restrict it. This argument for regulation, then, does not concern itself with the existence of limits on the operation of markets, such as spectrum scarcity, but assumes that markets will marginalise some sorts of programming and therefore in the long run diminish consumer choice.[16]

If this argument for regulation takes as its starting point the maximisation of individual consumer choice, a second argument starts from the need to promote a particular type of society with particular forms of democratic procedure. In an important article, Monroe Price has argued that the key problem will be the balance between different forms of communication, and in particular he asks us to:

[c]onsider a world of channels of communication that are transparent, commonly received, pervasive, and available everywhere. Think of these as a kind of open terrain, like the spaces that have been used for public speech in the mass media in recent decades (or, like the streets, from time immemorial). In opposition consider a closed terrain of channels of communication that are reserved and private, encrypted and privileged, channels in which important discourse takes place, but that are not so open to the public view.[17]

Current developments are resulting in 'a closing up of the open terrain, away from the broadcast channels, channels underwritten by advertising or government and therefore seemingly free—toward the narrowcast channels, encrypted pay channels and pay programs in which all information is metered and individuals pay for what they receive.'[18] He then used Habermas's concept of the public sphere as 'a zone for discourse in which ideas are explored and a public view is crystallized'[19] to characterise the open terrain, and to suggest that 'the very abundance of channels may mean more, not fewer, calls for government intervention to ensure that something remains of the public space.'[20]

This builds on an important area of social theory concerned with the

---

[16] For a developed reflection on the concept of choice in a variety of contexts see Lewis, N, *Choice and the Legal Order: Rising Above Politics* (London: Butterworths, 1996).

[17] Price, M, 'Free Expression and Digital Dreams: The Open and Closed Terrain of Speech' (1995) 22 *Critical Inquiry*, 64–89, at 67.

[18] ibid.

[19] ibid, 69.

[20] ibid, 79.

distinctive nature of the public sphere as a location for political and social debate; it is particularly associated with the work of the German social philosopher Jurgen Habermas.[21] The work is far too complex and dense to be treated here, but to give an (inadequate) summary from recent writings, '[t]he public sphere can best be described as a network for communicating information and points of view . . . ; the streams of communication are, in the process, filtered and synthesised in such a way that they coalesce into bundles of topically specified *public* opinions.'[22] This process involves a testing of claims through debate of a particularly demanding kind referred to as the 'ideal speech situation' in which the sole determinant of the outcome is the force of the better argument. Of course, such a situation is in practice unattainable but it can be used as a counterfactual critical tool for the assessment of actual existing institutions. In the context of the media,

[t]he diffusion of information and points of view via effective broadcasting media is not the only thing that matters in public processes of communication, nor is it the most important. . . . the rules of a *shared* practice of communication are of greater significance for structuring public opinion. Agreement on issues and contributions *develops* only as the result of more or less exhaustive controversy in which proposals, information, and reasons can be more or less rationally dealt with.[23]

The public sphere is partially constituted through basic rights including freedom of speech and freedom of the media and rights of access to the media; it may also form a basis for media regulation;

The *power of the media* is not sufficiently reined in by professional standards, but today, by fits and starts, the 'fourth branch of government' is being subjected to constitutional regulation. In the Federal Republic, for example, it is both the legal form and the institutional structure of television networks that determine whether they depend more on the influence of political parties and public interest groups or more on private firms with large advertising outlays.[24]

---

[21] The seminal work was Habermas, J, *The Structural Transformation of the Public Sphere* (Cambridge: Polity, 1989), and see more recently his *Between Facts and Norms* (Cambridge: Polity, 1996), esp chs 7–8. For applications of the theory to media see Garnham, N, 'The Media and the Public Sphere' in Golding, P, Murdock, G and Schlesinger, P (eds), *Communicating Politics: Mass Communications and the Political Process* (Leicester: Leicester University Press, 1986), and his different essay with the same title in Colhoun, C (ed), *Habermas and the Public Sphere* (London: MIT Press, 1992); for application to law see Prosser, T, 'Towards a Critical Public Law' (1982) 9 *J of Law and Society*, 1–19, and 'Democracy, Accountability and Institutional Design' in McAuslan, P and McEldowney, J (eds), *Law, Legitimacy and the Constitution* (London: Sweet and Maxwell, 1985), 170–90.

[22] Habermas, *Between Facts and Norms* (n 21 above), 360 (emphasis retained).

[23] ibid, 362 (emphasis retained).

[24] ibid, 376 (emphasis retained).

One justification for regulation, including constitutional regulation of the sort seen in a number of countries in this study, is thus to preserve a public sphere for debate of this kind, and it has been suggested that this is associated with the public service model of broadcasting.[25] Of course not all broadcasting will contribute; entertainment also plays a major role in viewing, after all! Nevertheless, the theme of maintaining a public sphere does support the argument made earlier that it will be important to preserve a plurality of different media forms and structures which provide access to a range of competing viewpoints and information sources; this may best be accomplished through regulatory action. As the Commission's Green Paper states, the success of convergence as one of the key 'enablers' of the Information Society '. . . will depend largely on the kind of regulatory framework devised to encourage it'.[26]

3 TYPES OF REGULATION

Forceful arguments for the retention of some types of regulation can also be found when we return to the four regulatory rationales described in our opening chapter; in particular, the need and demand for them does not appear to be withering away in the new media landscape. The first was social regulation of content; it would certainly not be possible to argue that concern with this is disappearing, and indeed if anything it would appear to be increasing. Examples which suggest this include the concern with the protection of children from violent and sexually explicit broadcast material, something of a high profile issue in the USA with the recent constitutional litigation described in the national chapter, and in the UK with the banning of overseas satellite stations broadcasting such material (action not limited to a concern for children but for adult decency also). Concern about pornography, and particularly child pornography, on the Internet has also had a high and growing profile. Similarly, concern with privacy issues and of the relationship between encryption and potentially criminal activities is growing, not disappearing. This is not of course to say that the traditional attempts to deal with these problems will remain appropriate in the changing media environment, but that expectations of action to deal with them will not die away. The problem in relation to, say, child pornography on the Internet is not the principle of regulation but rather practical problems of enforcement, on which more will be said below.

---

[25] Garnham, 'The Media and the Public Sphere' (n 21 above), 45–53.
[26] n 3 above, 8.

Regulation for competition is also the subject of increasing attention, as has already been made clear in this chapter. At one level this concerns the basic rules which make markets possible, for example those allocating intellectual property rights. However, with the move away from dominant state broadcasters and telecommunications operators to a multi-enterprise industry, issues of standardisation and interconnection have come to the forefront. In this context the European Community has done excellent work as part of its pioneering liberalisation of telecommunications; in other contexts the issue has become one of considerable legal controversy, notably in the United States as discussed in the national chapter but also in the UK and (outside the coverage of this study) in New Zealand.[27] Both these concerns are with the creation of markets; however, their policing raises further issues of competition policy and law, notably through the scrutiny of mergers. In the field of the media, as in others such as civil aviation, mergers are of an increasingly trans-national character and this has posed regulatory problems. The European Community has done something to address this issue but it is one which is going to continue to pose further problems given that, as suggested earlier, much consolidation has already taken place in the 'old' media and we are on the threshold of a major process of consolidation within the new media industry also. The need for clarifying problems of international jurisdiction in merger control is now urgent, and not just in the media. An issue of key importance within competition policy is that of interconnection and access to networks, which is addressed in, for instance, Open Network Provision (ONP) directives and resolutions of the EU with respect to some areas. All this requires supervision and structural safeguards.

A further problem will be caused by difficulties in using tests of ownership and of market share as a base for regulatory action in relation to the media, both on competition grounds and for reasons of democratic pluralism. However, as we noted in our introductory chapter, given the fragmentation of markets characteristic of the changing media, overall ownership figures will give little indication of dominance, and it will be difficult to assemble a general test of market share working across the different markets, as shown by the difficulty in constructing a 'media exchange rate' to permit this to be done. Moreover, as we have emphasised, control of key access points such as conditional access technology, billing, customer care and maintenance systems, and Internet search engines can give power to their controllers quite out of proportion to ownership or direct market participation.[28] We are not opposed to the

---

[27] See *Mercury Communications Ltd v Director General of Telecommunications* [1996] 1 All ER 575 (HL) and *Telecom Corporation of New Zealand v Clear Communications Ltd*, 19 Oct 1994 (LEXIS) (PC).

[28] For analysis of these issues see Graham, A, 'Exchange Rates and Gatekeepers', in

retention of structural regulation based on ownership and control over particular markets such as television viewing whilst the process of convergence remains as incomplete as we have suggested. However, we would expect there to be a gradual move away from such structural regulation towards more behavioural forms as new markets develop. A particularly good example of such action is that taken by the European Community in relation to conditional access and related systems (and which, in the UK at least, has been implemented effectively), which does appear to have been successful in producing a common European standard.[29] Other examples of behavioural regulation include action being taken to limit the degree of bundling permitted in the sale of programmes to cable companies in the UK and the action launched by the US justice department in relation to Microsoft's supply of Internet browsers. Another concern is with the institutional arrangements for regulation of competition; we have seen in the national reports that a combination exists of international, governmental, and sector-specific bodies with these responsibilities. Given the complexity of the new media and the need for close and continual scrutiny of their complex market structures, we see a strong case for entrusting these tasks to specialist regulatory bodies, as recognised recently in Germany and Italy, although in Australia important telecommunications responsibilities have passed to the general competition authority. Whatever the best instruments or regulatory arrangements, however, it is clear that regulation for competition is likely to remain as an important future concern.

Our third regulatory rationale was that of ensuring pluralism and diversity of the media on democratic grounds; we divided this between internal pluralism, to ensure that content covers a wide range of interests and tastes rather than offering only content which is cheap or appealing to advertisers, and external pluralism, concerned with the maintenance of a range of different services.[30] External pluralism might appear to be the rationale least appropriate for regulatory intervention because of the approaching diversity of niche channels to be made possible by the development of digitalisation, and because of the difficulties in controlling

Congden, T et al (eds), *The Cross Media Revolution* (London: John Libby, 1995), 38–49, and Goldberg, D, Prosser, T and Verhulst, S, *The Impact of New Communications Technologies on Media Concentrations and Pluralism* (Strasbourg: Council of Europe, 1997).

[29] 'Europeans Co-operate on Multi-Media', *Financial Times*, 29 Sept 1997.

[30] This was based upon the definition of the Committee of Experts on Media Concentration and Pluralism of the Council of Europe, which states that pluralism can be measured by four elements: (a) the existence of a plurality of autonomous and independent media; (b) diversity of media types and contents available to the public, resulting in a diversity of choice; (c) segments of society capable of addressing the public by means of media owned by, or affiliated to, them; (d) diversity of media contents in relation to media functions, issue covered, and audience groups served. See MM-CM (96) 11, Strasbourg, Sept 1996.

ownership and market share for the reasons outlined above. Moreover, it could be argued that if internal pluralism exists we need not worry about external pluralism as diversity is guaranteed. However, the opposite is clearly not true in the sense that a diversified ownership and even a dramatic increase in the number of channels available will not necessarily guarantee a diversified content; it is just as easy to imagine competition driving down profit margins so that market participants can only afford the cheapest forms of programming and those most likely to appeal to mass advertising markets. Moreover, it seems unlikely that future market structures will result in diversity of ownership; as we saw earlier the trend is towards consolidation.

All these arguments suggest that there will be strong arguments for ensuring internal pluralism, and this is where the arguments made above in favour of retaining elements of a 'public sphere' have particular importance. We would argue that this can best be achieved by regulatory interventions designed to maintain some form of public service broadcasting. This does not only mean public broadcasting in the sense of broadcasters completely insulated from the market through public ownership or through guaranteed subsidy; in the past programming requirements have been a way of maintaining internal pluralism even for broadcasters operating within what are basically market structures, for example in the UK. Interventions of this kind could do much to serve the basic justifications for regulation discussed early in this chapter, those of providing a more effective choice for consumers and of ensuring the maintenance of some form of public sphere for democratic debate. Something of the same sort of thinking indeed lies behind the Protocol on Public Service Broadcasting to the Amsterdam Treaty of the European Union.[31]

The question is whether this will remain feasible in a new environment of greatly enhanced media outlets. It could be the case that, if these become increasingly successful at attracting viewers, the audience figures for public service broadcasters will decline in such a way as to make public funding politically indefensible. Moreover, it is argued that those broadcasters subject to public service regulation but operating in the commercial marketplace will have no choice but to compete at the expense of their public service requirements; if the latter cannot be lifted the companies will go under. This may ultimately be the case, but the evidence that we have amassed in this study suggests that we are still far away from such a crisis; the conventional broadcasters remain dominant in terms of market share and the new forms of delivery are merely biting away at the edges, in the case of television-type services at least. This suggests that the maintenance of a distinctive model of public service

---

[31] *Treaty of Amsterdam Amending the Treaty on European Union* (1997), Protocol on the System of Public Broadcasting in the Member States.

broadcasting will not be unfeasible for a considerable time into the future.[32] Indeed, there are already signs that in some countries public service broadcasters, at first threatened by changes in the mass market, are successfully filling niches not covered by new commercial broadcasters; for example, in Germany at a national level public stations have lost market share and advertising revenue but have a growing role at regional level, as the national chapter above describes.

This leads on to our final rationale for regulation; that of universal service. This has been a major concern in telecommunications, as noted in some of the chapters above, especially in the United States, the European Community, and Australia. It has also been applied in some cases to new communications technologies such as the Internet, notably in the US through the FCC rule-making process. In the case of broadcasting it has also formed part of the basis for a number of regulatory interventions, for example the system of 'listed events' in some Member States of the European Union which prevent events of key national importance from being shown exclusively on subscription or pay-per-view services. A further example is that of 'must carry' rules requiring cable operators to provide access to other stations and, in the UK, the guaranteed access for public service broadcasters to digital terrestrial television. Not only can these be seen as examples of the application of principles of universal service, but also as attempts to protect the particular character of public service broadcasting in the new environment.

It would thus seem clear that regulation will have a considerable place in the new media environment; arguments that it will wither away are based on grossly simplistic assumptions as to the reasons for regulation and on over-optimism as to the likely openness of future market structures. This is particularly true in the case of mass broadcasting and the TV-type markets; some of the arguments described above will have less application in the on-line markets, though even here issues such as Internet pornography and consolidation of the industry suggest that the idea of leaving the net as simply a 'functioning anarchy' are themselves far too simplistic. The argument is thus not whether to regulate but how to do so. This is where an attempt can be made to analyse the future role of law.

4 THE ROLE OF LAW IN REGULATING THE CHANGING MEDIA

What role will law play in the future? We have seen in our national chapters a bewildering array of different types of legal intervention, and

[32] See Raboy, M (ed), *Public Service Broadcasting for the Twenty-first Century* (Luton: Luton University Press, 1996).

indeed some very different conclusions as to law's potential. For example, the author of our Hungarian chapter concluded that 'legal means of media regulation have serious limitations', and points to difficulties in using legal norms in such a rapidly changing context. On the other hand, our German contributor envisages an eventual move to an integrated network of legal norms, including traditional constitutional principles such as freedom of expression and universal service, but also including new and more specific norms. We cannot fully accept either conclusion. We do not see in the national chapters a general withering away of law in favour of an unregulated marketplace. Indeed, many of the controversial issues involved in creating and maintaining new media markets can only be resolved through law, for example the allocation of intellectual property rights, the availability of interconnection and maintaining open markets through competition law. It is of course possible to argue that to some extent these matters can be delegated to private agreement between different market actors; however the example of conditional access suggests that regulatory action may be necessary to provide incentives for this, and anyway contract is still law, with legal means of enforcement. Moreover, it would be bizarre to suggest that in the United States, home of many of the new developments in the media, law has been rejected or is withering away. One has only to look at the major constitutional litigation on such matters as freedom of speech on the Internet and obscenity in broadcasting, or at the mass of law spawned in telecommunications regulation, to see how law is maintaining its centrality. Indeed, the problems revealed in the Hungarian chapter appear to be largely due to an absence of a reasonably clear legal framework for the new media, not to the presence of too much law.

We suspect that attempts to argue for 'the end of law'[33] in the new media are based on an unduly narrow concept of law, basing it on criminal law or so-called 'command and control' regulation.[34] We shall argue in a moment that law's potential is much richer than these limited conceptions would suggest. However, we are also not able to accept that we are about to see a new rationalised and unified system of law applying across the new media; the future will be much more pragmatic and less tidy than this. We would in fact see four potential future roles for law.

The first role is that of setting out general frameworks of constitutional principle within which the media will operate; what one might call the 'moralisation' or 'constitutionalisation' role of law. This would include defining, and protecting, values such as freedom of expression and ac-

---

[33] This was the title of a book analysing the very different Marxist claims for the 'withering away' of law and the state; O'Hagan, T, *The End of Law?* (Oxford: Basil Blackwell, 1984).

[34] For elucidation of this concept see Ogus, A, *Regulation: Legal Form and Economic Theory* (Oxford: Clarendon Press, 1994), ch 11.

ceptable limitations to it, rights to privacy, and conceptions of public service. This is something which the courts, and in particular constitutional courts, have already carried out in a number of important jurisdictions, most notably the United States but also, amongst the countries covered in this book, in Germany, Italy, Hungary, and, to some extent, Australia.[35] The exception is of course the United Kingdom where, although there have been sporadic decisions of the courts on matters such as obscenity, 'the position . . . is striking because of the complete absence of constitutional principles and the relative dearth of case-law'.[36] Even in this jurisdiction, however, matters could change with the forthcoming incorporation of the European Convention on Human Rights (incorporating a right to freedom of expression) into domestic law and the greater willingness of senior judges to treat the common law as a source of constitutional principle.[37] This role of law could not have been better summed up than in a recent detailed study of broadcasting and fundamental rights:

The primary achievement of constitutional courts throughout Europe has been to give a clear signal that the audiovisual media should not be treated as just another commodity: radio and television have become central mechanisms through which we gain an understanding of ourselves and others. . . . First, there is the emphasis on the right of viewers and listeners to programme services which provide diverse and accurate information, information which, as far as possible, should be protected from distortion by either government or commercial influences. . . . Secondly, state regulation to ensure the provision of reliable and diverse audiovisual services is considered to be legitimate, even essential.[38]

This mirrors exactly the primary justifications for regulation of the electronic media outlined earlier in this chapter.

The second role of law which we see as continuing indefinitely is one which has already been discussed above; that of competition law to police markets. Indeed, this is a type of law whose importance is increasing with the growth of multi-enterprise markets rather than their being dominated by national telecommunications operators or a few public broadcasters, both categories often being exempt from the application of competition law. We have dealt with some of the problems of such regulation for competition above. It should be added, however, that older doctrines of competition law, such as those of the common carrier and of essential facilities, may have much to offer in the new digital world, especially in relation to gateway monopolies. As a commentator has stated, criticising

---

[35] For details from a number of jurisdictions see Barendt, E (n 8 above) and Craufurd-Smith, R, *Broadcasting Law and Fundamental Rights* (Oxford: Clarendon Press, 1997).
[36] Barendt (n 8 above), 10.
[37] See eg, *Derbyshire County Council v Times Newspapers* [1993] AC 534.
[38] Craufurd-Smith (n 35 above), 241–2.

share of voice regulation, '[a] different approach is required but one that is familiar to traditional US telecommunications regulation: come back common carrier, all is forgiven. In the digital age, all owners of servers, networks and set top boxes carrying on demand services and enjoying more than say 25% distribution market share, should be required to give common carrier access to all content and service providers.'[39] The essential facilities doctrine, building on earlier principles of the duties of a common carrier, has been developed in United States regulation and competition law and increasingly adopted by the European Community.[40] It provides a basis for enforcing third party access to such facilities needed by com-petitors. Thus if there is control of an essential facility by a monopolist, inability of competitors to duplicate the essential facility, denial of the use of the facility to a competitor of the monopolist and it is feasible or practical to provide third party access, the facility owner may be ordered by the courts to provide such access on fair terms. For example, in one case the European Court of Justice decided that companies with exclusive rights over port operations and the unloading of goods would breach the prohibition on abuse of a dominant position in the European Community Treaty if they engaged in overcharging, in failure to take up modern technology, or in undue discrimination.[41] The same concern also of course lies behinds policies of open network provision discussed in our Euro-pean chapter, and a similar approach played a central part in pioneering work by the UK Office of Telecommunications on how to facilitate fair competition in the process of convergence. This recommended different forms of regulation according to the extent of market dominance, reserv-ing the strictest controls for dominant operators.[42] Finally, of course, some means will have to be found of supporting universal service provision though, as we shall argue below, this may be better done through tech-niques involving delegation of regulatory responsibilities combined with setting of some more official standards.

Mention of such a specialist regulatory agency brings us on to the third role of law in the regulation of the changing media. We have noted that there has been a tendency towards the creation of specialist regulatory agencies for telecommunications and broadcasting regulation, and this

[39] Hooper, R, 'Media Concentrations in the Global Digital Media Environment', *Digital Media Forum*, 20–21 Mar 1995. For a further discussion of the potentiality of such doctrines see Prosser, T, *Law and the Regulators* (Oxford: Clarendon, 1997), 24–6.

[40] See eg, Hancher, L, 'Commission Decisions and "Essential Facilities"', (1994) 5 *Utilities Law Review* 62–4; Glasl, D, 'Essential Facilities in EC Antitrust Law: A Contribution to the Debate', (1994) 15 European Competition Law Review 306–14.

[41] Case 179/90, *Merci Convenzionali Porto di Genova SpA v Siderurgica Gabrielli SpA* [1994] 4 CMLR 422.

[42] Office of Telecommunications, *Beyond the Telephone, the Television and the PC* (London: Office of Telecommunications, 1995).

has replaced the older form of regulation by unitary government departments. This in fact creates the need for new law; whilst the internal workings of government could be left to administrative or political controls, law is necessary for new agencies in order to define their constitutions, set out their powers and jurisdictions, and to establish their procedures. Already we have massive experience of such agencies through the long experience of the Federal Communications Commission in the United States; Australia has also used this type of agency and is continuing to do so in the shape of the new Australian Communications Authority, although there has also been a move towards the use of the general competition authorities. Similar experience has occurred in Europe with the creation of the Federal telecommunications authority in Germany and the lengthy process of establishing the new authority covering both broadcasting and telecommunications in Italy. In the UK the Office of Telecommunications had been created as a direct result of privatisation, and in Hungary the absence of a clear regulatory structure of this kind is now causing problems. Finally, European Community telecommunications regulation, whilst not requiring the establishment of regulatory agencies at arms-length from government, has required the separation of regulatory and operating functions and so has encouraged such institutional change.

As this brief summary suggests, there is no agreement on the optimum jurisdiction of such regulatory bodies. The US model of the Federal Communications Commission combines telecommunications and broadcasting responsibilities; in other cases they are the responsibility of separate agencies, for example in Germany (complicated further by the split between Federal and *Länder* powers) and in the UK, where a considerable debate has taken place as to the best pattern for the division of functions. It has been suggested, for example in the European Commission Green Paper on convergence, that a more rational division of functions would be between infrastructure and delivery on the one hand and content on the other; the former could then be primarily a matter of competition law and policy whilst the latter could bring in the more social concerns which we have discussed earlier and which are likely to continue even after convergence has developed more fully. However, the two functions should not be regarded as completely separate, and, overall, the best solution may be to allocate these two functions to separate divisions in an overall super-regulator covering both, as in the case of the FCC. This was also the underlying rationale for the Italian Authority composed of a Commission for regulating infrastructure and networks and a Commission for regulating services and products. Clearly there is considerable need for legal construction of appropriate powers for such agencies; again the case of Hungary suggests the problems which can arise if this is neglected.

A final point about this role of law also needs making. The new agencies will of course be responsible for developing a considerable body of law of their own. Very obvious examples of these are the large rule-making procedures undertaken by the Federal Communications Commission on universal service, interconnection, and other matters; others are the work of OFTEL in the UK on the same issues, the issue of codes which have legal backing on programme standards and advertising practice by the Independent Television Commission also in the UK, and the development of codes of practice by the Australian Broadcasting Authority. If we accept the argument that regulation is likely to continue even as convergence develops further, the use of such techniques would seem to offer opportunities for the use of law in a more flexible and decentralised form which can better cope with the complexities of rapidly changing markets. The delegation of rule-making powers to agencies permits more effective study of the changing industries and markets, and more developed consultation, than does the use of more formal law in the form of primary legislation or judicial decision.

This concern with flexibility and decentralisation brings us to the final role of law which we would identify as becoming important as the process of convergence develops further. In a number of cases our national chapters have identified moves towards self-regulation, the most famous being that of regulation of content on the Internet.[43] At first sight this might appear to be the antithesis of legal regulation; however on closer examination this is far too simple a characterisation of the limits to law. Firstly, self-regulation is not a useful way of characterising a whole regulatory regime as almost inevitably it is accompanied by more direct interventions by public authorities including use of criminal or civil sanctions, as illustrated vividly by the example of Internet policing. Self-regulation is thus a technique of regulation rather than an alternative to regulation; it provides a type of technique to be used for regulatory purposes. Moreover, where self-regulation exists this often evolves towards more detailed official regulation as crises have to be faced and government cannot decline responsibility for their resolution. A striking example of this is that of the UK financial services industry; as a Parliamentary committee put it

---

[43] During November 1997 the European Commission adopted an Action Plan for 1998 to 2001 on promoting the safe use of the Internet which identifies key areas where measures are needed and could be supported by the European Union. This includes: for reporting illegal content, industry-led self-regulation and content-monitoring schemes, internationally compatible and interoperable rating and filtering systems, as well as awareness. See <http://www2.echo.lu/legal/en/internet/actplan.html> At more or less the same time, a Communication and a draft Council Recommendation on the protection of minors and of human dignity in audiovisual services was also adopted. The documents define common objectives and co-operation fields at Community level. The underlying idea is that self-regulation schemes at national level are the most appropriate answer as regards both television and the Internet. See <http://europa.eu.int/en/comm/dg10/avpolicy/new_srv/comlv-en.htm.>

in a study of the regulation of this area, *'the evidence we have received from the regulators has . . . stressed that the term "self regulation" is a misnomer and fails to reflect their independence or the statutory basis of their authority'*.[44] The stark opposition of self-regulation to statutory regulation is probably due to an over-reliance on the peculiar position of UK press regulation which has to some degree been arranged through the industry itself, although even this has changed in recent years.[45]

To argue for self-regulation is thus not to argue for no regulation or for no law. Moreover, where self-regulation exists, this does not indicate a lack of interest by the state, and in many cases self-regulatory techniques have been adopted to head off the alternative of government intervention; a celebrated example is that of the British Board of Film Censors (more recently of Film Classification), established by the industry precisely to avoid official censorship and later given statutory responsibility for classification of video cassettes. Indeed, as mentioned in our introduction, a strong case has been made for recognition of the interdependence of self-regulation and official regulation through the development of 'enforced self-regulation' involving negotiation between the state and individual firms to establish appropriate standards and regulations, which can then be publicly enforced.[46] A related approach is that of 'co-regulation' in which regulation is undertaken by an industry association with some oversight and/or ratification by government.[47] Our study has shown a number of examples of such a mixture of official regulation and self-regulation, notably in relation to regulation of content on the Internet and agreeing Internet standards. We suspect that a further important technique for law in the future will be setting the conditions for such enforced self-regulation or co-regulation through setting out basic standards to be followed, delegating the details of drafting and enforcement machinery to private actors and associations, and securing that enforcement takes place effectively. We are already seeing something of the sort in relation to universal service provision in the European Union where the authorities have favoured the setting of basic standards and then leaving the details of implementation to market actors, for example through a system of 'pay or play' in which enterprises may volunteer to provide the universal service or, if they do not do so, are required to pay a levy to support its provision by others. On a more general level, something of the sort has

---

[44] Treasury and Civil Service Committee, *The Regulation of Financial Services in the UK*, HC 332, 1994–5, para 25 (emphasis retained).

[45] See eg, Robertson, G and Nicol, A, *Media Law*, 3rd edn (London: Penguin, 1992).

[46] Ayres, I and Braithwaite, J, *Responsive Regulation: Transcending the Deregulation Debate* (Oxford: Oxford University Press, 1992); see also Michael, DC, 'Federal Agency Use of Audited Self-regulation as a Regulatory Technique' (1995) 47 *Administrative Law Review*, 171–253.

[47] Ayres and Braithwaite, ibid, 102.

been proposed by the European Commissioner responsible for telecommunications, when he proposed the creation of 'a new global framework for communications for the next millenium . . . [the] International Charter for Global Communications' which is foreseen as 'an international level [agreement] on a framework based on a range of principles and basic rules'[48] (that is, not based on detailed norms). Dr Bangemann has been quoted as saying that: '[w]e want something that's not legally binding, but which can embrace many different problems and is politically binding, like a charter.'[49]

5 CONCLUSION

No simple conclusions are evident from this work, except in the paradoxical sense that the lack of simple conclusions is itself worth emphasising. National and cultural differences do matter in shaping both the development of new media markets and their regulation. What we hope to have done, apart from having provided detailed snapshots of the way some nations are coping with change in the media, is to have suggested some of the key themes which should underlie both media regulation and media law. Of course, the future media world will be very different from that of today, but to suggest that this removes our responsibility to address issues of law and regulation would be to allow technological change (complex enough in itself) to mask even more difficult problems of economic, social, and legal organisation. We have suggested in these conclusions that legal regulation will, and should, continue to have an important place in the new media world; indeed, we suspect that political crises and political concerns so evident around issues such as Internet pornography will ensure that this remains high on the political agenda. We hope that we have at least clarified the purposes which we should seek through this regulation, and that our suggestions for more flexible legal responses will strike a chord amongst those who wish to combine the undoubted potential of the new media world with cultural values derived from the old.

---

[48] Speech delivered at Geneva, 8 Sept 1997, *A New World Order for Global Communications*, at <http://www.ispo.cec.be/infosoc/promo/speech/geneva.html>
[49] *European Voice* (27 Nov–3 Dec 1997). Survey: Information Society, 19.

Index

access, regulation for 21–3
  'gatekeepers' 21–2
  universal service principles 22
Australia 247–93
  ABA 257–8
  ACA 258
  ACCC 291–2
  advisory bodies 259–60
  ASEAN countries, and 289
  Austereo 254
  Australian content 276–7
  Australian Radio Network 254
  Broadcasting Services Act 1992 256
  broadcasting standards codes 274–6
  cable rollout 249–50
  classification of print, film and computer
    games 277
  codes of practice 274–6
  communications systems and
    developments 248–54
  competition law 266–8
    Trade Practices Act 1974 266–7
  content regulation 272–80
  control of radio and television 263–4
  copyright 282–4
    Act of 1968 282
    cable operators 283–4
    international context 282–3
  'cyberlaws' 292
  Davidson Report 1982 289–90
  electoral laws 280
  federal parliament 255
  film industry funding 281
  foreign control 265–6
    courts, and 272–4
  free communication, implied
    constitutional right to 272–4
  funding for local output 280–2
  future developments 288–93
  general trends 247–8
  government, role of 258–9
  Information Industries Taskforce 260
  Information Policy Advisory Council
    260
  internationalisation versus
    regionalisation 252
  legislative and policy environment 255–
    7
  licensing 262–3
    general carrier licences 262–3
    mobile carrier licences 263
  major players in media and
    communications 253–4
  market structure 261–8
  multimedia 251–2
  multimedia content 281–2
  National Office of the Information
    Economy 259–60
  new access regime 290
  News Ltd 254
  Nine Network 253
  on-line services 251–2
  Optus Communications 254
  political laws 280
  print media, control of 264–5
  privacy laws 284–8
    Australian legislation 284–5
    interception of communications 287
    Privacy Commissioner 286–7
    private sector communications 287–8
    telecommunications 285–6
    Telecommunications Privacy
      Committee 286
  Radiocommunications Act 1992 256
  regulation of on-line services 278–80
    ABA Report 278
    codes of practice 279–80
    international context 278
  regulators 257–9
  satellite communications 250
    international 250
    local 250
  Seven Network 253
  standards 260–1
    review of broadcasts 275–6
    support for local output 280–2
  tax law 280
  taxation 293
  technical regulation 260–1
  telecommunications access regime 268–9
  Telecommunications Act 1997 256
  Telecommunications Industry
    Ombudsman Scheme 259
  telecommunications structure 262–3
  Telstra 253–4
  Trade Practices Act 1974 256–7
  universal service 269–72
    legal structure 270–1
    level of service required 271–2
    origins 270
  unresolved tensions 290
autopoiesis 4

Bollinger
  regulation of media, on 300

child pornography
  regulation, and 303
comparative research
  problems 5–6
competition
  regulation, and 304
competition law
  role of 309–10
competition, regulation of 17–20
  domestic competition law, and 18
  external pluralism 19–20
  importance of 18–19
  internal pluralism 19
  scope 17–18
convergence in services
  variation of degree of 296
Council of Europe 150–1
  Committee of Ministers 150–1
  content regulation 172–3
  information society 161
  intellectual property 169–70
  International Secretariat 151
  licensing 168–9
  Parliamentary Assembly 151
  privacy 174
  sources of institutional competence 152–
    3
  universal service 175–6
courts
  regulation by 24

European Community
  audio-visual policy 156–8
    legal norms 157–8
    support systems 156–7
  commercial communications 170–1
  Commission 147–8
    Directorates-General 147–8
  Committee of Regions 148–9
  concentration 166–7
  content regulation 172–3
  copyright 169–70
  economic regulation 164–9
  ECOSOC 148
  electronic commerce 171–2
  ERO 168
  European Court of Auditors 148
  finance 169–72
  general telecommunications policy 155–
    6
  harmonisation of laws 154–61
  HLEG 149
  information society 158–61
    Action Plan 158–9

funding and research programmes
    160
  Green Paper 160
  policy objectives 159
  priority areas 159
  infrastructure 161–3
    wired 161–2
    wireless 162–3
  intellectual property 169–70
  interconnection of competing systems
    164–6
    WTO, and 165
  liberalisation of infrastructure 165–6
  licensing 167–9
  market structure 164–9
  media ownership 166–7
  non-governmental organisations 149–50
  open network provision 164–6
  overall approach 145
  policy 146
  privacy 174
  remuneration 169–72
  security 173–4
  Single European Market 154–61
  social regulation 172–6
  sources of institutional competence 152–
    4
  spectrum allocation 167–9
  standardisation 163–4
  technological regulation 161–4
  Television Without Frontiers directive
    157–8
  Treaty 152
  universal service 175–6
  user protection 173–6
European Convention of Human Rights
    and Fundamental Freedoms 153
European Court of Justice 148
European institutions 145–76
European Parliament 146

Germany 29–60
  advertising in private television 1996 30
  advertising in public broadcasting 50–1
  ARD 46–7
  Broadcasting Council 46
  Central and Eastern Europe, and 40–1
  competition between public and private
    sectors 33–5
  concentration 54–6
  consumer electronics companies 30
  cost of TV rights for Bundesliga 35
  definition of multimedia services 53
  development of new services 36–9
  digital radio 38
  digital revolution 29
  digital television 36–8

economic regulation 54–6
European integration, and 40–1
Federal Constitutional Court 48–9
federal system 44–5
future developments 58–60
globalisation 39–42
growing concentration and low quality
    programmes 35–6
growing privatisation and
    commercialisation 32–5
income of public broadcasters 50–1
instruments of policy 49–52
international co-operation in public
    sector 41–2
Internet 38–9
Internet access providers 32
ISDN 58–9
joint broadcasting authorities 47–8
joint public broadcasting stations 46
local television 42
market participants 30–6
Media Concentration Commission 54–5
media development 29–42
    general trends 29
media policies 42–58
multimedia content production 32
network operators 31–2
print sector 30–1
private broadcasting laws 47–9
proposals for change 52–3
public and private broadcasting
    institutions 30
public broadcasting laws 45–7
regional third programmes 42
regionalisation 39–42
regulation 42–58
'right to development' of private sector
    50
satellite operators 39
service providers 32
social regulation 56–8
    Internet 57
software development 32
sports television 33–4
State Treaty 43–4
technological regulation 54
    standardisation 54
Telecommunications Act 1996 43
telecommunications legislation 51–2
Telecommunications Regulations
    Authority 52
types of regulation 44–53
viewing rates for main television stations
    1997 33
ZDF 47
governments
    regulation by 24–5

Habermas, Jurgen
    public sphere, on 302
Hungary 177–99
    advertising market 184
    Bureau of Data Protection 189
    business communications 182
    competition 195–7
        broadcasting 196
        mobile services 196
        telecom market 196
    Compliance Committee 198
    concession agreement 192–3
    Constitutional Court 187
    content providers 183
    content regulation 197–8
    conveyance 179
    cross-subsidy 193
    developments in new services 180
    economic regulation 192–7
    first draft of Governmental Strategy on
        Realisation of the Information
        Society 186–7
    fixed telephone services 180–1
    General Communications
        Inspectorate 188
    general trends 177–80
    harmonisation with EU 199
    horizontal concentration 179–80
    information superhighway 179
    intellectual property 197
    Interdepartmental Committee on
        Information Technology 188
    internationalism 178
    Internet 182
    IT market 182
    key events 177
    key media legislation 189–90
    level of state ownership 194
    market participants 180–4
    media development 177–84
    media policies 184–99
    mobile telephone services 181
    narrowcasting 179
    National Information Infrastructure
        Development Project 186
    National Radio and Television Board
        188
    National Strategy on Development of
        Information Technology 186
    non-governmental organisations 189
    ownership regulation 193–5
        concessions 194
        political factors 195
        public foundations 194–5
    printed media 184
    privacy, protection of 198–9
    private companies 189

Hungary (*cont.*):
  privatisation 177–8
  radio programme distribution 181–2
  radio programme provision 183–4
  regulation 184–99
    aims 190–1
    institutions 184–5
    issues 190–9
    key strategies 185–7
    structure 184–5
    topics 190–9
  regulation of tariffs 193
  regulatory bodies 187–9
  social regulation 197–9
  technological regulation 191–2
  television programme distribution 181–2
  trade associations 189
  TV programme provision 183–4
  user protection 198–9
  vertical concentration 179–80

industrial diversification 297
Internet
  development of 298
  FCC, and 215–16
  indecency
    United States 235–8
  Germany 38–9, 57
  Italy 63–4, 65–8
  purposes of regulation 16–17
  US Telecommunications Act 1996 222
Italy 61–99
  advertising 97–9
    film production, and 98
    restrictions 97–9
  advertising and sponsorship regulation 88
  advertising controls 90
  anti-trust regime 85
  civil protection of information and privacy 90
  Commission for regulating infrastructure and networks 77–8
  Commission for services and products 78
  conditions for use of TLC services 91
  Constitutional Court decisions 74–5, 76
  constitutional rights 79–80
  content standards 89
  copyright law 86–7
  criticisms of proposals for change 79–82
  development of new services 65–9
  economic regulation 84–9
    print media 85–6
  electronic commerce, regulation of 88–9
  evolution of regulatory framework 74–6

  extra-contractual responsibilities 91
  fastest growing TLC sectors 72
  globalisation 63
  independent administrative authority 77–81
    anti-trust powers 81–2
    political composition 81
  information network 62
  initial state monopoly 61–2
  interactive telephony service 65
  Internet 63–4, 65–8
  legal and regulatory reforms 77–9
  legislative framework 92–3
    Constitutional Court 92
    'public service' 92–3
  Mammi Law 75–6, 77
  market participants 69–72
  market structure 84–9, 93–5
    channel rationing 95
    TV 94
  media development 61–72
    general trends 62–5
  media policies 72–91
  MEDIASET 69–72
  mobile telephone tariffs 73
  mobile telephony 68
  national television sector 70
  network infrastructure market prospects 68–9
  new regulatory framework 64–5
  on-line newspapers 65–6
  operators' revenue, limits to 87–8
  pay-TV 71–2
  political parties 90–1
  privatisation, limits to 95–7
  public interest groups 93–4
  'public service' 82
  RAI 62–3
  reduction in administrative powers 80–1
  regulation 72–91
  regulatory instruments 95–7
  revision of media laws 73–4
  social regulation 89–91
  state monopoly 74
  technological regulation 82–4
    infrastructure 82–4
    standardisation 82–4
  Telecom Italia 63–4
  television advertising 70–1
  topics and issues in media regulation 82–91
  TV audience 70
  TV financing 96–7
  types of regulation 73–82
  universal service, supply of 84
  user protection 89–91

law
  critique of regulatory capacity 3–4
law, role of 307–14
  competition law 309–10
  constitutionalisation 308–9
  decentralisation 312
  flexibility 312
  moralisation 308–9
  narrowness of concept 308
  self-regulation, and 312–13
  specialist regulatory agencies 310–11

macrotrends in changing media 8–14
  access application providers 13
  content and service providers 12
  content providers 12
  convergence 8–9
  diversification 10–11
  horizontal integrations 14
  layers of participants 12
  market development 9–10
  markets 12
  media exchange rate 14
  multimedia 11
  multiple media 11
  network builders 12
  network operators 12
  new communications industry 12–14
  new services 11
  on-line type services 10
  service providers 12–13
  site equipment providers 13
  technological determinism 13–14
  TV-type services 10
  types of application 11
  uncertainty 9–10
  vertical agreements 14
media markets
  distinct nature of 296–7
multimedia 1–2, 11

national and cultural differences
  importance of 295–6

Price, Monroe
  balance between different forms of
      communication, on 301
purposes of regulation 15–23
  access, regulation for 21–3
    see also access, regulation for
  complexity 23
  external pluralism 19–20
  internal pluralism 19–20
  Internet 16–17
  justifications 15–16
  oversimplification of discussion 15
  regulation of competition 17–20

  see also competition, regulation of
  social regulation of content 16–17

regulating the changing media 1–27
regulation
  child pornography, and 303
  competition, and 304
  external pluralism, and 305–6
  individual consumer choice, and 300–1
  internal pluralism, and 305–6
  market share, and 304–5
  need for 298–303
  public service 306–7
  public sphere, and 302–3
  scarcity problems 299
  types 303–7
  universal service 307
regulatory framework
  uncertainty as to 3–4
regulatory institutions 23–6
  courts 24
  diversity 23
  governments 24–5
  self-regulation 25–6
  United States 25
research methodology 5–8
  selection of countries 6–8
  template 6

self-regulation 25–6, 312–14
  role of law, and 312–13
Single European Market 154–61
specialist regulatory agencies
  role of 310–11

technological developments
  social impact, and 2–3

United Kingdom 101–43
  ACARD 114
  advertising 132–3
  ASA 111
  BBC 104–5
  BBFC 111
  broadcasting 104–7
    funding model 106–7
  BT 107–8
  Channel 4 105–6
  Channel 5 106
  child pornography 135
  CITU 122–3, 141–2
  COGs 112–13
  competition policy 126–9
  concentration and ownership rules 126–9
  Conservative government ideology 115–16

Index

United Kingdom (*cont.*):
  constitutional framework 116
  consumer interactive services 108–9
  content regulation 134–40
  context of government's communication
      policy 115–16
  copyright 130–1
    Shetland Times case 130–1
  courts 143
  data protection 139
  DCMS 110
  defamation 136–8
    innocent dissemination 137
    jurisdiction 137–8
  deregulation 118–19
  domain names 131–2
  DTI 110
  economic regulation 126–34
    B Sky B 128–9
    bottlenecks 127–8
    independent service providers 127
    media 126
    pay-TV 128–9
    telecommunications 126–7
  electronic commerce 133
  EMC regulations 125
  encryption 139–40
  European Union, and 115
  film industry 103
  future developments 142–3
  G7, and 115
  gradualism 101
  Information Society, and 101–3
  infrastructure regulation 123–5
    allocation 124–5
    duopoly review 123–4
    wired 123–4
    wireless 124–5
  instruments of policy 114–23
  integrity right 138–9
  intellectual property rights 129–32
  interest groups 112–14
  interoperability 125
  ISI 122
  IT industry 103
  ITC 110–11
  ITV 105
  Labour Government media policy 143
  market participants 103–9
  market structure 126–9
  media development 101–9
  media policies 110–42
  media strengths 102
  media unions 113–14
  MMC 111–12
  moral rights 138–9
  National Consumer Council 114
  obscenity 134–5
  Oftel 111
  PCC 111
  policy 116–18
    Conservative government 116–17
    House of Commons 118
    House of Lords 117–18
    Oftel 117
  policy makers 110
  pricing 133–4
  print media 104
  public access
    political process, and 141–2
  radio 107
  Radio Authority 110–11
  regulation 110–42
    broadcasting 120–2
    Broadcasting Acts 120–1
    institutions 110–14
    Public Telecommunications Operator
      Licence 119–20
    rationalisation 112
    structure 110–14
    telecommunications 119–20
  regulators 110–12
  regulatory framework 118–19
  roots of communications policy 114–15
  S4C 106
  satellite services 106
  self-regulation of content 135–6
  standards 125
  subsidy 122–3
  tax 133
  technological regulation 123–5
  telecommunications 107–8
  UKCOD 142
  Universal Service 140–1
United States 201–45
  advertising 232–4
    electronic commerce 232–3
    Lanham Act 233–4
  anti-trust law 226–8
    FCC, and 226
    mergers, and 226–8
    price, and 228
  broadband 204–5
  broadcasting versus narrowcasting 205
  Communications Decency Act 235
  concentration 205–8
    Disney/Capital Cities 206–7
    General Electric 206
    Time Warner 206
    Westinghouse 207
  content regulation 235–9
  copyright 228–31
    Act of 1976 228–9
    courts, and 229–30

'transmission' 231
  website 'framing' 230–1
  domain names 231–2
economic regulation 226–8
encryption 239–40
ensuring information security and
    network reliability 242
extension of 'universal service'
    concept 241
FCC 212–17
  broadcasting, and 213
  cable TV, and 213–14
court challenges 216
  Internet, and 215–16
  origin 212–13
  rulemaking procedures 216
  telecommunications, and 214–15
HDTV 224–5
HDTV debate 209
improvement of government
    procurement 243–4
improvement of management of radio
    frequency spectrum 242–3
information superhighway 204
intellectual property 228–32
interactive TV 202
Internet indecency 235–8
  distributor 237
  publisher 237
voluntary solution 236–7
market participants 210–11
  aggregation 211
  content 211
  infrastructure 210–11
  services 211
  software 211
media development 201–11
  convergence 202–4
  general trends 202–10
media policies 211–40

misappropriation 234
National Information Infrastructure 217
off-line 205
privacy 240
promotion of private sector investment
    241
promotion of seamless, interactive, user-
    driven operation of N11 242
promotion of technological innovation
    and new applications 241–2
protection of intellectual property
    rights 243
provision of access to government
    information 243–4
public versus private ownership 208–
    10
publicity rights 234
regulation 211–40
security 239–40
social regulation 235–40
spectrum auctions 225–6
technical convergence 202–4
technological regulation 224–6
Telecommunications Act 1996 217–24
  broadcast radio and TV 217–18
  cable TV 218–19
  Internet 222
  policies embodied by 222–4
  telephony 219–22
  interconnection 220
  unbundled access 220
  universal service 221–2
V-chip legislation 238–9
  'violence hypothesis' 238–9
Web-TV 203
wired versus wireless 204
universal service
  regulation, and 307

WorldCom 297–8